BROTHER
OUTSIDER,
**BROTHER
INSIDER**

# BROTHER OUTSIDER,

*The John Hope Franklin Series in*
*African American History and Culture*

Waldo E. Martin Jr. and Patricia Sullivan, editors

The best scholarship in African American history and culture
compels us to expand our sense of who we are as a nation and
forces us to engage seriously the experiences of all Americans
who have shaped the development of this country. By publishing
pathbreaking books informed by several disciplines, the John
Hope Franklin Series in African American History and Culture
seeks to illuminate America's multicultural past and the ways in
which it has informed the nation's democratic experiment.

A complete list of books published in the John Hope Franklin
Series in African American History and Culture is available at
https://uncpress.org/series/john-hope-franklin-series-african
-american-history-culture.

A POLITICAL
BIOGRAPHY OF
**LAWRENCE
GUYOT JR.**

—

**CHRIS
DANIELSON**

# BROTHER

# INSIDER

The University of North Carolina Press
CHAPEL HILL

Designed by Lindsay Starr
Set in Charis and HWT Unit Gothic
by codeMantra

Cover art courtesy of Herbert Randall Freedom Summer Photographs,
    University Libraries, University of Southern Mississippi

Library of Congress Cataloging-in-Publication Data
Names: Danielson, Chris, author.
Title: Brother outsider, brother insider : a political biography of
    Lawrence Guyot, Jr. / Chris Danielson.
Other titles: Political biography of Lawrence Guyot, Jr.
Description: [Chapel Hill, North Carolina] : The University of North Carolina
    Press, [2025] | Includes bibliographical references and index.
Identifiers: LCCN 2024050313 | ISBN 9781469685762 (cloth) |
    ISBN 9781469685779 (paperback) | ISBN 9781469685786 (epub) |
    ISBN 9781469685793 (pdf)
Subjects: LCSH: Guyot, Lawrence, 1939–2012. | African American civil
    rights workers—Biography. | Civil rights workers—United States—
    Biography. | Civil rights movements—United States—History—20th
    century. | African Americans—Civil rights—Mississippi—History—20th
    century. | Mississippi Freedom Democratic Party. | Student Nonviolent
    Coordinating Committee (US) | Mississippi—Race relations—Political
    aspects. | United States—Race relations—Political aspects. | BISAC:
    BIOGRAPHY & AUTOBIOGRAPHY / Cultural, Ethnic & Regional /
    African American & Black | BIOGRAPHY & AUTOBIOGRAPHY /
    Political
Classification: LCC E185.97.G97 D36 2025 | DDC 323.092 [B]—dc23/
    eng/20250102
LC record available at https://lccn.loc.gov/2024050313

For product safety concerns under the European Union's General Product
Safety Regulation (EU GPSR), please contact gpsr@mare-nostrum.co.uk or
write to the University of North Carolina Press and Mare Nostrum Group
B.V., Mauritskade 21D, 1091 GC Amsterdam, The Netherlands.

*To my mother, who made all of this possible*

# CONTENTS

LIST OF ILLUSTRATIONS · viii

ACKNOWLEDGMENTS · ix

INTRODUCTION · 1

CHAPTER 1. Guyot Will Never Do Anything Worthwhile, Anywhere: *The Making of an Atypical Activist* · 7

CHAPTER 2. There Was a War Going on, and the War Was a Very Simple One: *Guyot and the Student Nonviolent Coordinating Committee* · 38

CHAPTER 3. Who Is This Lawrence Guyot, Anyway? *The Birth of the Mississippi Freedom Democratic Party* · 67

CHAPTER 4. As Satisfying as Sex and as Addictive as Crack: *Political Power and Reform after the Student Nonviolent Coordinating Committee* · 102

CHAPTER 5. We'll Stay the Hell Out of the Goddamn Democratic Party: *The Failed Quest for Independent Black Political Power* · 141

CHAPTER 6. That's as Close to a Machine as You Can Get: *Fusion and the End of the Mississippi Freedom Democratic Party* · 179

CHAPTER 7. You Shouldn't Let Them Use You: *The Washington Years* · 209

CONCLUSION · 261

NOTES · 265

BIBLIOGRAPHY · 307

INDEX · 321

# ILLUSTRATIONS

Guyot showing reporters his injuries from the Winona beating,
14 June 1963 • 61

Guyot during Freedom Summer, August 1964 • 88

Freedom Democratic Party campaign headquarters during
the Freedom Vote, July 1964 • 96

Jean Wheeler and Guyot, with Mrs. Pinkey Hall, May 1964 • 148

Guyot with Jonathan Hutto, November 1997 • 241

Guyot in Hattiesburg, Mississippi, recalling the movement,
22 October 2010 • 256

# ACKNOWLEDGMENTS

The list of people who aided an author in the writing of a book is always long, and I apologize in advance for any omissions. The staff at the Montana Tech library deserves the first and highest mention, since they aided and assisted me in acquiring the books and microfilms I needed for research. Special thanks to head librarians Scott Juskiewicz and Ann St. Clair, and fellow librarians Conor Cote, Ulana Holtz, Debbie Todd, Kristi Carroll, and especially Francis Holmes and Karen Gerhardt from Interlibrary Loan. At my employer, my former department head Chip Todd deserves thanks for his support for my research, as does Beverly Hartline, the former vice chancellor of research.

I would like to thank other archives and archivists for their invaluable assistance, including Clarence Hunter and the rest of the William Winter State Archives and staff; Minnie Watson at the L. Zenobia Library at Tougaloo College; Paul Ortiz and the staff at the Samuel Proctor Oral History Program; Eileen Guthrie and Jena Shepard of the Pass Christian Historical Society; the Hancock County Historical Society; Jennifer Ford, Leigh McWhite, and Lauren Rodgers at the University of Mississippi; the staff of the Special Collections Department at Howard University; and Sara Brewer, archives specialist at the National Archives at Atlanta.

I spoke to many people who had connections to Guyot and thank them as well for the time they gave me out of their busy lives. Special thanks in particular to Jonathan Hutto, who enthusiastically backed this project and helped me scour the archives for material. Thanks also to Maybelle Taylor Bennett, John Brittain, Monique Guyot, Julie Guyot-Diangone, Jan Hillegas, Lorne Cress Love, Staughton Lynd, Peter Orris, Fannie Rushing, and Flonzie Brown Wright. Leslie Burl McLemore deserves special mention, both for being generous with interviews and for writing what is still the best dissertation on the Mississippi Freedom Democratic Party.

Many of my academic friends aided me as well. Billy Pritchard and Christopher Stacey gave me suggestions on Gulf Coast and Louisiana scholarship, and Victoria Bynum, Joe Crespino, and Michael Williams offered support and advice. Lauren Araiza at Denison University aided me in accessing student newspapers in Ohio. Douglas Bristol and Chuck Westmoreland helped me present parts of this work at conferences in Cleveland and Natchez, Mississippi, and I also thank Kevin Johnson of Grambling State for his comments.

The final acknowledgment goes to my mother, Nancy. Her love and support throughout this long project was essential, just as it was with my previous books. I do not exaggerate when I say I likely could not have written this book without her. I love you, Mom.

BROTHER
OUTSIDER,
**BROTHER
INSIDER**

# INTRODUCTION

On 26 February 2013, in the LeDroit Park neighborhood of Washington, DC, local residents and members of the Advisory Neighborhood Commission (ANC), a volunteer board of elected members, met to discuss business. The agenda topics were routine, including approving a market's license to sell organic produce in a city park and adopting parking regulations. Then someone put forth a motion to rename the 500 block of U Street as Lawrence Guyot Way, after the long-time neighborhood resident and ANC commissioner who had died the previous November. Because the meeting lacked a quorum, the motion was postponed until the next month, when the commissioners and the audience approved it overwhelmingly.[1]

The renaming of the street was not just an honor extended to a longtime local resident and activist. Lawrence Thomas Guyot Jr. — commonly referred to during his life as simply "Guyot" (pronounced GHEE-ot) — was so much more than that. Born on the Gulf Coast of Mississippi, he rose through the ranks of the Student Nonviolent Coordinating Committee (SNCC) in the 1960s to head the Mississippi Freedom Democratic Party (MFDP), a nearly all-Black political party birthed by SNCC to challenge the state's white segregationist regular Democrats. After years of organizing in the Magnolia State, he relocated to Washington, DC, where he held positions in the long-serving administration of fellow Mississippian and civil rights activist Marion Barry. By the time of his death in 2012, people remembered Guyot as a respected veteran of the civil rights movement who frequently lent his knowledge to scholars and activists, as well as a man held in high esteem by his community and city.

This book is a biography of that man. Civil rights biographies on movement figures are a rich and burgeoning field of historiography, and one on Guyot is long overdue. Throughout his political life, he labored as a "second tier" civil rights organizer, prominent but overshadowed by other movement figures. This overshadowing includes not just the heyday of his civil rights activism but the civil rights historiography as well. Fannie Lou Hamer, his close friend and colleague in the MFDP, has received at least six full-length biographical studies, one dual biography, a study of her rhetoric, and an edited collection of her speeches. Bob Moses, who worked with Guyot in Mississippi and organized Freedom Summer, has received biographical treatment as well, as has Stokely Carmichael, who organized with Guyot in SNCC. Medgar Evers, the Mississippi field secretary for the National Association for the Advancement of Colored People (NAACP), and T. R. M. Howard, his mentor, are also the subject of book-length studies.[2]

Guyot was an atypical civil rights activist, and one shaped by his unique upbringing. His Gulf Coast childhood was relatively comfortable compared to the grinding poverty of the Mississippi Delta, where Fannie Lou Hamer lived. But he did not grow up a product of middle-class privilege, like Martin Luther King Jr. in the Atlanta suburbs. Raised a Roman Catholic in a region resembling New Orleans more than Mississippi, Guyot did not experience the traditional milieu of African American Protestantism. He also came from a long political lineage, with relatives politically active since Reconstruction. The French Catholic influence, the space (albeit limited) allowed for Black political participation even during the worst years of Jim Crow, and the labor union presence all factored in his creation. The relative racial moderation of the Gulf Coast also gave him an outlook removed from that of many other Black Mississippians, in particular regarding class and education.

Guyot quickly abandoned these biases when he began his fieldwork for SNCC. Although he was no stranger to segregation, the brutal poverty and racism he saw in the Mississippi Delta was far removed from the coastal town of Pass Christian where he grew up. His evolution as a leader served as a testament to the transformative power of SNCC, which through its grassroots, bottom-up ethos sought to cultivate local leaders rather than impose them from the outside. Guyot rose to field secretary and then head of the MFDP. In the process, he almost met an early death in the Winona city jail. But the organizational needs of a political party, and the almost exclusive focus on voting and gaining political access, fed into the alienation of an increasingly incoherent and radicalized SNCC from the MFDP's mainstream orientation.

Guyot steered the new party through high-profile events like the congressional challenge to the state's white racist delegation. In the process, he likely played a major role in the passage of the Voting Rights Act, something not widely acknowledged in civil rights histories. Yet the MFDP's experience under Guyot showed the limits of the outsider approach. The party tried a variety of

approaches, from running general-election candidates for Congress to challenging white Democrats in primaries to running as independents and on the
local level. None of these approaches worked, and Guyot and the MFDP found
themselves losing ground to their rivals in the more centrist NAACP. The MFDP
struggled to win over many Black Mississippians who were intimidated by white
racist violence as well as by the taint of radicalism from Black Power and New
Left opposition to the Vietnam War, even though this was a militancy that Guyot
never fully embraced. Frustrated by the failure to build an independent Black
political base, Guyot ultimately chose to merge the party with the centrist civil
rights forces in the state to gain access to political power and influence—but at
a cost of the party's identity. But he saw the cost as worth paying, as Guyot and
the MFDP had existed as political outsiders for most of the 1960s.

The stresses of 1960s Mississippi took their toll on Guyot's health. In 1969, he
moved north to Washington, DC, to raise a family. Yet even there the transformative nature of his political work with SNCC emerged, as he rapidly changed roles
from southern rural civil rights organizer to big-city political operative, no longer in charge of a political party but now a cog in Barry's political machine. For
the rest of his life he bridged the southern and northern wings of the civil rights
movement, helping to keep the memory of the Mississippi civil rights movement
alive while cultivating new generations of leaders in the nation's capital. This
shift from political outsider to insider also testified to Guyot's political shrewd-
ness, as he now enjoyed access to the patronage that came with political power.

Often overshadowed by his contemporaries, Guyot also never developed the
star power of Carmichael or Hamer. He never published his memoirs, unlike his
fellow SNCC veteran Unita Blackwell.[3] It would be easy to call his 1960s leadership of the party a failure, since the NAACP ultimately became the political power
within the eventually integrated Mississippi Democratic Party and exercised a
traditional top-down rather than bottom-up leadership, but that misses the larger
issues of the awareness that Guyot and the MFDP raised through their electoral
campaigns, and the role they played in bringing about the historic civil rights
realignment of the 1960s. Such accomplishments cannot be easily quantified.

Why has Guyot been overlooked? Perhaps no one answered this question
better than Luvaghn Brown, who as a teenager in 1962 worked with Guyot in
Greenwood, Mississippi, organizing voters. In a 2022 oral history he told interviewer Paul Murray,

> Somewhere you asked why we don't hear more about a guy like Guyot.
> One of the things I'd like for people to understand is the people who
> came into Mississippi from wherever they came, when they came into

the South. You will notice, for the most part, the historians, the writers, they don't write about Mississippians other than Fannie Lou Hamer. I was asked a question once who was my hero. I said it then and I meant it then and I mean it now. "You've never heard of the people I consider my heroes because you've only heard about the people who came into the South. Diane [Nash] was one of them. Bevel is one. All those people did not ignore, but felt, that they had the right idea and we couldn't possibly. Guyot got caught up into that. The people that came in from colleges or from working someplace else, gave up what they did to come into Mississippi, it took them a while to understand there are people here. There are ideas here. There is a way of living. You need to know that. Then you can get people to do things. That's one of the reasons you don't hear about all of the "soldiers" who participated in the Movement. Books aren't written about them. Movies aren't made about them. But these were the people who did things. What about Fannie Lou for instance? I respect everything she did. But what about all those people who made that happen? What about the Guyots who worked in that environment?[4]

Perhaps this too is a reason why so many have overlooked Guyot, since he was a native Mississippian and not the proverbial "outside agitator."

While this book is a history of this overlooked man, it is not a history of the Mississippi Freedom Democratic Party. Although the party has been the subject of theses and dissertations, it mostly exists in studies of SNCC as an offshoot of that organization, usually with the 1964 Democratic National Convention in Atlantic City as the focus and little on the period after that. Only one published monograph on the party exists, and it is very short adaptation of a PhD dissertation that was not edited by the author.[5] I have attempted to shed as much light on the political workings of the party as possible in my study, in the hope that it can stand in as such until the definitive history of the MFDP is written.

This history means that unlike most other civil rights biographies, the focus here is not just on the civil rights years. Eric Burner's book on Bob Moses, for example, has only cursory coverage of his post–civil rights years with the Algebra Project. I aim to do more than that. Guyot defined himself as a civil rights activist, but he took his activism well beyond the 1960s, and his career in Washington, DC, fits within Jacquelyn Dowd Hall's conception of a long civil rights movement. Hall's analytical framework altered the historiographical understanding of the civil rights movement in at least six major ways, some of which apply to this biography. These six ways are (1) a focus that analyzes racism in the North and West, not just in the South, (2) tying race and class and civil rights and workers' rights together, (3) the centrality of women's activism and gender dynamics to the movement, (4) understanding the civil rights movements in the North and West, (5) how the movement's victories affected American society and politics in the 1970s, and (6) looking at the deeper historical roots of the Reagan-Bush backlash. Hall says that the longer and broader narrative in her first point undermines the idea of the South as the opposite of the North, which leads to an excessive focus on the Jim Crow South and obscures the institutional racism in the North. As a transitional figure, Guyot bridged the civil rights and post–civil rights years and linked rural southern activism and organizing to the urban machine politics of the North. Both activities expressed Black Power, just with different issues and in different settings and eras, and Guyot never saw his DC activism as separate from his Mississippi organizing. Washington, DC, had historically been more southern than northern, evolving from a plantation society to the nation's first Black-majority city. A study of Guyot therefore fits the first and fourth points of her framework. Also in keeping with Hall's analysis, Guyot conforms with the fifth point she argues, about the effort to use the 1960s reforms in the 1970s and beyond. He did this by working in the Barry administration on issues of Black political access and improving the lives of DC residents, in which he was aided by the growing Black political power in urban areas.[6]

While the bulk of the study is devoted to his years in Mississippi, this book also covers his years in Washington, DC, where he spent the last four decades of his life. Much of this period involved his raising a family, but he stayed active in politics, even if he did not organize a grassroots movement or head a political party anymore. In this approach, I echo Minion K. C. Morrison's notable biography of Aaron Henry, another Mississippi civil rights leader who had a long career after the movement.[7]

This is book is also not an intimate biography of Lawrence Guyot, like Fawn Brodie's of Thomas Jefferson, covering and analyzing details of his psyche and personal life.[8] Rather, it is a political one, examining his role as an organizer and civil rights activist, both in Mississippi and Washington. What I have included I have taken from whatever public sources I could access.

Finally, a note on sources. The ones I had access to overwhelmingly cover his public life as an organizer and political figure, and that dictated the direction of my research. They included the extensive interviews Guyot gave during his life, papers of civil rights activists, records from SNCC and the MFDP, coverage of Guyot in Mississippi's State Sovereignty Commission Files, and newspaper accounts. I have also used a considerable body of secondary sources on SNCC and the MFDP, including theses, dissertations, and published academic works and articles. While I have spent years researching this book and scrounging up whatever sources I could, any errors or oversights are mine alone.

# CHAPTER 1
# GUYOT WILL NEVER DO ANYTHING WORTHWHILE, ANYWHERE

THE MAKING OF AN ATYPICAL ACTIVIST

Lawrence Guyot Jr. grew up in the humid, subtropical climate of the Mississippi Gulf Coast, an area known today for its seafood industry and tourist beaches and quaint seaside towns with French names. Yet this area of the state, culturally and in some ways politically unlike the rest of Mississippi, nurtured a Black political tradition that lasted well beyond the end of Reconstruction and the decline of Black politics. But it is easy to overstate that continuity of Black politics on the coast. While white boosters ridiculously fantasized about the coast being a racially progressive oasis, it did provide a culture that shaped Guyot's ancestry and upbringing and gave him from an early age a political awareness that Black Mississippians in areas like the Delta lacked due to the more brutal and rigid boundaries of Jim Crow in those regions.[1] Specifically, the Roman Catholic influence on the coast, which largely radiated out from New Orleans and southern Louisiana, provided a limited check on the brutal white supremacy from elsewhere in the Magnolia State. The industrial development in coastal cities, which contributed to levels of unionization not normally seen in the South, added another influence that made white supremacy there less rigid. These factors all helped nurture a long political tradition that shaped not just Guyot but his entire family line. This political heritage primed the young Guyot for his leadership role in the civil rights movement, and provided an atypical upbringing for the activist. His experience differed from that of activists raised in the traditional Protestantism of the African American church, the rural upbringing of a sharecropper like Fannie Lou Hamer, or the comfortable middle-class suburbs that nurtured leaders like Martin Luther King Jr.

Politics ran deep in Guyot's lineage, providing him with a genealogical and historical foundation for his own activism. His great-great-uncle, Louis Joseph Piernas, provided the most prominent example of political involvement. Born in 1856 in Bay St. Louis to a Cuban-born father and a mother from Santo Domingo, Piernas's ancestors had received a grant of land from the Spanish government, and his grandmother owned land on the northern end of Bay St. Louis. He grew up speaking French, and he said he and his light-skinned family, conscious of their Spanish heritage, "kept ourselves separate from the real Negroes, and we had our own frolics and dances to which the white folks would come sometimes." He attended Our Lady of the Gulf Catholic Church with white parishioners, and was baptized there as well.[2]

Piernas's family, as free people, shared the color consciousness of the light-skinned free people of color on the Gulf Coast and in the New Orleans area, which meant a separate identity from the "real Negroes," one built upon privileging light-skinned Black people as "superior" to darker-skinned ones. The US annexation of the region in the early nineteenth century amplified this outlook on the Gulf Coast. Now the French-speaking mixed-race population in formerly French cities like New Orleans and Mobile enjoyed legal privileges that slaves and other free Blacks did not have, which reinforced their social distance from their darker-skinned brethren. In this sense the French Catholic Gulf Coast more resembled the Caribbean, where free people of color formed a distinct racial group in the island colonies of Great Britain and France. This superior attitude did not mean the Piernas family supported the Confederacy, however. The family sheltered white men evading the Confederate draft during the Civil War, at no doubt considerable risk to themselves. His family's behavior differed from that of Blacks in nearby Mobile, where pro-Confederate sentiment among the light-skinned free people of color was quite strong.[3]

A color line and limited citizenship rights for light-skinned free people of color did exist for Piernas and his kin on the antebellum Gulf Coast. Free Blacks in Pass Christian could own property, but they could not own weapons without the express permission of the mayor. Similar restrictions existed regarding the sale of alcohol and gambling. After the end of slavery, the color line extended to education, as young Piernas attended a private school at the church set up for both free Blacks and ex-slave children.[4]

Louis Piernas came of age on the Reconstruction-era Gulf Coast, an area of burgeoning Black politics during the 1860s and 1870s. Mississippi and Louisiana were two of the states with the largest number of Black elected officials. New Orleans, with its French-speaking, Catholic, light-skinned elite (or mulattos, quadroons, or octaroons, as whites called them in the nineteenth century, classifying them based on blood quantum)—what one historian called "the nation's most articulate and politicized Black community" at the close of the Civil War—was a center of Black political power, with influence radiating out to the Gulf Coast. Like Piernas, almost all the men of this community, more than 200 political leaders in all, had been born free. Unlike Piernas, they enjoyed legal rights before the Civil War even though they could not vote, due to old French legal privileges that eventually became state law in antebellum Louisiana. A few of them even owned slaves themselves. Much of their politicization came from the hardening color line that young Piernas himself experienced, as the 1864 constitutional convention in Louisiana denied the right to vote to mixed-race men and subjected them to the same harsh vagrancy laws and curfew regulations imposed on the freedmen and freedwomen. The free Black community responded by mobilizing politically and pushing Republican politicians in Washington, including President Abraham Lincoln, to back suffrage for free men of color—but not necessarily newly freed slaves, whose entrance into the political process some of the leaders opposed. Yet despite the often condescending and paternalistic tone of the light-skinned elite, most eventually threw their support to Black suffrage for all, born free or not, during Radical Reconstruction. Although the Black Republicans faced white violence, most notably the bloody New Orleans riot of 1866, Black political power grew with the franchise and military occupation during Radical Reconstruction, which Congress enacted with the Reconstruction Acts in 1867. In Louisiana and Mississippi, voters elected a total of thirty-four Black sheriffs, as well as Black men to numerous lesser offices. Even law enforcement reflected this rise of Black influence, with the New Orleans and Mobile police departments more than one-quarter Black by 1870, and Black captains in the former city empowered to give commands to white officers.[5]

Louis Piernas's own political rise built upon these earlier achievements. In Mississippi, Reconstruction ended violently in 1875 with the "Mississippi Plan" of "redemption" from the Radical Republican administration of Governor Adelbert Ames. White vigilantes intimidated and murdered Black and white Republicans during the statewide elections that year, and the administration of President Ulysses S. Grant did little to stop Democrats from regaining control of the state by these means. The Black Belt counties far from the Gulf Coast experienced the worst Republican losses. Even after "redemption," Black men held onto some elective offices, but even this declined sharply after 1890, the year the state adopted its infamous state constitution, which effectively stripped the right to vote from Black men using a variety of ostensibly nonracial mechanisms. Even the Gulf Coast counties experienced steep declines, with Harrison and Hancock Counties counting only 263 registered Black voters out of a Black voting age population of 1,312 in 1896.[6]

Yet even with the end of Reconstruction and the decline of Black political power, Piernas remained politically active and held elective office. His continued officeholding reflected the continuation of some Black political participation after the Compromise of 1877 and not an immediate onset of disfranchisement and segregation, but the Magnolia State had only minimal Black political participation after 1875. White violence diminished Black voting to only 38 percent of eligible Black voters in the 1881 gubernatorial election. Residing on the Gulf Coast helped Piernas stay in office, however. In 1887, he organized the Promete Benevolent Association for Black residents in Bay St. Louis, the first of twenty in the town by the 1930s, which covered medical aid, funeral expenses, and small pensions for needy families. He first entered politics in 1882, when he won election as secretary and auditor for Bay St. Louis. He ran successfully for the Hancock County Board of Supervisors in 1884, and won reelection in 1886. According to Piernas, local Republicans and Democrats agreed to a "coalition ticket" of both parties that allowed him to be elected. This process, known as "fusion" in Black-majority Mississippi counties, involved an alliance of white elites and Black candidates whereby the whites selected "acceptable" Black men for office, and relegated them to minor, low-paying offices, or to token appointments on white-majority boards. Although primarily a phenomenon of the heavily Black planter counties of the Delta, the arrangement seems to have fit the white paternalism of the Gulf Coast as well, where the counties had solid white majorities. Mayor August Keller appointed Piernas in 1887 to the school board to oversee the Black-only schools in the district. Another of Lawrence Guyot's ancestors also held political office in this era. Romain Morgan, the maternal grandfather of Margaret Piernas, Lawrence Guyot's mother, served as a city councilman in Pass Christian briefly in the 1880s.[7]

White Democratic Mississippi politicians found the presence of Black politicians, as well as their demands for more influence in state and local politics, intolerable, and the adoption of the Constitution of 1890 spelled the end of fusion. Although this ended Piernas's holding of elected office, federal appointments remained open for a handful of Black Republicans in the state. Republican president Benjamin Harrison appointed Piernas postmaster of Bay St. Louis after his election in 1888. Joseph Saucier, a white Democrat, replaced Piernas after the defeat of Harrison by Democrat Grover Cleveland in 1892, a move that reflected the partisan nature of federal patronage. Saucier and Piernas alternated with presidential administrations, with Piernas returning as postmaster during William McKinley's administration, but then replaced with Saucier again, until

President Theodore Roosevelt returned him to the office in 1902. He then held the office until William Howard Taft took office in 1909.[8]

Piernas's final years as postmaster, and the last public office he held, reflected the final hardening of white supremacy in Mississippi and the acquiescence of Republican presidential administrations to it at the turn of the century. The color line became more rigid not just politically but also socially for a light-skinned man like Piernas, as the *Plessy v. Ferguson* decision in 1896 gave legal sanction to segregation laws that classified people as Black who were as much as seven-eighths white. Despite the hardening attitudes, Roosevelt reappointed Piernas as Bay St. Louis postmaster in 1902, the same year as the Indianola affair. That event involved Minnie Cox, a college-educated Black woman who, like Piernas, had served as postmaster under Harrison and McKinley. But in 1902, James Kimble Vardaman, the newspaper editor-turned-gubernatorial candidate, joined with local whites to decry "nigger domination" in the Delta town. White Indianolans threatened violence against Cox, who then resigned and left the state. Theodore Roosevelt refused to accept her resignation and suspended postal service to the area, but local whites merely had their mail shipped to another postal facility. When Cox's commission expired in 1904, the post office reopened under a white postmaster.[9]

Piernas managed to hold onto his office as long as he did due to the relatively more tolerant Gulf Coast racial climate, which allowed for limited Black political participation in the early twentieth century. The 1908 voter rolls had 100 registered Black voters, including Armand Guyot, the great-grandfather of Lawrence Guyot. Piernas finally left office during the Taft administration. Taft himself acquiesced to white sentiments in Mississippi and his desire to build a viable Republican Party in the South by replacing Black postmasters with white ones. This included his refusal to reappoint a Black postmaster in nearby Ocean Springs. Piernas still remained active in Republican Party politics, serving as executive committeeman of the Hancock County Republican Party—a post he held for sixty-five years—and voted in every general election.[10]

This political background of a somewhat relaxed and limited space for Black Mississippians on the Gulf Coast during Jim Crow shaped the Guyot family's own development and eventually that of Lawrence. Black men, with few exceptions, could not vote in the Delta or Hill Country counties of the Magnolia State, but the "progressive" coast, including towns like Guyot's birthplace of Pass Christian, indulged a modicum of Black political activity—but not enough to threaten white supremacy. In many respects, it was the coast's version of the noblesse oblige of the Delta planter class. But those Delta planters, unlike the whites of Gulf Coast, did not allow even limited Black voting to continue in their fiefdoms after the 1890s, making the coastal counties all that much more atypical.[11]

Pass Christian is located in Harrison County on the Mississippi Gulf Coast. The French first settled the area in 1699, first establishing Biloxi and then spreading west to the areas of Long Branch and Pass Christian. The French then founded New Orleans, which established a French Catholic influence on the Mississippi Gulf Coast absent from much of the rest of the state. The Catholic presence came not just from New Orleans but also from upriver at Natchez, home to the only Catholic church in the entire state when Mississippi entered the Union in 1817. On the Gulf Coast, traveling priests from New Orleans and Mobile serviced communities like Pass Christian and Biloxi on an irregular basis, so the area contained small congregations of devout followers and far more numerous nominally Catholic settlers. Catholics in Pass Christian erected the town's first Catholic church by the early 1840s.[12]

White residents of the Gulf Coast, harboring paternalist fantasies, liked to consider their region to be a more tolerant area for African Americans than the rest of the state. William Peas, a visitor to Pass Christian in the 1850s, described a "colored population" that behaved with "great decorum, and are treated with much courtesy by the whites." John Lang, a local historian, published a history of Harrison County that cited antebellum court cases of slaveowners being prosecuted by local courts for "cruel and unusual punishment" of their slaves. Lang, born into a slaveholding family and in his eighties when he published the county history in 1936, lavished condescending praise on Pass Christian's Black population, calling them "the best negro population to be found in the state or any other state" who were "practically all good citizens, nearly all of them owning their own homes." Rather tellingly, Lang said that some of these families "are almost all white" and "descendants of the old French settlers," like in New Orleans. Apparently, the reason why Lang thought them so successful was their mixed-race backgrounds resulting from the rape of enslaved African women by their French owners, even if he did not state it so blatantly. Lang added to the Lost Cause romanticizing of the region when he mentioned the arrival of the Ku Klux Klan in the county during Reconstruction to frighten away "scalawags from the north-east" who had taken over county offices, indicating that the town's supposed progressivism did not exclude white terrorism and violence. And certainly, the coast did not see the intolerance directed at other ethnic groups, such as the hostility to Italian immigrants in Erwin, a town in the Mississippi Delta, where local whites murdered a Sicilian father and son in 1901, or the efforts by local parents to segregate Italian schoolchildren from other whites in Shelby and Sumrall in 1906 and 1907.[13]

The origins of the modern town of Pass Christian do not support Lang's rosy retelling. By the early 1800s, Mississippi's Gulf Coast contained a substantial population of free people of color, many of whom owned coastal property. Pass Christian itself came from one of these transactions, when Julia de La Brosse, a widow of a French settler, deeded 680 acres of her 14,500-acre estate upon her death in 1800 to two former slaves, Charles and Madelon Asmard. The Asmards went on to become slaveowners themselves. But the influx of wealthy white residents from New Orleans in the 1820s increased land speculation, which led to Pass Christian's development into a summer resort town for wealthy Louisiana planters and merchants by the 1840s. The Charlot tract, as the Asmards' land was called, stood in the midst of this coastal development. Charles Asmard resisted efforts by white speculators to acquire his land, but after his death his children sold off their patrimony in a series of unequal transactions to white developers. The land eventually became the town's beachfront downtown district. The acquisition of the Charlot tract symbolized locally the broader enclosure movement in the nineteenth and early twentieth centuries to push Black landowners away from the coast and turn it into a space for white luxury and entertainment.[14]

Economically, the region began as an agricultural hinterland, but the pine forests in the region gave rise to a lumber industry, a characteristic the coast shared with the Piney Woods region to the north around Hattiesburg. Moss Point in Jackson County contained most of the large mills, where overcutting left many of the forests stripped bare. The next major industrial development came in the late 1800s with the arrival of packing plants to can the fish, oysters, and shrimp plentiful in the Gulf. Pass Christian's first large-scale seafood plant opened in 1904.[15] The region had a mixed industrial economy that differed from the plantation-style agriculture of the Mississippi Delta, where the dense Black population and sharecropping system kept Black residents in feudal conditions.

The Catholic presence in the county meant that a substantial number of Black children from the more prosperous families attended parochial Catholic schools. In 1936 three Catholic schools specifically designated for Black pupils existed, out of a total of ten Catholic schools in the county. Only 374 Black Catholic pupils went to these schools, compared to the 1,800 Black children who attended Harrison County public schools. However, these schools contributed to the politically active and relatively well-off Black middle-class community that produced Lawrence Guyot, no small feat considering that the average Black public student attended school three months less than the average white student, and that only half the Black children in the state attended school daily in 1940.[16]

The earliest reference to the Guyot name is Joseph Guillot, a Frenchman born in the 1776 who later moved to Louisiana. Guillot owned twenty-three slaves by 1803, making him a quite successful planter. Around 1820, he fathered a son, Joseph Auguste, with an unknown woman, likely one of his slaves. Guillot died in 1838, and Joseph Auguste grew up and established himself as a carpenter in antebellum New Orleans, marrying Marie Lalande and raising eleven children. The spelling of the surname changed constantly for a number of reasons, including Joseph Auguste's illiteracy. At some point the spelling evolved to "Guyot," possibly because of a census taker's error.[17]

In 1858 in New Orleans, Marie Lalande gave birth to Lawrence Guyot's great-grandfather Armand Arthur Guyot, the ninth of her and Joseph's eleven children. During the Civil War, one of Armand's older brothers, Ernest, served in the Ninth Infantry of the United States Colored Troops. An August Guillot, age unknown and also possibly Joseph Auguste, served in the Seventy-Third US Colored Infantry. August Guillot's enlistment date of 1862 suggests that he first joined the First Louisiana Native Guard, which later became the Seventh-Third Colored Infantry. Arthur, another brother, also served in the Seventy-Third Colored Infantry. The 1910 census listed Armand Guyot as "mulatto." As a young man, he moved to Hancock County, Mississippi, and there married Mary Evaline Biami, also of Louisiana. The Guyots traveled back and forth between New Orleans and their residence on the Gulf Coast; the first four of their seven children were born in Louisiana. For at least the first two decades of the twentieth century, they lived in Pass Christian with their five surviving children (two of them, Armantine and Armand Guyot, died in the 1880s while still young). While in Pass Christian, both Armand and Mary—who usually went by her middle name in official documents—made their living in the service occupations that most Black Americans held. Armand worked as a hackman, or carriage-driver, while Mary worked out of their home as a laundress. Their oldest son, Leonard, also worked in his teenage years as a driver, before moving to New Orleans to start his own family and work as a freight hauler. Both Armand and Mary listed themselves as self-employed, indicating that Armand either rented or owned his own carriage. More important, the Guyots owned their own home by 1900. While the family enjoyed some self-sufficiency, the educational level that Lawrence Guyot would later attain largely eluded his great-grandparents and their children. Mary, illiterate for much of her adult life, did not list herself as literate until the 1920 census, and while Armand and his children could read, only Caesar, their youngest child, attended school in 1910. The political participation of Lawrence Guyot's lineage did not solely come from the Piernas line, as the

1908 Pass Christian voter registration rolls listed an "A. A. Guyot," apparently Armand, as a voter.[18]

The Guyots moved back to New Orleans in the 1910s with their daughter Elvina and four grandchildren, renting a house in Ward Five. Armand died there in 1918. Mary returned to Pass Christian and lived in her house with Elvina and six grandchildren, working as a cook for another family. She eventually returned to New Orleans, where she died in 1935.[19]

Thomas Eugene Guyot, the paternal grandfather of Lawrence Guyot, stayed in Pass Christian. Mary gave birth to him in 1894 in Mississippi. He was her and Armand's second-youngest child and matured into a tall, slender man. He worked as a wagon driver in the employ of his father, a position he held in 1917 when the United States entered World War I, and he registered with a civilian draft board. He worked as a civilian worker and not in uniform as a soldier. He had already married his wife Elinore by then, and she bore him a daughter, Rosie, in 1917 and son, Lawrence—father of Lawrence Guyot Jr.—in 1919. After World War I, Thomas worked as a laborer and rented a home in Pass Christian. By 1930, Thomas worked as a servant for another family, but he managed to purchase his own home, even as his wife bore two more children in the 1920s, Thomas Jr. and Edith. The children received schooling as well, and Elinore did not work, according to the 1930 census, a possible indication of Thomas's financial security.[20]

Or perhaps not. More likely, Elinore Guyot could not find a job. With the onset of the Great Depression by the time of the 1930 census, she plausibly could have been unable to find work and the family's relative gains from the 1920s eroded as the economy shrank. The Great Depression, as one historian has said, cast "the specter of starvation" over Black America. The collapse of the rural economy in the South, caused by an over 65 percent decline in cotton prices, hastened rural Black migration to the urban South, where Black people now competed with whites for the menial jobs once reserved for Black laborers. Maids, cooks, and housekeepers constituted nearly half the urban Black unemployed in the South, indicating the Depression's effect on Black women. By 1932, over half of Black Americans in southern cities could not find jobs. Rampant discrimination in both public relief and private charity only added to the desperate plight of Black southerners.[21]

For Thomas and Elinore's teenage children, the Depression meant that they had to provide for the family or themselves. The Guyot children achieved only a limited level of education, which was not unusual at the time for Black children in Mississippi because of white indifference (if not hostility) to Black education. Paid employment by all family members proved crucial for survival in the midst of declining fortunes and hastened the transition of Black children from schools to the workforce. The Guyot children actually benefited—compared to other Black residents of the state but not compared to white children—from living in the coastal counties, which appropriated more money for Black education than the state provided. Lawrence Sr. never made it beyond the seventh grade and went to work as a vender during the Depression. During that time, he met Margaret Piernas, daughter of Julius "Jules" and Mathilde Piernas, and married young, by 1935. Young Lawrence may have misrepresented his age, for although he was sixteen in 1935, the 1940 census for the Piernas household lists his birth year as 1917, making him eighteen in 1935—but still a year younger than his bride, who had more formal schooling than her husband, having made it through the first year of high school. She was fortunate: even by 1950, 75 percent of Black high-school-aged children in the state did not attend school.[22]

Julius Piernas, the son of Henri Piernas, an oyster dealer from nearby Bay St. Louis, and a nephew of Louis Joseph Piernas, benefited from New Deal relief programs. He had been an unemployed laborer beginning in 1935 but had managed to secure relief work in the New Deal's Works Progress Administration (WPA) by 1939, which provided him with an income three times his wife's salary as a part-time laundress. The Piernas family was one of 1 million Black families that year receiving WPA earnings, what Robert Weaver, a Black Roosevelt administration adviser, called "a godsend" for Black Americans. Julius Piernas benefited from a major shift in New Deal relief policy after 1935, when federal agencies like the WPA, the Public Works Administration, and the National Youth Administration, among others, advanced the economic livelihood of African Americans. Yet the income did not mean that the Piernas family avoided economic adversity. Like many white and Black families during the Depression, Lawrence Guyot Sr. and his new bride could not afford to live on their own, so after marrying they moved into Margaret's father's house at 335 Davis Avenue in Pass Christian, a no-doubt-crowded arrangement given that Jules and Mathilde also had five other children living with them. The neighborhood was integrated: Lawrence Guyot Jr. recalled a white family named Patalinas living on the same street.[23]

Despite the economic struggles the family faced, they remained politically involved, and the forces of modernization and industrialization contributed to a unique political climate. In addition to the long political involvement that the Piernas side of the family contributed to the Guyots, Lawrence Guyot Jr. recalled that the Catholic upbringing of his father and grandfather contributed to their political awareness, and that both men had no trouble voting in the 1920s and 1930s. A major change to the Gulf Coast also came in 1939, when

Ingalls Shipbuilding Corporation began operations in Pascagoula, Mississippi. The state's Balance Agriculture with Industry program, a municipal-subsidy incentive the state launched in 1936 to spur industrialization, had attracted the shipyard, the most successful industrial plant lured by the otherwise disappointing program. The arrival of Ingalls brought unionized industrial jobs to the coast, further influencing the Guyot family and making the political background in the coastal counties unlike the rest of heavily rural Mississippi. Ingalls eventually hired more than 1,000 Black workers, more than 10 percent of the company's workforce. Yet Jim Crow still affected the Mississippi coast, and Black workers at Ingalls frequently complained about being confined to unskilled labor or being paid at the unskilled rate even if they were promoted to skilled positions. Union organizers often ignored or received reluctantly complaints of racial discrimination lodged by Black workers at the shipyard, as the union leaders feared alienating white workers if they organized Black workers first or addressed their concerns.[24]

While organized labor did not spread beyond railroad workers and some craft unions in the larger cities of the state, a wider network of unionization in the Gulf Coast's port cities and towns drew in the coastal Mississippi counties. Guyot cited the International Longshoreman's Association (ILA), which first established its Gulf Coast District in 1911 in New Orleans, as a liberalizing factor on the coast. The Gulfport and Biloxi locals were very active in the district, even if dwarfed by those in New Orleans and Galveston. The ILA still operated within the confines of Jim Crow, meaning that while it may have politicized individuals, it did little to advance racial justice. Holt Ross, a state labor leader for the American Federation of Labor (AFL), recalled that the longshoremen held nonsegregated meetings due to the large numbers of Black members. Yet one labor historian questioned such claims, indicating that although the ILA organized both white and Black workers, the locals of the Gulf Coast District were segregated into racially separate branches. This unwillingness to challenge Jim Crow fit with the conservative philosophy of the Gulf Coast District, and some Black locals in larger cities like New Orleans and Houston in the early 1900s openly opposed both Jim Crow and the ILA leadership's quiet support for it. Still, both the white and Black local branches on the Gulf Coast participated in the district councils and apparently enjoyed equality of pay. Other coastal unions lacked the "enlightenment" of the ILA. In 1925 in Gulfport, a carpenter's union used violence and intimidation to force a contractor to dismiss his Black carpenters and hire white union members instead.[25]

Margaret gave birth to her and Lawrence's first child, Lawrence Thomas Guyot Jr., while living in the Piernas household. Born on 17 July 1939, the newborn joined a Piernas family that included his grandparents and five aunts and uncles. His brother Raymond was born two years later, followed by his brothers Jules, Raymond, and Albert. During Lawrence's first years, his family lived through the changes wrought by World War II, including the influx of people to the Gulf Coast. Larger urban areas on the coast experienced rapid growth in the 1940s due to shipbuilding and other defense-related industries, as migrants arrived looking for work. From 1940 to 1950, Biloxi's population grew from 17,475 to 37,425 (a 114.2 percent increase), the population of Gulfport from 15,195 to 22,659 (a 49.1 percent increase), and that of Pascagoula, home of the Ingalls Shipyard, from 5,900 to 10,805 (an 83.1 percent increase). Although the population of Harrison County rose from 50,799 in 1940 to 84,073 by 1950 (a 65.1 percent increase), Pass Christian did not experience the boom of its larger, more industrialized neighbors, its population rising from 3,338 to only 3,383 in the city and from 5,275 to 5,593 in the county's Beat (or District) Three, which included Pass Christian, indicating that Biloxi experienced the major increase related to war production.[26]

The changes created by the war included Lawrence Guyot Sr.'s enlistment in the US Army in February 1945 at Camp Shelby, an army base near Hattiesburg. Black workers benefited from the overall boom that the base brought to wartime Hattiesburg, as the federal wage scale far exceeded normal local hourly wages. Black soldiers had been stationed at Camp Shelby since the base's construction in 1940, but they still experienced racism, both from the local white community and from federally sanctioned segregation at the base. The local police chief warned Black soldiers to not go out at night and to stay in Black sections of town. The Army segregated recreational facilities, such as the USO centers, and spent less on the Black facilities. Lawrence Guyot Sr. likely experienced an adjustment, as he did his service and transitioned from the relatively cosmopolitan Gulf Coast to Hattiesburg, a Piney Woods city with little to no Black political participation and a firmer color line. He returned to Pass Christian once his enlistment ended.[27]

Far from weakening Jim Crow in Mississippi, World War II increased racial tensions as whites in the state held onto their system of Black subordination. Black men and women in the South experienced only marginal economic opportunities related to the war, so many—300,000 Black people in all—left the state for employment elsewhere, dropping the state's Black population from 54 percent to 45.3 percent. So many white men in uniform and away from the state led to white anxieties about a "race war" at home and concerns about returning Black veterans asserting their rights, especially after the battle against Nazi racism. The Mississippi Progressive Voters' League (MPVL) began to register

Black voters, targeting the state's small Black middle class. Fears of Black political influence led the legislature to tighten voting laws in 1947. These fears hardened the racial line even in the more tolerant Gulf Coast. Thomas Spencer, a Black veteran, registered to vote in Pass Christian in May 1946 as a Democrat, echoing MPVL president T. B. Wilson's advice to focus on the Democratic Party. The Mississippi Republican Party was a weak organization of "Black and Tan" Republicans under the leadership of Perry Howard, who did not even live in the state, so the Democrats were the only effective political party. Yet when Spencer actually tried to vote in the Democratic primary, election officials turned him away, saying, "Even if you paint your face white, you don't vote here."[28]

Black voters like Thomas Spencer seem to have suffered only a temporary setback on the coast, with the postwar attitudes somewhat relaxing again by the 1950s. By that decade, Lawrence Guyot Sr. and his family had moved out of his father-in-law's house to one down the street at 343 Davis. The elder Guyot now worked as a cement finisher in town, doing contracting work to support his family. Lawrence Guyot Jr. recalled postwar Pass Christian fondly, insisting that he "never experienced any racial violence for the first seventeen years of my life." He said he used public buses and libraries freely and that he did not know of any Black residents being turned away from voting. In fact, he said that he didn't even know that most Blacks in Mississippi could not vote until he was seventeen. His family also visited a local Black doctor, Felix Dunn, who confirmed relaxed coastal attitudes toward Black voting. He said that the Harrison County circuit clerk did not use the "understanding clause" of the Mississippi State Constitution of 1890 to create obstacles to Black voting, whereby potential Black (but not white) voter applicants were asked to interpret obscure sections of the state constitution. The toleration of limited Black voting appears not even to have been affected by the white backlash in the state after the Supreme Court issued the *Brown v. Board of Education* ruling in 1954, when the rise of anti-integration groups like the White Citizens' Councils created a wave of violence and intimidation that dropped the number of registered Black voters in the state from 22,000 to 12,000. Biloxi, by contrast, did not even have a chapter of the Citizens' Council until 1960, and none appeared to have existed anywhere in Harrison County in 1959, a dramatic difference from Jackson and the Delta, which experienced rapid Citizens' Council growth after the first branch opened in Indianola in 1954. The attitude in Harrison County thus differed sharply from clerks in the Delta counties and especially from that of Theron Lynd, the Forrest County circuit clerk—and later nemesis of Lawrence Guyot Jr.—who after his election in 1959 did not allow a single Black applicant to even *attempt* to take the registration test. Black votes in Harrison County played a role in electing more moderate white candidates, such as giving Curtis Dedeaux the margin of victory in the 1959 sheriff's race. Dedeaux replaced J. J. Whitman, an active collaborator with the Mississippi State Sovereignty Commission, the state's official investigative body to maintain segregation and white supremacy.[29]

Although the teenage Guyot grew up on the more tolerant Gulf Coast and enjoyed an education that sheltered him from many of the experiences of Black Mississippians elsewhere, this did not mean that he was unaware of segregation. Jim Crow was firmly in place on the coast, with segregated and unequal public schools and other public facilities, from buses to courtrooms. Gilbert Mason, a Black doctor living in Biloxi, reported that the poll tax and literacy tests still kept most Blacks away from the polls in local elections, and white political candidates would not address integrated audiences. White businessmen in the Biloxi Chamber of Commerce denied Mason membership, and his patients—all Black—experienced substandard and dangerous conditions at the local hospital, even though he received some hospital privileges, something Black doctors in Jackson did not enjoy. Despite the presence of Jim Crow on the coast, the toleration of Black voting, without the creative interpretations of the understanding clause by local registrars—as long as the legal and financial hurdles set by state law were met, of course—stands in sharp contrast to other areas of 1950s Mississippi. The Reverend George W. Lee, an activist with the National Association for the Advancement of Colored People (NAACP), publicly urged Black Mississippians to register to vote in the spring of 1955 in Mound Bayou, an all-Black Delta town. Two weeks later shotgun-wielding white men killed him in Belzoni. White assailants also shot Lee's friend and fellow NAACP member Gus Courts for his activism. Courts survived and fled to Chicago. That summer, a white man shot Lamar Smith, a Black farmer and World War II veteran, in Brookhaven in southwestern Mississippi for urging Black residents to register and vote in the Democratic primary. Despite his being murdered on the courthouse lawn on a busy Saturday afternoon, no one came forward as a witness.[30] In such a context, the Gulf Coast must have seemed a relative haven.

Mason's recollections suggest the role that class and education played in the Black community on the Gulf Coast. The Guyots and others in the social circle that Lawrence grew up in could pay the poll tax, something that many Black Mississippians, including fellow coastal residents, could not afford. Higher rates of illiteracy among poorer Blacks also kept them from voting. Jim Crow shadowed even the advantages that the Black middle class on the coast enjoyed over their less-fortunate neighbors and Black residents of other counties. The Catholic Church operated the Catholic schools in Gulfport as segregated institutions, but they were still superior to the Black public schools.[31]

Guyot's childhood appeared to have been a relatively sheltered one compared to many other Black Mississippians, given his fond recollections of his upbringing. His educational background, which included graduating from high school, reflected that. His mother, the most educated person in his immediate family, likely influenced the education that would play a major role in his outlook. He can hardly be blamed if he was less aware than others of the full extent of Mississippi racism and poverty, as his parents no doubt worked to blunt the harsh limitations that Jim Crow put on so many African Americans. He admitted that on the Gulf Coast there "was a more literate, a more open frame of political reference." Compared to the rest of the state that may have well been true, but even during Guyot's childhood white supremacists attempted to limit Black voting and participation, such as during the 1946 Democratic primary in the county (see below). His upbringing convinced him that voters should be literate, a belief he would take all the way to his first days of involvement in the civil rights movement. It would take exposure to a world beyond his Gulf Coast upbringing to make him shed this notion.[32]

Guyot's lineage made him well aware of the importance of Black political participation. Louis Piernas, who died in 1954, spent time with his great-grandnephew. Guyot learned from his elderly great-uncle about the importance of not just political participation but also self-help and community. Guyot attended J. W. Randolph High School, an all-Black high school, and Piernas told Guyot about the school's namesake. An attorney and former member of the state legislature, Randolph, nicknamed "Professor," became principal of the Harrison County Training School in 1891. He died in the 1920s, and his estate in 1930 willed money to renovate the building and purchase new furnishings and equipment. In 1939 the board renamed the school in honor of Randolph. Guyot said that Piernas told him "who Randolph was[,] . . . the kind of person he was and stuff like that," reminding him of the obligations that people had to help one another and the next generation, advice that Guyot would put into action during his adulthood.[33]

Guyot did live in reality, and, like other Black children, he worked from an early age out of either economic necessity or at the insistence of his parents, taking his first job at age seven. The outside world also crept in, with news of the inherent violence of Jim Crow. Mississippi, a state whose brutal history stood out even among the states of the old Confederacy, did little to hide its repression of Black people. The Magnolia State accounted for 476 lynchings from 1889 to 1945, almost 13 percent of the nation's total, the overwhelming majority of the victims being Black males. These statistics put the state ahead of more populous ones like Texas and Georgia, prompting the *Chicago Defender* to call Mississippi "the most brutal community in history." Even the Gulf Coast experienced the phenomenon, with eight lynchings in Guyot's native Harrison County in this period, more than neighboring Jackson County (five lynchings) and Hancock County (zero).[34]

Pass Christian itself had experienced a lynching in 1903, when a white woman visiting from New York suffered what a local historian called "a terrible crime"—apparently a rape—and a committee organized for the purpose lynched the Black man accused of the crime, before a hasty and questionable trial conducted by the local authorities. The execution was carried out in a highly organized fashion, with two local physicians present, and the leader of the mob "thanked the crowd for the orderly and quiet matter in which the whole matter was conducted." A jury commenced the following day and delivered a guilty verdict "as usual" and said that "the execution was committed by parties unknown." The episode fit the spectacle of the orderly lynching carried out by "respectable" members of the community as well as local whites' sense of noblesse oblige, as reportedly the unnamed leader of the mob used his influence to prevent further reprisals against the Black community. A local judge ordered a grand jury to investigate, but nothing came of the investigation. To John Lang, the local historian, this murder "did more to quiet any feeling between the races" and that "there has never been sufficient friction between the races to ignite a match," a paternalistic view that makes the lynching seem like a mutual agreement between local whites and Blacks rather than an episode of white terrorism that cowed the local Black community into compliance. The orderly manner of the lynching contrasted with the sadistic ritualized torture of other Mississippi lynchings of this era, such as the brutal murders of Luther and Annie Holbert in 1904 in the Delta, where a white mob severed their ears and fingers and ripped out hunks of their flesh with a corkscrew. To "progressive" whites in Pass Christian, the lack of bloodlust when hanging the suspected rapist proved the imagined racial liberalism of their town and region. The savagery of the Mississippi Delta counties further reinforced this idyllic viewpoint, since there the conflicts between Black sharecroppers and white landlords in those Black-majority plantation counties led to larger numbers of lynchings than on the more economically diversified Gulf Coast.[35] The Gulf Coast, then, could imagine itself as even more noblesse oblige than the Delta planters—but no less paternal than them. And torture or no torture, death was still the end result for the Black lynching victim, whether the mob was in Pass Christian or Pontotoc, Biloxi or Batesville.

The number of recorded lynchings in Mississippi declined during the Great Depression and World War II, but instead of a drop in violence, the murders became more secretive, with victims likely to be killed quietly rather than in a highly publicized spectacle. Nor did the "enlightened" coastal attitudes mean that Black people from that region had any illusions about white supremacy. One disgruntled Black soldier serving in Europe during World War II said in a letter that "if the Japs took America" he "would fare better," and that while he hoped the Germans would leave alone his mother's Harrison County home, they were welcome to have downtown Gulfport. Legal lynching began to replace the mob as well, vividly seen in the case of Willie McGee, a married father of four accused by a white housewife in Laurel of rape. The case and appeals dragged on for five years and led to McGee's eventual conviction. The guilty verdict came despite evidence that the woman, who was also McGee's employer, had coerced McGee into having an affair and that she had cried rape only when he broke it off. After appeals to the US Supreme Court were exhausted, McGee was executed in Laurel in 1951, in Mississippi's portable electric chair.[36] The wide publicity surrounding the trial no doubt reminded all Black Mississippians, who of course needed no reminding, of the perils of living in a Jim Crow society.

Emmett Till in August 1955 became the most famous lynching victim during Guyot's childhood. Till, a fourteen-year-old from Chicago, had traveled down to visit his grand-uncle Moses Wright, a sharecropper in the Delta. The northern-born Till, unfamiliar with the ways of Jim Crow Mississippi, whistled (or cat-called, depending on the account) at a white woman working in a local store in the tiny village of Money. He did this on a dare from his friends, who did not believe his boasts about having a white girlfriend in Chicago. The woman, Carolyn Bryant, did not tell her husband, Roy Bryant, about the incident. When he learned of it from others, he and his half-brother, J. W. Milam, sought revenge. The two men abducted Till from Wright's cabin and murdered him. When Till's decomposing body surfaced three days later in the Tallahatchie River, the authorities charged Milam and Bryant with murder. The widespread publicity made this case different since Till was from the North, and the murder occurred during the new scrutiny on the Magnolia State and the South in general after the *Brown* ruling. The trial of the two men attracted international attention, which became outrage as an all-white jury quickly acquitted Bryant and Milam. The next year, the two men admitted their guilt in a paid interview with *Look* magazine. The murder of Till resonated nationwide with Black Americans. Anne Moody, a Black teenager in Wilkinson County, Mississippi, said, "Before Emmett Till's murder, I had known the fear of hunger, hell, and the Devil. But now there was a new fear known to me—the fear of being killed because I was Black."[37] Such fears reached every Black teenager in Mississippi, no matter the region.

This awareness of racial injustice and violence, especially elsewhere in the Magnolia State, contributed to the political maturation of Guyot, adding to the already strong foundation his family had laid. One area that Guyot cited as influencing his political upbringing was his Roman Catholicism. He said that his family was "very involved" in the Church in Pass Christian, and that he "learned early" that he came from a "strong, Catholic family." At age seven, he read Paul's letters to the Galatians and the Ephesians before the congregation of St. Philomena's Catholic Church, the Black Catholic church in Pass Christian. The church also included a parish elementary school (formerly known as St. Joseph's Colored School) for Black children that provided free education, since many families could not afford tuition or even textbooks. Guyot said that he learned early from his family "the value of service and the interrelationship between religion and politics." His religious upbringing, like his educational and political background, gave him a life experience different from that of most Black Mississippians, reared in the various Protestant denominations that largely marked the Black religious experience. For example, race could be discussed more openly within the Catholic Church than other Mississippi churches. Beginning in 1954, he had worked as an attendant in his local church, and he said that he and the priest "had constant political discussions," including how the *Brown* decision would be implemented.[38]

Yet if Guyot cited his Catholic upbringing as an influence on his future civil rights activism, he apparently drew inspiration from local clergy and laity, for the Catholic Church in the United States offered little more than rhetoric in the fight against white supremacy. The Church finally took an unequivocal stand against racism in 1958 when US bishops approved a statement that "if our hearts are poisoned by hatred, or even indifference toward the welfare and rights of our fellow men, then our nation faces a grave internal crisis." The bishops went on to denounce segregation and racial discrimination and affirm the equality of all men before God, but then watered down their tone with fence-straddling moderation by criticizing both "a gradualism that is merely a cloak for inaction" and a "rash impetuosity that would sacrifice the achievements of decades in ill-timed and ill-considered ventures"—a repeat of the go-slow attitude of white moderates in the 1950s. While some bishops had taken proactive steps to integrate their parishes prior to *Brown*, these had come on the edges of the South, in areas like St. Louis and Washington, DC, and none on the Gulf Coast had done so. There were some individual actions of racial progress, such as when a Black priest said Mass at St. Clare's Parish, a white church in Waveland, on the Gulf Coast. When some white parishioners objected, Bishop Richard Gerow of Natchez (himself a native of Mobile) refused to budge, but this may have been as much about his not tolerating challenges to his authority as any commitment to equality. In 1951, Bishop Gerow also ordered the clergy to not allow segregation in church seating or communion in the diocese, in response to an integration resolution issued by the Catholic Committee of the South, an organization that lobbied for improved race relations within southern dioceses. These efforts were only partially successful. Gerow integrated only the first grade of parochial schools in 1964, after several public school districts had integrated under federal court order, showing him to be largely a follower rather than a leader. It was not until August 1965 that Gerow finally moved without prompting from secular authorities when he ordered all of Mississippi's seventy-five Catholic schools integrated. As for civil rights demonstrations, Catholic clergy and laity did not play a significant role prior to the Selma-to-Montgomery March in 1965. The low numbers of Black clergy in leadership positions, especially when compared to their more numerous Protestant counterparts, further added to Catholic inaction on civil rights.[39] Lay Catholics like Guyot, not the clergy, would defy the stereotype of Catholic passivity and disinterest in the civil rights movement. Other Black Catholics involved in the movement included his friend and Tougaloo classmate Ruben Anderson, who attended a Black Catholic school in Jackson. Anderson, who later became a civil rights attorney and the first Black person elected to the Mississippi Supreme Court, was also law partner with another Black Catholic, Fred Banks Jr. Banks, a fellow civil rights attorney and a schoolmate of Anderson, succeeded him on the court when he retired.[40]

Despite the mixed record of the Catholic Church on desegregation, it was still better than that of Catholics' more numerous evangelical brethren. The Mississippi Baptist Convention refused to endorse the *Brown* decision, openly defying the resolution of support for it from the Southern Baptist Convention's Christian Life Commission. The Methodist Council of Bishops supported the Supreme Court decision as well, but eight bishops in the Southeastern Jurisdiction (including Mississippi's bishop) issued a disclaimer saying that the council's declaration had little affect over southern Methodists. Mississippi presbyteries reacted with similar outrage when the General Assembly of the Southern Presbyterian Church echoed the Baptists and Methodists with a strong criticism of segregation.[41]

The limited steps of the Catholic Church toward desegregation, especially in neighboring Louisiana, alarmed Mississippi's segregationist ruling class. Archbishop Joseph Francis Rummel began to desegregate the New Orleans parish schools after *Brown* and threatened to excommunicate Catholic state legislators who acted to block desegregation efforts. Catholics were the third-largest denomination in Mississippi, behind the Southern Baptists and Methodists. The network of parochial schools and parishes the Church operated, as well as its three hospitals, appeared to have been the target of a pair of bills in Jackson that would have stripped any religious institutions "that offend against segregation" of their ad valorem tax exemptions. After vigorous debate, the bills were defeated largely due to the opposition of other denominations, who opposed the bills' violation of the separation of church and state.[42]

The local white Catholic clergy who likely provided inspiration for young Guyot included the Reverend George J. Strype, the Brooklyn-born parish priest of St. Philomena's since 1942. He testified before a special committee of the US Senate investigating Theodore Bilbo's 1946 US Senate campaign in Mississippi, during which Bilbo had openly called for county registrars to block Black applicants from registering to vote. Strype attended the hearing in Jackson and said he knew of attempts to prevent his parishioners from voting in Pass Christian, including recently returned Black veterans. He said that white election officials had not allowed them to vote in run-off elections for city officials, even though Black voters voted in the municipal primaries. He said they had also been turned away during the 2 July primary. When he asked Lester Garriga, the county patrolman, about this, Garriga told Strype that no Black voters were going to vote in Pass Christian "unless they paint their faces white." Strype blamed Bilbo's influence for the obstruction, as he said that the mayor of Pass Christian was "an intimate friend of the Senator's." Bilbo had also said at a rally in Greenwood that the mere fact that eighty-two Black voters had been permitted to vote in the 4 June municipal elections in Pass Christian represented "one of the most damnable demonstrations of demagoguery in our Southland." A New York Times photograph showed Strype testifying in the presence of Bilbo, who was eventually cleared by the committee. Strype's testimony, which included city officials telling him the local election commission had decided that "no Negroes could vote in Pass Christian," belied the reputation of the coast as being tolerant of African American voting and showed that voter suppression reached to every corner of the state. Despite these reports, the Sea Coast Echo, the newspaper for nearby Bay St. Louis, reported that a "false rumor" had circulated in the region that some areas would not conduct voting at all due to the possibility of Black voters showing up. The paper reported that "approximately fifty negroes" voted in the county during the 2 July Democratic primary. Bilbo and William Colmer, one of the candidates for the Democratic primary in the Sixth Congressional District, still carried the county by "tremendous majorities," the paper said. Colmer made no appeals for racial moderation, having earlier issued a campaign statement to the "sovereign white voters" of the district. The preference of the county's white voters for Bilbo and Colmer indicated that white moderation on the coast had its limits. Guyot may have later said that he "lived in an environment where Blacks could register to vote freely," but that did not make the coast immune to the pressures of white demagogues from elsewhere in Mississippi.[43]

Father John Rottermann replaced Strype as pastor in 1954, making him probably the priest with whom Guyot engaged in political discussions. But a lay Catholic, his grandfather Jules, played the key role in Guyot's religious and educational outlook. Guyot said that "he and I were buddies" and that they read the newspaper every day. Jules told his grandson in confidence that "there are two kinds of people in America: Catholics and the heathens." Guyot said that he "didn't entirely subscribe to that doctrine," and completely rejected it later in his life. But Jules, who described himself as a "Catholic's Catholic," taught his grandson the importance of communication and listening. Guyot said that Baptist friends of his grandfather would meet him at his house every Sunday and try to persuade him to convert to their faith. As this continued every Sunday, Guyot said, "Grandpa, you're smarter than all these people. Why do you do this?" Jules replied, "Boy, it gives me a way of saying, I listen to them. It also gives me a way to plan longer what I want to say." As Guyot recalled, "I just kept learning from him."[44]

Guyot mostly mentioned the influence of his family, like his grandfather and great uncle, in the interviews he gave later in his life. The undoubtedly important role that women played often did not rise to the level of recollection in his memories. For Lawrence, who had no sisters, his mother, with her education, likely had the greatest influence of all the women in his family.

Guyot's growing interest in civil rights involved people outside of his family as well, especially when he attended Randolph High School. The husky teenager befriended W. C. Ryals, the owner of a local grocery store, and in 1957, when Guyot was seventeen, the two of them invited Medgar Evers to Pass Christian. Evers, the field secretary for the state NAACP, had been tirelessly investigating lynchings and trying to register voters amid the post-*Brown* backlash. Evers discussed with them the racial climate in the state and on the Gulf Coast. As Guyot recalled, Evers told them that, "compared to the rest of Mississippi, there were no problems here at all."[45]

Despite the voter suppression during the era of Bilbo, Guyot cited an incident from his youth as an example of the coast's difference from the rest of Mississippi. One of his jobs in his teen years was bartending for white weddings, parties, and other events. He said that he "used to make a lot of money serving drinks" and was "a pretty good bartender." One Saturday in late 1960, Guyot bartended at a wedding reception, which occurred not long after the highly publicized nuptials of Sammy Davis Jr. and the Swedish actress May Britt, who had married that November. While thirty states banned interracial marriage by World War II, a state-by-state-campaign of gradual repeal began in the late 1940s, after the *Perez v. Sharp* decision by the California Supreme Court struck down that state's interracial marriage law. Still, Mississippi and numerous other states enforced bans against interracial marriage, and national prejudice against mixed-race unions was strong, with a 1963 poll indicating that 93 percent of white Americans would be upset if their teenage daughter dated a Black male.[46]

A white woman at the party approached Guyot and in the midst of the crowded room and asked him, "Look, don't you think those two people [Davis and Britt] should not have gotten married?" He thought, "Well, it's time to go home now because I know what I'm going to say and what the reaction is going to be" and then told the woman, "No, I think any two people who love each other or want to should get married." He said this in front of a room where all the guests were white, and then the host, a doctor from Pass Christian, walked over and said, "You're absolutely right. . . . I believe that, I always have." The doctor's reply "astounded" him.[47] Such a comment expressed openly by a white person would have been unthinkable anywhere else in the Magnolia State, but Guyot's refusal to tell the woman what she wanted to hear and agree with her foreshadowed his future civil rights leanings, as well as his own eventual marriage to a white woman.

Guyot did have a brush with the law as a teenager, and his unique upbringing on the coast with his politically active family ended up helping him. The police arrested him for selling black market slot machines. This violation would have gotten him sent up to the state prison farm in Parchman, a brutal and potentially fatal place for any Black man in Jim Crow Mississippi. Guyot's father called on his friend Bidwell Adam, a former lieutenant governor who eventually become head of the state party in the 1960s—ironically around the same time that Guyot would head the Mississippi Freedom Democratic Party (MFDP). His father was able to get Adam to intercede on his son's behalf with a phone call to Gaston Hewes, the county attorney, whom Guyot described as a "Presbyterian redneck fucker" who had a reputation for sending Black people to Parchman Farm. Adam secured young Guyot's release and at one point even invoked Guyot's light skin color, telling the police that he was creole, not Black. "I didn't correct him," Guyot later recalled, laughing. But he also reflected on the seriousness of the situation as well. "Here was political power being exercised in that one telephone call," he recalled later in his life. "Without that telephone call . . . I would never have been in SNCC [the Student Nonviolent Coordinating

Committee]. I'd never have gone to law school and I'd never been able to make the contribution that I have to America. . . . I believe that everything is political. There is no exception."[48]

The industrial and labor presence on the Gulf Coast also provided opportunities for Guyot not available to Black Mississippians in other parts of the state. He began working as a longshoreman for the Ingalls Shipyard, and there he became involved in union organizing for the AFL-CIO. He "worked on the pier," as the longshoremen say, beginning in the 1956–57 year. The ILA used a dating system for man-hours that runs from 1 October to 30 September, so Guyot likely began working right when he got out of high school. With a membership of only 24,000 in the state in 1959 and declining, as well as the racial prejudice of white locals against interracial organizing, labor had little impact on Mississippi's status quo. Still, the experience contributed to Guyot's political maturation, and he would put his union organizing skills to good use later in SNCC and the MFDP.[49]

Guyot knew he benefited from these various factors in his upbringing. "I consider myself very fortunate," he recalled. "I was born in the right town. I get to go to the right church. I get to go to the right college." When Guyot graduated from high school in 1957, he had an opportunity to go further than his parents or grandparents had. His good grades got him an academic scholarship to attend Tougaloo College near Jackson. For the teenage Guyot, Tougaloo College represented the most fitting place to nurture his nascent civil rights activism. The American Missionary Association, in cooperation with the Freedman's Bureau, founded Tougaloo in 1869 as a school for Black Mississippians. In 1871, the Reconstruction-era state government granted a charter of incorporation for Tougaloo University. Although the new school focused on training Black schoolteachers and enrolled primarily African American students, it had an open attendance policy. The school had a racially mixed faculty, staff, and board of trustees, although the college presidents at the time of Guyot's enrollment had all been white. Renamed Tougaloo College in 1916, it focused on agricultural and mechanical training in its formative years, but a liberal arts curriculum gained influence there, especially by the 1920s. In 1948 it became the first Black college in Mississippi to gain accreditation as a four-year liberal arts school.

The college also had a reputation for civil rights activism, seen when the school's Black chaplain, the Reverend William Albert Bender, filed a complaint with the state attorney general when a local registrar rebuffed his attempt to vote in the 1946 Democratic primary. Beginning in 1952, Ernst Borinski, a German Jewish sociology professor, attracted interracial audiences with his Social Science Forum, a series of speakers who discussed various contemporary issues, including race and politics. A rare space in Mississippi where Black and white people could gather freely to discuss racial issues, the forums even included interracial dinners, which for the Black and white participants was likely the first time they had ever shared a meal on equal terms with each other. The Reverend John Mangram, the school's new chaplain, continued this activism by organizing a regional NAACP conference in 1956. Tougaloo's reputation as the best Black college in the state and its history of opposing segregation made it, in Guyot's words, "the perfect place for me."[50]

It was perfect in another way, too. Guyot may not have been aware, but Tougaloo's reputation also included elitism and color consciousness, which it shared with the schools of the Black elite, like Howard University or Morehouse College. Tougaloo had many of the same biases of those better-known universities, despite being, in the words of Lawrence Otis Graham, "populated by poorer students from the Deep South." At campus religious services, light-skinned women students, as historians of the college have noted, "tended to sit together in church, pointedly excluding their darker sisters." This bias carried over to invitations to join campus clubs and even grading, as darker-skinned students believed that their lighter-skinned classmates received more favorable marks from teachers, even well into the 1960s. Anne Moody recalled that when she received a scholarship to the college in the early 1960s, a friend of hers told her, "Baby, you're too Black. You gotta be high yellow with a rich-ass daddy [to go to Tougaloo]." While not true, Moody did notice a lot of "yellow" students—but some darker ones, too—when she moved to the campus. Guyot, as a light-skinned Black man from a higher socioeconomic background than most Black Mississippians, fit well into the social world of Tougaloo, even if he did not necessarily share these biases.[51]

Guyot majored in chemistry and physics, and apparently focused on his studies in his early years at Tougaloo. There is no evidence of his participating in civil rights activities in the late 1950s, although he said he joined the NAACP campus chapter at some point and became its treasurer. His apparent lack of activism is not surprising, as the advances made by the civil rights movement elsewhere in the South—such as in Montgomery in 1956 and Little Rock in 1957—did not penetrate the seemingly impenetrable curtain of white supremacy in Mississippi. Activists like Medgar Evers exerted their energies in the 1950s investigating the murders of Black men in the state, and helped organize NAACP youth chapters, but only managed incremental, even glacial, change. Overall, there was an increase in the civil rights organization's statewide membership to 15,000 members by 1959, from a low of 8,000 in the mid-1950s.[52]

Of course, Guyot needed no reminding of what life was like for a Black man in Mississippi. No longer on the Gulf Coast, he now lived in proximity to the much more rigid Jim Crow environment of Jackson, a thoroughly segregated city. While Jackson did not have the same level of toleration of Black voting that the Gulf Coast did, Black voter registration crept up enough by the late 1950s to prove decisive in defeating two of the more extreme white supremacists in local politics. The transition to the city no doubt reminded him of the differences within the state regarding patterns of segregation and racial tolerance.[53]

As if Guyot needed any more reminding, the savagery of lynching hit closer to his hometown in 1959. In Poplarville, less than fifty miles from Pass Christian, a white mob broke into the local jail and abducted Mack Charles Parker, a Black man charged with raping a white woman. The evidence against Parker was dubious at best, built on coerced confessions from his friends and not supported by polygraph tests. His kidnappers beat and shot him, dumping his body into the Pearl River. A local grand jury, overseen by a judge who was a member of the White Citizens' Council, did not return any indictments, nor did a federal grand jury in Biloxi, despite identification of several of the lynchers by the Federal Bureau of Investigation (FBI). As the historian John Dittmer has noted, the police allowed the lynchers to take Parker from their custody, the first time this had happened in Mississippi since World War II. Medgar Evers told his wife that he wanted "to get a gun and just start shooting" after hearing about Parker's murder.[54] For Guyot and other Black residents of the Gulf Coast, the closeness of the lynching reinforced to them that no place in Mississippi was safe for a Black person.

The violence came even closer to home in 1960, when the first major anti-integration attacks occurred on the Gulf Coast. In April 1960, local Black residents in Harrison County held a "wade-in" at the segregated county beach, a peaceful action echoing the sit-in movement that had begun in February of that year in Greensboro, North Carolina. There, a sit-in by Black college students at a whites-only lunch counter triggered protests against segregated public and private accommodations all across the South. Local doctor Gilbert Mason had led the first wade-in the year before, in May 1959, but that one ended peacefully when police told the demonstrators to leave. Yet the April 1960 wade-in triggered a brutal white response. When a group of more than 100 local African Americans conducted the wade-in, a white mob attacked the beach protesters with clubs, chains, and other improvised weapons, inflicting serious injuries, while local police refused to maintain order or stop the assaults. White gunmen injured several people as the violence spread to nearby Biloxi. The riot attracted national attention from the press and condemnation from national civil rights leaders. It shattered the mirage of the Gulf Coast as an oasis of racial toleration, and Curtis Dedeaux, the sheriff whom Black Harrison County voters favored in

1959, privately intimidated demonstrators before the protests with threats of force and ordered his deputies to not make any arrests during the riot.[55]

Statewide, the arrival of direct action campaigns like the wade-ins in Mississippi pushed the state NAACP out of its conservative mindset. State president C. R. Darden of Meridian, who opposed the sit-ins and similar protests, resigned in the fall of 1960. He was replaced by Aaron Henry, a pharmacist from Clarksdale who favored greater militancy against Jim Crow. A World War II veteran and the first Black person in Coahoma County to vote in a Democratic primary, Henry was elected president of the local NAACP chapter in 1954.[56]

Tougaloo reflected these changes as well. In 1960, Reverend Mangram of Tougaloo College helped organize a youth branch of the NAACP on the campus. This coincided with the trustees' selection of Adam D. Beittel to be the new college president. Beittel, a white man from a Quaker family with an education from Oberlin College and the University of Chicago, had a long reputation for racial liberalism. His activism included writing antisegregation articles and hosting interracial conferences at Talladega College in Alabama during his presidency there from 1945 to 1952. His actions led to his dismissal from Talladega, but that did not seem to concern the Tougaloo trustees.[57]

Beittel arrived amid the burgeoning student activism of the sit-ins and turned Tougaloo into a safe space for civil rights activists. Yet the campus had only 500 students in 1960, so one of the students, Colia Liddell, asked a new sociology professor, John Salter Jr., to become involved with the North Jackson NAACP Youth Council. Liddell, the president of that organization, thought the Tougaloo branch too small to be effective. Salter, raised in Arizona by a white mother and Abenaki Indian father, had arrived in Jackson only weeks before Liddell asked him to become involved with the NAACP. He accepted her offer and became chapter adviser of the Youth Council, which grew in a year to include 500 members from Tougaloo, Jackson State, and local Black high schools. His wife Eldri helped revitalize the Tougaloo chapter as its campus adviser.[58]

The first major involvement of Tougaloo students with direct action came in 1961. Nine students, also NAACP members, launched a sit-in at the whites-only Jackson Municipal Library on 27 March. Police arrested the students, who became known as the "Tougaloo Nine." Jackson State College students, who did not enjoy administration support or toleration of their actions, soon joined the protests. The police responded violently to a protest march by the students, using tear gas and police dogs to disperse the marchers.[59]

Guyot did not take part in these demonstrations or sit-ins. He appeared to be an average student, never making the dean's lists posted in the college newspaper, even though he claimed that he "scored off the charts on everything."

Everything, that is, except mathematics and chemistry. His weaknesses in these areas did more than keep him off the dean's list—they also ended his initial plan to become a medical doctor. He then shifted his goal toward law school. He also played varsity football his freshman year but ceased involvement in campus athletics after that. During his junior year, fellow students elected him to serve as his class's sergeant-at-arms. An active member of the campus Greek system, Guyot pledged in the Omega Psi Phi Fraternity, Rho Epsilon Chapter, and served on the Pan-Hellenic Council. Guyot's joining a Black fraternity reflected his likely aspirations, as the organizations' membership eventually encompassed much of the Black professional class of college graduates, the "Talented Tenth" whom W. E. B. Du Bois had called upon to uplift the rest of Black America. Founded in 1911 by students at Howard University, Omega Psi Phi came to include famous members like Langston Hughes and Dr. Carter G. Woodson, founder of Negro History Week, later Black History Month. The fraternity did not have as strong a reputation for civil rights activism as other Black fraternities, being one of the few African American Greek-letter organizations that did not join the American Council on Human Rights, a civil rights lobbying group founded in 1948. However, its members promoted various causes, and as early as the 1920s the national fraternity promoted Negro History and Literature Week and sent a resolution to all US state governors condemning the activities of the Ku Klux Klan. Individual members of the fraternity took part in civil rights activities like the sit-ins, including undergraduate members.[60]

Young Guyot then experienced pledging for Omega Psi Phi, no doubt an interesting experience. Pledges in the fraternity's campus chapters initially wore Scottish kilts and carried lamps in their hands as part of their pledge uniforms, a practice that originated in the 1940s. By the 1950s, chapters began adopting canine-themed pledge garb. This hazing included brothers calling pledges "dogs," and making them wear dog collars and leashes, drink from bowls, and bark, all part of the public humiliation. This hazing reflected the call of the fraternity, "Ahr, Ahr!," a simulated dog bark that brothers used to greet each other. Omega Psi Phi members also dressed in paramilitary garb during stepping (public marches by Black Greek-letter organizations). This dress and the stepping itself came from military influences from campus Reserve Officers' Training Corps programs and the presence of many World War II veterans at Black universities. The fraternity also had traditions rooted in African American Christianity, such as the pledge song "Zoom," which alluded to crossing the river Jordan to get into Heaven.[61]

Like many other college students, Guyot also worked to make ends meet. He continued to work as a longshoreman intermittently from 1957 to 1961, most likely during the summer break back on the Gulf Coast. He only worked 18.5 hours during his freshman year, 31 hours his sophomore year, and just 5 his junior year. His time with the union ended in 1961, when he logged his most hours, 296.75, the equivalent of thirty-seven eight-hour days.[62] The year after that he would become a civil rights organizer and have no more time for a longshoreman's duties.

Guyot did not absent himself from discussions of civil rights and racial justice, despite his more traditional college extracurricular activities. By the early 1960s the Social Science Forums attracted more nationally renowned speakers than in the past, a result of Tougaloo's growing prominence as a civil rights movement center. James Baldwin, Ralph Bunche, Kenneth Galbraith, and other luminaries spoke at the forums, adding to the earlier list of local speakers like Medgar Evers and writer Eudora Welty. Guyot regularly attended these forums, where he saw the simple act of dining together as "radicalizing" due to the accompanying intellectual exchanges and debates between whites and Blacks over controversial issues. The radical nature of these forums is extraordinary considering the social and political pressure that white society and the state government put on all Mississippians, white and Black, to suppress any criticism of segregation. These forums introduced Guyot to local activism and organizing, where he met activists like Joyce and Dorie Ladner and Hollis Watkins, whom he would later work with in the Mississippi civil rights movement.[63]

While not involved in early civil rights activities at Tougaloo and in Jackson, the headstrong college student already had his own troubles on campus following an incident that showed his stubbornness and outspokenness, traits that would serve him well as a leader in the movement. Reverend Mangram left Tougaloo in the summer of 1961, and early in the fall term of 1961, the college's new chaplain, the Reverend J. Hawkins, clashed with Guyot. Hawkins, a Black man from Michigan, had little sympathy for the civil rights activities of some Tougaloo students. Salter recalled that Hawkins had even told students at one point to "obey all Mississippi laws." His conservative views led him to undertake as his first project the creation of a "Discipline Committee" aimed at students. Guyot became one of the committee's first targets due to what Salter called a "very minor" infraction committed by him. What really drew the chaplain's ire was Guyot's backtalking to him. He forced Guyot to appear before the committee, whose members had been picked by Beittel, and Salter said he "chose the members . . . wisely."[64]

Salter served as Guyot's defense attorney, his first interaction with the young student, in what the professor described as "a rather surreal situation." The committee held two different meetings on Guyot, both of which lasted for hours.

The committee members all voted to acquit Guyot, except for Reverend Hawkins, who pressed for his expulsion. Rose Branch, wife of Tougaloo dean A. A. Branch, defended Guyot by pointing out that he was from Pass Christian, and "those folks down there can be very feisty indeed." Branch, like Beittel, supported student demonstrations as long as academic standards did not suffer, and Guyot described the dean as "*very* political." By the spring of 1962, evidence surfaced that "Reverend" Hawkins had faked his credentials, so the Discipline Committee died and the president did not rehire him—something Salter approved of, since the chaplain was "not at all in tune with the spirit of Tougaloo." Before he left, he had yet another heated argument with Salter, and Hawkins told him that "Guyot will never do anything worthwhile, anywhere."[65]

John Salter had a considerable influence over Guyot, who took several of Salter's sociology courses. Salter said that he "was greatly impressed with his sharpness and his extremely strong commitment to social justice." Salter eventually gave him his personal copy of *Attorney for the Damned: Clarence Darrow in the Courtroom*, a biography by Arthur Weinberg. As Guyot eventually became a civil rights activist and political organizer, Salter said that he "saw that gift as a very effective investment."[66]

Ernest Borinski, the chair of the sociology department, also helped mold Guyot. As a Jew, Borinski knew about racial discrimination firsthand, having fled Nazi Germany in the late 1930s. Also a legal scholar, Borinski encouraged his students not to demonstrate but to work within the system to undo Jim Crow through legal means. A year after his arrival in 1947, he created the Social Science Laboratory, in which students connected classroom learning to current events and social conditions. In fact, white faculty at Tougaloo had more of an activist presence than the college's Black faculty, enjoying greater freedom and fewer constraints under Jim Crow, especially in their ability to find employment on other campuses. Still, Guyot said that there was a "brilliant compilation of very freedom-oriented, very well-educated faculty at Tougaloo," professors who had "the ability to bring out the best instincts of freedom and liberty and justice." He singled out Borinski for contributing to his future involvement and political development with the Freedom Democrats, declaring that the professor "taught me as much about politics as anyone else. [He] taught us that there are some institutions that are functional in their dysfunctionality, and this becomes one of the linchpins conceptually of the Mississippi Freedom Democratic Party." In all, Guyot remembered the college as "an oasis of academic excellence and individual and collective liberation."[67]

Guyot's recollections of his education at Tougaloo also suggest that it played a much larger role in his life than even his Catholic upbringing. The Protestant affiliation of Tougaloo also influenced him, as he recalled that he "got as much religious liberation out of the chapel at Tougaloo as I would have gotten at any other church anywhere. This was a school about liberation, about empowerment, unabashedly so." Much of that likely came from his education under Salter, Borinski, and other faculty, but the religious environment at the college, which allowed and encouraged activism and critical inquiry, likely differed considerably from the hesitant approach toward civil rights that the Catholic diocese in Mississippi was taking.[68]

That reputation as a civil rights center helped bring Dr. Martin Luther King Jr. to speak in the Tougaloo chapel, in a speech arranged by Aaron Henry during King's March 1962 "People-to-People" tour in Mississippi. Although Guyot attended the address, it was not King and his Southern Christian Leadership Conference (SCLC) but SNCC that drew Guyot into the civil rights movement, formed in April 1960 and born from the sit-in movement of college and high school students that year. Ella Baker, the executive director of SNCC, organized the founding conference in Raleigh, North Carolina. Frustrated with the top-down leadership of King and the SCLC, for which she served as executive secretary, she envisioned SNCC as a decentralized, grassroots organization to develop local leadership among people.[69]

SNCC emphasized both direct action and voter registration, employing college students as field secretaries to organize local civil rights campaigns. They became involved in the Freedom Rides in 1961, a series of nonviolent protests against segregated interstate public transportation, which quickly became violent as white mobs attacked the protesters in South Carolina and Alabama. Eventually the Riders arrived in Jackson, Mississippi, where police arrested them. Later that year, SNCC set up an organizing project in McComb, a town in southwestern Mississippi, under the leadership of Bob Moses, a Black mathematics teacher from New York City. Moses employed both white and Black college students in voter registration work and moved into the surrounding rural areas at the request of local residents. White violence halted this project, and the brutality claimed the life of Herbert Lee, a local Black resident murdered while assisting Moses and SNCC.[70]

Despite these setbacks, Moses remained committed to developing local Black leadership in Mississippi. He recruited Black field secretaries, since he felt the level of white violence made the use of white field secretaries unrealistic. Later in 1962, SNCC used locally recruited Black field secretaries to expand operations into Hattiesburg and the Mississippi Delta. Moses's charisma helped him immeasurably in this regard, as many SNCC members were in awe of him. Anne Moody said that she thought Moses "was Jesus Christ in the flesh."[71]

Tougaloo, with its civil rights activity now well-known due to the actions of the Tougaloo Nine during the Jackson library sit-ins, was well-suited to receive SNCC. SNCC and the college developed what one historian described as a "close relationship." Tougaloo students wrote articles for SNCC publications, volunteered for SNCC projects over the summer, and formed a campus affiliate. Joan Trumpauer, a white student at Tougaloo and a former Freedom Rider, served as SNCC's campus representative, and the college administration even approved a work-study program whereby students earned academic credit for movement volunteering.[72]

This period of expansion by SNCC brought Guyot into contact with the organization. Dorie Ladner, who with her sister Joyce was active in the student movement at Jackson State and worked closely with Medgar Evers on rallying support for the Tougaloo Nine sit-in, introduced Guyot to Bob Moses in 1962. Guyot recalled that "we talked about SNCC, and SNCC was exactly what I had been doing all my life and what my father had been doing." He connected this to the activism of his great-uncle Louis Piernas and in the Republican Party and saw joining SNCC as a continuation of the grassroots, local political activism that his family had practiced for decades. After his conversation with Moses, Guyot joined SNCC, only months before his graduation.[73] He later told fellow activist and historian Howard Zinn why he joined the movement: "I was rebelling against everything. I still am. I think we need to change every institution we know. I came to that conclusion when I was seventeen years old. . . . I'm not satisfied with any condition that I'm aware of in America."[74]

Lawrence Guyot Jr. may not have regarded his joining the Student Nonviolent Coordinating Committee as any different from his earlier activism or his family's long history of political involvement. However, his involvement in the organization and the broader civil rights movement in Mississippi would soon reveal this decision to be a turning point in his life, as he would soon rise from a newly recruited SNCC field secretary to the national spotlight as a leader of Black political empowerment—and almost become a martyr in the process.

# CHAPTER 2
# THERE WAS A WAR GOING ON, AND THE WAR WAS A VERY SIMPLE ONE

## GUYOT AND THE STUDENT NONVIOLENT COORDINATING COMMITTEE

Guyot's introduction to the Student Nonviolent Coordinating Committee (SNCC) at Tougaloo College in 1962 became his entry into full-time organizing and civil rights activism. From urban Jackson to Greenwood in the Mississippi Delta, Guyot's evolution into a grassroots leader reflected the transformative ethos of SNCC, which sought to cultivate local leaders rather than impose ones from outside the state or community. This transformation caused him to address some of the biases he inherited from his Gulf Coast birthplace, an area radically different from the brutal deprivation and white supremacy of the Mississippi Delta. But it would almost lead to young Guyot's death, as he and other SNCC activists would suffer near-martyrdom in the city jail in Winona for their efforts to register Black Mississippians to vote and break the bonds of segregation.

Lawrence Guyot began his work for SNCC in February 1962 in Jackson, at 714 Rhodes Street. At this time, the Freedom Riders had been returned to Jackson from Parchman Farm's maximum-security wing for retrial for attempting to integrate interstate terminals and buses in Mississippi. These appellate trials continued even though the Supreme Court issued a unanimous ruling on 26 February against Mississippi's segregation of transit facilities in *Bailey v. Patterson*, a class action suit that the National Association for the Advancement of Colored People (NAACP) had filed in June 1961 on behalf of four Black Jacksonians. Despite the ruling, the Court refused to issue an injunction staying the prosecution of the Freedom Riders, since none of the four plaintiffs were Riders themselves. Not surprisingly, state and local officials continued to resist the Court's ruling.[1]

The plight of the Freedom Riders and segregated interstate transportation did not attract the primary focus of Guyot and the other SNCC members. The reorganization of the Council of Federated Organizations (COFO) in February 1962 drew their attention instead. COFO was a united front of civil rights organizations in Mississippi that had been first formed in 1961 by Black leaders seeking a meeting with Governor Ross Barnett. At a meeting in Jackson in February, Aaron Henry, Medgar Evers, Bob Moses, and Tom Gaither agreed on a plan to revive the coalition and include SNCC and the Congress of Racial Equality (CORE), which along with the NAACP would now be the three main civil rights groups in COFO. Although composed of different civil rights groups, COFO effectively became one big civil rights organization, with overlapping memberships and a common vision of securing civil rights gains. Henry became the head of COFO, but the activists clashed over the appointment of others in the organization, specifically the role of non-Mississippians. According to Guyot, Henry and R. L. T. Smith—a Jackson grocer, minister, and fellow NAACP member—objected to Bob Moses, a New Yorker, being made an executive director in COFO. Guyot said that he and fellow SNCC member Hollis Watkins, as well as Dave Dennis of CORE and others, convinced Henry and Smith to accept Moses's appointment. Henry, however, made no such mention in his autobiography to any objection to Moses. Moses represented SNCC within the organization as the program director of COFO, while Dennis did the same for CORE as COFO's assistant director.[2]

COFO focused on securing the vote for Black Mississippians, which fit well with Guyot, who "was always very political," in the words of one fellow volunteer. Even before COFO, SNCC faced internal divisions over which direction would yield the most civil rights advances. SNCC as a protest organization spawned sit-ins first in the lunch counters and then in numerous other public and private accommodations. Yet some in the organization favored a more traditional focus on the ballot, a more conservative approach that received support from the Kennedy administration. The divisions in SNCC had been resolved by Ella Baker, the organizer of the meeting that created the organization, with the creation of separate direct action and voter registration wings.[3] SNCC's Mississippi organization, part of the larger COFO network, represented the voter registration wing. With much of the COFO organization made up of SNCC members using the networks and contacts established by NAACP veterans, the aims of the more conservative NAACP meshed with SNCC's voter registration arm. Guyot himself acknowledged this debt to his elders, such as Amzie Moore of the NAACP, who from his home in Cleveland had established "a hell of a network of individuals throughout the state and had had it for years," and critically could "provide contacts on a local basis" in the Delta. The federal government, seeking to channel civil rights activities away from disruptive protests that brought negative publicity, provided funds through the Voter Education Project (VEP) to COFO to help register voters. Guyot, along with other SNCC members, was skeptical about the Kennedy administration's VEP funding, fearing it was a ploy to co-opt the movement into the Democratic Party. Guyot suspected— correctly—that the real purpose was to stop public demonstrations, or, as he bluntly put it, to "get the niggers off the streets."[4]

Yet, as the white violence SNCC workers would face in Mississippi for voter registration work would soon show, the Kennedy administration's hopes that this strategy would be less disruptive proved ill-placed. Guyot said that in the eyes of white Mississippians, "anyone who tried to register somebody to vote was trouble." More trouble, he said, than desegregating a lunch counter, because "white folks understood—Black folks understood eventually—that the vote was really to bring about primary change, to make things happen. I mean, why else would people spend so much effort trying to prevent you from getting it?"[5]

Although a new member of SNCC, Guyot played an active role in the organization as a new field secretary. COFO's emphasis fit perfectly with his own family's tradition of political activism and voting. As he put it, the activists in COFO "were *not* concerned about hamburgers, about the beaches, or about the hotels . . . we left that to others." The shift to Greenwood and Hattiesburg in 1962 and 1963 to organize voter registration campaigns, he said, carried out the vital work of "getting, creating, facilitating, identifying, and promulgating leadership around the vote." He said that arrived in Greenwood from Jackson "with a specific agreement that we weren't going to desegregate anything along the way. We were going there around voter registration and nothing else."[6]

SNCC organizers had recruited Guyot as an example of that local leadership. But he said some Mississippi leaders, like Fannie Lou Hamer, his contemporary with whom he would work so closely in the Mississippi Freedom Democratic Party (MFDP), already existed. He insisted that "we didn't *produce* Fannie Lou Hamer, we simply found her." Moses and the Ladner sisters had also found Guyot and had not created him. Moses's recruitment of Guyot into SNCC in 1962 fit his goal of SNCC's developing local leadership rather than being a hierarchical, top-down organization. Ella Baker, one of the founders of SNCC, originated this approach, as she favored "group-centered" leadership as opposed to the charismatic leadership of groups like Dr. King's Southern Christian Leadership Conference. Moses did this with other SNCC workers, such as Hollis Watkins, a native of southwestern Mississippi, whom he and Marion Barry, another Mississippian, recruited into SNCC to do canvassing in McComb. Yet in keeping with

SNCC's decentralized, grassroots-centered ethos, Moses consciously avoided a heavy-handed leadership role, a position aided by his quiet and soft-spoken demeanor. The entire idea was to get local people to help themselves or, as Baker once said, showing people that "strong people don't need strong leaders."[7]

Yet leaders are human and not perfect, so effective ones learn and change over time. A grassroots local leader is no less biased or limited by his or her own experiences than a distant, national one. Guyot's life differed from that of most Black Mississippians, and it affected his attitudes in his early days in SNCC. He did not have as comfortable an existence growing up as someone like Martin Luther King Jr. in Atlanta, but in other ways Guyot resembled King more than he did Fannie Lou Hamer, who was raised as a Delta sharecropper and did not even know that she or other Black people could register to vote until SNCC canvassers arrived in Ruleville in August 1962 to conduct local organizing.[8] Guyot's upbringing, which he himself described as politicized due to the different culture of the Gulf Coast, put him closer to civil rights leaders like Aaron Henry and Medgar Evers.

Guyot's college education also contributed to his outlook. Most Black Mississippians did not even graduate from high school. Statewide, only one out of four Black Mississippi teenagers of high school age were enrolled, and of that only 13 percent were in their senior years. Yet most Black civil rights leaders in the state possessed an educational background like Guyot's. T. R. M. Howard, the founder of the Regional Council of Negro Leadership in Cleveland, Mississippi, in the 1930s, was an accomplished surgeon. Medgar Evers, who worked for Howard's Magnolia Mutual Insurance Company, used GI Bill of Rights benefits from his World War II service to attend and earn a business degree from Alcorn College. Aaron Henry used the same benefits to earn a pharmacy degree at Xavier University in New Orleans.[9] Many of the leaders of the civil rights movement, inside and outside of Mississippi, came not from abject poverty but from the Black middle class. While it is important to not exaggerate the wealth and privilege of these leaders, who still experienced the harsh stings and indignities of Jim Crow, their upbringing did give them an experience different from that of other poorer and less educated members of the Black community.

This class and educational background shaped Guyot's initial views regarding voting and political participation when he became a field secretary for SNCC. The Mississippi Gulf Coast, he said, had "a more literate, more open political frame of reference." Because of his upbringing, Guyot said that when he entered SNCC, he "firmly believed . . . that people should be able to read and write in order to vote." His experiences in Jackson, and then afterward in the Delta, with high illiteracy, poor education, and "a totally closed system," profoundly changed Guyot. The young man from the Gulf Coast who had grown up in a family of voters met people who had never voted in their lives, whom white Mississippi prevented from voting, and in the case of people like Fannie Lou Hamer, only recently knew that they *could* vote. Guyot recalled this challenge to his comparatively sheltered upbringing. "The literacy ramifications were very personal and very dramatic to me. . . . It took me about two weeks in SNCC to get disabused of that notion. I moved away from it, never to return to it in my life." His experience mirrored Medgar Evers's first job in the 1950s as a door-to-door-life insurance salesman in the Delta, where trying to sell life insurance to impoverished Black sharecroppers filled him with guilt and pushed him toward NAACP activism. Like Evers, Guyot used his Delta experience to become a better and more responsive leader.[10]

Guyot's shift also illustrated the effect that SNCC had on him, even early in his involvement. Historian Kay Hogan described the "cultural transformations" of SNCC workers as they "recognized the need for change, as well as the need to develop a democratic method of achieving it." For Guyot, this meant that his conception of democratic participation widened, leading to a removal of the conceptual barriers of his upbringing. Fannie Rushing, a member of Chicago's Friends of SNCC, called this the "transformative power of SNCC."[11]

Guyot's first major organizing campaign took him to Greenwood. This Delta town became the focus of a SNCC voter registration campaign in the summer of 1962 under the direction of Sam Block, a twenty-three-year-old vocational college student from Cleveland, Mississippi.[12] Leflore County had a population two-thirds Black (out of 47,000) in 1960, and Greenwood operated as an important site of the Delta's cotton economy. With a median income for Black families of $1,400 (compared to a median white income of $5,200) and an increasingly mechanized agriculture sector putting more and more Black farmers out of work, Greenwood combined to an even greater degree than other towns in Mississippi both the poverty and political marginalization of its Black residents. For a Black person to even register to vote required the backing of a white patron, meaning that the prospective voter had to be "a good nigger without a political thought in the world." An NAACP local, run by a service station owner named Richard West, had been leading a pay-the-poll-tax campaign among Black Greenwoodians since the 1950s, but the violent white backlash after the *Brown* decision forced West to leave the state. Some of the organizational network West and other civic leaders built remained when Block arrived in 1962.[13]

SNCC targeted six Mississippi counties, including Leflore, for voter registration drives using $5,000 of VEP funds. Bob Moses sent Sam Block to direct the

Greenwood project. Block trained at SNCC workshops in Tennessee on voter registration both at the Highlander Center and in Knoxville. The workshop leaders taught him some valuable lessons, including the importance of building personal relationships with local residents and avoiding class snobbery, especially since the preachers and other members of the Black "elite" would often be hostile to outside civil rights organizers. Block arrived alone in June 1962, left to his own devices to organize Greenwood. White pressure on Black landlords forced Block to stay in Cleveland and commute to Greenwood, but he forged relationships with some locals and by July began to take people to the registrar's office. Before he began taking people to the courthouse, he asked Moses for more manpower, and Moses promised to send Guyot and Luvaghn Brown, an eighteen-year-old volunteer. At the time, both Guyot and Brown resided in the Freedom House in Jackson, but they quickly headed to Greenwood. On their first day in town, Guyot rented a room at a boardinghouse and called the SNCC office to let them know they had arrived. The phone operator promptly contacted the landlady to inform her that a "troublemaker" had arrived at her house, and the landlady evicted them the next day. "So that was my beginning with Greenwood," Guyot recalled.[14]

Block desperately needed the presence of the two field secretaries. By the time Guyot and Brown arrived in Greenwood on 15 August, Block had organized the first mass meeting at a local Black church. By now, the Greenwood police were harassing Block and monitoring his activities. Three days before Guyot and Brown arrived, three white men beat up Block. On 16 August, their second day in town, Guyot and Brown joined Block to meet local volunteers at the SNCC office at 616 Avenue I. Block recruited the volunteers, all teenagers too young to vote, to canvass for prospective voters the next morning. Brown described "a tremendous amount of fear" among the workers. He said "our job was to go out each day and try to convince Black citizens especially to register to vote," but "Greenwood was a very dangerous place to be." Still, seven volunteers showed up the next morning, and they and the three field secretaries convinced ten people—out of a hundred contacted—to come register to vote. Of those ten, three, all women, actually showed up. Police harassment frightened the teenage volunteers away, so Guyot personally took the three women to the courthouse after a brief voter-education exercise. The police chief met them when the four arrived by taxi at the courthouse. He threatened and swore at the women, and successfully scared them away.[15]

That night, the three field secretaries stayed up late in the office to discuss the project, and as Brown put it, "find a way to get some of the fear out of the people we were working with." At about 1:00 a.m. on 17 August, when Block placed a call to Bob Moses in Cleveland, he saw an occupied police car parked outside. Fearing arrest, the men locked the door and watched the car until it drove off after ten minutes of waiting. Another car then stopped in front of the office and the workers noticed the driver was armed. At that point, fear of death replaced that of arrest, and Block unsuccessfully tried to call Moses again. After the Reverend R. L. T. Smith in Jackson and the US Justice Department both rebuffed Block's calls, the three men heard footsteps coming up the stairs, and they decided to make their escape out a window. They got to the roof just as intruders began to beat on the door and a car filled with white men pulled up. After they climbed down a TV antenna, Block led them through the local houses until they came to the home of a friendly minister, who sent them to his father's house to take refuge for the night. When the three men returned to the office in the morning, they found Bob Moses and Willie Peacock, another SNCC organizer, who arrived after the phone calls and found the office broken into and ransacked, with the records stolen.[16]

That incident showed just how alone Guyot and his fellow workers were in Greenwood. Not only did Guyot's call to Reverend Smith, a Jackson minister involved in COFO, go unanswered—Brown said that Smith said he did not know them and refused to accept any long distance collect calls—but the federal government also was no help. After being rebuffed by the Justice Department, Block had called the sole Federal Bureau of Investigation (FBI) agent stationed in Greenwood, who said he would come over. The agent did not show up until ten o'clock in the morning, apologizing for being late, and gave what Willie Peacock called a "lousy excuse." In fact, the agent had instead called the captain of the night shift at the Greenwood Police Department to ask about the incident, even though Block told the agent that they were convinced the police were behind the whole attack.[17]

Guyot later recalled, however, that the Department of Justice did provide some help, at least in areas other than Greenwood. He said that Justice Department contacts "told us what court decisions were coming down in terms of registrars, specifically Panola and Hattiesburg. We knew the decisions were coming before they came. And we had that on our side. I think that made the difference." This interaction indicates the federal government and its complex and often Janus-faced role with the movement, something amplified by the numerous different agencies of the government. While Justice lawyers provided some aid and information to the SNCC activists, such as when Guyot recalled a workshop at Mt. Beulah "pretty much run by the Department of Justice," at other times federal employees cooperated with the local white power structure. Guyot recalled seeing "with my own eyes a notice in a social security check, which you know is a federal issue, saying there are some troublemakers in this area." The notice threatened termination of benefits if the recipient helped any civil rights activists.[18]

None of this harassment deterred the SNCC men, and after the office burglary Guyot reported the incident to the *Greenwood Commonwealth*, the local newspaper, declaring that he didn't "have any doubt what their [the attackers'] intentions were." The police chief dismissed the entire incident as "trumped up" by "these outside agitators," and the paper, in a front-page editorial, echoed the chief and identified Moses and the three field secretaries by name, accusing them of wanting to "spark racial strife, without which their whole movement will wither and die." The men had to relocate their office after the nighttime attack, for the police arrested the landlord on a charge of bigamy, which the local prosecutor dropped in return for the landlord's evicting the SNCC workers from their office.[19]

Although the men now commuted from Cleveland for the time being, they continued voter registration work in Greenwood, and Block, Guyot, and Brown took thirty-one local residents to the courthouse to register in the following week. Guyot showed his characteristic defiance in a letter to the Greenwood police chief, declaring that he "must compliment you and the other members of the pseudo gestapo [*sic*] that is now commonly reffered [*sic*] to as a police department. . . . I would like to remind you that Mississippi is still a member of these United States." Other SNCC activists engaged in similar acts of defiance, such as Block telling the Leflore county sheriff, before a group of potential registrants, that "if you don't want to see me here, you better pack up and leave, because I'll be here." Movement historian John Dittmer called the bravado "calculated" so that news of the confrontation "would quickly circulate through the Black community." Mary King, a SNCC volunteer, described Guyot as "robust and feisty . . . smart, ebullient, tenacious, and someone that I never in four years saw intimidated." Brown said of Guyot that "it was almost like at times he wasn't afraid of dying. He would do stuff most of us would say 'You shouldn't do that; or 'You shouldn't talk to a person that way.' And Guyot had a lot of nerve. I liked him a lot."[20]

Only Peacock volunteered to stay full-time in Greenwood to work with Block, but Guyot and Brown, along with Moses, constantly traveled in and out of town. By now Guyot had attracted the attention of the State Sovereignty Commission (SSC), the state-funded agency pledged to defend segregation and white supremacy. His letter to the police chief ended up in the files and labeled as a "threat," and by September 1962 Tom Scarbrough, an SSC investigator in the Delta, included Guyot and his activities in his written reports. Guyot attended a trial in early September in Indianola of five defendants, including Moses and

Block, whom police arrested for "handing out literature without a city permit." The work of SNCC in Indianola had so alarmed the local white power structure that the county bar association issued a resolution—carried on the front page of the local newspaper—advising citizens of their right not to cooperate with FBI agents or investigators.[21] Scarbrough commented on Guyot's appearance, describing him as "a heavy-set yellow Negro who looked to be about White, age around 26 or 27." In addition to getting his age wrong (Guyot was twenty-three at the time), Scarbrough also literally identified Guyot as an outside agitator, reporting that "it is my thinking that he is not a native of this state." Scarbrough expanded on this belief in another report later that same month, when Guyot, Moses, Block, and others held meetings at Williams Chapel in Sunflower County to organize local residents. He now gave a more elaborate misidentification, referring to Guyot as a "Negro attorney from Atlanta, Georgia"—a misidentification that the Sovereignty Commission would continue to make as late as April 1965.[22]

In the coming months, Scarbrough continued to misidentify Guyot, describing him in an April 1963 report as "Lawrence Guyap" of Chicago and then as "Lawrence Guyat" in another report that same month. The next month, Scarbrough said that Guyot's home address was Chicago, but that he was "working out of the Central Student Non-violent Coordinating Committee Office in Atlanta, Georgia." In another of his reports, Guyot became "a mulatto Negro voter registration worker from Atlanta." Scarbrough, a former commissioner of public safety, had a long history of actively opposing integration, including helping in 1958 to prevent the integration of the University of Mississippi by Clennon King, a Black history professor at Alcorn College. Scarbrough's lackluster investigative skills are even more laughable given that he had served as the sheriff of Chickasaw County from 1944 to 1948.[23]

White southerners like Scarbrough commonly made such errors about civil rights activists. White segregationists across the South constantly labeled civil rights workers as "outside agitators," regardless of their birthplace. While some, like Bob Moses, certainly came from outside the state, other organizers did not, such as SNCC chairman Marion Barry, a native of Itta Bena. The local men and women that out-of-state field organizers recruited, like Sam Block, certainly did not fit the "outside agitator" mold. Tom Scarbrough and his fellow white Mississippians could not fathom the actions of people like Guyot, native Black Mississippians who did not accept white supremacy. As the historian Jason Sokol noted, white southern paternalism "rested on a conviction that southern whites knew 'their Negroes' intimately, understood their needs and desires, and fulfilled those needs whenever they could." White southerners interpreted Black deference as friendship and acceptance of the status quo, and thus expressed shock and resentment when Black southerners acted contrary to these deeply held white beliefs.[24]

With this in mind, Scarbrough appears to have engaged in a selective reading of evidence from his investigation of Guyot, insisting that he was "not a native of this state" and ignoring evidence to the contrary. The designation of Guyot as an attorney, as well as the near-obsessive attention to his skin color, illuminates further the racial anxieties of white southerners like Scarbrough. Guyot's formidable intellect made a distinct impression on the investigator, not surprising since the SNCC field secretary studied at the most prestigious institution of higher education for Black people in Mississippi. Although fears of federal intervention forced the Mississippi state government to increase funding for public education of Black children in the years after World War II, little overall improvement came to Black education due to minimal efforts designed only to stave off desegregation of public schools. For many, if not most, white Mississippians, attitudes toward Black education had not changed much from the days of Governor James K. Vardaman at the turn of the century, who said that "in educating the negro we implant in him all matter of aspirations and ambitions which we then refuse to allow him to gratify. . . . Their education only spoils a good field hand and makes a shyster lawyer or a fourth-rate teacher." Or as the historian Neil McMillen said, "Educated Blacks were thought to be less dependent and deferential . . . [and] more likely to challenge white supremacy."[25] Guyot's obvious education and intelligence served as a red flag to Scarbrough of an "outside agitator," and given the poor state of Black education in Mississippi, he likely assumed that no Black Mississippian could "rise" to Guyot's intellect.

The investigator's attention to Guyot's skin color, identifying him as "yellow" and "about White," also indicates white southerners' obsessions with interracial mixing. Scarbrough and other whites so feared a "yellow" man like Guyot, obviously a product of "race-mixing." As historians like Jane Dailey and Neil McMillen have demonstrated, white segregationists obsessed over "miscegenation" or interracial sex. But his comments on Guyot's skin color also suggested that Scarbrough worried that white ancestry in Guyot's family tree might give him more intelligence than the average Black civil rights activist. White southerners' near-hysterical fears of interracial sex arose not just from the threat they believed it posed (at least sex between Black men and white women), as the literature of segregationist organizations like the Citizens' Councils readily indicated. The children of such unions alarmed them, too. Many white people, and not just southerners, long assumed that intelligence was linked to skin color. Racial scientists from the era of European and American imperialism in the late nineteenth and early twentieth centuries maintained that Africans of lighter skin tones could advance beyond simple manual farm labor to professions such as mechanics and preachers. These prejudices were likely why Scarbrough regularly misidentified the "heavyset yellow Negro" as an attorney.[26]

Guyot certainly fulfilled the fears of white segregationists that as an educated Black man he defied the deference they expected from Black people under Jim Crow. The opposite of the soft-spoken Bob Moses, Guyot resisted white racists in both word and action, as his letter to the Greenwood police chief shows. He did not spare his allies his bluntness, either. When Charles Cobb, a freshman at Howard University and volunteer with CORE, stopped in Jackson in the summer of 1962 while on the way to a civil rights workshop in Houston, he visited the SNCC office. When told SNCC workers that he was headed to Texas, Cobb later wrote, Guyot "rose from his seat and gave me a stern look. . . . 'Civil rights workshop in Texas!' he scoffed. 'What's the point of doing that when you're standing right here in Mississippi?'" Cobb said that Guyot "was a big, intense guy, and his tone was disdainful, almost bullying, conveying without further words what was at once a challenge and a demand." Cobb never got back on his Greyhound bus and instead joined SNCC's Mississippi efforts, becoming a field secretary by the end of the summer. As Guyot recalled later, Cobb stayed five years in Mississippi, and "he tells people I kidnapped him. I didn't kidnap him. I just creatively brought him in."[27]

Guyot did show deference and respect to his elders in the movement. He in particular praised Amzie Moore. Guyot said that Moore acted as "an entrée for us into the counties. . . . We met at his house, we stayed at his house. . . . Whenever anyone was threatened, Amzie Moore was sort of an individual protection agency." Other young activists shared Guyot's respect for him, and Moore acted as a mentor to Bob Moses.[28]

The SNCC activists continued their work in Greenwood, establishing a presence there despite harassment and violence. They continued to register voters, an action that Guyot recalled as far more threatening to white Mississippians than desegregating a lunch counter, and thus dangerous to civil rights workers. Registration work also moved slowly. Guyot said that in Greenwood "there was a war going on, and the war was a very simple one — surviving and just walkin' around talkin' to [Black] people about what *they're* interested in. . . . If it was fishing, how do you turn that conversation into when are you gonna register to vote? If it was religion, that was an easier one to turn to registering. . . . Our basic verbal mien was that there's nothin' that's not involved with politics."[29]

This approach also meant the SNCC canvassers dealt with locals too afraid of white authorities or distrustful of activists to register. "You learned very quickly that if you got that door slammed in your face, it just takes a day or two of talking to people to find out whose face the door won't be slammed in," Guyot said. This meant he and other canvassers had to not be pushy and also respect the attitudes of locals, which he said meant that "you don't alter the basic format you walk into. Let's say you're riding past a picnic, and people are cuttin' watermelons. You don't immediately go and say, 'Stop the watermelon cuttin', and let's talk about voter registration.' You cut some watermelons, or you help somebody else serve 'em."[30]

Guyot credited the relative success of the Greenwood campaign to two factors. One was the support of the churches, the operational base of the movement. In Greenwood, he said, "we first cracked the churches." After that, he and his fellow SNCC field workers organized "the kids, then the women, then the men." Second, SNCC singularly focused on voter registration in Greenwood, avoiding other activities like sit-ins. He said that "our objectives were very clear. It was not to desegregate the two or three good local white restaurants. It was simply to register people to vote." Gradually, the approach paid off. The stream of applicants to the courthouse grew and continued, even if the Leflore County registrar turned most away by invoking the "interpretation clause" of the Mississippi Constitution. Guyot said that "cracking the fear of each individual, going with them. Never asking anybody to do anything we wouldn't do" proved the key to success. Hardy Lott, a local white attorney who later gained fame for defending Byron De La Beckwith during the first two trials for the murder of Medgar Evers, told Guyot that he and SNCC "should be very satisfied. You haven't registered any voters here but more people have applied here than anywhere else in the state." Guyot, nonplussed, replied, "Well, we are interested in registration."[31]

By working through the churches, Guyot and the SNCC activists mobilized people through "the only institution owned, controlled, paid for, directed and given importance by Blacks regardless of how the rest of the economy went." White economic reprisals that individual Black people in Greenwood often faced did not as readily affect the Black churches. There, activists could mobilize from the bottom up, bypass the more conservative male minsters, and concentrate on recruiting women and children. Guyot said that this approach put Black community leaders "in such a position that they had to be on our side or be against the community." When he later recalled the lessons of Greenwood, he said that "you have to involve local leaders as much as possible," but their self-interest has to be addressed. "You have to have programs that were geared right towards their needs."[32]

SNCC's success canvassing and getting some locals to attempt to register led the local white power structure to retaliate harshly against Greenwood's Black community. In October 1962 the Leflore County Board of Supervisors voted to end its participation in a federal surplus food distribution program, which meant that 22,000 people, half the county's population and mostly African Americans, lost access to desperately needed food. COFO now moved in to run a food distribution program of its own, to provide "food for those who want to be free," in Bob Moses's words. SNCC sent out word to its other chapters to send help, but police harassment now tried to disrupt their efforts. Guyot actively participated in the food program, sometimes handling difficult cases of local residents lying about their circumstances to receive food. He and several other SNCC staffers began to contribute their fifteen-dollar weekly salaries to pay for food for emergency cases. Help came from volunteers up north as well. Ivanhoe Donaldson and Ben Taylor, two Black Michigan State University students, drove a truck full of food, clothing, and medicine to the state in late December, but police arrested them and confiscated the cargo. The prosecutor charged them with narcotics possession, due to the presence of aspirin and vitamins in the shipment.[33]

The food distribution efforts became the major focus of the Greenwood campaign through the winter of 1962–63, and coverage in major newspapers, as well as the efforts of Black celebrities like Dick Gregory and Harry Belafonte, kept the stream of relief supplies going. White retaliation continued, including arson against suspected food storage warehouses in February 1963, and police arrested Sam Block for vocally criticizing the arson attack, accusing him of inciting a "breach of the peace." That same month, assailants shot and seriously injured Jimmy Travis, a SNCC volunteer, in an ambush, and Sam Block narrowly escaped being hit by a shotgun blast in a separate attack. Yet as movement participant and historian Howard Zinn has pointed out, the use of hunger as a weapon by the county supervisors backfired, as it changed the image of SNCC workers from "outside agitators" to relief workers in the eyes of local Black residents. As a result, the number of applicants heading to the courthouse grew, and the SSC investigator Tom Scarbrough reported that "Negroes have been coming to the Circuit Clerk's Office in sizeable numbers for the last two or three months" to register to vote. He also reported high attendance at the meetings at a local Baptist church, reaching at least 500 attendees.[34]

During this crisis John Salter, Guyot's old college professor from Tougaloo, came up to see him in Greenwood. As Guyot recalled, Salter asked him,

> Guyot, why are you doing all this, you and I have read a lot of books, we have done a lot of studies together. Why are you feeding these people? You should not feed them and let them get out and revolt. I said,

"John, I will [tell] you what. We have got two decisions to make. One if do we get these people to fight around their own self-interest, at their own time frame when they are ready to fight. Or do we put them in a no-win situation simply to prove the system can't work." I said, "I think it is very clear where I stand on that."[35]

To Guyot, people would come before principle or abstract ideologies of revolution.

In March 1963, the harassment and intimidation of SNCC continued. On 24 March, fire gutted SNCC's voter registration office, destroying all the equipment and records. The Greenwood fire chief dismissed Block's claims that the fire was arson. When two nights later, gunmen shot up the home of George Greene, a SNCC worker—with three children inside narrowly escaping injury—SNCC activists decided to protest the shooting. Moses led a march the morning of 27 March, accompanied by Guyot and nine other SNCC members. Moses called the march "not planned" and undertaken to request police protection after the attack on Greene's family. The eleven civil rights workers led about a hundred Black men, women, and children from a local church to the courthouse. The marchers were met by riot police and police dogs. Guyot said, "The dogs were snapping at us, and we just moved ahead. . . . The highway patrolmen saw I wasn't afraid of the dogs." Police arrested the eleven workers for disorderly conduct, yet the marches to the courthouse continued, with another group of fifty arriving the next day to register.[36]

Judge O. L. Kimbrough tried the SNCC workers in his courtroom, and Guyot, the second one of the group put on trial, put his defiance on full display for white Greenwood. Police Chief Curtis Lary took the stand as the first witness, and Guyot (misidentified as "Guyat" from Chicago by the local newspaper) interrupted his testimony. An irritated Judge Kimbrough told him that, "If you don't stop interrupting the witness, I will cite you for contempt of court." Guyot continued to interrupt Chief Lary, and the judge declared him in contempt of court and sent him back to his jail cell. By the end of the week, eight of the SNCC members arrested received four months in the county jail and a $200 fine, with Guyot receiving an extra day and a $50 fine for his contempt of court charge. The eight activists refused bail and remained in jail to force the Justice Department to file suit against the local officials.[37]

Meanwhile, the Greenwood arrests and demonstrations made national news. When comedian Dick Gregory spoke to and actively assisted and took part in the demonstrations, his celebrity led local police to avoid arresting him. Governor Ross Barnett pledged state support for the Greenwood authorities, calling the nonviolent marches "a loaded bomb lying in the city's streets." The Justice Department, in turn, sought to prevent the local authorities from blocking the marches and filed an injunction, which drew harsh criticism on the floor of the US Senate from John Stennis, one of Mississippi's two Democratic senators. The violence and arrests had attracted the attention of the Justice Department, largely after Wiley Brandon, a Black civil rights attorney and head of the VEP, sent an angry telegram to Attorney General Robert Kennedy demanding "immediate action by the federal government" after Jimmy Travis's brush with death. COFO also responded, pulling workers from other projects and sending them into Greenwood to canvass for voters and set up citizenship classes to teach civics and basic literacy to local residents.[38]

While the eight SNCC workers were in jail, the staff treated them decently, likely due to the heightened public and federal attention on Greenwood and the jailed workers specifically. Some locals who participated in the Greenwood movement said that Chief Lary appeared scared and indecisive during the entire civil rights campaign, so that likely contributed to a lack of brutality against the imprisoned workers. James Foreman, one of those jailed, received several visits from a local Black doctor to treat his ulcers. "[Local] people came to start visiting the jail, bringing food, bringing cakes," Guyot said. To pass the time, they engaged in educated discussions and workshops, with Foreman lecturing on writing, Bob Moses on mathematics, and Guyot on biology.[39]

The Justice Department reached an agreement with the city in early April, just as the Greenwood city jail had been filled to capacity. According to VEP records, 513 local residents tried to register, with hundreds more taking registration classes. The 4 April agreement had the city release the eight SNCC workers in return for the federal injunction being dropped, and the city agreed to stop harassing applicants and even provide a bus to transport them. The county supervisors also agreed to restore the surplus food program. While the police released Guyot and his fellow activists, the Justice Department disappointed SNCC when it did little to enforce the agreement. John Doar, the Justice Department official who directed negotiations with Greenwood officials, said that enforcement could have drawn the federal government into serving as a policeman across the South. Movement historian Charles Payne called the agreement "a promise to be nicer [in] the ways they [Greenwood officials] disfranchised Negroes." Not surprisingly, the *Greenwood Commonwealth*, a strongly prosegregation newspaper, endorsed the deal and congratulated the Justice Department in a front-page editorial.[40]

Despite this setback and the dwindling national attention on Greenwood, the movement continued, even after many of the SNCC workers left to organize and direct other projects. SNCC achieved its goal of helping to facilitate and organize a local project, which was then taken over by local activists. Harassment at the voter registration office dropped off by May, and arrests in June—arrests of local people, not SNCC activists—continued and even exceeded the arrest numbers for March. The process of building the movement moved slowly, but it continued even after the news cameras and reporters went elsewhere.[41]

But some SNCC organizers remained. After their release, Moses and Guyot continued their work in Greenwood and continued to experience intimidation and violence. Guyot's duties included working as the main instructor in a voter registration school at the Hopewell Baptist Church in Itta Bena, a town outside Greenwood. The church experienced a bomb attack during a meeting on 3 May. Guyot retrieved the bomb and refused to turn it over to the local sheriff, instead declaring that he would only give it to federal authorities. He also began to canvass outside of Leflore County, heading over to Lexington, the county seat of neighboring Holmes County. Early in 1963 several Black residents of Holmes County attended some of the mass meetings in Greenwood, and soon they began to organize their own movement. Sam Block traveled to the town of Mileston and began to hold meetings there, and soon another SNCC worker joined him to conduct citizenship classes. A group of fourteen of these local residents—the "First 14," as they became known—attempted to register at the county courthouse in Lexington on 9 April. Hartman Turnbow, an outspoken and independent land-owning farmer, attempted to register first. Eventually all fourteen took the test, but none passed the byzantine registration process. One month after his attempt, night riders firebombed Turnbow's home, and the farmer returned gunfire. When Bob Moses came to investigate the following morning, the deputy sheriff arrested him and later Turnbow and three other workers, charging them with the arson attack. This official harassment, unlike so many other attacks, brought a federal response by John Doar from the Justice Department, who filed suit and got the charges dropped. After the attack on the Turnbow homestead, Guyot arrived and lent aid to voter registration efforts, doing door-to-door canvassing in Lexington. He also played a key role in securing Turnbow's release, as he contacted Doar about using a reciprocity bond to bail him out of the Tchula jail.[42]

With Guyot's intense dedication to his work as a SNCC field secretary, it is easy to forget that he still had classes to attend. Civil rights activism may have delayed his formal graduation, but he did not neglect his studies while he was in the movement. Indeed, Adam Beittel, the Tougaloo president, while not discouraging off-campus activities, did not allow civil rights activities to hurt academic standards either, as he refused to grant excused absences from class or academic credit for sit-ins. Guyot adhered to that standard during his hectic days of organizing and graduated with a bachelor of science in chemistry and biology in 1963.[43]

Guyot had a background in science, but like his colleague Marion Barry, SNCC's first chairman (who had gone to graduate school at Fisk University to study chemistry, where he then joined the sit-in movement), he did not consider a career as a science teacher or researcher. The passion for social and racial justice now superseded his earlier academic interests. He had contemplated attending law school after graduating from Tougaloo, but Bob Moses said that "I think [he] altered those plans with the idea that it was more important to work than to go to law school." Guyot told Howard Zinn that "at first I thought of being a teacher, or a doctor; now I would like to get married, and do just what I'm doing now." In a 1965 interview, he said that he originally wanted to become a teacher and then later wanted to become a doctor, but then "learned how ineffectual and useless both those positions were in Mississippi" under the system of white supremacy. "Then the only thing left for me to do was to find out more about Mississippi and more about myself," he said.[44]

The summer of 1963 proved to be a defining moment in Guyot's life, and an opportunity to find out more about himself, as he continued his work after graduation. As a SNCC field secretary, he had been chased, threatened, verbally abused, arrested, and jailed by white supremacists. Luvaghn Brown said of Guyot that there were "times it was like dying didn't occur to him. I don't know how to explain that . . . but he had a lot of courage." He had also escaped any serious physical violence, but that changed in June 1963. On 9 June, Fannie Lou Hamer and six other SNCC activists headed to Greenwood on a Continental Trailways bus from a Southern Christian Leadership Conference (SCLC) citizenship school workshop in South Carolina. The bus stopped in Winona, a small town on the highway between Jackson and Memphis. When some of the passengers entered the bus station and asked to be served at the lunch counter, several Winona policemen and state highway patrolmen forced them to leave. One of the group, a young Black voter registration worker named Annelle Ponder, began writing down the license number of one of the patrol cars, which prompted the police chief to arrest five of the activists, leaving the other two to finish their trip to Greenwood. Hamer came off the bus to investigate, and she too was arrested, with the entire group taken to the county jail. There the policemen brutally beat Ponder and June Johnson, a fifteen-year-old Black voter registration worker. The violence, in its sheer sadism, rivaled the worst of Mississippi's treatment of civil rights workers. Hamer said that one of the policemen beat Ponder with a blackjack, shouting at her, "Cain't you say yes sir, you nigger bitch?" Hamer said that "her eyes looked like blood, and her mouth was swollen . . . it was horrifying." Johnson received a personal beating from the sheriff, the police chief, and finally two other white men. James West, another of the arrested passengers, suffered the same fate. Two highway patrolman and two Black prisoners forced by the police beat him severely.[45]

The police then beat Hamer next. One of the policemen, after realizing that she was *the* Fannie Lou Hamer of Ruleville, the SNCC field secretary, told her, "You bitch, we gon' make you wish you was dead." He ordered two Black inmates to beat her with a blackjack, beating her all over her body, till she was "as navy blue as anything you ever seen." She said she "began to bury my head in the mattress and hugged it to kill out the sound of my screams." By the time the beating ended, Hamer had suffered numerous injuries, including permanent kidney damage. Only later did the police bother charging the activists with a crime—disorderly conduct and resisting arrest.[46]

Back in Greenwood, the two other passengers arrived and quickly informed Willie Peacock of the arrests. Peacock immediately got on the phone to call the Justice Department and others to seek help for the Winona prisoners. Guyot called the Montgomery County jail to ask about bail, to which Sheriff Earl Patridge replied, "Well, if you are so interested, you come on down here and find out." He immediately departed for Winona but since he did not drive or have a driver's license, SNCC members Milton Hancock and Willie Shaw accompanied him as drivers to bail the group out of jail. They parked in front of the courthouse but the police had locked the front doors, it being a Sunday. He walked around to the back and entered the building, and walked into a room filled with policemen. Guyot said, "Sheriff, I come to see about these people," and read off their names. He replied, "I got 'em. What you gon' do about it?" Guyot replied, "All I want to do is find out what the charges are so we can raise the money to get them out." "You get the fuck out of here," Sheriff Patridge replied. "So I decided to do that—just that," and he left, but not before politely telling the sheriff, "Thank you." But before he did so, State Highway Patrolman John Basinger stopped Guyot and asked him if he was part of "that shit in Greenwood" and if he was a member of the NAACP. He said he was not a member but had been involved in voter registration, to which the patrolman asked him if it would "hurt your mouth" to say "yes sir" or "no sir." Still defiant, Guyot replied "No it won't." Basinger then slugged him in the mouth, a blow powerful enough to knock the heavyset Guyot into the street. The sheriff arrested him and brought him inside the jail.[47]

Inside the jail, the terror escalated to horrendous levels. At least nine policemen took turns beating Guyot. They hit him with gun butts, blackjacks, and their fists. He recalled that one man was a prize fighter, "and he just stood me up against the wall and just beat on me." They then stripped him naked and "threatened to burn [his] genitals with fire and a sharp stick." As Hamer later recalled, the men had "taken a piece of paper and tried to burn Guyot's private[s] off." The sexualized torture did not stop there. Guyot recalled that one of his captors wielded a long knife and said "we should castrate all you Black bastards, and that might begin to solve some of the problems." Another man "played with a gun behind my head and he kept moving it across the back of my head." Determined not to fall unconscious and then presumably die, Guyot endured four hours of torture and abuse, until he couldn't lift his arms up and his eyes swelled shut. He said that he knew he had to "remain conscious, but if I get unconscious, they're going to kill me." Finally, the sheriff called in a doctor, and the police asked if he "can take anymore." The doctor said, "Well, I'm not going to be responsible if you do," which Guyot said made them hesitate, fortunately for him. "I don't think I could have taken much more," he said.[48]

Guyot's notoriety among the white power structure in Greenwood and the State Sovereignty Commission likely meant that the police singled him and Hamer and the rest out for special treatment, as the beatings went well beyond the routine ones state law enforcement typically gave to Black men or women. When he arrived at the jail, he found that his reputation, no doubt spread by agents of the SSC and members of the Citizens' Councils, had preceded him. One of the police, recalling the marches he led in Greenwood, said, "Oh, you the nigger who wasn't afraid of the dogs." That, combined with his lack of deference to the police officers, led Chief Patridge to single him out as an example, as the police did not arrest Guyot's driver, Milton Hancock. Guyot also took advantage of his name, knowing that if he vanished anonymously, he would end up like so many other Black Mississippians, a forgotten casualty of Jim Crow. After the hours of brutality ended and police put him in a cell, Guyot identified himself to the other prisoners, since he "didn't expect to come outa there [alive]." Hamer had the same fear, for she overheard her tormentors discussing killing the group and throwing their bodies into a nearby river. He said he identified himself to the others so that if the police did murder him, "at least they would know I *was* there, and if they were not too afraid, they might talk. . . . I played like I was out, ok?" His jailers tried a ruse to kill him—leaving a knife outside his open cell door, with two guards with shotguns "standing right outside the hall waiting for me to act a goddamn fool and try to come on outa there. I didn't fall for that one." Hamer caught a glimpse of him while her jail door was open. She said that he "looked like he was in bad shape and it was on my nerve, too, because that was the first time I had seen him . . . not smiling." But the beating did not break his spirit, even if it almost destroyed his body. Hamer began to sing a freedom song in jail the next day after her own beating, and Guyot joined her, Ponder, and the others in singing the spiritual "The Gospel Train."[49]

Guyot could thank Willie Peacock for keeping him from dying in a small-town Mississippi jail. Peacock and SNCC's well-organized network of volunteers and phonebanks sprang into action when Guyot failed to report back, as Peacock feared Guyot's imminent murder. Even before Guyot could call the SNCC office, Peacock organized SNCC supporters from out of state—in California, Chicago, New York, Detroit, and other northern states and cities—to continually place calls to the Winona city jail, asking, "Do you have Lawrence Guyot? I want to speak to Lawrence Guyot." He also credited Roberta Galler, a SNCC operative from New York, for organizing many of the long-distance calls. When the calls flooded the jail, the police moved Guyot to other jails in nearby town and county jails, including to Carroll County. While in the county jail, the police finally allowed him to make a phone call, and he called the SNCC office in Greenwood and asked to speak to "Squeaky Sandus," a code phrase used by SNCC workers to indicate their dire straits, which further galvanized the SNCC phonebanks and their pressure on the federal government to intervene. When the phone lines at the Winona jail and elsewhere kept ringing, H. L. Howard, a local physician, visited Guyot at one of the jails and tried to pass off his injuries as resulting from an auto wreck. "You came to Winona, and you got to drinking a little bit, and you had an accident," Howard said, an excuse even more ridiculous since Guyot did not drive or even have a driver's license. Still, he said that "I wasn't at that time about to argue the facts. . . . He treated me . . . it was quite a beating, that was about it." Even so, he still refused to sign the statement when the police demanded he do so. His refusal angered Patridge, who kicked him in the flank and said that he had "earned . . . a long trip to Whitfield [the state mental hospital] and Parchman."[50]

The doctor's feeble excuse indicated that the white policemen worried about federal attention to their crimes. Guyot said after the doctor visited him, "it became really funny to me because the chief of police, after having received a lot of long-distance phone calls brought me some aspirin because he didn't want me to die in that jail." What Guyot did not know is that the FBI had begun an investigation into their beating and detention, and knew of Guyot's injuries, as J. Edgar Hoover ordered agents to interview the doctor and policemen involved in the arrest. The police also considered beating Euvenester Simpson, a Black teenager arrested with Hamer and the others on the bus, but June Johnson said that they spared her over their concern that, due to her light-skinned complexion, the bruises would provide evidence of the beating. This restraint indicated that the police had no desire to leave any physical evidence to aid federal prosecutors. Although Guyot's light skin tone did not save him from a brutal beating, as the police left him covered in visible bruises upon his release, the policemen apparently had enough intellect to know that *two* "automobile accidents" would not convince federal investigators. Not surprisingly, the sheriff told Tom Scarbrough, the SSC investigator, that "no brutality was used on Guyot in his presence and it was his thinking Guyot was lying which is the customary thing for all of the outside agitators to do when arrested."[51]

Even before the visit from the doctor, the police tried to cover up their crimes and enlisted the rest of Winona's white power structure to aid them. The sheriff had Guyot taken outside to be seen by F. C. Ewing and his son Clay. The elder Ewing operated the local TV and radio station, and handled news stories for NBC's wire service. Sheriff Patridge asked Ewing if he should release him, and he replied, "Keep him, by all means, because he was involved in that mess in Greenwood." After Dr. Howard's examination, B. F. Heath, president of the Winona bank, visited Guyot and asked him leading questions to try to get him to admit that the injuries came from an automobile. He refused to answer, so Heath told the policemen and other whites present—about fifteen to twenty others—that Guyot "obviously" had fallen out of a car, to which a newsman, presumably the elder Ewing, said, "Well that's good. I'll get it out on the wires."[52] Clearly the city fathers of Winona worried about the attention the beatings could bring down on their town and themselves, and sought to manipulate the emerging media narrative.

In addition to Hamer, another Black prisoner in the cellblock also saw Guyot's injuries after the beating and later told the FBI during their investigation that his "arm and shoulders were purple as was one side of his body." He said that Guyot "obviously feared for his life, and told the other Negro prisoners to call his 'folks' in Greenwood if he did not live."[53]

Eleanor Katherine Holmes, a young Black Yale Law School student who arrived in Mississippi after Guyot's arrest, played a critical role in securing his release and probably saving his life. After conferring with SNCC members, she walked over to the office of the Greenwood police chief and asked him to call the Winona chief and let him know of her impending arrival—and to tell the Winona chief that she had called people and told them her destination to protect herself. "I do not intend to be the third person to enter your jails," she said. The next morning, she arrived at the jail, a place "hotter than hell" and visited the incarcerated activists. She said that "Guyot had to get some clothes on because they had beat him so bad he was virtually naked." Although unable to secure his release that day, her presence as an observer helped put the local authorities on notice that the death of any of the SNCC workers would have repercussions.[54]

When Guyot was in the Carroll County jail, an FBI agent visited him and asked what happened. But he knew that the "little gold badge" the so-called agent flashed was fake due to his past dealings with FBI agents. He said, "Oh I don't have anything to say, talk to the sheriff." The imposter—later revealed to be the sheriff of Carroll County—became angry and said, "You smart mother-fucker," then walked away. Meanwhile, the real FBI promised to investigate the Winona arrests. Yet the Bureau had few agents in the state to do the job, as the FBI did not have a field office in Mississippi, the only state in the country to lack one. The national headquarters had only dispatched a few agents to Jackson to deal with the Jackson protests and the recent murder of Medgar Evers. But J. Edgar Hoover felt enough political pressure that on June he ordered the Memphis FBI office to send agents to investigate and determine if police brutality did take place and to "immediately proceed with preliminary investigation of each such instance." Agents arrived in Carrollton that night to interview Guyot but could not find the sheriff at his home or the jail. Events elsewhere also hindered federal action. Governor George Wallace's recent efforts to block the desegregation of the University of Alabama drew John Doar from the Justice Department to that state, so he did not visit Winona.[55]

When the police eventually returned Guyot to the Winona jail, they charged him with attempted murder. The basis for this came from a written note they found in his pocket that said that someone had been stabbed to death, which the police then used to accuse him of murder. Guyot said that he had been given the piece of paper by someone in Greenwood "concerned about voter registration," who asked that he turn it over to the FBI. He had not yet had a chance to turn over the note, which was about two white people he did not know who had been murdered two weeks earlier. The police then took the imprisoned SNCC activists to court on Tuesday morning. The judge denied them legal counsel and, after entering not guilty pleas, convicted and fined the group arrested on the bus for disorderly conduct and resisting arrest. That same day FBI agents, sent after SNCC communications director Julian Bond sent a telegram to Attorney General Robert Kennedy alerting him of the group's arrest, arrived at the jail to take pictures and question all of the arrested activists. From her cell, Ponder witnessed the agents taking pictures of Guyot's battered body. Given the past unwillingness of the Bureau to investigate violence against civil rights workers, the detained group did not give the agents much information. As Ponder said later, it appeared that "they were cooperating with the [Winona police] chief."

That night, after the agents left, the police forced the group to sign statements at gunpoint that the police had not beaten or mistreated them while in jail, and that their injuries came from them attacking *each other*.[56]

The FBI visit showed that the phone calls and the visit by Holmes, followed by subsequent visits to the jail by SNCC workers as well as calls to the national news media, were having an effect. The police allowed Andrew Young from the SCLC to post bail for the civil rights workers when he arrived on Wednesday. Young said an FBI agent arrived during his visit and informed the sheriff about the federal brutality case and investigation against him, but "we soon discovered to our dismay that the agent was also the brother-in-law of the sheriff." The groups had their radio access cut off during their four-day stay, and they found out why when Young bailed them out. A white supremacist had shot Medgar Evers on 11 June outside his Jackson home. Evers had organized boycotts and sit-ins in downtown Jackson in May and June, including sit-ins with Tougaloo students and Guyot's old professor John Salter. Guyot said the jailers "didn't want that known in jail." He credited Evers's assassination and the barrage of phone calls organized by Peacock and Galler as the reasons the police did not murder him or the others.[57]

Dorie Ladner saw Hamer, Guyot, and the others soon after their release. She said that Guyot's "face looked like a piece of raw steak." Guyot said that his injuries included "two gashes in the frontal and coronal area of my skull" and "bleeding from the nose and mouth," and that he "was bruised throughout the chest and stomach area." He also had "what appeared to be small blood clots" on his calf, thigh, and shin from being kicked repeatedly while he was on the floor. He went to a physician, who examined him and told him that he had hematomas in several different places, blood in both eardrums, but no concussion. According to the FBI reports, he also had bruises and swelling around his eyes and temples, a large bruise stretching from his shoulder down his entire back to his waist, and bruises on his elbows, right buttock, and right leg. Two days after his release, reporters interviewed him and he posed shirtless for photographers, showing them his bruised upper body. While Guyot obviously went through a severe trauma, what he experienced also deeply impacted those who came to his aid. Years later, Eleanor Katherine Holmes (by then Eleanor Holmes Norton, the District of Columbia's delegate to the US House of Representatives) said that "because of Larry Guyot, I understood what it meant to live with terror and walk straight into it." Guyot himself never forgot the critical aid that she gave him in his hour of need. Recalling her boldness, he said her "involvement in building a bridge between political activism, academia, and her ability to deal with anyone she met on her terms is what ties me to Eleanor."[58]

Guyot showing reporters his injuries
from the Winona beating, 14 June 1963.
Associated Press Photo/Jim Bourdier.

Although reporters interviewed and spoke with Guyot, the media gave relatively little coverage to the Winona arrests and beatings. The *Delta Democrat-Times* of Greenville mentioned their release but not the beatings, as did the fiercely segregationist *Winona Times*. Some wire services carried the story, and the *New York Times* ran two brief articles, one mentioning the beating of "Lawrence Guyat." The *Chicago Daily News* mentioned Guyot and his beating as part of a larger story on SNCC it ran in July 1963. As movement historians have noted, when white supremacists victimized only Black people, the national media attention paid little attention. This inattention became one of the reasons why COFO leaders later would decide to enlist white college students in their cause.[59]

It is worth analyzing the specific nature of the torture the SNCC workers received in Winona, as it is heavily rooted in the racial and sexual anxieties and psyches of white men in the Jim Crow South. The white policemen chose the sexualized torture of Hamer and Guyot for a reason. Charles Marsh, in his biographical study of the people involved in Freedom Summer, extensively analyzed the sexualized nature of the abuse the police inflicted on Hamer. She was degraded verbally, called a "whore" and "bitch" by the officers, and beaten with "a large, Black iron phallus," as Marsh described the blackjack wielded by the Black prisoner ordered to beat her. "The significance of the pantomime could not have been lost on Mrs. Hamer," Marsh insisted, linking the beating to her involuntary sterilization in 1961 when she went to a local hospital to have a uterine tumor removed. Now, "the state was recreating a savage mockery of her sexual barrenness."[60]

Whether or not Marsh's psychosexual analysis of Hamer's beating is on target, such echoes were very clear in Guyot's ordeal. Guyot's manhood, literally and figuratively, threatened these white men. As Winthrop Jordan and Deborah Gray White have ably demonstrated, white people have long had a fascination with Black sexuality, going back to English travels to Africa for exploration and slave-buying. Just as whites hypersexualized or desexualized Black women during slavery into the respective myths of Jezebel and Mammy, Black men were viewed as "virile, promiscuous, and lusty," especially toward white women. This manifested itself in antebellum times in white male fears of enslaved Black men raping white women during slave revolts. The sexual anxieties of white men focused in particular on Black genitalia. As far back as sixteenth-century English explorations of Africa, white travelers reported on the alleged size of Black penises, and the idea that the Black man had an unnaturally large member seems to have been an article of faith with white men by the antebellum period. This belief continued after emancipation, with Mississippi Delta planters occasionally reporting their astonishment—what James Cobb called both "anxiety and envy"—at the size of their sharecroppers' manhood, as well as their alleged superhuman virility and sexual prowess. This obsession continued during civil rights organizing in the Delta, and even was aimed at white civil rights activists. For example, a white policeman in Greenwood threatened to emasculate a white male volunteer when he came into the station to report a beating he had received, and the Black woman he was with was subjected to crude sexual comments as well.[61]

The threat Guyot's manhood posed to his tormentors' white male supremacy led them to threaten and attempt castration. Castration had been a legal punishment for enslaved men since the colonial era, even for crimes that were not sexual in nature. It was a punishment that had been reserved disproportionately for Black men and, according to Jordan, "clearly indicated a desperate, generalized need in white men to persuade themselves that were really masters and in all ways masterful, and it illustrated dramatically the ease with which white men slipped over into treating their Negroes like their bulls and stallions whose 'spirit' could be subdued by emasculation." This practice continued postemancipation with the spectacle of lynching, as white mobs castrated, tortured, and executed hundreds of Black men in the most horrific fashion to make them submit to the social caste of Jim Crow, in particular its sexual order.[62] In the 1960s, these anxieties were still firmly embedded in the psyche of Mississippi's white men. They attempted to emasculate Guyot with fire, and threatened to do so with a blade, in the desperate hope that this would "solve some of the problems" created by civil rights workers challenging their racial order. It is not a leap to then see how these white men perceived this attempted castration as an act of physical violence to break Guyot's "spirit" and metaphorically protect southern white womanhood.

The events in Winona finally compelled the Kennedy administration to take concrete action. John Doar and the Justice Department moved quickly after the release of the activists, filing a civil action on 17 June ordering the mayor, sheriff, and police chief not to interfere with integration at the bus station and to dismiss the charges against the arrested activists. On 9 September, Robert F. Kennedy indicted the sheriff, police chief, and three other policemen for the beatings, charging them with seven counts of conspiracy to deprive the arrested of their civil rights. The arrest, not surprisingly, triggered a front-page editorial on the cover of the Winona newspaper, insisting that the police lawfully arrested the "trained racial agitators" who "could easily have caused a riot."[63]

Guyot only enjoyed a brief respite from jail, but he did not spend it recuperating. He did not let his injuries deter him from organizing, and after Winona he returned to Greenwood to continue his voter registration activities. He spent the rest of June registering voters in Leflore County. SNCC registered voters in nearby Itta Bena, where members conducted voter workshops at Hopewell Baptist Church. On 18 June, June Johnson spoke at a voter registration meeting at the church, describing her ordeal in the Winona jail only nine days earlier. During the singing of a freedom song later, a someone threw a bomb into the church—Guyot called it a firebomb, but the local paper called it "poisonous fumes." The several dozen members in attendance fled the church and headed en masse to the home of Ed Weber, the city marshal of Itta Bena and a deputy sheriff in Leflore County, to demand protection. The crowd was angry, as several members of the congregation suffered injuries caused by the panic in the church and reported to the hospital. The marchers soon encountered armed white men, and a deputy sheriff arrested the demonstrators for "disturbing the peace." According to the sheriff, Guyot and Samuel Block escaped arrest.[64]

The following day, the courts sentenced forty-five of those arrested to six-month jail terms in the Parchman penitentiary, where they spent the next two months before being released on bail, with money provided by the National Council of Churches (NCC). The courts sent demonstrators as young as sixteen to Parchman, and Howard Zinn, who arrived in Greenwood with his wife when the prisoners posted bail, described the poor condition of many of them. Prison staff had denied them medical treatment, and Zinn mentioned teenage boys with infections, swollen feet, and loss of vision caused by dietary deficiencies.[65]

COFO workers knew well of Parchman's notoriety. The state sent Clyde Kennard, who tried to become the first Black man to enroll in Mississippi Southern College (now the University of Southern Mississippi) there on trumped-up charges, where he developed colon cancer in 1962 and was denied medical care, leading to his death the following year. In 1961, the state sent the Freedom Riders arrested in Jackson to Parchman, including James Farmer of CORE, who called it "the most fabled state prison in the South," where they were put two to each eight-by-ten-foot cell and only allowed to shower twice a week.[66]

Guyot soon became intimately familiar with Parchman. A week after the Itta Bena arrests, SNCC worker MacArthur Cotton led 200 Black people in Greenwood to the county courthouse to register to vote. At noon, a deputy sheriff ordered the crowd, which included Lawrence Guyot, MacArthur Cotton, and Hollis Watkins, to disperse. According to SSC investigator Tom Scarbrough, some of them dispersed but then returned after they ate the lunches they brought with them. When the police told them again to leave, "Guyot began to jump up and down and stomp his feet and told the officers they had no right to tell him what to do; that he was well within his constitutional rights." The police then swept in, arresting Guyot on the courthouse steps and the rest of the SNCC members and would-be registrants. Their trial was swift, occurring at 1:30 p.m. the same day and lasting only a few minutes, with the courts sentencing all of them to four-month sentences for disturbing the peace. The judge sent Guyot, Cotton, Watkins, and several local Greenwood activists to jail. For Guyot, the new arrest came only two weeks after his arrest and beating in Winona.[67]

Guyot and the others initially went to the county work farm, but there he took part in a "sit-down" strike, where he and twenty-two other prisoners refused to obey orders to work. After that, authorities sent them all to Parchman, where they spent the next two months, "naked without any bunks, any sheets, or what have you." Willie Rodgers, one of the teenagers arrested with Guyot, told of being put in the "hot box" for two nights. He stayed in a six-foot-square cell with "no openings for light or air" and "a little round hole in the floor which was a commode." Prison staff confined several inmates in there at one time, and Rodgers said as "long as they don't turn the heat on—with three in there—you can make it." Jesse James Glover, another teenager, spent thirteen days in the box. The prison staff used the box and other punishments for infractions like being too loud or singing freedom songs, which is what happened to MacArthur Cotton, who was "hung . . . on the bars," as Glover described it. Guyot spoke matter-of-factly about his time in the infamous prison. "We sleep on steel cots and that's the way it happens." He said that the "only reason we get out is because there is sixty-eight of us," suggesting that the large number of prisoners could not be locked away indefinitely or gotten rid because this would attract too much outside scrutiny. Guyot also had an outside benefactor—the white doctor from Pass Christian who hosted the wedding party that the teenage Guyot had worked as a bartender. Guyot said the doctor "put a lot of pressure on the Civil Rights Commission to find out, you know, check on me and see if everything was all right." At one point during his incarceration, prison guards escorted away Guyot and Hollis Watkins, who told the other imprisoned activists that they were going to kill them both. Instead, the guards took the two SNCC men to the courthouse to meet with Justice Department attorneys who wanted to hear their testimony on the Winona arrests and beatings. The brief respite did not lead to freedom, for the guards returned the two men to the prison to finish their sentences. The main impact that Guyot's stint in Parchman had on his health was on his figure—he lost a substantial amount of weight in the prison, enough that Stokely Carmichael teased Guyot about it on his release, calling it an improvement over his normally husky look. "Ol' Guyot had lost one hundred pounds," Carmichael recalled. But "he could afford that better than any of us, 'cause he usually hovered up around three hundred pounds."[68]

While in Parchman, Guyot also received a visit from FBI agents, who spoke to him about his beating in Winona. They interviewed him on 2 August, when he identified the officers who beat him from photographs to provide evidence for the Justice Department's investigation of the beatings of Guyot, Hamer, and the others. While he cooperated with the FBI in the investigation, he remained justifiably suspicious of the FBI's lack of action to protect civil rights workers or investigate violations of their rights. In an earlier interview with FBI agents, he refused to name the author of the note that he had with him when he was arrested in Winona.[69]

Guyot probably did not know that the police officers who beat him feared they might be punished as well, unlike the Emmett Till days when the federal government refused to get involved. The FBI, acting at the behest of the Justice Department and Attorney General Robert Kennedy, conducted an investigation for a federal civil rights trial against the officers. Aware of the possibility of charges, a hostile Sheriff Patridge refused to cooperate with the FBI agents. He told two of the investigating agents that they "had better be extremely careful of their activities" and that if agents violated local laws, he would "take action that would attract a great deal of publicity." Patridge and his officers refused to allow themselves to be photographed by agents to create photo arrays for Guyot and the others to identify them, which forced the agents to find back issues of the *Winona Times* to find pictures of them. Prison authorities also stonewalled the agents when they tried to interview Guyot at Parchman by citing jurisdictional technicalities and forcing the agents to get permission from the Leflore County sheriff before they could conduct an interview.[70]

As Guyot recovered from his ordeals in Winona and Parchman in 1963, COFO prepared to expand its voter registration efforts in the coming year, but not like its previous efforts in either scope or ambition. The organizing of 1964 led to two of the major events of the Mississippi civil rights movement—Freedom Summer and the creation of the Mississippi Freedom Democratic Party (MFDP). The latter event in particular thrust Guyot into an entirely new area of responsibility and political leadership.

# CHAPTER 3
# WHO IS THIS LAWRENCE GUYOT, ANYWAY?

## THE BIRTH OF THE MISSISSIPPI FREEDOM DEMOCRATIC PARTY

Late 1963 marked planning by the Council of Federated Organizations (COFO) for the seminal event of 1964, the Freedom Summer campaign. First came the mock Freedom Vote in the fall of 1963, coinciding with Mississippi's gubernatorial election, with the goal of demystifying the process and motivating Black Mississippians to exercise the courage to register and vote in a real election. Freedom Summer, the brainchild of Bob Moses, would generate national publicity for the Mississippi movement by using white northern volunteers to register Black Mississippians to vote. The efforts of the Student Nonviolent Coordinating Committee (SNCC) in this, which included Guyot moving into a new position in Hattiesburg, led the organization to give birth to the Mississippi Freedom Democratic Party (MFDP), with the Magnolia State acting as unintentional midwife. The MFDP gave Guyot new prominence as he rose to head it. But the bitterness over Freedom Summer stemming from the failed challenge at the Democratic National Convention in Atlantic City, as well as the more explicitly mainstream political direction of the MFDP, soon led to a rift between parent and child, one that would move Guyot into a post-SNCC world as that organization went into decline in Mississippi.

By the time the National Council of Churches (NCC) bailed out the activists, Mississippi was well into its gubernatorial election season. Allard K. Lowenstein, a white Yale Law School graduate and college professor, arrived in the state to assist with COFO's voter registration efforts and provide legal assistance after the murder of Medgar Evers. After meetings with Bob Moses and other COFO members, he and others in the organization spearheaded a series of protest votes by Black Mississippians that would culminate in a mock "Freedom Ballot" election in November. The activists saw the election as a way to educate Black Mississippians about voting and their own potential as a voting bloc. The first protests came from Black Mississippians (733 in all, including 400 from Greenwood, indicating the effect the movement had there) who presented affidavits at the polls during the 6 August Democratic primary that said white registrars had illegally denied them the right to register. Three weeks later, during the gubernatorial runoff, 27,000 unregistered Blacks cast protest ballots at separate ballot boxes in Black churches and businesses.[1]

Guyot aided with the "Freedom Vote" campaign that COFO activists organized in September in preparation for the general election. Fannie Lou Hamer and John Lewis of SNCC proposed making the vote interracial by putting ballot boxes in white neighborhoods around the state as well, but Guyot preferred a focus on Black political empowerment. Hamer argued that all Mississippians suffered from their out-of-touch elected leaders, and by reaching out to poor white people a truly interracial democracy could be created. Such views reflected Hamer's commitment to integration, one that would later bring her into conflict with younger activists. Guyot shared her integrationist vison but opposed her and Lewis's proposal. He argued that it would be too dangerous, with the white community so hostile to any Black political activity. His views won out, and the Freedom Vote only targeted Black Mississippians.[2]

The campaign held a statewide COFO convention in Jackson in October, which included a platform of civil rights proposals and economic and antipoverty programs. Delegates chose Aaron Henry as their gubernatorial candidate and a week later selected Ed King, the white chaplain of Tougaloo College, to be his running mate. These nominations differed from the August primaries, where voters cast mock ballots for J. P. Coleman, a moderate—by Mississippi standards—on the race issue, who lost in the real primary to Lieutenant Governor Paul Johnson, the Citizens' Councils' candidate. Johnson beat Coleman due to the latter's support for John F. Kennedy in 1960, whom white Mississippians largely despised for sending troops in 1962 to admit James Meredith to the University of Mississippi. Still, in the words of movement activist and historian James Marshall, the August Freedom Vote only gave Black voters a choice between "a moderate racist and a racist." The November Freedom ballots included Henry as a choice against Johnson and Rubel Phillips, the Republican candidate who also ran as a segregationist.[3]

Official harassment accompanied the rallies for Henry and King as they campaigned in the fall. Henry described a rally in Hattiesburg where the police department closed down the local civil rights headquarters on the day of a rally for a fire code violation. Henry relocated the rally to a church, where the police followed and arrested a white girl who tried to join the rally. The police circled the church in their cars with sirens blaring, and then fire trucks joined as well. Henry said "it was impossible to speak above the roar of the official harassment." Guyot spoke after Henry, and city firemen interrupted his speech "looking for a fire." Henry said they "stood in front of the group, in full regalia, some snickering and some actually looking around for a fire, but all looking like damn fools." The firemen asked their captain, a man named Moore, what to do. Guyot said, "We're going to have a meeting here tonight, and we don't give a damn what you do." Captain Moore said nothing, and he and his men left.[4]

Despite his bravado, the official harassment did concern Guyot. On 23 October, Hattiesburg police raided the Whirly Bird Café, a restaurant that served student volunteers from Yale University. In multiple incidents, the police arrested the owner for possession of alcohol, as well as the local and student volunteers. Mary King recalled that "Guyot was worried" and that this "troubled me because [he] was normally optimistic." She said that the reprisals made him worry that the mock election would fail, as some people were returning ballot boxes early out of fear of police harassment.[5]

Local whites and police harassed, jailed, and attacked SNCC organizers and canvassers for the Freedom Vote throughout the state, and the state's major newspapers provided almost no coverage of the campaign. Yet some local ones did, such as when the Greenwood paper reported on a rally of almost 1,000 coming to hear Henry speak in Leflore County. Despite these suppression efforts, Henry and King spoke at rallies around the state, and voters cast more than 83,000 Freedom Votes in November for the two men. Movement activists focused on the positive aspects of the campaign, glossing over the fact that they fell short of their stated goal of 200,000 votes cast. Lowenstein lamented the low number of votes and considered it a failure, but Guyot argued otherwise, insisting that COFO had "been able to tear down the terror and bring it just to normal fear, given the conditions we're operating under in Mississippi." The Freedom Vote also laid the groundwork for two events to come in 1964. Freedom Summer came first, since Lowenstein had brought down white college students from northern universities, mostly from Yale and Stanford, to help organize the campaign. As Guyot himself noted, consideration of a summer project followed the Freedom Vote. This would lead to hundreds of white college students coming down to help with voter registration in 1964 and increase national attention on the problems of Mississippi by bringing privileged white youths to the state since violence against Black SNCC activists was usually ignored by the national media.[6]

The Mississippi Freedom Democratic Party also resulted from the Freedom Vote. The mobilization of Black voters by COFO, in the words of James Marshall, "clearly represented a breakthrough in establishing a statewide movement." Guyot echoed this, declaring that the election "accomplished the purpose we have set out to achieve. We now have a local grass roots political organization throughout the state of Mississippi." The mock election also educated Black Mississippians about the actual practice of voting. As he said later, "We wanted to reconnect Mississippians with their voting heritage," specifically the period of Black political power during Reconstruction. The Freedom Vote was in his view a success because it "was mobile, politically agile, and worked at the local level." Instigators like Lowenstein wanted the Freedom Vote to lead to Black Mississippians voting for the liberal wing of the Democratic Party, not building an organization that could become a potential third-party movement independent of white control. Yet despite his intentions, Lowenstein helped cultivate a political movement that Black Mississippians used to further their own ends instead of those of white liberals.[7]

The momentum from the Freedom Vote led COFO workers to expand operations to new counties, and the umbrella organization began holding monthly conventions. During the week following the Freedom Vote, COFO staff met in Greenville at a three-day strategy workshop sponsored by the Highlander Folk School. The first day of the workshop centered on what participant Howard Zinn called "a lively discussion on the role of whites in the movement." By the summer of 1963 SNCC leaders had assigned several whites to the central and field offices of COFO and SNCC, so the question that the workshop participants—thirty-five Blacks and seven whites—debated concerned whether or not more whites should be brought in for the summer of 1964. The major advantage of using white volunteers is that it involved publicity, since the media paid attention to violence against whites while ignoring it when it affected Black workers, as the scant media attention to Guyot and Hamer and the others' arrest and beating in Winona had shown. By contrast, when police arrested John Else, a white Yale University student, in Hattiesburg during the Freedom Vote rallies, the local paper gave his arrest and trial—and the presence of a delegation of his classmates—front-page coverage.[8]

The debate exposed growing racial tensions within COFO, with some Black activists resentful of the growing white presence and the plans to bring more whites next summer. Zinn said that "four or five" of the Black staffers urged that the role of whites be limited. They complained that whites had tried to "take over" the Jackson office, a charge that Bob Moses denied. Al Lowenstein, who had brought the white college students to the state for the Freedom Vote, received criticism, with some organizers charging that the students he recruited would only take orders from him, not from veteran organizers. They feared that white students from privileged backgrounds would gravitate into leadership positions and unconsciously benefit from the notions of white superiority that Jim Crow had ingrained into so many Black Mississippians, thus stunting the local leadership and participatory democracy they were nurturing among Black Mississippians.[9]

Guyot and other Black organizers took a dim view of Lowenstein. Jim Forman, SNCC's executive secretary, had prior experience with Lowenstein and disliked him. Guyot did not like Lowenstein's complaints about SNCC's decentralized structure, in particular with regards to decision making. To Guyot, Lowenstein represented an elitist view of leadership, one that said "every man must be led," while he and SNCC wanted "every man a leader." He complained to Bob Moses about Lowenstein's involvement, asking him, "Why are you dealing with this guy? . . . This is contrary to everything we live by." Moses, however, defended Lowenstein's ability to recruit the necessary white northern college students for the summer project.[10]

Despite his differences with Lowenstein, Guyot agreed on the need for white volunteers and spoke out against limiting white participation, saying that bringing more whites into the movement would be good, as "a lot of Negroes in Mississippi meeting a lot of white people, on a human individual to human individual relationship," would further the goal of an integrated society. Fannie Lou Hamer also spoke for inclusion, arguing that "we can't segregate ourselves." Moses, usually reserved, spoke forcefully for more whites as well, declaring that if "no white person can be head of any project, [then] I don't want to be part of an operation like that."[11]

Despite Zinn's claims that only a few Black staffers opposed expanded white participation, it seems that that many Black civil rights workers resented white involvement. As Guyot recalled, the arguments, while about race, really dealt with "turf," or the question of "why bring in well-tutored, well-trained people who have a sense-value relationship to the power to compete with me for my constituency." Some of this jealousy, Guyot said, boiled down to "I've earned my right" and "I've taken the risks," which a middle-class white college student had not. Staffers who shared this sentiment included Charlie Cobb and Ivanhoe Donaldson, both northerners, as well as native Mississippians recruited into the movement by Moses like Willie Peacock and Hollis Watkins. They opposed the use of white volunteers and the expansive summer project, which they feared would undermine local organizing and indigenous leadership. Guyot and Hamer strongly backed Moses, but no other staffers offered their level of support.

The Greenville meeting ended with no decision on the question of white volunteers, but subsequent meetings over the winter gave shape to the idea of Freedom Summer as a voter registration project that included community centers for Black residents and "freedom schools" to provide literacy and citizenship training to Black voters and children.[12]

Guyot was busy with other matters that winter besides the planning for Freedom Summer. That December, Guyot, Hamer, and the others jailed and beaten at Winona hoped to see justice served. At the federal courthouse in Oxford, the criminal trial against the Winona policemen, *U.S. v. Patridge, Herrod, Surrell, Basinger and Perkins*, began that month. The SNCC plaintiffs attended the trial, but white resistance in Oxford—where James Meredith's admission to the University of Mississippi a year earlier triggered white violence that led to two deaths—kept them from staying in the college town. They stayed instead in nearby Holly Springs and when they attended the trial, had their food brought to them in the Justice Department office since even a Black-owned café in Oxford would not serve them.[13]

Judge Claude F. Clayton, an Eisenhower-appointed jurist, did not have the racist reputation of other southern-born federal judges, but John Doar and the Black plaintiffs believed he showed bias, and Clayton selected an all-white jury for the trial. White students from the University of Mississippi attended and waved Confederate flags in the courtroom, adding to the racially charged climate. The media largely ignored the trial, which took place in the aftermath of the Kennedy assassination. Annelle Ponder testified first about her beating, followed by Hamer. When John Basinger testified, the highway patrolman claimed that Hamer resisted arrest and fought with the officers, a direct contradiction of Hamer's testimony. Sole Poe, one of the Black inmates who was ordered by the guards to beat Hamer, testified for the prosecution, corroborating Hamer's account. A doctor who had examined Hamer and Ponder after the beating also testified that their injuries resulted from physical violence and not an accident. The defense team relied on the time-honored contention that the plaintiffs were "professional agitators" who provoked the police with a sit-in and linked them to Dr. King, the Southern Christian Leadership Conference, and the Highlander Folk School in Tennessee, which to the mind of the white southern jurors meant "communist."[14]

Guyot testified about his arrest and beating in Winona, identifying the officers who struck him. Will S. Wells, an assistant attorney general for Mississippi, cross-examined Guyot and, like a typical white southerner of his day, refused to call him "Mr. Guyot," just as he referred to the female witnesses by their first names. Wells began his cross-examination by asking Guyot about his background but then obsessively focused on his salary as a SNCC field secretary, which originally was $10.00 a week but in December 1963 stood at $9.64 per week. He kept asking Guyot if income taxes and Social Security had been withdrawn and if Guyot had filed federal income taxes, apparently in an attempt to suggest he was being paid under the table to dodge taxes. Wells dropped the line of inquiry after a prosecution objection, and then questioned him about his arrests and fines for civil rights activities in Greenwood. The second time Guyot took the stand, Wells tried to get him to admit that he stated in the presence of the sheriff that he had sustained his injuries from "falling out of your automobile Saturday night" (the night before his arrest in Winona), a charge that he denied. On 6 December, the jury acquitted the policemen after deliberating for slightly over an hour. Guyot said that "we identified them, we told them exactly what had happened, told them how it had happened and when it had happened. The jury didn't convict them." Septima Clark and Ella Baker counseled him to move on from his bitterness over the verdict. "Look beyond this foolishness," Baker said. "Don't let it stop you."[15]

Guyot took the women's words to heart. By the end of 1963, COFO stationed him full-time in Hattiesburg in Forrest County, where he worked as coordinator for the Fifth Congressional District, which included the Piney Woods counties around Hattiesburg that stretched down to the Mississippi Gulf Coast. There he met one of his and SNCC's most formidable opponents, Forrest County registrar Theron Lynd. Even larger than Guyot, Lynd was a Citizens' Council member and former football player with 330 pounds filling out his intimidating frame, and he used that and the power of his office to, in the words of historian John Dittmer, "put his Delta counterparts to shame" in the obstruction of Black voting rights. He took office in 1959, and the Justice Department sued him in January 1961 for refusing to allow federal examination of county voter registration files. During his first two years in office, Lynd did not allow a single Black person to even attempt to register, and Forrest County had only 25 Black voters registered out of its 7,495 eligible ones. Even after another federal lawsuit and a ruling from the Fifth Circuit Court of Appeals, Lynd defied the courts and refused to register Black applicants.[16]

The federal action prompted SNCC to begin a voter registration drive in Hattiesburg, with the goal to "prod the Justice Department a bit," according to John Pratt, a lawyer from the NCC representing Black plaintiffs in the county. Since 3,500 Black people in Forrest County had cast Freedom Votes in 1963, the county and town seemed to be a good place to organize. Aaron Henry said that "we don't plan on leaving Hattiesburg until the Justice Department takes Registrar Lynd in hand." In March 1962 Hollis Watkins and Curtis Haynes, another

SNCC recruit, arrived and began to work with Vernon Dahmer, a local leader in the National Association for the Advancement of Colored People (NAACP). Dahmer, by nature more confrontational than the stereotypical NAACP officer, initially had little support from other NAACP officials, mostly distrustful of SNCC and reflecting the growing tensions within COFO. But Dahmer's local leadership role was critical, and Guyot called him "tough, aggressive and at the same time very stabilizing. . . . Once he said it was all right the rest of the NAACP came around." After Watkins and Haynes left in September 1962 to work in the Delta, Victoria Gray, owner of a successful local cosmetics business, took over as project director. Gray conducted citizenship classes, where she taught local Black residents literacy and civics education. While essential to political empowerment and developing local leadership, these classes also consumed large amounts of time, so the Hattiesburg movement grew slowly throughout 1963. Positive steps continued though, and the NAACP joined the project after its initial reluctance.[17]

Mrs. L. E. Woods, a widow and member of one of the city's more prominent Black families, owned SNCC's Freedom House on Mobile Street in Hattiesburg. While nowhere near the white population in income levels, Hattiesburg's Black community enjoyed more prosperity than its counterparts in the Delta counties, and the town had a reputation for being more moderate than Greenwood or other places. Guyot said that "what we found in Hattiesburg was a very literate group of people, willing to be organized and mobilized, and they already had established leaders there." He said the town, unlike Greenwood, had "a different setting. Not agricultural." Guyot recalled that the people there "had more what I would safely describe as middle-class expectations." By January, Moses, Guyot, Hamer, Charlie Cobb, Dave Dennis, and many of the other prominent organizers in SNCC and the Congress of Racial Equality (CORE) had arrived in the city to organize. Guyot headed up the COFO special project in Hattiesburg and planned direct action in the city to bring pressure on Lynd to register Black voters, and on the federal government to enforce the Fifth Circuit's ruling.[18]

The "Freedom Day," a tactic that COFO borrowed from SNCC's voter registration drive in Selma, Alabama, became a central part of the Hattiesburg campaign. Set for 22 January, the day involved a mass march of Black residents to the courthouse to attempt to register, accompanied by a demonstration against Lynd's obstructionism. The third leg of demonstrations that day included a student boycott of classes. These actions came on the heels of a ruling by the Supreme Court on 6 January upholding the Fifth Circuit's ruling against the Forrest County registrar. Lynd's continuing defiance of the federal courts prompted the local organizing by COFO. "We can't ask people to go down and take a test which is going to be reviewed by a man who has no regard for federal court orders," Guyot said. "The only recourse is federal intervention or community action."[19]

Guyot prepared to go to jail once again during the Freedom Day. He told COFO that he needed about ten staff members prepared to go to jail, and he included himself among that number. During a planning meeting at the Freedom House, COFO staffers decided that Bob Moses would join Guyot on the picket line and be one of those arrested. At a mass meeting at a church the night of 21 January, Aaron Henry, John Lewis, Ella Baker, and others addressed the crowd about the need to make Hattiesburg a turning point in the Mississippi movement.[20] Howard Zinn recounted Guyot's fiery address in the church, which combined the emotionalism of a revival with his academic knowledge, and attested to his rising status in the movement:

> Everyone in the church stood and applauded when he came down the aisle; it was a spontaneous expression of the kind of love SNCC organizers receive when they have become part of a community in the Deep South. Guyot combines a pensive intellectualism with a fierce and radical activism. He stood before the audience, his large frame trembling, raised a fist high over his head, and shouted, pronouncing slowly and carefully: "Immanuel Kant . . ." The church was hushed. "Immanuel Kant asks—Do you exist?" In the front row, teen-age [sic] boys and girls stared at Guyot; a young woman was holding two babies. Guyot paused. "Kant says, every speck of earth must be treated as important!" His audience waited, somewhat awed, and he went on to get very specific about instructions for the Freedom Day at the county courthouse.[21]

The church meeting reflected the growing white involvement in the movement, continuing on the example of the Freedom Vote and further building support for white involvement in civil rights work planned for that summer. A number of white clergymen from the National Council of Churches attended the meeting—Guyot said he requested them, but Moses played a role in their invitation as well. From mid-January to mid-June 1964 over 100 ministers from around the county came to Hattiesburg to join in demonstrations and serve as voting canvassers. Many of these clergymen came from the Presbyterian Church, but Episcopal priests and Jewish rabbis also took part. The NCC's role, Guyot said, helped significantly with the summer project that came later, as the organization "was instrumental in training and providing the training, money, and the site for the volunteers."[22]

Guyot's church address also showed his development into a Black leader unlike many of the other leaders of the civil rights movement. A Roman Catholic with a college education, Guyot, while often fiery like Black Protestant preachers such as Martin Luther King Jr. and Alabama's Fred Shuttlesworth, preferred to quote philosophers like Kant rather than Christ or Scripture. While King possessed more education than Guyot and drew on that education when he engaged white liberal audiences in his writings, his sermons were still rooted in the long tradition of Black preaching and borrowed from other Black ministers. Guyot instead drew on the both the intellectual traditions of his Catholic upbringing and his Tougaloo education to inspire grassroots activists and everyday people. As Michael Paul Sistrom noted in his study of the MFDP, Guyot, at least in his rhetoric, rejected the religious themes of Black preachers as well as the growing Marxist language of SNCC revolutionaries and instead "sounded much more like a pure political animal."[23]

Guyot's organizing of the Freedom Day also highlighted strains on COFO resources. He said that Lynd was a "symbol to Negro and white communities of resistance to federal authority" and that his defiance encouraged other registrars to follow his example. Therefore, "Freedom Day will symbolize our resistance just as Lynd symbolizes theirs." Toward that end, he advocated concentrating COFO staff there, and the COFO committee complied and sent a request for ten more staffers to arrive after 22 January, but this maintained what Ivanhoe Donaldson called "a skeleton crew" in the rest of the state to cover projects. Staff shortages also increased support for bringing more white volunteers into the state, due to the demands of the Hattiesburg and proposed summer projects. Already, white volunteers from other COFO offices, such as Mickey and Rita Schwerner from the one in Meridian, helped to organize in Hattiesburg. Amzie Moore drove down from the Delta to join to project as well, as did Fannie Lou Hamer.[24]

Planning for the Freedom Day included distributing circulars to people to notify them of the upcoming events, which alerted the Hattiesburg police department to COFO's actions. After police arrested Robert Plump and Lafayette Surney, two Black volunteers, Guyot asked the Justice Department to investigate police harassment of canvassers. Police arrested a white Tougaloo student, Peter Stoner, in a separate incident. Chief of Police Hugh Herring publicly warned of "agitators" passing out leaflets that urged civil disobedience, and the *Hattiesburg American,* the local newspaper, accused COFO of trying to "whip up" a demonstration.[25]

On 22 January, the marchers gathered for their trek to the courthouse, with a downpour opening up on them. Despite the weather, nearly 200 people arrived at the Forrest County Courthouse by late morning, including fifty NCC clergymen. Picketers marched while applicants attempted to register to vote, and Aaron Henry and Charles Evers both addressed the crowd. Evers, the brother of Medgar Evers, had recently taken over as field secretary for the Mississippi NAACP after the murder of his brother. Unlike at other demonstrations, the Hattiesburg Police Department did not conduct mass arrests, and Theron Lynd made a point of allowing Black applicants to take the test. The local authorities no doubt complied because of the heavy media presence in the city, which included television cameras in the courthouse and reporters interviewing Lynd, who said on the air that "I will treat all applicants alike, just as I have always done." Black children boycotted classes in solidarity with the protests, with the local paper reporting 700 more absences than average that day.[26]

Despite the lack of violence, official obstruction continued in Hattiesburg. Lynd had only allowed twelve applicants to take the voting test by noon, and a policeman arrested Bob Moses for breach of the peace when he refused a policeman's order to move off the sidewalk. Police also began to harass picketers by the afternoon, but only arrested Moses that day. The COFO forces kept up their demonstrations on the subsequent days, sending more applicants to the courthouse. By the end of the week 150 people had taken the test, while a judge sentenced Moses to sixty days in jail and a $200 fine.[27]

The city obtained an injunction against the picketing, and on 29 January, police arrested nine Presbyterian ministers—eight white and one Black, all there at the behest of the NCC—for violating the order. By this time the national media lost interest, so the police widened their crackdown on the COFO project and its leaders. Guyot himself soon fell afoul of the law and saw his name and face splashed across the front of the *Hattiesburg American*. On 28 January, police arrested him for "contributing to the delinquency of a minor." While on the surface it sounded like a salacious charge of statutory rape, the reality was far less lurid. The charge specifically related to the school boycotts, for prosecutors accused him of encouraging a thirteen-year-old Black girl, Barbara Ann Thomas, to skip school to take part in a civil rights demonstration. County prosecutors claimed she left home without her mother's consent, joined the demonstrations and then spent the night away from home with a resident on Mobile Street, near the Freedom House. Her mother and a youth counselor found her with the COFO demonstrators at the courthouse.[28]

The charges appeared questionable at best, as the girl's mother apparently worked part-time as a maid for a sergeant in the police department. Even though police picked up the girl at her mother's home, they placed her in protective custody. The court, not the mother, had the sole right to appoint an attorney for her defense, and COFO already reported that other children had claimed coercion by authorities into making false statements against civil rights workers. Investigators for the State Sovereignty Commission (SSC) considered Guyot a prime target, as the director of the Hattiesburg project. Tom Scarbrough, already familiar with Guyot's work in Greenwood, monitored the Hattiesburg Project with Virgil Downing, another SSC investigator. They reported that he "is a big factor in instigating and pushing for the demonstration" in Hattiesburg and, in words that dripped with sarcasm, charged that "the sanctimonious white ministers who come from various parts of the United States have taken orders from this distinguished gentlemen, Guyot." Certainly, the COFO workers considered the case to be bogus. In a report on the Hattiesburg Project, COFO called the case "substantially weak." Unita Blackwell, not in SNCC at the time but who joined the following year and worked with Guyot on political organizing, said that police had him "in jail half of the time; they gave him some of the charge that he looked at some girl and molest her or something. They just arrest us for anything."[29]

Local authorities stopped Black people from attending Guyot's arraignment. They did this to prevent the integrated audience that attended Moses's trial a few days earlier, where COFO attendees successfully defied the judge's order to segregate the courtroom. Guyot pled not guilty and waived his right to a jury trial, no doubt knowing it would be all-white and pointless as an exercise in judicial fairness. The girl's mother claimed that Guyot bribed her daughter with money and food, and that the girl looked "dirty and wet and everything" when she found her at the courthouse (it had been raining that day). She admitted that her daughter had prior problems with truancy, and once "ran away and stayed right next door [to her house]." Guyot testified that he had never met Barbara Ann Thomas, who herself testified that he had encouraged her with money to join the demonstrations and asked her to spread word of the demonstrations to her classmates. She wavered under cross-examination by Guyot's attorney, claiming that she never met Guyot and participated in the Freedom Day of her own free will. Even the newspaper reporter covering the case reported on the contradictions and weaknesses in her testimony, writing that "when the state questioned her she said whatever was expected of her. When the defense interrogated her she did likewise." District Attorney James Finch accused her of changing the earlier testimony she gave him and asked why she had done this, to which she simply replied, "I don't know." Judge William Haralson still found Guyot guilty, sentencing to him to six months in jail and a $500 fine, with five months suspended on the condition of good behavior. Despite the efforts of authorities to crush the movement by arresting its directors, local demonstrations continued after Guyot's arrest and imprisonment. The NCC continued to send ministers to support the project, and Dick Gregory, a frequent supporter of the Mississippi civil rights movement, also arrived in Hattiesburg.[30]

Peter Stoner, a white SNCC staffer and graduate of Tougaloo College, tried to visit Guyot in jail. Stoner had already served time in jail in Hattiesburg, arrested by the police on 7 January, the first day of his arrival in the city, for obstructing traffic, illegal parking, and other charges. A court convicted him of the traffic charges and he spent six days in jail rather than pay the fines, and then three more days when police rearrested him after his release. He tried to visit his friend and fellow alumnus in the Forrest County jail on 5 February, during Guyot's stay there. When Stoner refused the jailer's order to leave the premises, the jailer detained him without charge, and an hour later police charged him with disturbing the peace, resisting arrest, and other offenses. The jailer, Print Jones, claimed during the subsequent trial that Stoner had arrived after visiting hours and said, "I God damn well am going to see Guyot." Stoner disputed that charge, insisting that Jones denied him the right to visit Guyot during regular visiting hours. The judge found Stoner guilty, and Stoner served 107 days in jail and at the Forrest County Work Camp, during which time fellow inmates and guards beat him, and jailers even bribed an inmate with cigarettes to try and rape him.[31]

Guyot spent the first part of February in jail, then later in the same work camp with Stoner. Despite his health problems from the Winona beating, Guyot worked at hard labor until his release on bail. Stoner said that despite inmate hostility, Guyot did not suffer the same abuse that he received in Winona. Guyot confirmed this comparatively benign treatment—of course anything short of death looked benign compared to the ordeal in the Winona jail. "I was never beaten in jail," he recalled. "I was threatened a couple of times. I would have to say I was treated better in the jails of Hattiesburg than any other jail." Meanwhile, the Freedom Day demonstrations continued in Hattiesburg, including pickets and attempts to register to vote. By 13 March, 196 Blacks had successfully registered to vote, and 700 in total applied to take the registration test. Governor Paul Johnson signed into law in April a harsh antipicketing law at the behest of a Forrest County legislator, which provided for a maximum six-month jail sentence and $500 fine for picketing on state, county, or municipal property. The draconian law quelled many of the Hattiesburg protests by mid-April. The Justice Department kept up the pressure on Lynd, with John Doar arguing the case against the registrar, but the case dragged on in judicial delays while the discrimination against Black applicants continued. As Patricia Buzard-Boyett, a historian of the civil rights movement in Forrest County, has noted, "non-violent massive resistance" by the white establishment was working. COFO needed a broader project, beyond a single county or city. The glacial approach of the federal government combined with unyielding white resistance thus led directly to the 1964 COFO summer project, better known as Freedom Summer, and its related creation: an interracial political party to challenge the all-white Mississippi Democratic Party.[32]

Guyot did not stay in Hattiesburg in April, however. After his release, SNCC advertised that it sent him on a speaking tour of the Midwest, to visit public and private universities in Illinois, Indiana, and Ohio to raise northern support for Freedom Summer. At Southern Illinois University, he gave a campus reporter an indication of his future critiques of the US government, telling her that it "was no longer possible for the U.S. to sell the commodity of freedom on the foreign market when it does not exist in this country." The campus reporter was none other than Minniejean Brown, one of the Little Rock Nine from the 1957 integration of Central High School in Arkansas, now majoring in journalism at the university. In addition to the interview, he also addressed several classes and the campus's chapter of SNCC.[33]

The Mississippi Freedom Democratic Party was created in the spring of 1964, as authorities stymied the Hattiesburg demonstrations and Guyot returned to the state. Movement leaders, including Guyot, decided as far back as 1963 that some kind of challenge to the state Democratic Party had to be made, due to single-digit Black voter registration in Mississippi. They had indications by early 1964 that white supporters outside the state would lend a hand. In February, 2,600 delegates to the California Democratic Council at Long Beach unanimously adopted a resolution calling for the seating of the MFDP and the denying of credentials to the "traditional Democratic Party of Mississippi." At the monthly COFO state convention in Jackson on 15 March, COFO officially approved a formal challenge of the state Democratic delegation and also announced a "freedom registration" campaign for the summer—Freedom Summer.[34]

At the Masonic Temple in Jackson, on a rainy Sunday—26 April—COFO leaders formally established the party. Len Holt, a Black attorney assisting COFO, gave a pessimistic view of the convention, noting that a mere 200 people showed up. He said that their belief they could challenge the state Democrats, and by extension all Southern Democrats and President Lyndon Baines Johnson and even potentially the mainstream civil rights establishment, created "a sense of impertinence and irrelevance" at the gathering. "The scene bordered on the ridiculous . . . ridiculous by any standard other than that of SNCC. But one could [only] wonder if SNCC had gone beyond the pale of rationality in this case." Moses arrived late to the convention, returning from a trip to the North that failed to drum up much outside support for the new party and its challenge. Holt summed up the underwhelming nature of the rally when he said that Moses returned to his lodgings and "withdrew in relative quietness for three days." Holt called the startup of the MFDP "not overly impressive."[35]

As inauspicious as the beginnings of the party were, the MFDP still had all the formal structure of a political party. The delegates elected twelve native Black Mississippians from all five of the state's congressional districts to serve as a temporary state committee, with Aaron Henry as the chairman. The delegates approved the creation of a party "open to all Democrats in Mississippi of voting age, regardless of race, creed or color." Les McLemore, one of the committee members, said that local whites attended "but they refused to take an active part in the Party, because the of fear of harassment and intimidation" from their white neighbors.[36]

At the founding convention, the stress of Guyot's past two years of involvement with SNCC, the near-fatal beating in Winona, and the continuing threat of violence from white supremacists finally took its toll. He said that he left the meeting, and "I just got against the wall, and I couldn't move the left side of my body—just, just couldn't move it. A couple of people picked me up." They took him to an apartment, where a doctor arrived to treat him. The doctor said, "You're just exhausted. Just get some rest." Guyot later recalled that the daily pressure of organizing, the "very personalness of the operation," just proved too much for some activists. He said that "*you* stayed at someone's house and then that house was blown up or burned because of that. Take a couple of months of that and it begins to wear you down." Robert Coles, a psychologist who worked in Mississippi during Freedom Summer, called this condition "battle fatigue," which crippled the work of many veteran activists. Sam Block suffered insomnia, depression, anorexia, and other ills brought on by the beatings, arrests, and threats he experienced in Greenwood. He left the state after Freedom Summer when he began to experience ringing in his ears and hallucinations.[37]

The nascent MFDP meanwhile tried to expand its ties to other civil rights groups within COFO. In May, the temporary executive committee appointed Charles Evers of the NAACP as an ex-officio member and also elected him treasurer. McLemore said that "this was done in the hope of avoiding a public clash with the NAACP." The MFDP made the overture because of growing tensions within COFO. COFO's expansion across the state as a result of the Freedom Vote raised fears among some out-of-state SNCC members that COFO would "swallow" SNCC during the summer project, especially in fundraising. James Forman of SNCC distrusted the more conservative, hierarchical NAACP and the "Toms" in COFO. Guyot himself argued for COFO, assuring COFO critics that "in Mississippi SNCC *is* COFO." Despite the appointment of Evers, the NAACP did not send any personnel to assist the MFDP, and Evers, according to McLemore, "never did function with any kind of consistency" as treasurer. Evers himself had little interest in cooperating with the MFDP or SNCC, an attitude that became even more apparent in subsequent years. McLemore said Evers was "so hard to get along with" and was always "the one guy who never agrees with anybody about any goddamn thing."[38]

Guyot threw his energies into preparing for Freedom Summer. In May, assisted by Len Holt and two other attorneys, he filed a petition with the Fifth Circuit Court of Appeals in New Orleans requesting that five additional US district judges, accompanied by "at least" five US marshals, be assigned to Mississippi from June to September 1964 to protect the incoming northern volunteers. He based his argument on the expected growth of the number of voter registration workers in state, in particular the Fifth Congressional District where he was field secretary. Guyot said that he expected the voter registration workers he supervised to grow from the 20 he currently oversaw to more than 200. He summarized the long history of violence against civil rights workers as another need for the federal officials, indicating that the threat was so grave that "the only restrictions seem to be the imagination of the perpetrators of violence." The two federal judges in the state, who also vacationed part of the summer, could not handle all this increased activity, he argued. One of the judges, Harold Cox, had a particularly racist reputation and the Fifth Court had already overruled his decisions supporting Theron Lynd's refusal to register Black voters. Guyot closed by invoking the name of civil rights martyrs in Mississippi and declaring that "the only protection these 2,000 young people from the North can hope for is a willing and able federal judiciary." Nothing came of the request. The next month in Oxford, Ohio, at the orientation and training for Freedom Summer, the Justice Department's John Doar told the assembled volunteers not to expect any federal protection, as "maintaining law and order is a state responsibility."[39]

Guyot and other SNCC staff also worked on the congressional campaigns of MFDP members. Fannie Lou Hamer, Victoria Gray, James Monroe Houston, and the Reverend John Cameron all represented the MFDP and COFO as candidates in the 2 June Democratic primary, challenging the white Democratic incumbents. Hamer ran against Jamie Whitten of the Second House District, Gray challenged Senator John Stennis, and Cameron opposed William Colmer in the Fifth District. Houston, a retired machinist from Vicksburg, ran in the Third

District. Although their success was impossible given that only 28,000 Black voters were on the registration rolls, they ran to raise awareness of the plight of Black Mississippians. "We feel the time is ripe to begin to let people know that we're serious about this whole thing of becoming first class citizens," Gray said. White authorities retaliated against the candidates despite the impossibility of a MFDP victory. On 4 May, the Hattiesburg city government fired Victoria Gray's husband Tony, a plumber, from his job in the city's Water Works Division. The threat of violence against the candidates prompted a Hamer supporter to write a letter to J. Edgar Hoover requesting—unsuccessfully—Federal Bureau of Investigation (FBI) protection for the candidate. "We can show her that America is worth living for," pleaded the unidentified letter-writer.[40]

The staff executive committee of SNCC, which included Guyot and Charlie Cobb, met in Jackson on 15 May. They planned how to assist campaigns, focusing on Hamer's and Gray's, and planned for the Democratic precinct meetings in June and July that followed the 2 June election. According to Cobb, SNCC planned to mobilize Black Mississippians politically and "break down the fear of, and get the Negro communities accustomed to going to the polling places." The MFDP had held mock conventions earlier that month to educate potential voters about the political process.[41]

Kay Mills, a biographer of Hamer, summed up the June primary as "the end of one campaign and the beginning of another, far from unremarkable, that would change the state forever: Freedom Summer." After the defeat of the candidates, COFO organizers worked on bringing white student volunteers from the North down to register voters and engage in other civil rights activities. To raise publicity for Freedom Summer, Guyot, Hamer, and other COFO members held a hearing in Washington, DC, on 8 June. They failed to get a congressional hearing, so they instead set up a panel that included a New York judge and other luminaries. Guyot spoke first, describing his beating in Winona and the federal trial and acquittal of the officers. He gave the panel a critical assessment of the federal government's inaction on civil rights, taking a direct shot at Senator James Eastland's cozy relationship with the White House. He said that "in Mississippi, as long as you have Federal district judges who are appointed by senatorial courtesy, a white man doesn't have to worry about the Federal Government. The Federal Government in Mississippi is the white man." Hamer followed him and described her ordeal in Winona and the loss of her job and other harassment by police and white civilians. Elizabeth Allen of Liberty also testified, speaking about her husband, Louis Allen, whom whites murdered when he reported to the FBI his witnessing the murder of Herbert Lee, a Black civil rights worker. Hartman Turnbow testified last, describing the intimidation he faced when trying to register to vote in Lexington and how the sheriff arrested him after white men firebombed his home. The testimony of Guyot and the civil rights workers prompted Representative William F. Ryan (D-NY) to ask the Justice Department to send federal marshals to protect the volunteers, but like Guyot's application to the Fifth Circuit, the department denied the request.[42]

As COFO commenced preparations for training and organizing volunteers for Freedom Summer, the MFDP prepared its challenge against the all-white Mississippi delegation at the Atlantic City Democratic National Convention that summer. The grassroots strategy involved sending volunteers to attend precinct meetings of the state Democratic Party, something that had not been done before due to violence and intimidation. The refusal of local white party officials, activists hoped, would give the MFDP ample evidence for its seating challenge at the national convention. These meetings expressed the local power of the state party, since the precincts decided which delegates went to the re-spective county conventions and then the state convention. In some precincts, MFDP members found that the meetings had been moved or changed to keep them from attending, while in others white Democrats simply refused them entry. Only in ten precincts did officials admit Black MFDP members, but those same officials wholly or partially restricted their voting during the delegate selection process. Despite these obstacles, some Black delegates won election, and one Black member won on the county level from an integrated precinct in Jackson at the Hinds County Democratic Convention. In general, white officials in heavily Black counties like Leflore and Madison proved more hostile to the presence of Black participants, while most counties, according to Les McLem-ore, had enough white participants to simply ignore or outvote the handful of Black participants.[43]

The MFDP then held its own precinct meetings after the state Democrats held theirs, but did not hold them in every county. In rural areas, fear kept many local Blacks away, and they often refused to take part if nominated by the party. The local residents had good reason to be fearful, as whites firebombed the home of two MFDP leaders in Hattiesburg in the early morning hours of 25 July. Despite the intimidation and violence, counties like Madison, Lafayette, and Leflore held successful conventions and elected delegates, many of them women, to attend the state convention.[44]

Despite the MFDP's successes in holding the conventions and organizing for the challenge in Atlantic City, the party faced what could be generously described as an uphill battle. A less generous observer would have called the battle futile. Bob Moses sounded a note of alarm in July in a memo to COFO field staff and volunteers, warning that "the various political programs which comprise the Freedom Democratic Party's Convention Challenge are in very bad shape all around the state." Staff either did not think the challenge important or were unaware of the amount of work the challenge would take. Moses urged all staff not working in the Freedom Schools or community centers to devote all their time to the challenge, as "all of us must now pull together behind the program in order to make it at least a partial success."[45]

As the MFDP readied itself for its state convention in August, Guyot organized in a part of the Fifth District that had not received much attention from COFO: his native Gulf Coast. Hattiesburg and the organizing there had long overshadowed the rest of the Fifth District, while the coastal counties experienced violence over beach integration but nothing at near the level of the Delta counties. The smaller Black populations of the Gulf Coast contributed to the lack of attention there, compared to the majority-Black (and more repressive) Delta, where COFO resources seemed better utilized. But the Gulf Coast offered another area of potential, the organizing of *white* Mississippians. At a 15 May meeting of COFO staff in Jackson, including Guyot, the discussion covered mobilizing the white community, as they said "there is next to no program" there and "it was felt that we should begin now to start dialogue and communication with the white community."[46]

With only a staff of ten and eleven volunteers for the entire Fifth District for Freedom Summer, Guyot lent assistance to COFO's White Community (or "White Folks") Project. Directed by Sam Shirah, a twenty-two-year-old white Alabamian, the effort sent integrated teams into five Mississippi cities with the goal of unifying poor Blacks and whites on the common theme of their poverty, echoing similar attempts by the Populist Party in the late nineteenth century. One leaflet declared that "We Must Be Allies. . . . Race Has Led Us Both to Poverty." Like the efforts of the Populists, the results were not encouraging, as the deep-seated racism of poor whites hindered any meaningful cross-racial alliances. The most notable success was Robert W. Williams of Biloxi, a white man who became an MFDP delegate to the Democratic National Convention in Atlantic City.[47]

Of the twenty-five volunteers assigned to the project, COFO sent eighteen to Gulfport and Biloxi. Despite the belief of white coastal residents that their area was more racially enlightened than the rest of Mississippi, local officials and white residents threatened the integrated COFO teams and employed violence. At Moss Point, a community outside Pascagoula, COFO held a voter registration rally on 9 July, and Guyot addressed the crowd of around 300 people. Elizabeth Sutherland, a white SNCC staffer, said that he gave "a terrific speech."

He criticized Black apathy in Moss Point, and asked, "What will it take to make you people move? A rape? A shooting? A murder? What will it take?" At the end of the meeting, during the singing of "We Shall Overcome," four white men opened fire on the building. A bullet hit Jessie Mae Stallworth, a seventeen-year-old Black girl, in her side. She recovered, but the sheriff—who had been watching the meeting but left shortly before the shooting—returned and later arrested five Black men. The men had returned home to get firearms and then went in search of the gunmen's car, underscoring the angry willingness of local Black residents to defend Black lives and property.[48]

The Moss Point speech and others by Guyot, as well as his defiance toward white officials, earned him a reputation for being aggressive and combative. His size added to this, with his colleagues frequently commenting on the role it played in his dealings with white supremacists. Andrew Young described Guyot as "massive and physically intimidating." Movement historian Charles Payne said that some SNCC members who worked with him found him "forceful," like his contemporary Stokely Carmichael, sometimes to the point that they felt he imposed his views on them. John Dittmer called Guyot "a strong, forceful, person whose vocabulary matched his imposing physical stature" and who "developed both a loyal following and bitter enemies within the movement." Dittmer criticized Guyot's temperament as not suitable for a leadership role in the MFDP, suggesting that his personality "better equipped him to confront sheriffs than to deal with the subtleties of movement politics." While some critics might view Guyot's leadership style and personality as contrary to the SNCC ethos of developing local leadership and participatory democracy, it is important to note that Guyot himself was not an outsider like Moses but a native Mississippian recruited by him, and thus an example of the local leadership developed by SNCC. It also remains open to interpretation how "forceful" Guyot could be with other people. Bob Zellner, a white Alabamian who had been with SNCC since the McComb campaign in 1961 and was brutally beaten by local whites himself, said that "a lasting gift from Greenwood was getting to know Lawrence Guyot during that brutal summer of '64." He "did not take anything from anyone. . . . He was a good movement leader, and what better way to forget the terror around us and the total frustration of trying to light a fire in the middle of iceberg, than having a good poker game every time Guyot rode into town."[49]

Peter Orris, a white medical student who met Guyot during a visit to New York City and then later in Atlanta, gave a very different perspective of the MFDP leader. He described Guyot during the earlier debates in SNCC over direct action versus voter registration as "a quiet, gentle giant" who "had that style of local, southern community organizing in which he frequently didn't talk until others talked, and when he had something to say was relatively profound." Orris added that "most of [Guyot's] contributions were quiet and he engendered a lot of respect in the group itself," a leadership style very different from many other recollections. When he encountered Guyot in the South, Orris said Guyot came across as a "classic SNCC community organizer. Patient, eloquent, but with the style of listening to other people and working from that and not being angry and aggressive with everyone that he talked to."[50]

These differing observations of Guyot do not mean that ones like Orris's are incorrect. Instead, they suggest Guyot's skill as a politician and organizer, specifically his ability to speak differently to different audiences depending on the circumstances. Fannie Rushing, another SNCC activist, said that she never ran into anyone "more sarcastic, acerbic or arrogant than Stokely [Carmichael], but when Stokely was talking with local people he was a completely different person. Never, ever, was he arrogant with anyone on a project. And of course older people just loved him because he always seemed to be listening." She said that "people can be very different in different circumstances," and she suggested Guyot was acting the same way in his interactions with people.[51] This ability to listen to and behave differently with different people became a defining characteristic of political leaders like Guyot, who would head the MFDP, and Carmichael, who would eventually lead SNCC.

As SNCC volunteers registered Black voters and taught at Freedom Schools in the summer of 1964, they faced brutal white retaliation. By August, white Mississippians had killed four volunteers and beat up around eighty others, while police arrested over 1,000 people, and arsonists had firebombed or dynamited sixty-seven homes, churches, and businesses. The widely publicized disappearance and murder of COFO workers Mickey Schwerner, Andrew Goodman, and James Chaney, whom officers in the Neshoba County Sheriff's Department had handed over to the Ku Klux Klan, set the overall tone of terror and intimidation for the COFO activists. As Clayborne Carson noted, "A summer's effort could not undo the psychological consequences of generations of racial oppression." Instead, it was the beginning of a long and slow process of Black political mobilization in Mississippi. That summer COFO volunteers convinced about 17,000 Black Mississippians to apply for voter registration at courthouses, but white registrars allowed only about 1,600 to register. However, more than 80,000 Black residents registered as members of the MFDP.[52]

In July, Martin Luther King Jr. made a five-day tour of Mississippi to lend support to Freedom Summer and the MFDP's recruitment of an integrated delegation to go to Atlantic City. Andrew Young had extended the offer of a King visit to the SNCC and MFDP organizers, and they accepted. King flew into

Guyot during Freedom Summer,
August 1964. Herbert Randall
Freedom Summer Photographs,
University of Southern Mississippi.

Greenwood and began a speaking tour that included helping MFDP workers in their local canvassing. He also caucused with local civil rights organizers at Tougaloo College and visited Vicksburg, Meridian, and Philadelphia, with the tour concluding in Jackson.[53]

King came to Mississippi at great personal risk. He did not want to make the trip, but his staff convinced him to go. The Klan had promised to kill him if he set foot in the Magnolia State, which prompted President Johnson to order FBI director J. Edgar Hoover to assign a detail of agents to shadow King and make sure he avoided the fate of Cheney, Schwerner, and Goodman. Guyot commended King for the risks he took by visiting the state during the violence of Freedom Summer, calling his record with regard to the state "impeccable." "He was frightened to death of Mississippi," Guyot recalled. But "we ask him to support the summer project. He comes into Mississippi, moves across the state, and he vigorously supports it."[54]

The MFDP prepared for Atlantic City in the midst of the voter canvassing by Freedom Summer workers and white violence directed against them. On 6 August, only two days after FBI agents unearthed the bodies of the three men from a Neshoba County dam, the MFDP held its statewide convention in Jackson. The importance of this event should not be underestimated, as it was, in the words of MFDP member and historian Les McLemore, "the first time since Reconstruction that Blacks had gathered in such numbers to challenge Mississippi's political structure" and "probably the first time since Reconstruction that an essentially Black political party had assembled in such large numbers." Eight hundred delegates from forty of Mississippi's eighty-two counties attended. They selected sixty-eight delegates and alternates—including Guyot, Aaron Henry, and Fannie Lou Hamer—to go to Atlantic City. Joseph Rauh Jr., a Washington attorney who had agreed to represent the MFDP at the Democratic Convention, gave a speech to the attendees, and SNCC founder Ella Baker gave the keynote address. The attendees also elected the leadership of the MFDP, replacing the interim committee set up in the spring. The members elected Aaron Henry to head the Atlantic City delegation, with Hamer as vice chair, and Ed King and Victoria Gray won election to the positions of national committeeman and committeewoman. But one of the most important offices—party chairman—went to Guyot, who now found himself head of the insurgent MFDP, or what Freedom Summer volunteer and later historian James Marshall called "the political organization of protest politics." Members elected Les McLemore as vice chairman.[55]

Aaron Henry opposed Guyot in the race for chairman—with a distant third-place challenge by McLemore—but Guyot won, in the words of historian Michael Paul Sistrom, because "he had the allegiance of the majority of poor Black delegates and he wished to see the Freedom Party live on after Atlantic City." Henry, viewed as more moderate—and thus more palatable to white Democrats in the national Democratic Party—received support from Joseph Rauh, who lobbied for him. Guyot won the support of SNCC women he had worked with, such as Hamer, Victoria Gray, Peggy Jean Connor, and Annie Devine. Henry "seemed to be of two minds" on the future of the MFDP, wanting it to continue the spirit of COFO but at the same time become a part of the state Democratic Party, integrating it and moderating the racism of white elected Democratic officials rather than existing as a mostly Black independent party. Despite these philosophical differences, the attendees and candidates remained civil, even friendly, during the debates and elections.[56]

Guyot moved quickly in his new leadership role, sending a letter to John Bailey, the chairman of the Democratic National Convention, requesting that the MFDP delegation be seated in place of the traditional state Mississippi delegation. This letter, which Guyot sent at the request of the MFDP members, echoed an earlier letter sent by interim MFDP chairman Aaron Henry and pledged loyalty to the national Democratic Party as well as support for President Johnson in the November election. The MFDP platform reflected the liberal wing of the national Democratic Party, with calls for civil rights legislation, legislative reapportionment, antipoverty programs, full employment, collective bargaining, Medicare, and other reforms. Much of this agenda had originated either from the Supreme Court rulings of *Baker v. Carr* and *Reynolds v. Sims* (in the case of reapportionment), or in the civil rights, antipoverty, and medical insurance proposals of the Kennedy administration, which then went on to become the centerpiece of Johnson's Great Society.[57]

The state Democrats moved to squelch any challenge to their authority after the MFDP's convention by filing an injunction in state court to prevent any use of the word *Democratic* by the MFDP, claiming that state law did allow not more than one party with that word in their title. According to Guyot, the writ had a negative effect on the MFDP, as it caused "utter chaos" for three months as members argued whether or not to disobey the injunction. Mississippi attorney general Joe Patterson won a permanent injunction in the state's favor after Atlantic City, which led to a two-year legal battle until the state finally dropped its exclusive claim to the word.[58]

Guyot and other MFDP members now began to solicit support from Democratic state delegations outside of the South in their bid to unseat the Mississippi white delegation. He cosigned a letter with Aaron Henry, Victoria Gray, and Ed King to all the convention delegates, urging them to support the MFDP delegation, arguing that "it would be a mockery of both justice and logic if the National Democratic Convention votes to seat the racist and treacherously disloyal delegation that represents the political power-bloc responsible for the murder of James Chaney, Andrew Goodman, and Michael Schwerner." This powerful argument of moral suasion became the major rhetorical argument for the seating of the MFDP, an appeal to white liberal conscience. Fannie Lou Hamer would dramatically highlight this in Atlantic City, when she testified before the Credentials Committee on national television and famously said that "if the Freedom Democratic Party is not seated now, I question America."[59]

Liberal state delegations in Minnesota, New York, California, and other states—nine in all—supported the MFDP's position, as twenty-five Democratic House members and Martin Luther King Jr. lobbied for the party's seating at the convention. SNCC veterans like Ella Baker and Marion Barry also rallied northern support for the challenge. More conservative civil rights groups like the National Urban League and the NAACP hesitated at first but eventually joined as momentum for the challenge built. But Guyot did not see the drama in Atlantic City. Hattiesburg police arrested him shortly before the delegation left Mississippi, on the charges that he violated the terms of his suspended sentence from his Hattiesburg conviction. While the rest of the delegation went to Atlantic City, he spent thirty days in a Hattiesburg jail. Two local Black landowners had bonded their property for his release from jail back in January, so Guyot chose not to go and accepted the jail time so that the two citizens would not lose their land. He told fellow MFDP member Peggy Jean Conner, before she went to Atlantic City, that he opposed a compromise on seating the party.[60]

As for Freedom Summer, many capable historians have told the story of the MFDP in Atlantic City. President Johnson, not wanting a controversy to disrupt the convention, actively worked to undermine the MFDP. He ordered the FBI to use surveillance on the pro-MFDP forces, including wiretapping of SNCC offices in Atlantic City. Rauh begin to feel the pressure from his liberal allies to abandon the challenge, and the White House rejected his compromise offer to seat both delegations. After the television publicity of Hamer's moving testimony before the Credentials Committee, Johnson began to bend, and offered the MFDP nonvoting status at the convention, which the delegates rejected. Liberal pressure from Senator Hubert Humphrey (D-MN) and his protégé Walter Mondale on the MFDP to accept a compromise that would give Aaron Henry and Ed King two seats at the convention, with a promise that no discrimination in state delegations would be allowed at the 1968 convention. Humphrey pleaded with the MFDP delegates to accept the compromise, but Hamer and the others refused. Johnson's behind-the-scenes pressure prevailed, however, and the Credentials Committee approved the two-seat compromise. This action enraged Moses and the others, who had not accepted the compromise, but by now even Martin Luther King Jr. had switched to Johnson's side and urged acceptance of the deal. In the end, Aaron Henry and Ed King accepted the compromise, but Hamer and the rank-and-file-delegates overwhelmingly rejected it. "We didn't come all this way for no two seats," Hamer declared.[61]

The absence of Guyot from Atlantic City had a "profound effect" on the events at the convention, according to historian Vanessa Lynn Davis. With Guyot not present, Fannie Lou Hamer took on a larger share of the leadership of the MFDP delegation, which meant that there would be "more opportunities" for her and Aaron Henry to "butt heads over the question of FDP goals and strategy," namely acceptance of the eventual compromise.[62] Davis implies that Guyot's presence would have had a moderating influence on the convention and thus led to less friction and discord, but that is conjecture at best and questionable given the strong passions and emotions among activists heavily politicized by the events of Freedom Summer.

The experience in Atlantic City was a bitter pill for SNCC and the MFDP. For Bob Moses, it increased his dissatisfaction with working with established political parties and organizations, and marked the beginning of his withdrawal from the Mississippi movement. But Les McLemore, one of the rank-and-file delegates at Atlantic City, delivered a sharp rebuke of Moses's role in the compromise. In his study of the MFDP, he said that Moses, who had always sought the counsel of local Black Mississippians while organizing there, had little patience for the opinions of the delegates at Atlantic City. Instead, he and the other "so-called purists," such as James Forman and John Lewis of SNCC, composed a "hierarchy"—a notion very at odds with the entire idea of SNCC—who debated the compromise mostly among themselves and not the other delegates. The MFDP leaders then handed their plan for rejection to the delegates, who had only a limited time to consider it. "Moses and company, for all practical purposes, refused to listen to the counsel they had sought before the Atlantic City convention," McLemore concluded—charges that would eventually be leveled at Guyot as he headed the MFDP. The "so-called purists" of the MFDP regarded Dr. King, Rauh, and others who urged acceptance of the compromise as traitors in this ideologically rigid environment. McLemore said that the "real Purists" consisted of delegation members whose opinions Moses and other MFDP leaders dismissed, "the very people they were suddenly treating with disdain." McLemore ultimately supported the rejection of the compromise, but he questioned the hierarchical, top-down way in which Moses and others handled it.[63]

Joyce Ladner called the two groups in Mississippi the "locals" and the "cosmopolitans." The locals consisted of uneducated, unskilled long-term residents of the state, people like Hamer, Hartman Turnbow, and others. The cosmopolitans, by contrast, included educated, skilled activists, "usually newcomers to Mississippi." McLemore said that according to her categorization, Guyot fell in the cosmopolitan category, and McLemore speculated that she classified him as one too, likely due to his college education. Ladner said that the cosmopolitans controlled the delegation and made the decisions.[64] Such a characterization is unfair and overly simplistic, given that Guyot and McLemore both came from Mississippi, while Moses, a college-educated northerner, passionately opposed the compromise.

Hamer returned home unrepentant and angry about the compromise, even condemning Aaron Henry as a sellout in a speech in Ruleville. Other delegates, like Unita Blackwell, had more positive viewpoints. She argued that Atlantic City provided valuable political education for MFDP members. Henry, not surprisingly, proved more effusive in his support for the events in Atlantic City, writing to President Johnson that "the problems we have here in Mississippi will come nearer to being solved by the national Democratic Party than any other unit in America." Guyot shared that viewpoint and rejected the bitterness of Hamer and Moses over the failure to be seated. He called Atlantic City "a great victory, because for the first time it told our story to the country and demonstrated our growing strength." To him, the fact that Johnson tried to stop the MFDP showed their strength, for if the president of the United States moved against this nascent party of protest politics, then they did something right.[65] While Guyot continued working with Hamer in the MFDP, his comments indicated his practical ability to compromise, something necessary for a political leader and also foreshadowing his future rift with the uncompromising Moses.

Guyot's absence from Atlantic City, according to fellow activist Staughton Lynd, significantly affected his future involvement with the MFDP. Whereas Atlantic City left Moses embittered, Guyot missed the betrayal by white liberals and thus did not come back with the negative experience of electoral politics that Moses developed. Guyot and Casey Hayden, a white SNCC activist, involved themselves heavily in setting up the MFDP as a parallel political process to the SNCC organization. Guyot's commitment to electoral politics meant that he stressed the legitimacy of the MFDP over the Mississippi Democrats but also supported the Johnson-Humphrey ticket due to the national Democrats' commitment to an integrated delegation in 1968. He criticized Moses, who he said "thought the purpose of the MFDP was to simply go to Atlantic City and disband." But to Guyot, "the real power in Mississippi was the Democratic Party . . . so why don't we simply go back and build a base."[66]

Guyot's support for the national ticket did not earn him any goodwill with the Johnson administration. The Department of Justice issued a list of "responsible Mississippi leaders" in August 1964. Under the subheading "People Who Have Especially Impressed Us," it named not only moderate civil rights leaders like Aaron Henry, R. L. T. Smith but also, interestingly enough, more confrontational ones like Hartman Turnbow (who was described as "a very attractive man, but hard-headed and strong-willed"). The subheading also included Fannie Lou Hamer, a surprising designation that likely changed after her Atlantic City testimony. She remained the highest-profile MFDP member on the list described in favorable terms by the Department of Justice. Under different subheadings, the authors of the list labeled Ed King as "not reliable" and Guyot "a Kenyatta type Negro. Large. Bitter toward the federal government. One of the state leaders in COFO. Believes in large-scale street demonstrations." The comparison of Guyot to Jomo Kenyatta, the Kenyan independence leader jailed by the British for accusations that he supported the Mau Mau insurrection, represented the Department of Justice's crude attempt to portray Guyot as a potential violent figure, a depiction that did an injustice to both Guyot and Kenyatta.[67]

After Guyot's release from jail, he reassumed his role as MFDP chair and mobilized for the fall election. This included supporting the Johnson-Humphrey ticket against the anti–civil rights campaign of Republican nominee Barry Goldwater as well as organizing another Freedom Vote. The support for the Democratic presidential ticket rankled many SNCC field secretaries after the experience of Atlantic City, but the MFDP, despite no support or official recognition from the national party, issued leaflets and canvassed in support of the Johnson-Humphrey ticket. In a break from his actions in Atlantic City, Moses resisted imposing his views on this new party that his own organization and development of indigenous leadership had helped create. Guyot recalled that some staff in SNCC, angry over the support for the Johnson-Humphrey ticket, wanted to "go to Mississippi and clean [the] MFDP up." Moses did not want to clash with the formidable Guyot, telling the staff to drop the issue and saying, "No, if we do that, we got to take on Guyot. We're not going to take on Guyot."[68]

Like Moses, Stokely Carmichael knew all too well the full force of Guyot's personality and his persuasiveness. Charlie Cobb said, "When ol' Guyot gets into that Southern backslapping, good-to-see-ya-fella, kingfish political-boss bag, it's best you keep your hand on your wallet." Carmichael recalled Guyot's phoning the Greenwood SNCC office and telling him, "The 'peoples' need ya, my brother." When Guyot arrived, Carmichael said he

> walked in, this broad, poker-shark, bluffing-for-the-pot grin of his plastered over his moon face, squeezed my hand, pumped my arm—"You a great American, Bro Stokely"—and announced that the MFDP needed SNCC help to campaign across the state for the Johnson-Humphrey ticket.
>
> After dropping that little bombshell, he sat back, glasses glinting, grin widening, all three hundred pounds quivering with excitement and glee as he peered intently into my face, clearly waiting for a response. But I wasn't gonna play his game by repeating stupidly, "You want SNCC to campaign for LBJ?" So I pretended I hadn't really heard.
>
> "I'm sorry, my man, what did you say?"
>
> We stared at each other.
>
> "As the only loyal Democrats in this state, the MFDP is going to campaign for the national ticket."
>
> He stared at me some more, panting and wheezing with suppressed laughter. I still couldn't believe my ears. Obviously Guyot was now stone crazy. But actually, even if he was crazy, "If this be madness there be method in it." As Polonius said about Hamlet."[69]

Carmichael, in his position as SNCC project director for Mississippi's Second Congressional District, acquiesced to Guyot and used SNCC resources to campaign for the ticket.[70]

Despite overbearing Carmichael into helping with the election, Guyot now led the party in a direction increasingly separate from SNCC. He never lost sight of the grassroots organizing of the MFDP and its goal to increase Black political consciousness in Mississippi. The MFDP did not focus most of its strength on the Johnson-Humphrey ticket, since it was clear that white Mississippi, from Democratic governor Paul Johnson on down, supported Goldwater. The MFDP's energies instead went toward the Freedom Vote, which featured a challenge to the state's congressional delegation in the November election. The Johnson-Humphrey campaign ignored an MFDP invitation to appear at a Jackson rally—as Carmichael recollected, the MFDP "never received the courtesy of a reply"—even though the MFDP and SNCC distributed posters with the two Democratic candidates at the top of the MFDP slate selected for Congress. This slate included Aaron Henry running for the Senate against John Stennis, while for the House Fannie Lou Hamer ran in the Second District, Victoria Gray

Freedom Democratic Party campaign
headquarters during the Freedom Vote,
July 1964. Herbert Randall Freedom
Summer Photographs, University of
Southern Mississippi.

in the Fifth, and Annie Devine in the Fourth. The party secured legal counsel for the challenge to the seating of the white Democrats after the expected loss of the MFDP candidates, retaining William Kunstler, Arthur Kinoy, and Benjamin Smith, the latter two attorneys with the National Lawyers Guild, which due to its leftist orientation drew criticism from the NAACP, the most conservative of the civil rights groups in COFO.[71]

The congressional challenge signaled as well growing discord within COFO in the wake of Atlantic City. The NAACP and other civil rights organizations had urged acceptance of the two-seat compromise, and now they began to raise concerns about the MFDP's direction. At a NCC meeting on 18 September in New York that included Joe Rauh, James Farmer, Al Lowenstein, and others, Gloster Current of the NAACP echoed McLemore's critique of Moses and the "so called purists" in SNCC and complained that "all compromisers [are] castigated as appeasers" and called the MFDP "a delusion." John Morsell of the NAACP, one of those in attendance, criticized Bob Moses (who was not present) and SNCC's "need for [a] single-minded approach." They also raised concerns about the influence of the National Lawyers Guild in SNCC, with Rauh declaring that he wanted them out due to their suspected communist influence. Lowenstein cited the influence of the National Lawyers Guild as a reason for dropping out of the planning for Freedom Summer, calling the guild "a communist infiltrated organization." Lowenstein's red-baiting had rankled Guyot in particular, who claimed that Lowenstein had spread charges that SNCC had been infiltrated by Maoists, something he continued to do when he returned to Yale that fall. Courtland Cox of SNCC responded to Current and Rauh by telling them that "it doesn't help to engage in a diatribe against Bob [Moses] and SNCC." Jack Pratt of the NCC clashed with Cox, disagreeing with Cox's argument that "the people" rejected the Atlantic City compromise, and said that instead SNCC "railroaded" the Mississippi delegation.[72]

Regarding the MFDP's congressional challenge specifically, Lowenstein questioned how the party selected the candidates for the challenge and said he heard complaints from two Black Mississippians that the MFDP excluded local people from its decision-making process. Mendy Samstein, a white activist from SNCC, fired back that members chose Henry and the others at MFDP meetings and that "it is essential that you be in Mississippi and know what the facts are rather than make accusations without knowing what is really going on." The anti-SNCC/MFDP forces indicated that their real problem lay with participatory democracy and its naturally slow-paced decision making. Current complained about that, noting that "the NAACP is a disciplined army. No decision is made on lower levels without authorization from on top. Henry has got to get into line," an ironic statement given that Lowenstein was criticizing the MFDP for being too top-down. Lowenstein's complaints veered into hypocrisy since he had quit the Freedom Summer project earlier that year partly over his frustrations with the decentralized decision-making process of SNCC and its devotion to participatory democracy. The critics of SNCC and the MFDP agreed that COFO needed a central committee to direct resources and organizing in a more centralized fashion, something at odds with SNCC's ethos.[73]

James Forman described a meeting at the Justice Department in Washington related to the Freedom Summer. Assistant Attorney General Burke Marshall presided over the meeting, which included Bob Moses and Guyot. Marshall urged a go-slow approach in the organizing, which the COFO leaders rejected. Then Arthur Schlesinger Jr., the former adviser to President Kennedy, spoke and addressed the National Lawyers Guild controversy, declaring that "many of us have spent years fighting the communists . . . fighting forces such as the National Lawyers Guild . . . we find it unpardonable that you would work with them." Forman said that the remarks "came out of the blue." The meeting then focused on that issue, and Moses and Marshall had "a hot exchange" when Moses indicated that COFO took aid from the National Lawyers Guild since the NAACP and Justice Department provided so little. Forman said that the meeting was an example of "the white liberal-labor syndrome and its Black sellouts" putting pressure on SNCC.[74]

SNCC faced internal problems as well. At an October meeting in Atlanta, SNCC organizers met to discuss the future organizing efforts. Forman and Moses had previously agreed on the summer project for 1965, the proposed Black Belt Program, in which SNCC would organize across heavily Black regions of the Deep South using only Black volunteers. Moses, who had supported white volunteers for Freedom Summer, now agreed that the racial tensions within projects and Black dependence on white volunteers should be avoided in future projects. Former Mississippi SNCC staffer Frank Smith asked who decided on the projects, and then the meeting "took a disastrous turn," particularly after Guyot attacked the project. "Who made that decision?" was the refrain from the critics. Forman said that the critics were "not fundamentally the rural, Southern Black staff members of the organization but Northern, middle-class elements—both Black and white," but that characterization did not apply to Guyot, one of the sharpest critics of the project. Guyot then "walked out of the room, throwing his hands up in the air." Guyot's actions rattled Mendy Samstein, who planned to present a preliminary report on the project, because he "had great respect" for Guyot. Samstein then refused to present his report until those present reached a consensus on the project. Adding to Forman's frustration, Moses, one of the chief backers of the project, remained true to his nonconfrontational style and never spoke up in support of it at the meeting. He "remained absolutely silent," Forman lamented. The attendees eventually tabled the project and never debated it before SNCC again. To Forman, this motion represented a "crucial defeat" and signaled the problems with SNCC's structure, one that put him closer to the viewpoints of Gloster Current and other SNCC critics. He said that toleration of Frank Smith's interjection—even though he was no longer a SNCC staffer—as well as concern about Guyot's opposition meant that meetings could be "tyrannized by a minority," since SNCC made decisions by consensus rather than by voting.[75]

The next day Forman spoke to Guyot, who had left the meeting while the Black Belt Project was still under discussion. He told Forman he "was not really worried about decision making, he just didn't want the Black Belt Project to take SNCC resources from Mississippi." Forman denied that was the intention of the project and lamented that "if Guyot had expressed his objections in a principled, clear statement from the floor, we could have dealt with them positively. Instead he told me his true feelings in a side meeting between the two of us." Forman particularly resented that Guyot made this comment about resources as Forman was handing him a "substantial" check from SNCC to the MFDP for party support.[76]

Guyot returned to Mississippi to work on the Freedom Vote, which the party held from 30 October to 2 November. The MFDP mailed out letters signed by Guyot and other materials to promote the project, including ballots to potential Freedom Voters to cast in polling locations. As for the previous Freedom Vote, about fifty volunteers, mostly white northern college students, arrived to help with the vote and other COFO projects. Guyot said that the election "will give local Negroes and whites a choice between the segregationist candidates of the closed regular Mississippi Democratic Party and a slate of MFDP candidates. It will also give the majority of the state's voting-age Negroes a chance to participate in the election process for the first time since Reconstruction." At the same time, he discussed plans for the congressional challenge, which the MFDP formally decided to go forth with after a statewide meeting in Mileston, after Mississippi secretary of state Heber Ladner rejected a petition asking that the MFDP candidates be put on the regular ballot. The MFDP already looked ahead to the congressional challenge, its major campaign in 1965. The MFDP hoped that the Freedom Vote, a largely symbolic election, would raise consciousness about voting, as Guyot indicated, and thus build on Freedom Summer and the first Freedom Vote. With so many Black Mississippians afraid to even register to vote, the Freedom Vote campaigns aimed to lift the veil of mystery and white entitlement surrounding the political process, or what Steven Lawson called loosening the "mental knot keeping Blacks away from citizenship."[77]

Yet the 1964 Freedom Vote differed from its predecessor. As James Marshall mentioned, the campaign represented a "way station" between Atlantic City and the upcoming congressional challenge. The 1964 nominees also came from a formal party structure, with precinct meetings and a statewide organization. The MFDP saw much of the reason for the election, besides consciousness-raising, as being an opportunity to collect evidence of voter suppression for the congressional challenge and hopefully spur federal action. Guyot's strategy included directives to county chairs to collect information on who voted as well as data on harassment of voters and campaign workers.[78]

And the voters and workers experienced real intimidation. Despite being a mock election, white Mississippi still saw it as dangerous. Guyot sent a telegram to the national Democratic Party asking for an investigation into attempts to suppress the Freedom Vote, including twenty incidents of violence, arrest, and harassment of campaign workers. Police arrested some of the workers for simply handing out Johnson-Humphrey leaflets. Local MFDP officials had to deal with the still-prevalent fear in this election, as Guyot sent county chairmen instructions on how to conduct the election, which included a directive to allow people to vote even if they were afraid to sign their names, and to keep a record of those so intimidated for affidavit purposes. Racial tensions led to balloting being canceled in thirteen counties.[79]

In all, about 68,000 people participated in the 1964 Freedom Vote, a disappointing drop from the 83,000 votes cast in 1963. Speculative explanations for the low turnout ranged from disappointment following Atlantic City, to lack of interest due to the vote's symbolic nature, to the growing problems within the COFO coalition, as Moses began to withdraw himself from SNCC and Dave Dennis of CORE left the state in September. Under the pressure of these factors and the internal debates in SNCC over the Black Belt Project, the COFO coalition by November 1964 was showing the cracks that shattered it in 1965.[80]

The MFDP put as positive a spin as it could on the Freedom Vote. Guyot said that "this election has accomplished the purposes we have set out to achieve. We now have a local grassroots political organization throughout the state of Mississippi." He congratulated the volunteers but said that "the real heroes are the local people. They are the ones who have the most to gain but also the most to lose." And a drop in the votes from the previous year did not mean that white Mississippians saw Guyot and the MFDP as less threatening. S. T. Roebuck, an attorney and chairman of the Newton County Democratic Executive Committee, received an MFDP mailing signed by Guyot. He angrily fired off a letter to

Erle Johnston Jr., director of the State Sovereignty Commission, complaining about receiving this "trash" that addressed him as "Dear Member." Livid at the suggestion that he belonged to the MFDP, he asked Johnston, "Who is this Lawrence Guyot, anyway?"[81]

Who indeed but the head of the first truly independent Black political organization in twentieth-century Mississippi, one that sought to reclaim the memory of grassroots Black political power from Reconstruction and apply it to the modern era? Guyot and the members of the Mississippi Freedom Democratic Party, having built a political party and laid the groundwork for what would become the landmark Voting Rights Act of 1965, now sought to increase their challenges to white supremacy in Mississippi on both the national and local level by creating a parallel political force that promised the hope of a biracial democracy and just society in Mississippi. Yet local activists had birthed an MFDP still in its infancy, and a tough period of maturation lay ahead for it and its chairman in 1965.

# CHAPTER 4
# AS SATISFYING AS SEX AND AS ADDICTIVE AS CRACK

## POLITICAL POWER AND REFORM AFTER THE STUDENT NONVIOLENT COORDINATING COMMITTEE

The creation of the Mississippi Freedom Democratic Party (MFDP) represented both a birth and a break from the Student Nonviolent Coordinating Committee (SNCC). The establishment of a political party that registered voters and ran candidates to challenge the power monopoly of the segregationist Mississippi Democratic Party inevitably meant a move from grassroots bottom-up organizing and participatory democracy toward a more mainstream vision of Black political empowerment. While the MFDP's politics seemed still too left-of-center for more centrist civil rights organizations like the National Association for the Advancement of Colored People (NAACP), Guyot led the party in a direction that SNCC, with its growing rejection of the "establishment," did not want to go. The new party entailed a move away from projects like 1964's Freedom Summer and toward ones like the congressional challenge, which consumed the MFDP's attention in 1965. This tension with both the Right and the Left would contribute heavily to the collapse of the Council of Federated Organizations (COFO) coalition and the growing rivalry between the NAACP and MFDP as SNCC faded into irrelevance. It would also contribute to the MFDP's losing ground to the state NAACP under the leadership of the charismatic Charles Evers, who effectively outfoxed Guyot during a major civil rights campaign in Natchez. Yet the actions of Guyot at the MFDP with the challenge likely played a significant, if overlooked, role in the passage of the landmark Voting Rights Act of 1965.

By the fall of 1964, SNCC staffers reflected and engaged in self-criticism regarding their past accomplishments and future courses of action. The experience of Freedom Summer and Atlantic City left many disillusioned and wondering what the next steps should be in their organizing. With internal discord growing in the wake of the October meeting, James Forman and others planned a November retreat in the Mississippi Gulf Coast town of Waveland to address long-range strategies and internal issues. In the thirty-seven position papers issued at the retreat, a common theme was SNCC's loss of direction and failure to act effectively in the wake of the summer of 1964. Charles Sherrod proposed in his paper that SNCC create a more rigid ideology and structure to resist conservative backlash against the movement. Yet this call would lead away from the SNCC ethos of local organizing and participatory, grassroots democracy. Frank Smith criticized the college-educated backgrounds of SNCC workers and proposals to centralize decision making away from local people and community organizers.[1]

James Forman called the views of Smith and other SNCC staffers a "freedom high" or "poor people-itis," meaning that they exalted individual freedom and romanticized poor Black Mississippians. This viewpoint resulted from the tendency of outsiders, especially white volunteers, to dominate SNCC projects, but Forman felt that the pendulum had swung too far toward anarchy and inaction. The result was that volunteers would not follow orders, abandoned projects, and believed that "local people could do no wrong." Organizational structure vanished as these sentiments set in and "became almost a religion" among the staffers. Bob Moses's retreat from his leadership role, Forman said, only exacerbated the situation.[2]

Although Forman criticized Guyot's dissension at the October meeting as an example of SNCC's ability to be "tyrannized by a minority," the two men shared a desire for a more organized approach to political action and organizing. Guyot presided over a political party, the precise structure that would put it at odds with SNCC's participatory democracy, which empowered local voices but rendered decision making anarchic. Guyot's college education, the kind of background that staffers like Frank Smith so pointedly criticized, suggested that his emergence as leader of the MFDP fit the pattern of more centralized civil rights organizations carrying on the civil rights struggle.

Ironically, Forman criticized Guyot for the "objectionable" way he ran the party, even as he scored SNCC poorly for its lack of leadership. Forman appeared to have more problems with Guyot's moderation and his scuttling of the Black Belt Project for 1965 than with his actual leadership style. After Atlantic City, Forman, disenchanted with white liberals and their attack on the National

Lawyers Guild's support for SNCC, did not like the MFDP's support for the Johnson-Humphrey ticket in 1964. He said that SNCC's failure to exert leadership in the MFDP, which he said "many people in the MFDP wanted," helped drive a wedge between the two organizations. Yet Forman contradicted himself again when he also said that the MFDP "needed to have its own character, to take its own positions," which is exactly what it was doing under Guyot—just not to Forman's liking. Forman simply did not like Guyot's politics, as he said the MFDP under him became "just another reform institution" and that SNCC had failed "to make [the MFDP] realize its fabulous revolutionary potential."[3]

Guyot remained convinced that the MFDP had a commitment to group decision making due to the party's origins in SNCC. He rejected the notion that the party had a hierarchy and later recalled that "our hierarchy was who is doing the most to empower people. And we believed very strongly that anyone had the right to empower anyone else. We believed that empowerment was as satisfying as sex and as addictive as crack." Yet the MFDP had a middle-class orientation that belied its image as an organization of impoverished sharecroppers. As Alan Draper demonstrated in his study of the MFDP's Atlantic City delegation, the delegates disproportionately represented entrepreneurs, teachers, preachers, and independent farmers, not the rural poor. More than half had some college education, and in general very few came from poverty. That the MFDP organized the upper echelons of Black Mississippi rather than the sharecroppers was not surprising, Draper pointed out, since "political activism required not only uncommon courage but also time, social skills, and economic security that relatively privileged Black Mississippians were more likely to possess."[4] Guyot, as leader of the party, reflected this class background.

The lack of discipline in SNCC that Forman complained about hurt the efforts of the MFDP as well. Staughton Lynd said that when the MFDP members came back from Atlantic City "there was no Plan B." The conflicts in SNCC reemerged, since many delegates assumed they would be victorious at the convention. As a result, the Waveland retreat was "all over the place," with no unified strategy, and thus the emphasis on voter registration passed to the Southern Christian Leadership Conference (SCLC) and Selma in 1965. As members abandoned projects, some Freedom Schools and other institutions created by SNCC ceased to exist. Marion Barry said that some members worked while others didn't, and at any rate there were few ways for officers to compel or punish recalcitrant or lazy volunteers. As a result, SNCC offered no new programs in the fall of 1964, which meant that the MFDP, still overlapping significantly with SNCC at this point, did little as well. This inertia contributed to the disappointing turnout for the 1964 Freedom Vote. Guyot lamented that a "crucial time" had been allowed to slip away, since after Freedom Summer and Atlantic City, "the state of Mississippi was on the defensive." The activists lost the moment that fall because of the shadow of Atlantic City. "For three months there was nothing but anger [and] frustration," he said. The organizers were so disillusioned, he said, that they "would have been better absent than in Mississippi."[5]

But Guyot was also done with SNCC. He later said that "we had to make a break with SNCC. And I'm very proud of the fact we made it. SNCC after 1964 was a spent force, God bless them. I love every one of them." But he rejected SNCC's disdain for electoral politics and for the compromises that came along with it. Ever the practical politician, he alienated what he called the SNCC people who were "too pure for politics." Guyot also wanted a party that was independent not just from white Democrats but from SNCC too, an organization with its own fundraising, staff, and even basics like offices and equipment. Mary King, active in SNCC, called these "legitimate administrative concerns." She herself became disillusioned with SNCC staff meetings as they drifted into the esoteric realm of the "floaters" and others who resisted any organizational structure. At one point she told fellow SNCC staffer Casey Hayden that the meetings were "beginning to remind me of the Marquis de Sade's account of an eighteenth-century French insane asylum." She recalled a staff meeting in autumn 1965 where the participants debated building Black political power. She said that Guyot accused SNCC of cutting off ties with the MFDP and openly criticizing the party. "SNCC," he said, "should be destroyed. This is what happens when people bring about change that they can't keep up with."[6] SNCC, in his view, did not have the structure to meaningfully exploit and harness the change it had unleashed. Instead of measurable political and economic power, the result in SNCC's hands became raw chaos.

Guyot himself favored action over ideology, despite his own intellectualism. This put him squarely against the "floaters" and "freedom high" volunteers in SNCC. As Luvaghn Brown recalled, "Guyot was a character. He didn't give in to people easily. He would discuss strategy. If somebody else's idea was better, fine. But if his idea was better, he'd make it known what he thought about that. He didn't get as much credit as he should have gotten for a lot of his ideas and a lot of the things he did. But Guyot was busy being a fighter in the beginning as opposed to an idea person. He had an idea of what should happen and he would go make it happen. That's who he was."[7]

Despite his rhetoric, Guyot did not have universally poor experiences with SNCC. On the contrary, his years with SNCC had changed him. Doug McAdam, in his study of the Freedom Summer volunteers, wrote of the "dramatic change experienced by the volunteers and America during this era[,] . . . for Freedom Summer marked a critical turning point in both the lives of those who participated in the campaign and the New Left as a whole." SNCC became the catalyst that turned Mario Savio into the leader of the free speech movement at Berkeley, and Tom Hayden's work in McComb with SNCC directly influenced his drafting of the Port Huron Statement and founding of Students for a Democratic Society. Fannie Rushing spoke in a similar vein about the broader effect that belonging to and organizing SNCC had on the volunteers, and on other civil rights leaders, such as Martin Luther King Jr., who worked with SNCC. As Rushing said, "It moved people from one place to another."[8] Certainly SNCC had this effect on Guyot, moving him from a worldview shaped by his upbringing on the Gulf Coast, where he believed in barriers to voting such as literacy tests, to a more inclusive, universal view of democratic participation where citizens could use the franchise unfettered. While this may merely be a "reformist" position rather than the revolutionary one that people like Forman wanted, it was an example of how SNCC changed those who worked in the organization.

The MFDP reflected its clearest example of the reformist rather than revolutionary nature of the MFDP in the congressional challenge in 1965, which highlighted its role as a political party working within the existing political system. The congressional challenge developed out of the second Freedom Vote and the MFDP's campaigning for the Johnson-Humphrey ticket in November 1964. MFDP workers canvassed for the national ticket but also obtained signatures for a petition to Mississippi secretary of state Heber Ladner asking that MFDP members and supporters be put on the ballot as congressional candidates. Henry opposed Senator John Stennis, Hamer opposed Jamie Whitten of the Second District, Victoria Jackson Gray (the MFDP national committeewoman) ran against William Colmer in the Fifth District, and Annie Devine ran against Arthur Winstead in the Fourth District. Harold Roby, a Tupelo businessman and active member of the Lee County FDP, was the final candidate, challenging Thomas Abernethy in the First District. Not surprisingly, all did well in the mock Freedom Vote against their white racist opponents.[9]

Attorney Arthur Kinoy recalls that the MFDP planned the congressional challenge at a two-day meeting in Oxford after the election. Kinoy and his partners William Kunstler and Ben Smith met with COFO leadership to decide how to capitalize on the momentum from the Atlantic City challenge. Bob Moses stressed the need for the southern civil rights movement to form coalitions with other movements and social organizations to keep the conditions in Mississippi and the issue of voting rights and political participation in the national spotlight, and therefore counter the alliance of northern liberals and southern segregationists in the Democratic Party that had forced the MFDP to compromise at Atlantic City. According to Kinoy, Moses's argument led to the congressional challenge: "Suddenly an idea took hold of everyone at the meeting. Why not challenge head-on the legitimacy of the regular elections?" The MFDP decided that Hamer, Gray, and Devine, who had been defeated in the Democratic primary due to the exclusion of Black voters, would become the more legitimate alternatives seated in the place of the regular Democrats.[10]

Kinoy, using a Reconstruction-era statute, drew up a memo that explained how to challenge the congressmen. After formally challenging the seating of the five men in Congress, the MFDP would use federal subpoenas against white elected officials and collect testimony from Black Mississippians to argue that potential voters in the state were being denied the ability to register based on race. Kinoy said that when he presented the memo to the MFDP leadership, Guyot's response was "wildly enthusiastic." From this memo came the collection of votes for the second Freedom Vote from 31 October to 2 November to prove that Black Mississippians wanted to vote.[11]

Guyot, Hamer, Devine, Gray, and others in the MFDP then met in Washington, DC, on 13 November with Kinoy to discuss the planned challenge. Kinoy did not want to take time away from legal preparation to go to Washington, but Guyot told him that "we need a Challenge lawyer to help explain why it's really important" to the community organizers. Guyot "was absolutely right," recalled Kinoy, and Hamer personally praised his address to them. To aid with the organizing and planning for the challenge, the MFDP also opened a Washington office headed by Mike Thelwell from SNCC, who attended the November meeting. The MFDP plan involved challenging the seating of the Mississippi delegation, with Hamer, Devine, and Gray filing a challenge over their exclusion from the regular election ballot. At this meeting and another one on 28 November, members of the NAACP, the SCLC, and the Congress of Racial Equality (CORE) were "noticeably absent," as Les McLemore put it.[12]

A Jackson COFO meeting on 23 November vividly showed the tensions and personality clashes among movement leaders. The Jackson COFO office suffered numerous problems, notably staff dysfunction and personality conflicts. Jesse Morris, a Black activist from California, reluctantly managed the Jackson office. He oversaw volunteer office workers there, mostly white women, who provided critical support since they managed the communications that had become increasingly channeled through the central office. Hunter Morey, a white SNCC worker who coordinated COFO's legal assistance program during Freedom Summer, complained about the lack of discipline at the office, including theft of cash and supplies, and that "white workers are often subject to severe racial abuse and even violence from Negro workers." The state headquarters operated "completely dysfunctionaly [*sic*]." Although John Dittmer said that Morey's claims were "perhaps exaggerated," CORE's Matt Suarez, brought in to investigate problems, concluded that Black volunteers, especially local teenagers, sexually harassed white female office staff.[13]

Morris shut down the COFO office for a week, and eventually Muriel Tillinghast, a former Howard student, left her position as project director in Greenville and took over managing the Jackson office and restored a measure of stability. At the 23 November meeting, Morris clashed with other COFO members, including Guyot, over his management of the Jackson office. The MFDP's use of COFO office space and his perception that the party was taking over COFO became a major point of contention. Guyot defended the use, arguing that "no other space is available to the FDP." Morris said he had no problem with the FDP using the office but insisted that "FDP is just another program—like Freedom Schools—despite the fact that the people involved in FDP may think otherwise." Guyot, irritated at this barb, said, "Jesse, what do you suggest we begin to think of ourselves as?" He responded that Guyot should "consider that one person's attitude can affect all other people in the organization. Be a little more broadminded; think of other people's work, too." "I'll work on that, Jesse," Guyot replied sarcastically. The tensions at the meeting took on racial and gendered tones too, when Liz Fusco, who dealt with the Freedom Schools, accused Morris of suggesting she wasn't doing her job. She finally told him that she "may not be from Mississippi and . . . may not be a Negro, but I do know Freedom Schools and what they can do."[14]

The contentious meeting—whose agenda included trying to improve the communications situation regarding the central office—did underscore the fact that the MFDP's activities apparently diverted attention away from other COFO activities and organizing, which disturbed some members. Theresa del Pozzo, a white volunteer, said that "listening to all this talk gives me a smothering feeling; I feel so guilty just sitting here listening to all these plans knowing that the FDP in the next month—with the mechanics of the Challenge coming up—is going to upset all this schedule." Bob Moses, who withdrew from SNCC and the MFDP over the experience of Atlantic City and his discomfort with the MFDP's campaigning for the Johnson-Humphrey ticket, cited the congressional challenge as another issue on which he differed with Guyot. To Moses, the challenge took too much energy and resources away from local organizing: "They [the MFDP] were following the national programs, programs geared at the national level—the Congressional Challenge." Moses felt that the MFDP "needed to retrench" and "begin at the local level in electing people, building the party like that." But the mild-mannered Moses had no wish to confront the brash, outspoken Guyot, insisting that "there was no way I could take that disagreement to the people without clashing with Guyot at that point." Guyot and Moses had clashed in the past, or "used to get into it now and then," as fellow SNCC worker Luvaghn Brown recalled. "Bob grew up in a different world," apparently referring to his New York upbringing. "Guyot used to have his own ideas about what needed to happen or what the people were like." Aside from the personality clashes, Moses also felt that airing his criticisms would violate the principle of local leadership, as he risked local people deferring to his views if he became involved. Local leadership, Moses felt, had to be free to make its own decisions, even if they were ones that he did not feel were in the best interests of the movement.[15] Still, it was clear that, like Forman with the Black Belt Project, Moses felt the MFDP squandered its resources in high-profile cases rather than doing the less glamorous but hard and necessary work of local organizing.

Aaron Henry, farther to the right politically than Moses, also had his problems with the MFDP and began to distance himself from Guyot and the party. Henry already faced pressure from the national NAACP over his involvement with COFO. As an NAACP state leader, he became increasingly uncomfortable with the left-leaning politics of SNCC and the MFDP. His acceptance of the Atlantic City compromise represented his more moderate political outlook, and the hostility he experienced from SNCC members in Atlantic City upset him. According to Henry, they said "the political and economic systems of this country were no good and that the systems had to be replaced before any progress could be made," views he said were "as foreign to the American system as white supremacy." The political leanings of the MFDP became apparent with the choice of counsel for the congressional challenge. The party dismissed its legal counsel Joseph Rauh, who had urged acceptance of the Atlantic City two-seat compromise, in favor of the more radical attorneys Arthur Kinoy and William Kunstler, two lawyers who had already built a reputation as seasoned civil rights litigators.[16] Whether one perceived the MFDP as too radical or too centrist obviously depended on one's orientation, but the fissures showed the growing problems of maintaining the COFO coalition as well as the personality and ideological rifts in the Mississippi movement.

Guyot threw his full support behind the congressional challenge, issuing a statement criticizing Representatives Thomas Abernethy and Arthur Winsted, declaring that they "both have been in the House over 20 years and have risen to positions of power where they've been able to block legislation affecting the entire country. The only reason they have been around so long is because they and the entire Mississippi Democratic Party have been responsible for excluding

Negroes from the ballot." In a separate statement, he emphasized that the MFDP "was not asking Congress to punish Mississippi" but instead asking that "the House recognize the simple fact that the rigidly segregated and undemocratic political system in that state which disenfranchises 428,600 Negroes has by that fact disqualified itself from participation in the U.S. Congress." The party also contacted supporters in northern cities, creating ad hoc committees to pressure northern House members into supporting the challenge, and Guyot asked field staff to help collect testimonies. Arthur Kinoy proved instrumental with the deposition-collecting, convincing 250 lawyers to come to Mississippi to interview hundreds of Black Mississippians about local registrars denying them the right to register to vote.[17]

While the congressional challenge became the main focus of MFDP energies, Guyot continued to address other civil rights issues. During the MFDP delegation visit to Washington in January to push the congressional challenge, members also visited the Department of Agriculture to protest discrimination in cotton allotments that favored large planters, and met with the assistant secretary of the Department of Health, Education, and Welfare to complain about welfare cutoffs by county officials in retaliation for registering to vote or joining the MFDP. During the gathering of the depositions—which spread outside of Mississippi as the interviewers deposed former Freedom Summer volunteers back on their northern campuses—Guyot also corresponded with other civil rights leaders. In February, he attended a conference titled "The Civil Rights Movement: Reform or Revolution?" sponsored by students at Amherst, Smith, and Mount Holyoke Colleges and the University of Massachusetts. Speakers listed in promotional materials for the conference included Malcolm X, Andrew Young, Ossie Davis, former Mississippi civil rights lawyer Bill Higgs, and Howard Zinn (who was now teaching government at Boston University), among others. Guyot spoke on the MFDP, but his speech received no press coverage, which focused on Davis, Higgs, and the other participants (Malcolm X and Andrew Young, while scheduled, did not appear). Higgs, whom the state of Mississippi disbarred due to a morals charge and hounded him out of the state, now worked as a civil rights lawyer in Washington. He spoke on the MFDP and the congressional challenge, saying that "because of the challenge, a political revolution could be brought about this summer." He stated that he hoped that the MFDP would launch a summer project in 1965, but the challenge consumed many of the available resources. In fact, the Massachusetts conference only involved giving speeches and raising awareness of issues, and its organizers advertised it as an "educational endeavor." It did not actively recruit any students at the heavily white colleges into organizing—unwilling to repeat the controversies over white student involvement that marked Freedom Summer, and not wanting to exacerbate the growing tensions between white and Black volunteers currently straining COFO.[18]

The MFDP served the actual challenge to the clerk of the House of Representatives on 4 December and argued that violations of the Fourteenth and Fifteenth Amendments by the state of Mississippi, as well as the conditions under which the Union readmitted the state to the Union in 1870 during Radical Reconstruction, meant that the state had denied Black voters their rights, which rendered the election of the House members unconstitutional. In December 1964 and early January 1965, the MFDP garnered prominent support for the challenge, including press conferences by Martin Luther King Jr. and James Farmer, with King declaring that denying the representatives their seats would "remedy the root cause of Mississippi injustice." The *Washington Post* also wrote an editorial supporting the challenge. However, groups that made up much of the centrist civil rights and Democratic establishment—the blue-Black coalition of organizations like the NAACP and major labor unions, did not join the effort. This lack of mainstream support, like the failure of the national Democratic Party and President Johnson to support the MFDP in Atlantic City, meant that the challenge faced an uphill battle. The publicity also worsened the financial straits of the MFDP in late 1964. COFO sent out letters asking supporters to please send money rather than volunteers or goods, as it was "very short of funds." Ads in newspapers like the *New York Times* also stretched the MFDP's budget, as Guyot noted with worry in handwritten comments to donors.[19]

The 4 January vote, in which the House decided on seating the Mississippi delegation, combined the legal challenge by MFDP lawyers and the public demonstrations of civil rights organizing. Guyot led a meeting the day before the vote to coordinate strategies for lobbying the members of Congress. Although the Democratic leadership closed off debate on the seating challenge, 148 representatives—more than one-third of the House—voted to keep debating. At the same time as the debate, some 600 MFDP supporters held a silent vigil outside, and Guyot told the *Washington Post* that "to vote for the seating of these five men is to condone the murder and terrorism that have occurred in Mississippi." The three MFDP candidates also tried, unsuccessfully, to enter the floor of the Capitol. Yet Guyot abandoned plans to hold sit-ins at the Justice Department and Federal Bureau of Investigation (FBI) offices, in what looked like a nod to political moderation. The MFDP apparently abandoned the sit-ins in favor of less disruptive—and less controversial—vigils, a decision reminiscent of the way civil rights leaders and their liberal allies had pressured SNCC members at the March on Washington to accept limitations on their speeches and public demonstrations. One of these vigils took place at the Lincoln Memorial, where Guyot told the over 600 Mississippians who came to support the challenge, along with other supporters from across the country, that the challenge "will once again bring to America's attention the repression and intimidation under which Mississippi's Negroes live and die." While the Johnson administration did not support the challenge, the president remained publicly civil to the MFDP delegation, inviting ten of the MFDP members, including the three women, to his inauguration.[20]

The challenge and the negative publicity it brought to the Magnolia State affected the rhetoric of the state's politicians. A staff writer for the *Jackson Clarion-Ledger* complained that "the party's top dog[s] might not be great political strategists, but they are bona-fide top dogs when it comes to attracting lets-slam-Mississippi attention." From Governor Paul Johnson on down, elected officials in the state began to make public pronouncements against racial violence and in favor of law and order, a sign that they were taking the challenge seriously, given the large number of representatives who voted against the Mississippi delegation. Both the MFDP and the white delegation gathered testimony from state residents to support their respective sides. Guyot best summed up the mood among the MFDP forces at a church rally in Washington after the vote. The support from the House elated those at the rally, but Guyot reminded them of the long road ahead. He said that the MFDP had sent a small army of lawyers down to Mississippi to collect the needed testimony, and that they needed the members' help. He ended the rally by declaring, "Back to work!"[21]

The US Commission on Civil Rights announced after the vote that it would hold hearings in Mississippi to gather testimony on voter discrimination, which Guyot hailed as "the first tangible sign of official federal concern about disfranchisement of Negro citizens in Mississippi." Aided by more than 150 attorneys recruited pro bono with the help of the National Lawyers Guild, the MFDP held public hearings across the state and deposed state and local officials, including the governor and Erle Johnston Jr., head of the State Sovereignty Commission, for the testimony the party gathered throughout February and March. Guyot also continued to reach out to local people, such as in February when he and Annie Devine spoke in Jackson at a Black church, and an MFDP newsletter paraphrased him as saying that he "didn't want anyone to pull out of the church, but he wants to pull the church into what we are doing."[22] The hearings indicated that the challenge had the desired effect of attracting federal scrutiny and national attention to voter discrimination in Mississippi.

The MFDP gathered thousands of pages of documented evidence for their depositions, held in Jackson in April 1965. The Mississippi congressmen boycotted the depositions, an action Guyot called "entirely consistent with the Congressmen's failure to take evidence of their own. . . . They have nothing to say. They have no answer." He said that the depositions would "expose the ugly reality we are determined to change—with or without the help of Congress."[23]

Political realities forced the MFDP to scale back its expectations. As far back as late December cracks appeared in the civil rights coalition, as the various liberal organizations agreed on unseating the Mississippi delegation but not on giving the MFDP slate the seats. The liberal group Americans for Democratic Action (ADA) warned that the effort to seat Hamer, Devine, and Gray lacked legal support since they were elected in the mock Freedom Vote, not a regular state election. The NAACP and the *New York Times* echoed ADA's concerns, agreeing that using a symbolic vote to seat the three women would be constitutionally suspect. The MFDP eventually modified its position and suggested that vacating the elections and ordering new ones would be a more realistic accomplishment.[24]

Guyot and the rest of MFDP and COFO leadership knew these realities. Arthur Kinoy said that "time and again the MFDP and COFO leadership stressed that the legislative showdown on the Challenge in September would probably not result in total victory, the repudiation of the elected representatives of the white power structure and the seating of the representatives of the Freedom Movement." Kinoy wrote that the real victory would be to establish the MFDP as an alternative to the white Democrats, and to exploit the publicity to strengthen the party's relationship with other movements.[25]

While this may have been political reality, the congressional challenge followed the same course of deal-making that marked the Atlantic City compromise. Guyot said that the House Democratic leadership "was determined at all costs to avoid any vote on the issue of the Mississippi elections. . . . Any vote in favor of the Mississippi delegation could not help but appear to be the most cynical disregard for that document [the Constitution]." Since no way around that issue could be found, the House voted to temporarily seat the delegation. Guyot also charged that the Mississippi delegation "received the full support and protection" of the Johnson administration and that the White House pressured potential supporters of the challenge in the House. Drew Pearson, the Washington columnist, backed up Guyot's claims by reporting that Speaker of the House John McCormack used his influence to save the Mississippi delegation.[26]

As the congressional challenge continued across the state, COFO was falling apart. Not surprisingly, segregationists like Senator James Eastland red-baited the MFDP over the congressional challenge, calling the challenge and depositions "an invasion which the Communists regard as only the opening maneuver in the coming Negro revolution." Prentiss Walker, the sole Republican in the contested delegation, also echoed these charges, arguing that the "deposition caravan" was staffed with communists or "those affiliated with communist front organizations," a reference to the involvement of the National Lawyers Guild. But the salvos came from onetime allies as well. Roy Wilkins of the NAACP charged that "Chinese communist elements" had exerted influence inside SNCC, an accusation repeated by nationally syndicated columnists Rowland Evans and Robert Novak. Much of Wilkins's attack came from the NAACP's unwillingness to share power with SNCC within COFO, as well as the resentment of older NAACP leaders in Mississippi toward the younger, more militant SNCC activists who often railed against "Uncle Toms" in the state. Aaron Henry's growing estrangement from the MFDP and the pressure the national office of the NAACP put on him also factored into this split. The state NAACP withdrew from COFO in January, but Henry stayed on as COFO president, and the NAACP's withdrawal forced him to explain the departure when COFO held a statewide convention in Jackson on 7 March. Henry defended the decision, claiming that the other organizations excluded the NAACP from COFO planning. Later that day, Henry left the COFO meeting to help the NAACP plan a separate summer project. With the MFDP focused on its own course and the NAACP gone, COFO's decline accelerated.[27]

The dissolution of COFO had as much to do with the MFDP delegation's independent political course, seen in its opposition to the Atlantic City compromise the previous year, as it did with red-baiting or clashes with the NAACP or other factors. Arthur Kinoy, now representing the MFDP in the congressional challenge, later recalled that the red-baiting arose because of the MFDP's rejection of white liberal guidance from Joseph Rauh and Hubert Humphrey, which could only mean that wily communists were manipulating the "uneducated Mississippi Blacks." In his 1983 book *Rights on Trial*, Kinoy wrote that "what became clearer after Atlantic City was that what the national power structure, both North and South, really feared was the potential lesson of the Mississippi experience for all America, the possibility of a truly independent political party, controlled not by the establishment but by the people at the grass roots. The United States had not seen a political party like this for years."[28]

Guyot recognized that even with the independent course of the MFDP, they still needed allies, as mainstream liberal organizations deserted the challenge. Despite the splintering of COFO, he attempted to keep a civil rights coalition alive through the congressional challenge. While in Washington, he issued a call for a conference to be held on 24 April in the nation's capital. He said that the party sought to bring together "grassroots representation" from civil rights, church, political, and labor organizations to "plan the final national effort to unseat the Mississippi congressional delegation." The success of the challenge, he said, "can very much depend on this conference." Later in March he continued to speak on the challenge and the proposed voting rights legislation, and announced plans for a summer project organized by the MFDP. Victoria Gray also appeared before the House Judiciary Committee in late March to testify in favor of proposed voting rights legislation. She linked it to the congressional challenge by urging that provisions to call new elections as a remedy against disfranchisement be written into the bill.[29]

Guyot himself, along with Hamer, Devine, and Gray, gave their testimony on 1 April in Jackson. Guyot described the systematic repression of voter registration in Mississippi by the state government. He told the panel that the federal courts also obstructed them, since Judge Harold Cox, a Kennedy appointee who once roomed with James Eastland, threw out civil rights suits brought by COFO requesting federal protection for their work. He also referred to the "genocide bill," a bill in the Mississippi state legislature that proposed imprisoning women who had two illegitimate children, then coercing them into choosing incarceration for two months at Parchman or sterilization. Legislators defeated the bill in the state House but only after it attracted significant negative publicity. "It is completely impossible to attempt to organize politically in a State that is controlled on every level like this," he said. The panel questioned him about the challenge and its constitutionality, which he defended, declaring that "what is really at question is how political power is going to be distributed in this country, because there is no comparison between the election of any of the five pretenders in Mississippi and Congressmen from any other State in this country." The testimony later shifted to a long discussion of his ordeals at Winona and Parchman, and his imprisonment that prevented him from going to Atlantic City.[30]

Yet new events undermined the congressional challenge, taking much-needed publicity away from it. By March, much of the nation's attention was captured by Bloody Sunday in Selma, Alabama, where the voting rights campaign of the SCLC and SNCC resulted in televised beatings by Sheriff Jim Clark's troopers of peaceful demonstrators at the Edmund Pettus Bridge. The violence and the subsequent Selma-to-Montgomery March, along with the presence and involvement of Martin Luther King Jr., generated publicity that no other civil rights demonstration could equal.[31]

Although Guyot joined John Lewis of SNCC and James Farmer of CORE in endorsing both the Selma march and Johnson's proposed voting rights legislation, some in the MFDP worried about this shift in publicity and suggested new direct action to bring media attention back to them. The Reverend Leroy Johnson, the chair of the Cleveland, Mississippi FDP, wrote a letter to Guyot and the three congressional candidates and cited Selma and the proposed voting legislation as having undermined support for the challenge. He suggested "a massive protest demonstration" in Jackson to show mass support for unseating the white House delegation. But not all in the Mississippi movement thought the congressional challenge should be drawing away so many resources. The Fifth District of COFO—Guyot's former jurisdiction from his SNCC field secretary days—held a meeting in Waveland in April and expressed concerns about "the amount of FDP work being done outside the state and the lack of organizing going [on] in the state." The COFO members wondered why the MFDP had an office in Washington, and "why is all the activity centered around it?" Some also expressed unhappiness about the MFDP's planned summer project, and confusion over the blurry boundaries between the MFDP and COFO.[32]

The Fifth District meeting of COFO showed that the tensions slowly dismantling COFO came from places besides the NAACP. The growing top-down structure of the MFDP as it lobbied in Washington and took on the features of a political organization distressed the SNCC members at the meeting, who, like Bob Moses, saw this development as moving away from SNCC's participatory democracy. James Forman and others expressed their frustrations with Guyot's leadership of the MFDP. Doug Smith complained that the MFDP "is given to people on a silver platter. People don't make decisions because they don't feel the need for decisions to be made." Forman said that they "needed to make chairman [Guyot] responsible to membership and made membership recognize that it's just as strong as anybody else." The Fifth District COFO ended up sending a letter to the MFDP complaining that party leaders made many of the decisions from the top down, decisions "imposed on communities by the FDP 'power structure.'" They suggested that the MFDP engage in greater activity on the local and precinct level, including running candidates on the local level. They did not recommend abandoning the congressional challenge but instead suggested mobilizing greater local support to better involve chapters and their membership, such as more direct action, like Reverend Johnson had suggested. The letter closed with the hope that the MFDP and COFO could "work effectively together."[33]

In the shadow of these events, the MFDP held its 24 April conference in Washington, titled "Free Elections in 1965." Four hundred people attended the rally and heard Hamer, Gray, Devine, and Guyot give speeches, as well as attorneys Kunstler and Kinoy and Ella Baker, who spoke almost a year earlier at the MFDP's founding. James Forman, despite his misgivings about Guyot's leadership, spoke in favor of the challenge, and James Farmer endorsed creating more FDPs to expand voter registration and run more local candidates. Although the attendees mostly discussed the congressional challenge and the proposed voting rights legislation, Lee Dilworth, a member of the MFDP executive committee, gave a report on the planned summer project. It included plans for voter registration and the establishment of community workshops from the county to the district level—perhaps a sign that the concerns of local FDPs were being heeded. Guyot addressed some of the issues brought up by Farmer, mentioning voter registration drives in Sunflower County as well as eight MFDP candidates running in the state's municipal elections that year. He described the power of the MFDP as coming from organizing the unorganized, those people "written off by this country."[34]

Just two days after the conference, the MFDP forces received encouraging news from the Supreme Court. Prior to assisting the MFDP with the congressional challenge, Kunstler and Kinoy worked on a case out of Louisiana, *Dombrowski v. Pfister*. Police there had arrested James Dombrowski, a white southern civil rights activist and director of the Southern Conference Education Fund (SCEF), charging him with belonging to a "subversive" organization, as the Joint Un-American Activities Committee of the Louisiana Legislature had labeled the SCEF. Louisiana police raided and ransacked the SCEF office and arrested Ben Smith and Bruce Waltzer, respectively an attorney for the organization and its treasurer. The state charged all three men with violating the Louisiana Subversive Activities and Communist Control Law and the separate Communist Propaganda Control Law, both of which the state passed in 1962 to combat civil rights organizations. The SCEF officers filed a suit alleging that the arrests challenged their First and Fourteenth Amendment rights and constituted a pattern of harassment of civil rights activists in the state. Kunstler and Kinoy represented the plaintiffs and continued to do so as they worked on the Mississippi challenge. A three-judge federal panel initially dismissed the case, but the Supreme Court took it and on 26 April ruled for the plaintiffs, declaring the Louisiana statutes unconstitutional and in violation of the First Amendment. Kinoy said that the "immediate impact on the morale of the entire Freedom Movement was overwhelming," even though the case did not directly involve Mississippi. He said that Guyot called him from Jackson to get the details of the case and told Kinoy that the ruling "is going to be great for the Challenge work."[35]

On 17 May, the MFDP filed its depositions with the US House clerk, over 600 collected testimonies in all, which recounted stories of intimidation and violence against Black voter applicants in the state. Guyot called the over 15,000 pages of evidence "an incontrovertible body of evidence proving that the general

elections of November, 1964, in Mississippi were unconstitutional." He continued to emphasize solidarity with the national Democratic Party and the Johnson administration, arguing that the depositions proved that the state denied
people the right to vote based on their race and skin color, just as Johnson had
outlined in his 15 March voting rights speech. Martin Luther King Jr. and John
Lewis quickly issued statements through the SCLC and SNCC, respectively, that
reaffirmed their support for the challenge.[36]

The MFDP now planned to lobby House members over the summer to vote
to unseat the Mississippi delegation. This included lobbying representatives that
Guyot said "voted with us on the 4th of January but were very weak kneed and
would love an excuse to get out of their commitment." But in June Governor
Johnson derailed the MFDP's focus on the congressional challenge, as well as
its plans to launch a voter registration drive as its summer project, when he
called the legislature into session to repeal the state's racially discriminatory
voting laws. These laws included the infamous "understanding clause" that
empowered registrars like Theron Lynd to block Black applicants, as well as the
requirement that prospective voters have their names published in the newspaper as they applied, which invited economic and physical retaliation. Johnson,
a committed segregationist, called for the repeals in the hopes of undermining
both the congressional challenge and to prepare for a court challenge to the
voting rights legislation making its way through Congress.[37]

The MFDP saw Johnson's actions as an opportunity to generate the publicity
they needed. Building on the legal arguments of the congressional challenge,
they claimed that the disfranchisement of Black voters rendered the special
session illegal. On 14 June in Jackson, Guyot led 500 demonstrators, many of
them teenagers, from a Baptist church in a mile-long silent protest to the state
capitol. They included about 75 white volunteers recently arrived from outside the state. The police intercepted the marchers and began mass arrests for
parading without a permit, carting them off to the state fairgrounds in paddy
wagons and garbage trucks. Police arrested 482 people and detained them in
two large exhibit buildings. The front-page publicity brought even more supporters to Jackson, including John Lewis and Charles Evers. Evers, along with
Henry, opposed the MFDP's influence in COFO, but he agreed to show solidarity
with the MFDP on this matter, since these demonstrations dealt with the larger
issue of the proposed Voting Rights Act. By the end of the week police had arrested 856 demonstrators, including Guyot, Evers, and Lewis. Thelma Glover, an
MFDP leader in Batesville who went to Brooklyn to speak at a pro-MFDP rally
after her release, said that state authorities kept her and the other prisoners
in "abominable" conditions, including crowded and unsanitary facilities, with

poor food. Others described police brutality and mistreatment, and guards reportedly beat Guyot and Ed King, along with many other members. She and other MFDP members rallied supporters from outside Mississippi to come to the state, and they used the demonstrations to pressure House members to support the congressional challenge.[38]

Claudia Shropshire, head of the National Lawyers Guild law office in Jackson, used the Court's decision in *Dombrowski* to the benefit of the protesters. Specifically, she challenged the antidemonstration ordinances invoked to arrest and detain the demonstrators, citing a denial of their First Amendment rights. As Arthur Kinoy recalled, this use of the case brought it "into the daily reality of the political activities of the thousands of people who were responding to the Mississippi Challenge."[39]

Although the MFDP hoped to rally the nation's attention to what the National Council of Churches described as a "concentration camp" and make Jackson another Selma, this did not come to pass. After the first week media attention shifted elsewhere, even though the marches continued into July, with Charles Evers and SNCC still participating. By 24 June, Guyot described press coverage as "practically non-existent." The Fifth Circuit Court of Appeals ordered the city on 30 June to make no further arrests, citing *Dombrowski*, but there was now little media attention for the resumed marches. After some peaceful marches in July the MFDP turned its attention back to the congressional challenge in Washington. The main significance of the Jackson demonstrations, said Les McLemore, was the cooperation between the NAACP and the fraying MFDP-SNCC alliance. The fissures in the COFO coalition managed to hold together for six more months due to the participation of Evers and the NAACP, and led the Mississippi NAACP to endorse the congressional challenge later that summer, the first time it had issued a statement on the matter.[40]

But another conflict with the Johnson administration had developed, one that continued to show the tensions between a grassroots party of civil rights activists and Black Mississippians committed to social and racial justice, on the one hand, and the practical realities of politics within a national, pluralistic party, on the other. Johnson nominated former Governor James Coleman, now employed as legal counsel for the Mississippi Democratic congressmen, to the Fifth Circuit Court of Appeals in the midst of the congressional challenge. Coleman, an old friend of Johnson's from their days as House congressional aides, held moderate segregationist views, at least by Mississippi standards. While not a rabid demagogue like Ross Barnett or Theodore Bilbo, he did sign the bill creating the State Sovereignty Commission (SSC) and arranged for Clennon King, a Black man who had tried to integrate the University of Mississippi, to be committed to Whitfield, the state mental hospital. Johnson continued Kennedy's tradition of nominating segregationists recommended by political allies like James Eastland (Stennis nominated Coleman), who headed important committees like the Judiciary and had amassed considerable seniority. Johnson needed senators like Eastland and Stennis to win passage of non–civil rights legislation, especially the slew of Great Society bills introduced that year. Ironically, President Dwight Eisenhower—who held a less stellar reputation than JFK and LBJ when it came to civil rights—had a better track record of appointing civil rights progressives to the courts, such as John Minor Wisdom, Elbert Tuttle, and John R. Brown to the Fifth Circuit.[41]

Victoria Gray, speaking on behalf of the MFDP, expressed "great shock" at Coleman's nomination. She outlined his record of opposing civil rights for Black Mississippians and said that the "only claim that Mr. Coleman has to the appointment is his position in the power structure of Mississippi and the blessing of the illegally elected Senators Eastland and Stennis." Here she linked opposition to Coleman to the congressional challenge, calling for Congress to reject both Coleman and the Mississippi delegation. She declared that the challenge's success would secure Black voting rights and that "only then will we have any say over who gets federal appointments." She expanded on this message on 29 June with testimony before the House, recounting the story of Clyde Kennard, the Black serviceman who tried to enroll in Mississippi Southern College (now the University of Southern Mississippi). During Coleman's tenure as governor, police arrested Kennard and a judge sentenced him to seven years in prison for allegedly stealing chicken feed, all on the testimony of the teenager originally arrested for the crime. Forced to work on a cotton plantation, he fell ill with cancer and prison authorities denied him treatment. He died in 1963, shortly after his release on a suspended sentence. Coleman convinced Kennard to delay his application to the university, duping him into believing that he would back his enrollment when he had no intention of doing so. Aaron Henry, Martin Luther King Jr., and other civil rights activists also lobbying against Coleman's appointment, but Johnson, not wanting to alienate two powerful senators and his reelection in 1968, continued to back Coleman's ultimately successful appointment to the Fifth Circuit.[42]

The MFDP obviously opposed Coleman given his record, but in the middle of the congressional challenge their lobbying against him did not increase any chances for affection from Johnson. Like in Atlantic City, the Coleman affair showed that in the White House moral arguments ran up against the political realities and larger considerations facing the presidential administration, and those realities won out.

Although the MFDP saw Democratic support for the challenge waver, many civil rights and labor groups provided at least some backing as the date of the final vote drew closer. The Leadership Conference on Civil Rights (LCCR), a coalition of about forty civil rights and labor groups headed by Roy Wilkins of the NAACP, initially favored dismissing the challenge after the Voting Rights Act passed, but Martin Luther King Jr. convinced the LCCR to support the MFDP. McLemore said that this alliance provided "at least a slim chance" of success for the challenge, but the passage of the Voting Rights Act that summer shifted media attention away from Mississippi.[43]

In addition to the Voting Rights Act, a new issue—the rapidly escalating war in Vietnam—created problems by the summer of 1965 for the MFDP and the congressional challenge. President Johnson authorized limited airstrikes against communist North Vietnam in 1964 and Congress passed the Gulf of Tonkin Resolution that year, which allowed him to use further force to prop up the Republic of South Vietnam, the shaky US Cold War client, to contain the spread of communism in Southeast Asia. Increasing instability and North Vietnamese military actions in South Vietnam led to further escalation, first with Operation Rolling Thunder in February 1965, a sustained bombing campaign against North Vietnamese military and industrial targets. By March, Johnson ordered US Marines deployed to South Vietnam to provide security for airbases launching the attacks, followed by regular US ground forces in April to engage North Vietnamese and communist guerrilla forces in South Vietnam. In July 1965, in what historian George Herring called "the closest thing to a formal decision for war in Vietnam," the president publicly committed 50,000 troops to Vietnam, with another 50,000 to follow at the end of the year.[44]

Most, but not all, Americans supported Johnson's escalation. Some members of Congress urged peace negotiations, and the first large-scale student protest against the war occurred in Washington, DC, in April. The MFDP came into contact with antiwar groups as it sought to build coalitions with other progressive organizations during the congressional challenge. At a strategy meeting with the MFDP lawyers at the end of July, Guyot told them—"with some hesitation," Arthur Kinoy recalled—that the MFDP executive committee had agreed to participate in an "Assembly of Unrepresented People," which was a planned demonstration against US involvement in Vietnam. He also informed the attorneys about local MFDP actions against the war back in Mississippi. The FDP in McComb began distributing leaflets urging young Black men to resist registering for the draft, including endorsing civil disobedience to avoid military service. The fliers cited the recent case of a white soldier in New Jersey discharged after conducting a hunger strike to avoid deployment. Much of the opposition to the war by the McComb FDP resulted from anger over the death of John Shaw, who was killed in action in Vietnam in late July. Shaw, a Black Mississippian, had worked four years earlier on SNCC's McComb project, its first major program in the state. Two local MFDP members—Clint Hopson, a summer volunteer and law student at Howard University, and Joe Martin, a SNCC worker and former candidate for city selectman—wrote and circulated the leaflets throughout the town's Black community. As Les McLemore noted, the McComb statement "was the first time that a civil rights and/or indigenous political organization had formally spoken out against the Vietnam War." The statement did not attract much media attention or criticism until it was reprinted in the MFDP's official newsletter.[45]

Guyot faced a tension between his need to be an effective leader for the party—which meant making compromises and forging alliances—and the growing militancy of the party grassroots. Kinoy said that Guyot "seemed a little uncertain as how to respond" to the McComb FDP. He hesitated in part over fears of a new line of attack against the MFDP by its critics, this time questioning their patriotism and lack of support for US foreign policy. Bob Moses, despite his distance from COFO, headed a Mississippi delegation for the antiwar march. In the end, the MFDP executive board took no position on the war and did not endorse the McComb leaflets, but in keeping with its roots in participatory democracy and grassroots activism, it did not censure or muzzle the local activists. Ed King, serving as national committeeman of the MFDP, issued a statement that the leaflet did not represent official MFDP policy, and Guyot declared that he would fight in the war if drafted, but both men defended the right of their members to hold antiwar views. They also offered their own implicit criticism of the war when they said that they understood why Black residents of McComb "should resent the death of a citizen of McComb while fighting in Viet Nam for freedom not enjoyed by the Negro community of McComb." Guyot also said that volunteers and students at some of the Freedom Schools had discussed draft evasion, defending this as "the free and uninhibited inquiry on a number of political and economic questions."[46]

Guyot also showed the Janus face that running a political party and making compromises often entailed. Hopson, coauthor of the leaflet, said that when he presented it to the MFDP headquarters, "they told me it was great . . . beautiful," and that he informed them the flyer represented the position of the students and staff involved in the Freedom Schools in the McComb area. Guyot admitted later that the circulation of the antiwar statement hurt the MFDP politically, and led the party to not take an official position, which Hopson criticized as keeping the party "off the line" of the McComb statement. While it is easy to criticize

Guyot for his lack of an endorsement, he and King did not try to squelch the leaflet and acknowledged locals' right to free speech. Les McLemore noted that the McComb statement did "reflect the grass-roots aspects of the Party" and its "loose nature," a reflection of its SNCC origins. A more established party would have demanded that any public expression be cleared first with party leaders. The way the MFDP leadership dealt with the McComb statement meant that the party allowed "the greatest possible degree of expression by its members." Soon MFDP leaders would add their voices to the antiwar opposition. By the end of the year, Fannie Lou Hamer had spoken at an antiwar demonstration in Washington, DC, and sent a telegram to President Johnson asking him to bring US troops home from Vietnam and the Dominican Republic.[47]

Not surprisingly, segregationists pounced on the linkage between the MFDP and the antiwar movement to try to wreck the challenge. Senators and Eastland and Stennis called the challenge a "most dangerous Communist conspiracy," and the Mississippi American Legion called the leaflets "open treason." Thomas Abernethy and Prentiss Walker, two of the congressmen challenged by the MFDP, also denounced it, with Abernethy calling it "treasonable." Even Black civil rights supporters blasted the McComb statement, with Charles Evers declaring that resisting the draft would undermine the fight for equal rights, and Michigan congressman Charles Diggs calling it "ridiculous and completely irresponsible." While the McComb statement foreshadowed later, more highly publicized opposition to the Vietnam War by activists like Stokely Carmichael and Martin Luther King Jr., the early issuance of an antiwar position hurt the MFDP with moderates. White moderates like Hodding Carter III red-baited Ed King and Guyot in the *Delta Democrat-Times*, and Claude Ramsey of the state AFL-CIO called the MFDP board "anarchists" and compared them to the Klan. The McComb statement gave further ammunition to challenge opponents, as congressmen now accused the MFDP of a lack of patriotism, along with the argument that the new Voting Rights Act made the challenge unnecessary.[48]

Guyot remained optimistic despite the challenge's likely defeat. To him, simply getting the challenge heard toppled important barriers. One of these included the granting of floor privileges to the MFDP contestants during the debate on the challenge. This meant that the House sergeant-at-arms escorted Hamer, Gray, and Devine onto the floor of the House, the first time the House had granted Black women such a privilege, and the first time it had granted it to Black people since the nineteenth century. Guyot, upon seeing the three women escorted onto the House floor, exclaimed to Kinoy, "We did it! We did it!" The MFDP kept up the pressure with public demonstrations during the closed hearings by the House Elections Subcommittee, including a rally of over

1,000 supporters near the Capitol. In addition to public demonstrations, MFDP members in straw hats and other sharecropping attire joined with college students to testify for the challenge before the subcommittee.[49]

The subcommittee's report on 15 September recommended dismissal of the challenge. The only concession it gave to the MFDP was a provision that the House should "scrutinize all elections more thoroughly in the future, particularly under the Voting Rights Act," language almost identical to that in the Atlantic City compromise of the year before. In all, the subcommittee only held two meetings on the challenge, with no full hearings or discussions in the full House. Two days after the subcommittee's recommendation, the House voted 228–143 to dismiss the challenge.[50]

The coalition that supported the challenge, from the conservative LCCR to the left-leaning SNCC, condemned the subcommittee's ruling. In speeches on the evening of the defeat of the challenge, Guyot and the three women spoke, all of them emphasizing that the struggle would continue. Hamer told Kinoy that the next step was to "take the Challenge right to them in the Sunflower County elections this November." Guyot echoed Hamer, telling supporters at a 16 September vigil that "we haven't begun to fight" and urged people to attend precinct meetings and remain politically active. In a press release, he condemned the Johnson administration for not forcefully implementing the Voting Rights Act, and said that "we do not regard either our lives or our constitutional rights as negotiable items. We have nothing left to compromise away." The MFDP leaders remained committed to local organizing and developing the MFDP into a viable political party, and hoped to build on the publicity and coalition-building of the challenge.[51]

Yet the bitterness lingered. Fannie Lou Hamer said during a vigil after the vote that "we have been robbed, killed, and murdered in Mississippi, [and] we have also been robbed in America." Guyot said that the challenge showed that "the very institutions and men whom we petitioned for relief are very deeply implicated in the crimes committed daily against us." He accused Congress of dodging the central issue of the treatment of Black Mississippians. "Was the Congress of the United States going to allow to sit among them men elected by a system of murder, terror and economic slavery?" he wrote in an MFDP letter mailed after the vote. "Rather than face those questions, Congress found that we, the Negro citizens of Mississippi, did not have the legal authority to bring these questions to the floor." The costs of the challenge and other MFDP organizing had also severely depleted its meager reserves. The cost of printing and distributing the brief they developed from the over 600 depositions alone was "staggering," according to Guyot. The state office of the MFDP in Jackson admitted in July that it had exhausted its funds and that any more would have to be raised locally from the Black community. Securing funds from outside the state, the office admitted, "doesn't look very good right now." By August, the MFDP advised its local chapters to contact SNCC headquarters in Atlanta for help instead of them.[52]

In his study of Black political parties, Hanes Walton Jr. criticized the MFDP for the failure of the challenge. He called the entire effort "'quixotic' and unrealistic." He called the leadership's decision to base the entire challenge on the mock election a "questionable strategy, for it put the House of Representatives in an untenable position." He said that to approve the challenge on those grounds would set a precedent for similar challenges around the country.[53]

For all the resources and effort Guyot and others put into the challenge, it also went against the grassroots nature of the party, and consumed funds and manpower that the local FDPs might have better spent on organizing. Larry Gamble, a SNCC volunteer in Carroll County, described the statewide coordination of the MFDP as "very weak," even though the county had what a SNCC newspaper called "one of the best organized MFDP counties in Mississippi." The local members paid little attention to the challenge and focused instead on local issues like school integration.[54] The MFDP may have hoped to use the publicity from the challenge to boost local organizing, but it also helped to stunt it by diverting scarce resources away from that same organizing.

The publicity from the challenge did bring more attention to the MFDP, and Guyot in particular. In August, Robert Baker of the *Washington Post* interviewed him during a visit Guyot made to the MFDP's Washington office. He deflected Baker's questions about the party being mostly Black and infiltrated by radical SNCC activists. Guyot said that "our platform and political structure are open-ended" and that "it is very radical for Negroes to attempt to register and vote in Mississippi or . . . run for office." As for communist infiltration, Guyot said that that charge "simply does not matter" to Black Mississippians. "They'd be more concerned about being bad Baptists than with political affiliation." When Baker asked about the congressional challenge, Guyot said that "Black people and deprived people are really watching which party is our friend." And that friend may not have been a state Democrat—Baker pointed out that the MFDP loyalty was to the national, not state, Democrats. "Do you mean the FDP could conceivably vote Republican?" Baker asked. Guyot simply smiled in reply.[55]

Guyot also sat down for an interview that summer with the *New York Times* Oral History Program, part of a project by Stanford University to chronicle the civil rights movement in the South. This would be the first of many interviews that Guyot would give in the years ahead on his participation in

SNCC and the MFDP. In the interview, he boldly predicted a MFDP victory in the congressional challenge. Yet later in the interview he left open the possibility of defeat, declaring that "if the thing does fail, we simply come back to Mississippi" and continue to register voters. Despite his differences with Aaron Henry, he refused to go on the record criticizing him—but he had no compunctions about pointing out the NAACP's lack of support for the MFDP. He also linked Mississippi to the nation as a whole, stating that "the political oppression and control in Mississippi is much more conspicuous, much more overt . . . but it's just as clinical, just as effective throughout the rest of America."[56]

The congressional challenge overshadowed much of the other activities the MFDP did during 1965, but the collapse of the COFO civil rights coalition and the growing alienation of moderates like Aaron Henry from the MFDP contributed to new political controversies that drew in the party. The creation of the Mississippi Democratic Conference (MDC) became one such flashpoint. Claude Ramsey, the state president of the state AFL-CIO, conceived of the new organization. In his letter, sent out in July 1965 to 100 white and Black political and civic leaders, Ramsey proposed creating a "Loyalist Mississippi Democratic group to restore relations with the national party." Ramsey, a paper mill worker from Ocean Springs, grew up in the same less racially stratified Gulf Coast environment as Guyot, except of course for his key advantage of being white. He worked to oppose the Citizens' Councils and other extreme segregationists as a labor leader in the 1950s and early 1960s, but backlash from the rabid white supremacists in Mississippi's white working class kept him from taking too strong a position on the civil rights movement. That moderation led him to decline an invitation from the MFDP to participate in the Atlantic City challenge. Ramsey joined with other white moderates, such as Hodding Carter III, the editor of the *Delta Democrat-Times*, in the goal of creating an interracial state party out of Black reenfranchisement created by Voting Rights Act.[57]

Despite their mutual labor backgrounds, Ramsey held little interest in making common cause with Guyot. His invitation to create the MDC went out to only middle-class Black businessmen and political leaders, such as Aaron Henry and Charles Evers, both affiliated with the NAACP and opposed to MFDP/SNCC influence in COFO. Ramsey did not invite any members of the Black working class—the maids and sharecroppers of Mississippi—either. This new organization opposed the grassroots, participatory democracy of the MFDP and the greater voice and participation it sought for the Black working class. Ed King and other MFDP leaders commented on the class barriers that emerged after Atlantic City, where "the old Negro leadership class refused to work with the Freedom Party."[58]

Yet a deeper level of complexity and nuance marked these divisions. Alan Draper, in his study of the MFDP delegation to Atlantic City, pointed out that most of the MFDP delegates had some college education, owned their own homes, and had middle-class backgrounds in business and education, and that the delegation vastly underrepresented low-income Black Mississippians like farmworkers. Rather than social class being the main divider between the NAACP and MFDP, Draper argues that patronage—the coming clash between the two organizations over control of federal War on Poverty funds—is what drove the rivalry between the two organizations, including the MDC controversy.[59]

In response to Ramsey's call, about 125 people, three-quarters of them white, met at the Heidelberg Hotel in downtown Jackson on 18 July to create the MDC. The Johnson administration withheld recognition since it needed the support of the state's two powerful Democratic senators, John Stennis (chair of the Defense Preparedness Subcommittee, which had oversight on Vietnam War issues) and James Eastland (chair of the Senate Judiciary Committee, which oversaw judicial appointments). Some whites, including the MDC's short-lived president, attorney Robert Oswald, did not like the organization's liberal and labor orientation, which some members, including Ramsey, wanted to use to increase Black voter registration to defeat antilabor white legislators. Oswald resigned when he failed to convince MDC members to support segregationist state Democrats like Governor Johnson and accept voting restrictions on illiterate citizens while opposing federal registrars—a position anathema to Henry and other civil rights leaders. While Sargent Shriver, the director of the Office of Economic Opportunity, promised the MDC veto power over state poverty programs, this power never materialized. The state AFL-CIO provided the major financial support for the MDC, but it hemorrhaged locals who were disaffiliating out of anger over Ramsey's public opposition to segregation. The MFDP had little interest in the MDC and Ramsey's efforts. The MFDP newsletter criticized the heavily white makeup of the MDC and Ramsey's segregated locals, with one editorial writer declaring that "in the race for the Negro vote Claude Ramsey has got off to a bad start." With little local and no national support forthcoming, the MDC quickly faded from the political scene.[60]

A similar schism between the MFDP and the NAACP and AFL-CIO moderates erupted over the Young Democratic Clubs of Mississippi (YDCM), a feud emblematic of the COFO breakup. The YDCM, an all-white group under Robert Oswald, lost its charter in 1963. Three days before the Atlantic City Convention, a civil rights activist named Melvin Whitfield, connected to SNCC, the MFDP, and the Mississippi Student Union, a Black youth organization, applied for a new YDCM charter, this time as an integrated group, with the Young Democratic Clubs of America (YDCA). The YDCA denied the application over the MFDP's role in organizing the new YDCM but encouraged reapplication at its national committee meeting in April 1965.[61]

The YDCM did reapply, but under a different leader. In April, Whitfield appointed R. Hunter Morey, a white SNCC field secretary, to be the executive secretary of the YDCM. Morey, a Princeton graduate, first came to Mississippi with SNCC to work in Greenville in 1963, and then served as the coordinator of the COFO legal department beginning in 1964. Whitfield later gave up active leadership of the group and moved to California, leaving Morey in control.[62]

Morey reached out to both Vice President Humphrey and Claude Ramsey in an effort to get recognition for the YDCM, but Ramsey rebuffed him, suspicious that the group was a front for civil rights activity and not interested in creating a "bona-fide Democratic Party in this state." Morey also directly addressed an inquiry from SNCC officer Ruby Doris Smith Robinson on the relationship of the YDCM to the MFDP, indicating that "Guyot suggests . . . not having a formal relationship with FDP." Yet Morey said that his interests with the YDCM mirrored those of the MFDP, with the intent to "use the political process to gain justice, political democracy, economic opportunity and advancement, etc."[63]

Morey's close association with the MFDP and his leadership role in the Young Democrats caused considerable controversy. His use of the title "Executive Secretary" angered some, to the point that John Sexton, a Washington, DC-based SNCC attorney, sent him a letter advising him to drop the title. According to Spencer Oliver, a member of the National Membership Committee of the YDCA—and an opponent of the Whitfield faction—the meeting of the YDCM held at Tougaloo on 2 May erupted in chaos. According to columnists Rowland Evans and Robert Novak, MFDP leaders "controlled" the meeting of about 200 Black participants and 10 white Mississippians. Oliver said that little happened at the meeting and, in a foreshadowing of the Vietnam flyer at McComb, that statements "were made attacking Johnson's policy on Viet Nam and the Dominican Republic." Sexton warned Morey that "this line is political death." In a similar vein, he told Morey that he supported a challenge of the seating of the Mississippi congressmen, but that seating the MFDP delegation "is tactically unwise." Morey's association with the MFDP even confused Whitfield, who wrote to Morey from California and inquired about the YDCM's using the MFDP phone number, saying that he thought that "Guyot had disagreed to this" and he wanted to know if the YDCM received any support from the MFDP.[64]

In the spring of 1965, the YDCA held its national committee meeting in Kansas City and rejected the YDCM application for a charter. Oliver led the campaign against the YDCM, with the backing of Ramsey and Charles Evers. Morey responded by filing a complaint against the YDCA Membership Practices Committee on the grounds of discrimination, specifically attacking Spencer Oliver (who was white) as having "too much racial feeling to handle such a case as Mississippi" and saying that Oliver's racism caused his "extreme emotionalism" and "outbursts of anger that were quite unusual" at a 4 April meeting in Jackson. He also launched a broad attack against the moderate forces like Ramsey, calling them "supposed liberal whites" who handpicked their Black members. Morey had a similar sharp exchange of letters with Robert Oswald of the MDC, with each man accusing the other of unwillingness to compromise. Morey received little help on this matter from Edwin Kruse, the national secretary of the YDCA, who urged the YDCM not to support any resolutions critical of the Vietnam War. He avoiding taking sides in the dispute and instead suggesting they focus wholeheartedly on backing President Johnson's Great Society.[65]

Morey dove deeper into the civil rights schism when he tried to get involved with the MDC as well. He tried to attend a meeting of the Lauderdale County Democratic Club on 23 May, but the chairman, a wealthy Black businessman named Charles Young, blocked his entry. MDC leaders like Ramsey, Oswald, and Evers attended, however. Ramsey and Oswald both told Morey that he could not attend the MDC meeting on 18 July at the Heidelberg Hotel in Jackson. MFDP press reports called the MDC conference a "fraud" and an "Uncle Tom/ White Opportunist Alliance." White segregationists eagerly watched the feud. Mack Smith, a white MFDP volunteer from New York, told an investigator for the State Sovereignty Commission that Guyot and Evers openly clashed and that Guyot "is very much against Evers." By July an SSC investigator reported that Guyot and Evers worked together on voter registration in Jackson, but Evers apparently canceled the plans for a joint march and then conducted his registration campaign separately.[66]

Shortly after the failed joint march, COFO, on life support for months, finally died. The MFDP held a meeting in July at Tougaloo College and agreed to dissolve COFO and turn over all local projects to local FDPs. The MFDP now filled the void left by COFO. At the meeting, Guyot kept the focus clearly on voter registration and mobilization as the keys to change. He said that "until the Negro in Mississippi has some political power everything else we do is useless." At the same time, he warned of the MFDP's becoming too top-down. Despite his differences with Moses, he echoed concerns about civil rights workers exerting too much influence over Black Mississippians. "There is X amount of political power in Mississippi and we need to give it to the people to use," Guyot said. "Even if they use it unwisely."[67]

Guyot, despite reportedly not wanting a formal arrangement between the MFDP and the YDCM, did play an active role in the feuds regarding both the YDCM and the MDC. The MFDP gave active but not financial support, as the MFDP had spent so much on the congressional challenge that it turned down a request from the YDCM for money. In April, Guyot issued a statement of support for the YDCM and its charter, writing that "we urge this very strongly although we are not officially affiliated with the group." He attended the Kansas City meeting with Morey to try to get a charter for the group. At the 4 April meeting where Oliver clashed with the YDCM leaders, Guyot attended even though he did not have an invitation. He and Morey then met with Evers in Jackson before the 18 July meeting in an unsuccessful effort to get MFDP members invited to the conference. He made no effort to stop COFO-issued press releases unabashedly pro-MFDP and anti-Ramsey and anti-Evers. On the question of the feud with the liberals, Guyot said, "We will accept help from anyone, but we will accept guidance from no one. The only coalition I am responsible to is the Negroes of Mississippi."[68] Guyot's actions and words indicate the blurry relationship between the civil rights groups, an overlap originally encouraged by the establishment of COFO.

The MFDP-YDCM overlap occurred with other organizations as well. In 1965, another affiliated group, the Mississippi Freedom Labor Union (MFLU), went on strike against Delta plantation owners. The MFLU had formed in the Delta town of Shaw in April 1965 with the goal of raising wages for ill-paid cotton choppers and tractor drivers. The MFLU went on strike in May in Greenville for a $1.25 hourly wage for its members. Mass firings by the planters spread the strike to other towns and professions. While the members fought bravely, by September the MFLU strike had failed due to police repression and a lack of resources and leverage, the latter exacerbated by the growing mechanization of Delta agriculture. The strike showed the cross-organizational efforts of the MFDP, including its push for economic rights. Most of the strikers belonged to the MFDP, took part in voter registration drives, and lent active support to the congressional challenge. As movement historian Michael Paul Sistrom noted, "The members and local leaders of the Freedom Labor Unions did not make organizational distinctions."[69]

The schism between the NAACP-AFL-CIO liberal faction and the MFDP-YDCM activists came to a head at the 14 August meeting in Jackson, once again held at the Heidelberg Hotel. MFDP supporters, many of them Black college students, arrived in sufficient numbers to dominate the meeting, which led Hodding Carter III, the newspaper editor and a member of the liberal faction, to lead a walkout to another room. The two factions proceeded to elect their own slates of officers and appeal for national recognition. The elected slate further underscored the overlap between the YDCM and the MFDP, as delegates elected Robert Smith, a Black FDP worker from Brookhaven, and Ed King as president and vice president, respectively. Morey and the YDCM made their final attempt at recognition in October at the annual Young Democrats convention in New York City, but the YDCA sided with the liberal faction and recognized it as the legitimate Mississippi Young Democrats club.[70]

The MFDP efforts to win national recognition might have failed, but Guyot and his supporters did not give up. They tried once again in the fall of 1965, when the Democratic National Committee's Equal Rights Committee held hearings in southern states, including Mississippi. The national Democrats used the hearings to determine how much progress the state parties had made toward creating integrated delegations for the 1968 national convention. Not surprisingly, the Mississippi Democratic Party had not created and had no intention of sending an integrated delegation. When the committee held hearings in Jackson, Guyot and Victoria Gray testified and claimed that the Democratic Party had pledged at Atlantic City to seat the MFDP in 1968. This was untrue, as the pledge was only to seat integrated delegations, not a specific organization. Guyot still maintained his loyalty to the national Democrats despite the lack of official recognition, declaring that "we are by no means a third party. We are maintaining that our party is the Democratic Party of the state. We will run candidates in the municipal elections this year and continue organizing so that by 1966 we will be able to take on Senator Eastland." He urged the national party to help fund the MFDP voter registration drives and even asked them to block the state Democratic Party from conducting the 1966 primaries as official Democratic campaigns. Guyot asked for something he would never get, as Sistrom noted that the latter action "would have been an unprecedented and unthinkable level of intervention in a state party's affairs." The Equal Rights Committee took no action on Guyot's proposal, and in general continued to regard the MFDP as a group of uncontrollable militants. National Democrats sent their funds to the AFL-CIO and MDC, who backed the NAACP's voter registration drives. Doug Wynn, a white Delta political organizer allied with the Hodding-Ramsey faction, told Hubert Humphrey that any effort to have a connection to "Mr. Guyot or the so-called Mississippi Freedom Democratic Party" would only undermine the efforts of the liberals.[71]

While white liberals (and some Black ones, too) thought Guyot and the MFDP too radical and thus blamed them for the lack of a broad-based coalition, it is important to note that those same liberals had no interest in dealing with the MFDP in any appearance of good faith. Their reticence likely resulted from the continuing fallout over the Atlantic City convention. Bayard Rustin, the Black pacifist involved in organizing the March on Washington, published an editorial in the liberal journal *Commentary* in February 1965 titled "From Protest to Politics: The Future of the Civil Rights Movement." Writing in the wake of Atlantic City and Johnson's landslide election victory, Rustin endorsed increasing involvement in electoral politics by the MFDP and the movement in general. He credited this new political orientation in Mississippi to Bob Moses, apparently unaware of Moses's growing withdrawal from the state after Atlantic City. And Rustin warned against an independent political course, declaring that "neither that movement nor the country's twenty million black people can win political power alone. We need allies . . . I speak of the coalition which staged the March on Washington, passed the Civil Rights Act, and laid the basis for the Johnson landslide—Negroes, trade unionists, liberals, and religious groups." He said that the Black vote can never be independent, as Black voters must necessarily be a swing vote for a (presumably white) candidate from either of the major parties. This meant that "there will be compromise" and the political leader "who shrinks from this task reveals not his purity but his lack of political sense."[72]

The problem with Rustin's analysis is that in Mississippi, Black voters could not build such a coalition due to near-unified white hostility, a state of affairs that constrained the options of not just Guyot but also of leaders like Ramsey, Evers, and Henry. The racism within the white working class, as seen earlier, hindered the state AFL-CIO's opposition to Jim Crow, and that same racism made it exceptionally difficult to recruit white Mississippians into pro–civil rights organizations like the Young Democrats and the national Democratic Party, much less actual civil rights groups like the NAACP and MFDP. And Guyot long distrusted Rustin for his close association with Al Lowenstein and others who tried to manipulate SNCC and the MFDP. In late 1963, SNCC had held a conference on in Washington, DC, that focused on "providing jobs and food for the people of depressed rural areas." Guyot recalled that Rustin urged SNCC to work with labor unions and offered it funding. Guyot said "that is when the AFL-CIO tried to buy us out." James Forman echoed Guyot's sentiments, dismissing the efforts of Rustin and Norman Thomas, of the Young People's Socialist League (which, despite its name, was in Forman's words "a strictly reformist outfit of social democrats who were more vehemently anticommunist than the loudest rightwingers") as liberal co-opting. "The entire conference represented a thrust to pull SNCC closer to the liberal-labor syndrome," and he said that "within a year, all of SNCC would be disenchanted with Bayard Rustin."[73]

Just as the congressional challenge ended, the MFDP also played a part in events in Natchez. The small city on the river bluffs in Adams County became a flashpoint of violence against civil rights activists in the late summer of 1965. The events in Natchez highlighted not only the NAACP-MFDP rift but also questions over the growing militancy in the MFDP, specifically the question of armed self-defense. Coming on the heels of the McComb statement on the Vietnam War, the Natchez movement underscored a growing restlessness among the young activists of the party, one that presaged the events of the Meredith March and Stokely Carmichael's famous "Black Power" speech of 1966.

Despite the rivalry between the NAACP and MFDP on the state level, the two organizations worked together locally in Natchez in 1963 and 1964. Dorie Ladner and George Greene of SNCC had good relations with George Metcalf, the president of the Natchez NAACP branch. Metcalf even supported a COFO project in the city in the summer of 1964. But he worked at Armstrong Tire and Rubber, a plant that mostly confined Black workers to menial jobs and employed many Klan members and supporters. On 27 August 1965, Metcalf barely survived an attempt on his life when a car bomb demolished his car after his shift at the plant. Plant management had just promoted him to the position of shipping clerk—a traditionally whites-only position—and he had recently petitioned the Natchez school board to comply with the *Brown* decision.[74] These actions meant the local Klan marked him for death.

The terrorist act prompted mass protests by Black residents in Natchez and drew Charles Evers there, who openly advocated armed self-defense. His arrival angered the local FDP, given the Evers's history opposing the MFDP across the state. But Evers had his own problems with the national NAACP, as his unpredictable nature and refusal to follow NAACP policies had almost cost him his job as Mississippi field secretary by the time he arrived in town. The white violence in Natchez gave him an opportunity to save his position.[75]

Although Evers occupied the civil rights mainstream, he had openly advocated armed self-defense since 1964, one of the reasons why NAACP head Roy Wilkins wanted him fired. He had an armed security team accompany him to Natchez during a spring visit before the attempt on Metcalf's life. While he and other activists calmed local residents who wanted revenge after the attack on Metcalf, he continued to endorse armed self-defense, and hundreds of local Black residents began to openly carry firearms in public. Evers said that "we're not going to start any riots, but we've got guns and we're going to fight back." Evers said these words only weeks after the Watts riot in Los Angeles, which raised fears of a race riot in the small river city. Governor Paul Johnson ordered 650 National Guardsmen into Natchez to quell any disturbances.[76]

Historian Akinyele Omowale Umoja points out that Evers may have simply recognized the growing militancy among activists from the rival MFDP and local Black residents, many of them NAACP members themselves. Of course, a Black person carrying a firearm hardly meant an endorsement of militancy—for a Black person in Mississippi, such an action reflected good sense. Movement participants and historians have noted the prevalence of guns while organizing in Mississippi, particularly from local Blacks who protected civil rights workers. Chuck McDew of SNCC traveled to Natchez in 1964 and gave a .32 pistol to Dorie Ladner and trained her in its use. In the weeks before the attack on Metcalf, local Black residents, most of them affiliated with the NAACP, formed an armed self-defense group.[77]

In the wake of Metcalf's near-murder, Evers asked Robert Hicks, a leader of the Deacons of Defense and Justice, to establish a chapter in Natchez. The Deacons originated in Jonesboro and Bogalusa, Louisiana, in 1964 to protect local Blacks and CORE activists from Klan violence. But the Deacons and armed self-defense also attracted the MFDP's interest. On 29 August, nine members of the Bogalusa Deacons attended an MFDP meeting in Jackson, where two of the leaders of the group spoke to about 175 people. One of those leaders, Charles Sims, then traveled to Natchez. Local activists in Natchez renamed their armed self-defense group the Natchez Deacons but did not affiliate with the Louisiana Deacons—largely because Sims wanted a percentage of their dues if they did. The Natchez Deacons took advantage of Mississippi open carry laws to protect the Black community and movement activists.[78]

The MFDP sent additional activists to Natchez to help with the demonstrations there, and Guyot tried to get Martin Luther King Jr. to visit to bring national attention to the city. In particular, he hoped to link the congressional challenge to the events in Natchez and undercut Evers's influence. That came to naught, as Andrew Young of the SCLC visited at Evers's invitation instead. SCLC staffers arrived in the town and assisted Evers and the NAACP with organizing demonstrations, but after a couple of weeks the SCLC staffers clashed with the NAACP, apparently in part a generational dispute between the younger SCLC staffers and older NAACP members. The feud led Evers and the NAACP to demand in October that the SCLC leave. Al Sampson, one of the SCLC staffers, denounced the NAACP by name at a meeting as "unreliable, untrustworthy, and incapable." Not surprisingly, King never visited Natchez during the campaign.[79]

Ultimately, Evers gained the upper hand over the MFDP in Natchez. He presented a list of demands to Mayor John Nosser and the Board of Aldermen, calling for full integration of the city government, schools, and local businesses. The city government rejected the demands, which prompted Evers to call for a boycott of white-owned businesses—but not a march downtown like he origi-nally planned. This infuriated local MFDP activists, shut out of Evers's decision making. The local NAACP, through Evers, effectively wrested control of the Natchez movement from the MFDP. The power grab included freezing out the SCLC, as Sampson had tried to bring the MFDP and Delta Ministry into the strat-egy and planning sessions but Evers blocked him. Ultimately, Evers organized marches and maintained the boycott, forcing the city leaders to negotiate with him. MFDP organizers tried their best, highlighting Evers's abuse of power, but the attacks only made Evers appear to be the reasonable moderate. Class played an issue in the MFDP's lack of appeal, as most of the NAACP members in Natchez, despite their endorsement of self-defense, were middle-class adult males, not young college students like the MFDP and SNCC members. Evers eventually ended the boycott with some token concessions from the city, and by late December the Natchez movement's momentum had fizzled, ending the last major mobilizing campaign of the Mississippi movement.[80]

Guyot insisted on a tactical commitment to strict nonviolence that local residents found unrealistic and irrelevant to their needs. This tension erupted vividly when Guyot visited Natchez and spoke at Bright Star Baptist Church in September. A documentary crew recording footage for *Black Natchez*, a film released two years later on the Natchez movement, captured the drama, as the film contained a heavy emphasis on the NAACP-MFDP rivalry. During the church meeting, a Black woman stood up during the address by MFDP speakers and rejected the MFDP's call for nonviolent picketing and marching, saying that "if a man or woman hits me; I'm going to hit him back. And so I don't want to get in there since it's non-violent." Guyot called for the local people to demonstrate by "being quiet and doing nothing" and "sitting back and staying in your places." These calls for passivity did not go well with the crowd, who began to leave the church as Guyot spoke. His final comments showed how badly he misread the local situation, when he said, "The most cowardly thing I have ever heard is for someone to say, 'I would go with you all but I ain't non-violent.'" By the end of his speech, most of his audience had left the church.[81]

The church scene in *Black Natchez* dramatically showed that in the politi-cal struggle between Evers and Guyot, Evers soundly defeated Guyot. Despite Evers holding the mantle of the "mainstream" civil rights leader through his NAACP position, he recognized and exploited Black anger in Natchez—not an anger confined to younger activists but part of the mainstream itself, among the middle-class Black residents comprising Natchez's NAACP branch. Guyot and the MFDP did not recognize that or did not want to embrace a stance of armed self-defense, and thus lost the local community.

The confrontation at Bright Star Baptist Church also contradicted the MFDP's ethos of participatory democracy. As Guyot candidly acknowledged in later recollections, when he first began working with SNCC he believed that Mississippi Blacks should be literate before being able to vote. His Gulf Coast upbringing ran up against the conditions and realties of the Mississippi Delta, and he quickly abandoned that unrealistic position. But he and other MFDP activists still brought unrealistic attitudes into Natchez in 1965, this time over armed self-defense. The local population rejected their commitment to strict tactical nonviolence. The attempt to impose these ideals on the local community stands in sharp contrast to what Guyot said about SNCC's organizing in McComb. He said that what SNCC discovered was that "the Black community will protect and support them," a lesson they took to the Delta when they organized there. Guyot also said on his SNCC years that he was "very proud that SNCC took the position that we were not going to let anyone tell us what to do." But apparently that maxim did not extend to the Black residents of Natchez, who rejected what Guyot told them to do and did not support him or the MFDP. Of course, one can be too hard on Guyot over this position, one likely shaped by his own recent history. If he had a gun in his possession at Winona, for example, the police would surely have killed him and claimed a justified shooting. That is exactly what he said during earlier debates among SNCC staff about arming activists during Freedom Summer: "Don't you see? They'll shoot us quicker if we're armed!" He also declared that he would "leave Mississippi" if he decided to take up arms.[82] That experience likely shaped his reasoning as he sparred with the locals in the Natchez church. In his own upbringing, Guyot did not show a reverence for "pure" nonviolence. He recalled that as a boy he could move freely in Pass Christian because "my father would've killed any twenty people that had anything to say to me." And MFDP members themselves hardly remained committed to nonviolence. Robert Miles, an MFDP leader in Panola County, physically struck down a white man in a group that attacked a COFO worker outside the courthouse in Batesville during a demonstration in 1965.[83] But whatever the reason, Natchez and the failure of the MFDP there proved to be a lesson ignored or forgotten by Guyot in later years, as discussions of the Natchez organizing campaign are absent in his oral histories and interviews. More broadly for the party, Guyot and the MFDP failed in Natchez similar to the way that Martin Luther King Jr. and the SCLC failed during the Albany Movement in Georgia in 1962. But King and the SCLC rebounded from that defeat with Project C in Birmingham the following year, which proved to be the campaign that motivated the Kennedy administration to introduce what would eventually become the Civil Rights Act of 1964. The MFDP did not win any much-needed victories in 1966 or 1967.

The tone of the Natchez movement, from the armed self-defense of the Deacons to the more ominous violence and intimidation of the boycott enforcers (organized by Evers associate Rudy Shields, whose job was to punish Black residents who shopped at white businesses), reflected the growing militancy among the younger activists as a whole, in SNCC, the MFDP, and all across the South. And as Natchez showed, Guyot and the MFDP viewed this insurgent activism ambivalently, as seen in his handling of the Vietnam draft flyer in McComb. The groundswell of youth activism often left Guyot and other MFDP leaders like Ed King caught in the middle. Even with his fellow MFDP activists, Guyot sometimes found himself caught on the more accommodationist side of issues and playing the role of the pragmatic politician. On 18 September, Guyot suggested at an MFDP Executive Committee meeting that Percy Greene, the editor of the Black state newspaper the *Jackson Advocate*, be invited to the MFDP's state convention in October. Greene had used his paper to denounce the civil rights movement, not surprisingly since he was in the pay of the State Sovereignty Commission. According to the minutes, "It caused so much protest that a vote was taken." Guyot's motion was defeated, 8–5, with Annie Devine and Fannie Lou Hamer among those opposed. Why Guyot wanted to invite Greene—a man who had lost credibility with the Black community back in the 1950s—is unclear, as his opinion of the movement had not changed. Later that month, the *Jackson Advocate* ran an editorial denouncing the congressional challenge and declaring that the MFDP wanted to dominate the Black Belt with all-Black governments and then "spark a revolution to overthrow the established United States government, and thus bring about the establishment of Communism in this country."[84]

In his future assessment of the events of the summers of 1964 and 1965, Guyot believed firmly that Freedom Summer and the Atlantic City challenge, and the congressional challenges related to it, played the major role in the passage of the Voting Rights Act in 1965. He cited the strengthening of the act with Section 5 during the debates over the challenge as proof, and that "we didn't want to be beaten by the passage of the Voting Rights Act because we felt that those two things could complement one another rather than being an alternative to one another, which is what they turned out to be." Stokely Carmichael also saw a link between the two, recollecting in his autobiography years later that "technically the MFDP lost . . . but I tell you what, it helped pass the Voting Rights Act." Volunteers who worked in the party, such as Lisa Anderson Todd, a white woman from New Jersey who later wrote a memoir of her involvement in Freedom Summer, shared Guyot's viewpoint. Todd argued that the SNCC and MFDP work "heightened awareness in the country of the treatment of Blacks as second-class citizens and led to a moral imperative to enforce the right to vote. . . . Thus the MFDP should be credited for its role in the passage of the Voting Rights Act of 1965." Ed King said that the challenge was "a victory because it had to be treated as valid; for Congress not to throw the challenge out on the first day meant that there was a legal foundation for it." Mary King, another SNCC activist, also said that the congressional challenge made the passage of the Voting Rights Act possible, citing the intensive lobbying efforts on House members by SNCC volunteers. David Langun, in his biography of William Kunstler, the attorney who aided the MFDP after Atlantic City, credits the thousands of depositions collected by the MFDP attorneys and activists during the congressional challenge in 1965 (and the resulting publicity), which grew directly out of Atlantic City, as being of "crucial importance" to the passage of the act.[85]

These assessments are ones that scholars of the movement have largely avoided. The traditional interpretation in civil rights historiography—which Todd laments in her memoir—is that the Selma campaign in 1965, in which Martin Luther King Jr. played the most prominent role, proved the catalyst for the passage of the Voting Rights Act. David Garrow, one of King's biographers and author of one of the first academic studies of Selma and the act, seconded this viewpoint in his scholarship. Garrow gives the MFDP only a few passing mentions in his work, portraying it as marginal compared to the SCLC. King is shown as working with the MFDP, such as when he delayed a ten-county voter registration drive in Alabama's Black Belt so as to not take media attention away from the congressional challenge, but nowhere is the MFDP credited with playing a role in the passage of the Voting Rights Act through either the Atlantic City or congressional challenges. The only role the MFDP plays in Garrow's analysis is the fear their February memo on voting rights created in Washington, when Roy Wilkins of the NAACP told Lee White, a legal counsel to President Johnson, that the memo—incorrectly—included plans for sit-ins in the Capitol. White then suggested to the president that pressure needed to be put on King to exercise "some restraint" on the MFDP lest the voting rights bill become derailed. In his recent study of Selma, Robert Pratt echoes Garrow and gives only scant mention to the MFDP and none to the congressional challenge, situating the passage of the act within the sole context of Alabama. A recent collection of essays on Selma also reinforces the centrality of Selma to the passage of the Voting Rights Act, with not a single mention of the congressional challenge and scant mention of the MFDP.[86]

Les McLemore, the vice chairman of the Atlantic City MFDP delegation, differs from the movement activists who credit the challenges for the passage of the Voting Rights Act. In his doctoral dissertation on the party, he sees the Atlantic City and congressional challenges as two distinct events, and credits Atlantic City with creating a change that "had an impact on the body politic of the nation." But he said that King "more than anyone was responsible for the passage of the [Voting Rights] Act, because of his dramatic march from Selma to Montgomery, Alabama." McLemore in fact says that the act's passage during the summer of 1965 *hurt* the congressional challenge, since it allowed a number of House liberals to "use it as an excuse" for not voting for the MFDP. He says that the act proved "the political undoing" of the congressional challenge. To McLemore, the impact on both white and Black radicals represented the real legacy of Atlantic City and the congressional challenge, a view echoed by Clayborne Carson, who highlighted the bitterness SNCC activists and MFDP delegates felt after Atlantic City. McLemore ultimately argues that "a new Black politics emerged out of the 1965 challenge," and that this politics became the major long-term effect.[87]

On the role of the MFDP, Clayborne Carson, John Dittmer, Charles Payne, and other movement historians do not attribute the passage of the act to Atlantic City, although Dittmer said that the congressional challenge "kept the issue of voter discrimination on the agenda, reinforcing the hand of congressional liberals who succeeded in enacting a strong bill." Some lesser-known scholars of the movement are more favorable in their view of the MFDP, such as Steven Gentine, who wrote in his study of the congressional challenge that "there is no question Selma provided invaluable images in pushing the [Voting Rights Act] to passage, but discounting the role of the MFDP Congressional challenge is a disservice to history and the people who shaped it." The opinions of contemporaries and participants in Atlantic City vary. Joseph Califano Jr., who served as LBJ's domestic adviser, followed the traditional interpretation and credited the president and King with the passage of the act, emphasizing the Selma campaign and Johnson's legislative maneuvering. Like LBJ, Califano did not even mention the MFDP in his memoirs of his time in the White House.[88]

Who gets the credit for the Voting Rights Act probably has more to do with the viewpoint of the observer. Political historians and liberals who focus on top-down studies of government and institutional structure and partisans of LBJ or King will give them or the federal government or the SCLC more credit than historians and activists who sympathize with the grassroots, bottom-up approach of SNCC and the MFDP. It is easy to dismiss the perspective of Guyot, Todd, and other MFDP members as hopelessly biased or prone to exaggerating their own importance in the civil rights struggle. Such a casual dismissal is short-sighted and neglects the influence and contributions of the grassroots organizing and local activists in sustaining the movement, while at the same time overplaying the role of prominent national leaders. While the MFDP may not have been the sole reason the Voting Rights Act passed, it played a key role in highlighting voter discrimination and white supremacy in Mississippi, and thus reminded the rest of the country of why the vote was important—and helped the eventual passage of the Voting Rights Act. To give sole credit to LBJ and King does a disservice to the grassroots activists who often labored out of the media spotlight.

As the fall of 1965 approached, Guyot looked ahead to the next year's elections in Mississippi. He announced at the end of the congressional challenge that the MFDP would be nominating candidates to oppose all five Mississippi House members as well as Senator James Eastland, who would be standing for reelection. In a mailing to supporters, Guyot referenced what was to come in 1966 by saying that "our challenge to illegal representation is not ended."[89] He sought to continue with high-profile campaigns similar to the congressional challenge with the goal of achieving an electoral breakthrough in Mississippi. But the years 1966 and 1967 would test the MFDP and show its limits as an alternate party to the state Democrats, and eventually force Guyot and other MFDP leaders to reconsider their strategy.

# CHAPTER 5
# WE'LL STAY THE HELL OUT OF THE GODDAMN DEMOCRATIC PARTY

## THE FAILED QUEST FOR INDEPENDENT BLACK POLITICAL POWER

The passage of the Voting Rights Act of 1965 focused the Mississippi Freedom Democratic Party (MFDP) even more on electing Black candidates. Yet Guyot's leadership would be marked by shifting priorities even with this goal of creating Black political power and access. The focus in 1966 on higher-profile congressional elections, including a run for office by Guyot himself, came at the expense of the grassroots organizing and local election campaigns. The Black political electorate, still in a minority in much of the state compared to white voter registration and facing intimidation from the white power structure, could not deliver the kinds of results that the MFDP wanted. This necessitated a change in focus in 1967 toward local elections in heavily Black counties and towns, but even there it faltered. White resistance slowly accommodated to Black voting, as white elected officials and candidates successfully appealed to segments of the Black electorate who considered the MFDP too radical. Meanwhile, Charles Evers and the state chapter of the National Association for the Advancement of Colored People (NAACP) continued to outflank the MFDP, making local gains while the MFDP had few tangible ones. This state of affairs gave Guyot and the MFDP bitter results by the summer of 1967.

At a meeting of the MFDP Executive Committee shortly after the failure of the congressional challenge, Guyot announced that he would spend more time fundraising for the party outside of the state. He realized that the challenge generated a great deal of sympathy with white liberals, and he wanted the party to profit from the postchallenge climate of goodwill. In November he appeared on a panel on Mississippi with Bill Higgs and William Kunstler, as part of a week-long fundraising effort for unemployed Mississippi workers called the "Fast for Freedom," put on by Oberlin College's student civil rights organization, Oberlin Action for Civil Rights. At the meeting at the Ohio college, Guyot discussed organizing in Mississippi in the wake of the Voting Rights Act, and specifically criticized the two-party system and the lack of input local people had in selecting candidates and writing the policy platform. Guyot continued to work toward building a strong local political structure for the MFDP. In October he spoke at the Harrison County FDP and urged its members to continue activism and pressure on white authorities, such as supporting a group of Black citizens on trial in Biloxi for picketing stores in Hattiesburg the previous year. He advised the FDP to hold regular meetings and helped it set up structures like a finance committee. That same month, the MFDP also began a voter registration drive in Bolivar County, the first part of a broader effort to register large numbers of Black voters.[1]

Guyot also looked to the 1966 congressional primary elections. On 6 October, Guyot and Victoria Gray spoke before the Democratic National Committee's Equal Rights Committee, where they continued to make the case for the illegitimacy of the Mississippi Democratic Party, based on its white supremacist history and defiance of the national party. Guyot continued to press for the recognition of the MFDP by the national party and called for the suspension of the June primary elections. Clarence Mitchell of the NAACP arranged the witnesses, and they made the common plea for more registrars to be sent South. Yet they still ran up against the reluctance of the national Democratic Party to take on the white Mississippi Democrats. The committee, headed by former governor David Lawrence of Pennsylvania, deferred the issue of registrars to US Attorney General Nicolas Katzenbach, who feared offending Jim Eastland if he sent registrars to Mississippi. In October 1965, just as the MFDP was waging its voter registration drive in Bolivar County, the Johnson administration withdrew federal registrars, apparently in to avoid antagonizing Senator Eastland. When Guyot pressed the issue of the 1966 congressional primaries and the lack of Black participation with Lawrence, the former governor dismissed his concerns, replying that "if you've got the votes, you'll win the election."[2]

Despite his criticism of the two-party system, Guyot did not consider the MFDP to be a third party. In the Stanford oral history he gave the previous summer, he said that "as long as the national Democratic Party remains the amorphous monolith that it is, there's no need for a third party." On 19 October, he gave a lengthy address to staffers in Greenwood, where he outlined MFDP strategy for the future. A "period of transition," now defined the MFDP, and he predicted that the public demonstrations of the civil rights movement would now decline. "Civil rights as such is on its way out; the question now will be an attempt to gain political power and an attempt to see that it's not misused." He warned that a problem was "personality-oriented" politics. This spoke to the question of organizing, and the MFDP's need to avoid "the possibility of a sellout," which Guyot considered to be a real problem. He said that the organizers in Mississippi had to be prepared to leave the counties they were organizing and relinquish control to others. If they didn't, Guyot said—in a jab likely aimed at Evers and Natchez—that "we are simply building parochial kingdoms of individualistic, personality-oriented power." To avoid this fate, he said that the MFDP must "work within the existing procedural steps, political steps, attempting to revamp or change them on every level. Now whether or not that can happen depends upon the kind of work and the kind of energy that we can release around the political regime." Further reflecting the desire to work within the political system, Guyot attended a White House Civil Rights Planning Conference in November with Unita Blackwell, Annie Devine, Ralthus Hayes, and Andrew Hawkins, the latter two a Holmes County farmer and a Freedom Labor Union activist, respectively.[3]

Guyot's warning about personality-oriented politics corrupting the MFDP reminded staffers not to forget that the Student Nonviolent Coordinating Committee (SNCC) and the MFDP rested on the ethos of participatory democracy. Guyot correctly predicted the decline of mass organizing and the demonstrations of the civil rights movement and the shift toward creating Black political power—the "period of transition"—and the new challenges that political participation brought in the wake of the Voting Rights Act. He again framed the MFDP as a party working within the political process and not as an upstart third political party. Given the scant presence of the GOP in Mississippi, the MFDP effectively *was* the other political party to rival the state Democratic Party. Guyot had previously warned about the MFDP becoming a top-down "savior" of local people. In a July 1965 meeting at Tougaloo College, he cautioned civil rights workers that they "really need to look at the folks they are freeing. The most dangerous thing in Mississippi is the people the community people trust. . . . You can no longer lead the people around by the nose. The question is one of skilled versus unskilled."[4]

Keeping with this ethos of participatory democracy, Guyot in later years recalled his vision of the MFDP, which combined democracy with a religious message: "We were to be the party of the unrepresented. We were to be the party that fought openly for them and aligned with them. We were to be the nonreligious church of the needy. We bring you the message that you can be part of your salvation. Everything we did was built around that. We were either litigating, mobilizing, educating, proselytizing, or coalescing."[5]

The MFDP did not just focus on the upcoming congressional elections as a way to increase political power for Black Mississippians. In late 1965, the US Department of Agriculture held elections for the Agricultural Stabilization and Conservation Service (ASCS) in the rural areas of Mississippi. The ASCS controlled production of basic commodities and set allotments for farmers with the goal of stabilizing prices. County ASCS committees could also provide additional acreage to farmers, so not surprisingly Black farmers received disproportionately smaller allotments from the all-white boards. The elections had the added advantage of not requiring registration, literacy tests, or poll taxes.[6]

The Council of Federated Organizations (COFO) had first run Black candidates in a number of majority or heavily Black counties in the 1964 ASCS elections, but harassment and intimidation, as well the complex election process of the ASCS, stymied Black candidates. Voters elected fourteen Black farmers to the community committees in six counties, but none made it to the county committees, where the real power lay. The MFDP brought in Joseph Resnick, a first-term Democratic US representative from New York, to observe the ASCS elections. Resnick, who represented a rural district, toured four counties, and visited striking Mississippi Freedom Labor Union (MFLU) sharecroppers and Black farmers whom the government denied federal loans for registering to vote. He spoke at a press conference alongside Guyot at the Jackson MFDP office and endorsed suspending the ASCS elections due to the pervasive discrimination he witnessed. Resnick, who had voted to support the congressional challenge, said that "the policy of the State of Mississippi is to drive the Negro out."[7]

The MFDP ran about 240 candidates in 22 counties in Mississippi and reported continuing problems of racist intimidation. In Quitman County, no candidates stepped up to run for ASCS offices due to fear of reprisal. Like the previous year, the MFDP could not change the direction of the ASCS. Indeed, civil rights leaders and Black farmers well into the 1970s criticized the ASCS across the South, particularly over the lack of Black representation on committees and discrimination in the county elections. However, some Black farmers did win committee seats. Three farmers in Benton County won, as well as at least one farmer each in Holmes County and Marshall County.[8]

In addition to the ASCS elections, the MFDP focused on state legislative seats. In October the MFDP filed a lawsuit over reapportionment. The state of Mississippi had apportioned its state legislative districts in 1963, after a seventy-three-year period that saw significant population increases in the Jackson area and the Gulf Coast. The state's urban areas suffered gross underrepresentation, and the 1963 reapportionment only occurred due to a lawsuit, *Fortner v. Barnett*, filed by white residents of the Gulf Coast. The case became an *amicus curiae* in the much more famous *Baker v. Carr* in 1962, when the Supreme Court ruled against the state of Tennessee on unequal reapportionment and triggered an avalanche of reapportionment cases around the country.[9]

The Warren Court, along with the passage of the Voting Rights Act, paved the way for the MFDP legal challenge with its 1964 ruling in *Reynolds v. Sims*, an Alabama case that established the "one man, one vote" principle and set population as the main standard for representation and apportionment. At Guyot's suggestion, the Lawyers' Constitutional Defense Committee filed a lawsuit on behalf of the MFDP in the US District Court in Jackson, in the wake of the passage of the Voting Rights Act. William Kunstler represented the eight MFDP plaintiffs in *Conner v. Johnson*, named after MFDP secretary Peggy Jean Conner. Guyot recruited Conner, a native of Hattiesburg, into SNCC when he was a field secretary there in 1963, and she later served as an MFDP delegate at the 1964 state convention and at Atlantic City, where she opposed the two-seat compromise. The suit challenged congressional and state legislative districts on the grounds that their unequal population figures diluted Black voting strength.[10]

Despite the MFDP's differences with Charles Evers, he supported the lawsuit and argued that the state's use of multimember districts, where voters elected multiple legislators for the same district, diluted Black voting strength. Even as the case went to trial, the state passed a new law that split the Black-majority Delta among three congressional districts. The court ruled against the MFDP on the congressional districting plan in late 1966 and only ordered the state to create a new apportionment plan for its state legislative districts, yet one that still had multimember districts. The case then dragged on as the MFDP challenged the new apportionment plan the legislature created.[11]

The MFDP's broader political strategy in 1966 included *Conner v. Johnson* as well as running candidates for office. The MFDP held a nominating convention in October to nominate a slate for that year's elections. It planned to run candidates for the 7 June Democratic primary, but at the convention, the MFDP still showed an internal split between working in the two-party system and existing as an independent political party. The party decided that if the candidates lost the June primary, they would run as independents in the general election. Guyot said that despite the "inconsistencies within the Democratic Party," the MFDP was "not building a third party, but a first party run by the people." Since the MFDP already dealt with the taint of radicalism and militancy due to the draft controversy, it did not wish to contribute to that image any further by severing itself completely from the national Democratic Party. The slate consisted of five Black candidates and one white. Heading the delegation was Clifton Whitley, a minister and professor at Rust College in Holly Springs, who ran for the US Senate seat held by James Eastland. The five House seats included Dock Drummond, a retired plumber running in the First District; Ralthus Hayes, in the Second District; Clinton Collier, a Philadelphia minister running in the Fourth District; and Ed King, the only white candidate, in the Third District. In the Fifth District, Guyot, the final candidate and the youngest of the nominees at age twenty-six, challenged William Colmer, the powerful chairman of the House Rules Committee and a man fifty years his senior.[12]

The MFDP marked the beginning of the new year of 1966 with a statewide convention in Jackson on 2 January. Approximately 300 people attended the meeting at the Masonic Temple on Lynch Street. The First District did not have enough members present to hold a caucus. The caucuses for the individual districts focused on the upcoming congressional campaign, setting up local campaign structures and planning fundraising. Guyot then addressed the entire assembly, telling them that 1965 had been a year of "big fights and small victories." Referencing the congressional challenge, he said that "we tried to unseat those five killers but were unsuccessful." He emphasized the positive, declaring that "we shook them up and made them afraid." Concerning the reapportionment suit and other activities, he indicated that the party would increasingly have to rely on the federal courts, as "we shouldn't have that much faith in the federal government" after Atlantic City and the congressional challenge. Alluding to conflict within the MFDP, he called for people to work together and put aside their personality differences to help the party organize local people who had no political voice. Looking toward 1966, Guyot reiterated his desire for community organizing, urging local people to mobilize politically with voter registration and paying poll taxes. He said that the MFDP needed to emphasize voter registration and political education rather than demonstrations, now "a thing of the past."[13]

The gender makeup of the 1966 slate of candidates also stood out. Unlike the woman-dominated congressional challenge of the previous year, the MFDP this time ran an all-male slate. Why the party did so is not clear, but it appeared that as part of its quest to become a viable political party, the MFDP pursued a more traditional form of Black leadership—one skewed toward Black men of middle-class backgrounds. Three of the candidates, including the only white one, came from the clergy, while Ralthus Hayes owned his own farm, having purchased his land under a Farm Security Administration loan program in 1941. Guyot had a college degree, and only Drummond, a plumber, came from the working class—and the skilled working class at that. This slate reflected continuity with the Atlantic City delegation, whose members also predominately hailed from the Black middle class.[14]

Aside from class, the selection of an all-male slate also suggested an attempt to use "traditional" male leaders rather than women who did much of the organizing work for civil rights groups. As Belinda Robnett shows, women were "bridge leaders" based on their grassroots organizing and community work, not through traditional hierarchies of power like the Black church. Male leaders largely excluded women from formal leadership positions, at least in the top tier of movement organizations.[15] The MFDP's approach marked another move away from SNCC's ethos, like Guyot's decision to run the party in a more centralized fashion in the wake of Atlantic City. By running respected men of the Black middle class, especially ministers, MFDP leaders likely hoped to make the party more appealing to Black Mississippians.

These developments do not mean the MFDP had succumbed to sexism, or that by comparison SNCC embodied gender equality. The Waveland retreat famously exposed the problems of sexism within SNCC when Mary King and Casey Hayden authored a memo confronting sex discrimination in the movement, a story that has been told extensively by Sara Evans, Clayborne Carson, and other movement historians. On gender equality, SNCC had a better record than the more conservative Southern Christian Leadership Conference (SCLC), where male ministers like Martin Luther King Jr. and Ralph Abernathy did not treat women as equals and often ignored their input.[16]

Guyot candidly expressed how his views on the role of women in the movement changed over time, much like his how his class orientation and views on literacy tests changed when he became a SNCC volunteer and experienced the harsh realities of the Delta. He recalled telling a group of women, including Hamer, Victoria Gray, and Unita Blackwell, to "step back a bit and let the men move in now. Fortunately, they didn't kill me." He credited Ella Baker for disabusing him of his sexist notions. He made a similar comment to her about the need for women to step aside for the men, and she replied that he needed to learn to "never, never make the mistake of substituting men in quantity for women of quality." "I haven't done that shit anymore," he said. "In fact, I've gone the other way around." Guyot once made a sexist comment in her presence, and she corrected him with a history lesson about the role of women in the freedom struggle. Guyot called his comment "one of the most idiotic statements I ever made, and I have never said anything like that since."[17]

Guyot also acknowledged the critical role that the support of women played in his election in April 1964 as chair of the MFDP. He worked closely with Victoria Gray Adams, and her daily schedule at the SNCC office in Hattiesburg

Jean Wheeler and Guyot, with
Mrs. Pinkey Hall, May 1964.
Sheila Michaels Papers Collection,
University of Southern Mississippi.

indicates she met and worked regularly with him, even visiting him during his stint in jail in the summer of 1964. In addition to Adams, other women he worked with in Hattiesburg, like Peggy Jean Conner, backed him, as did Annie Devine. Their support gave him the edge over Aaron Henry and Leslie Burl McLemore. He said of the women, "They know me, because I worked for them. . . . I'll never forget that."[18]

Obviously, some women in the movement meant a great deal to Guyot. But some women became more than just professional associates and friends. During his time in Mississippi, he dated Jean Wheeler, a Black Howard University student from Detroit whom Stokely Carmichael sent in 1963 to work in southwestern Georgia. The large number of white volunteers working in Georgia alienated her, so by 1964 she was working in Mississippi, where she met Guyot while doing voter registration work in Hattiesburg.[19]

Guyot and Wheeler soon became seriously involved, even getting engaged, but like many relationships during the movement, theirs proved fleeting. By the end of 1965, Guyot's relationship with Wheeler had ended, and he was dating a woman named Monica Klein—a white woman. Klein came from San Francisco and met Guyot during one of his visits to California. She joined him in Mississippi and began working in the MFDP offices, handling budgetary issues and orientations for new civil rights workers. Interracial relationships and dating in the civil rights movement occurred frequently but also caused tensions. The obvious danger came from Black men associating publicly with white women, which, as David Dennis of CORE noted, sent white Mississippi men into a rage and led SNCC to avoid recruiting white women volunteers. Nor was white segregationist fury and obsession over interracial sex confined to the Magnolia State, as white reactions to the civil rights marches in Selma and elsewhere showed. But interracial sex also caused problems among the volunteers, and jealousy over affairs and sexual harassment plagued movement projects. Much of this tension resulted from volunteers engaging in casual sexual relationships, however. Guyot and Klein's relationship became a serious rather than a transitory one, eventually leading to a marriage that lasted the rest of their lives.[20] Indeed, Guyot's and Klein's romance came just as Black Power waxed, with its call for Black self-sufficiency and separation from white society. Rather than embrace that path, Guyot showed his commitment to an interracial society not just through his political organizing but through his own romantic relationships. His love for Klein also became a natural expression of the political and social integration of the civil rights movement.

But the relationship carried real risks. Mississippi had exonerated two white men for killing Emmett Till over even the suggestion of interracial intimacy.

Mississippi outlawed interracial marriage since 1880 by statute, and in 1890 delegates inserted the ban into the same state constitution that largely disenfranchised Black men. By the twentieth century, state law outlawed those with at least one "Negro or Mongolian" great-grandparent from marrying whites, a crime that carried a maximum of ten years in prison. State law even prevented distribution of printed material favoring interracial marriage, a misdemeanor prosecutable with a maximum six-month jail sentence.[21]

The *Loving v. Virginia* decision in 1967, where the US Supreme Court unanimously struck down the remaining sixteen state interracial bans in the United States, finally ended Mississippi's marriage ban. Unsurprisingly, Mississippi resisted this decision as well, and the social stigma against interracial marriage guaranteed that Guyot and Klein would marry outside of the state. Even two years after the decision, Charles Evers, the first Black mayor of Fayette, opposed the planned marriage of Martha Wood, his white city attorney, to Monroe Jenkins, one of the town's Black police officers. Evers said he had no problem with the union, but the openness of their relationship made him concerned for their safety and for others in the town. He said in his autobiography that "public safety comes before personal rights." He fired both of them, and they subsequently left the state. Not until 1970, in the face of continued obstruction by white supremacists through the local courts, did the federal courts order the granting of interracial marriage licenses in the state. The state still did not drop its antimiscegenation statutes until 1972, and not until 1987 did Mississippi voters narrowly repeal the now-unenforceable constitutional prohibition against interracial marriage.[22]

Not surprisingly, State Sovereignty Commission (SSC) investigators obsessed over interracial romances. The relationship between Guyot and Klein drew the scrutiny of the SSC, which reported on their unmarried cohabitation in Jackson, including one time when a potential landlord refused to rent them an apartment.[23]

Many "movement marriages," not just the union of Guyot and Klein, developed from Freedom Summer and other civil rights campaigns. Doug McAdam, in his study of Freedom Summer, noted that the volunteers "were no less interested in getting married than their peers, but . . . they now were looking for a partner who shared their commitment to the struggle." By 1967, thirty-one marriages of project veterans of Freedom Summer to each other had occurred, as highly politicized people found each other and made a union of love and politics. Many of the marriages of activists did not last as long as Guyot and Klein's.[24]

The year 1966 opened with yet another martyrdom of a Mississippi civil rights activist. Vernon Dahmer of Hattiesburg, the NAACP member who had invited SNCC workers to his town against the wishes of the state and local NAACP organization, played a key part in the movement in the Piney Woods town. By January 1966, Dahmer had organized a major voter registration campaign in Forrest County, including using his store as a place to collect poll taxes. This campaign attracted the ire of the local Klan and Imperial Wizard Sam Bowers, who ordered Dahmer's murder. On 10 January, Klansmen firebombed the Dahmer family home. Although his wife and children survived the attack, Dahmer died of burns and smoke inhalation.[25]

Guyot joined other state and local civil rights leaders and condemned the murder. He wrote Governor Paul Johnson Jr. and demanded that he and the state government end the "atmosphere of terror." Hattiesburg's Black residents poured into the streets to protest Dahmer's slaying, and Charles Evers urged them to boycott white businesses and register to vote. Guyot arrived in Hattiesburg for Dahmer's funeral and participated in the demonstrations as well. According to Patricia Buzard-Boyett, the Dahmer murder marked a change from earlier murders of civil rights activists, as by 1966 white Mississippi—now dealing with the Voting Rights Act and increased federal scrutiny—could not ignore the Klan violence. Indeed, white politicians from the governor on down condemned Dahmer's murder. The FBI and Department of Justice took an active role, with the latter handing down federal indictments against Bowers and thirteen other Klansmen and the former taking all of the men into custody.[26]

Although the MFDP had yet to win any concrete victories against the Mississippi Democratic Party, the segregationists still viewed Guyot and the party as a menace. Guyot still received death threats, and in January 1966 Senator James Eastland called the MFDP a "stooge" of the Communist Party. In remarks entered into the Congressional Record, Eastland falsely claimed, in a reference to the Vietnam issue last summer, that the MFDP urged its members to avoid the draft. He also directly attacked Guyot over the 2 January MFDP meeting, claiming that Guyot invited Herbert Aptheker, "a notorious communist" who had recently traveled to Hanoi "to discredit U.S. policy with respect to Vietnam." Eastland apparently received this information from the SSC, which reported on the 2 January meeting in its internal communications before Eastland's speech, and the SSC also had a copy of Eastland's remarks in advance.[27]

The renewed red-baiting of the MFDP came just as the party expanded its efforts to include a broader agenda of social change and antipoverty measures. In the area of federal welfare for poor Black Mississippians, the MFDP voiced support for the Child Development Group of Mississippi (CDGM). The CDGM began in the summer of 1965 as a preschool program set up by white activists in Mississippi and grew into eighty-four Head Start centers in twenty-four counties, funded with almost $1.5 million from the Office of Economic Opportunity (OEO). Employees ran the program out of Mount Beulah, a center of both Delta Ministry and MFDP activity. The CDGM, SNCC, and MFDP all overlapped significantly, despite the increasing division over political organizing between SNCC and the MFDP. Local activists controlled the CDGM, so it reflected the SNCC ethos of grassroots control. SNCC members looked with suspicion on the influx of federal funds, but local Black Mississippians, many of them women who wanted to further their children's education, welcomed the money.[28]

Movement activists' involvement in the CGDM drew the ire of white supremacists and even the NAACP, resulting from its rivalry for control over the movement in Mississippi. Many MFDP activists worked in the child centers, and the financial independence this gave to a largely Black female workforce emboldened them to do additional civil rights work like registering to vote and pressing for school desegregation. Some of these activists pressed OEO officials to be firmer in their support for the poor, such as at a 20 February meeting of the MFDP in Jackson, where a Black woman (identified only as "Wilson" from Philadelphia, Pennsylvania, by an SSC informant) assailed Tom Carter, an OEO official, over why "the government spends 13 million a day on Vietnam and won't spend 10 cents a day at home for hungry people." Her exchange with Carter continued until Guyot cut it off. Senator John Stennis used his seat on the Senate Appropriations Committee to begin a major campaign against the CDGM. Assisted by SSC informants, he accused the program of mismanagement, while James Eastland red-baited its organizers. The OEO refunded the CDGM in February 1966, but over the summer of 1966 diverted the funds to a new antipoverty agency, Mississippi Action for Progress (MAP), composed of prominent whites from the Delta and more moderate civil rights leaders like Aaron Henry and R. L. T. Smith, opponents of the MFDP. MAP eventually assumed control of the Head Start program in Mississippi, and its integrated boards represented a remarkable concession by white segregationists, who accepted the more conservative MAP—identified with the NAACP—as a lesser evil than the "radical" CDGM, with its MFDP connections.[29]

The MFDP's support for the impoverished also led to a conference at Mount Beulah in late January 1966 with the Mississippi Freedom Labor Union and the Delta Ministry, where 700 people created the Poor Peoples' Conference. The three organizations sent a telegram to President Johnson asking for financial support to buy land and build houses and farms to become self-sufficient. The Reverend Art Thomas of the Delta Ministry proposed direct action, endorsing squatters' occupation of the abandoned Greenville Air Force Base, where 300 buildings lay vacant. On 31 January, the squatters occupied the base and demanded assistance from the federal government. The occupation built on the demands echoed during the MFLU plantation strike the previous summer. Military police soon evicted them from the federal property. While the federal government agreed to release substantial food commodities to the poor residents of the Delta—Attorney General Nicolas Katzenbach worried that Mississippi could become "the Selma, Alabama of 1966"—political pressure from Senator John Stennis led the administration to abandon its plans for job training programs and housing for unemployed sharecroppers.[30]

Guyot's refusal to oppose the direct action of the Delta Ministry alarmed the State Sovereignty Commission. SSC director Erle Johnston Jr. sent a memo to Senator Eastland reporting on Guyot's statements at the meeting. The red-baiting continued when Representative William Colmer of Mississippi upped the rhetoric and accused Guyot of sanctioning the teaching of "draft dodging techniques" in the Freedom Schools and of not supporting the war in Vietnam. Colmer said that the MFDP was part of "the Communist conspiracy" to "enslave the world."[31]

Although the Greenville sit-in briefly attracted national attention and led Martin Luther King Jr. to personally request aid from President Johnson for the farmworkers, Stennis's threats to target Department of Health, Education, and Welfare funds in Congress succeeded in blocking any aid. Not only did the White House not provide any aid at the time, but federal policies going back to the New Deal actively, if unintentionally, worsened the position of Black share-croppers in the Delta. Federal price supports for cotton and acreage-reduction efforts only swelled the bank accounts of white planters while reducing their demand for Black labor. Mechanization after World War II decreased the labor demands, and the federal minimum wage law that went into effect in February 1967—which covered agricultural employment—further drove white planters to cut their workforces. Other antipoverty efforts, like food stamps, proved more costly for Black families than the old commodities programs, and the channeling of War on Poverty funds through white-controlled welfare boards meant that many Black Mississippians saw the federal government as an abettor rather than a savior in their poverty and oppression.[32]

With Black voter registration now increasing due to the Voting Rights Act, the MFDP lent support to some of the first local Black candidates who emerged in the 1966 elections. These first candidates the party endorsed ran in several spring school board races across the state. After civil rights activists won a suit in federal court blocking a state election law that required candidates to file a petition prior to running for the school board, several Black candidates ran for their local boards in March. In Panola County, Cleveland Williams, a Black farmer active in the MFDP (he had been a delegate to Atlantic City and voted against the compromise), challenged a white incumbent in the South Panola School District. After he entered the race, another Black candidate, Stanley Edmonds, ran for a seat in North Panola. The races generated what the local paper described as "extremely crowded" voting conditions in Batesville, likely due to white turnout to defeat the candidates. In Bolivar County, Minnie Barnes ran against a white planter, and the paper there too reported "record" turnout. In West Point, the presence of a Black candidate on the ballot spurred the local paper to urge white citizens to vote. Charlie Graves, a local Black man and MFDP member, sought a seat on the board, and when the MFDP sent out a flyer urging Black residents to "elect a Negro candidate," the city's *Daily Times Leader* accused the party of playing the race card and being "only concerned . . . that the chairman be a Negro." The higher white voter registration numbers meant that the Black candidates could not win. In addition to a unified white voting bloc, the Black voter turnout in areas like West Point exceeded the number of votes actually cast for the Black candidate, indicating that some Black Mississippians did not support the MFDP, probably due to its perceived association with Black militancy and the antiwar movement. These early contests foreshadowed the problems that the party experienced in upcoming elections. All the school board candidates lost overwhelmingly.[33]

The MFDP spent most of its energies in the spring on the 1966 congressional elections. Guyot told the press that "we will campaign hard and we will start our campaigning early," and that the candidates would also hold rallies at courthouses in their respective districts. Guyot continued to raise support for the 1966 MFDP congressional candidates, and in late February departed for California to raise money for them. He and Monica Klein spent the rest of February and much of March in Berkeley. They raised funds for an April push for the candidates, as the slate of six MFDP members qualified with the Mississippi secretary of state on 4 April for the June primary. The MFDP had put itself in debt during the congressional challenge and now relied on donations from individuals and other liberal and labor organizations. The war in Vietnam also emerged as a competitor for funds and attention. The trip to UC Berkeley showed how much the Vietnam War now overshadowed the Black freedom struggle, at least outside the South. The *Daily Californian*, the official campus student newspaper, did not even mention Guyot and Klein's visit, instead giving heavy coverage to the now-daily antiwar rallies and attempts by the university administration to restrict them. The New Left did take notice of Guyot's visit, however. The *Berkeley Barb*, an underground newspaper launched in the Bay Area in 1965, advertised a radio interview that Guyot and Stokely Carmichael gave in late April to local radio station KPFA.[34] Still, the escalation of the war by the White House in 1965 and 1966 did not bode well for MFDP fundraising efforts, as the left-of-center political forces that had supported the party and SNCC during Freedom Summer now focused on protests against the draft.

The MFDP candidates each campaigned vigorously in their respective districts. The elections lacked the brutality of Freedom Summer but still attracted white violence. Three white men attacked Clifton Collier in the Neshoba County stockyard when he refused to leave a seating area designated for whites. The assault, which included one of the men striking Collier with brass knuckles, opened a gash in his head that required stitches. No one attacked Guyot in his Fifth District, representing Hattiesburg and the relatively placid Gulf Coast. Local whites treated him to some degree like any other candidate. He attended an AFL-CIO meeting in Hattiesburg and answered questions on his support for labor legislation, alongside Edward Khayat, a "moderate" Democrat from Jackson County challenging Colmer in the primary, as well as a token Republican challenger. Guyot fell eight votes shy of winning the union's endorsement. In May, he campaigned throughout the district, appearing in Columbia, Moss Point, and Gulfport.[35]

The hostility of AFL-CIO head Claude Ramsey to the MFDP likely killed potential labor support for Guyot. At the 24 April meeting in Jackson to celebrate the second anniversary of the MFDP's founding, Guyot reported that Aaron Henry and Ramsey were trying to form an alliance—a new COFO—to "kill" the MFDP. Guyot said that if they succeeded in their scheme, then the MFDP would sever all its ties with them and become "a completely independent party." Guyot, ever defiant, declared to the crowd that he "will fight until I die to stand up for the MFDP."[36]

Despite these clashes among the leaders of the labor and civil rights groups, the organizations still overlapped to a considerable degree, especially on the local level with voter registration. In the spring, Henry, Evers, Guyot, and Owen Brooks of the Delta Ministry met with Ramsey to form the Mississippi Voter Registration and Education League (MVREL), which dispersed funds from a $100,000 grant from the NAACP as well as additional funds from the AFL-CIO and other groups. The executive board included Henry, Guyot, Unita Blackwell, and two white labor leaders. The blue-Black alliance alarmed the segregationist media in the state enough that newspapers like the *Greenwood Commonwealth* gave it front-page coverage. Yet the league, given its liberal donation base, inevitably favored Evers and the NAACP over Guyot and the MFDP. The Evers-led voter registration drive in southwestern Mississippi received a disproportionate share of the funds, which Evers used to build his political fiefdom.[37]

The six Freedom Democrats ran on a progressive platform, indeed a "radical" one by Mississippi standards, as MFDP member Les McLemore put it. It included repealing the state's right-to-work law, enacting a federal jobs program to help agricultural workers displaced by mechanization, expanded aid to public education, legislative reapportionment, desegregation of all public facilities, and expansion of Medicare. FDP campaign literature outlined these social and political programs, as well as other proposals like lowering the voting age to eighteen and an end to the Vietnam War. The flyers also included a speech from Guyot where he spoke of the potential of the Black vote in the state, and of the MFDP's intention to acquire political power within the existing political process. "You cannot think of Mississippi politics if you register 250,000 Negroes in the same frame of reference that you thought of it when 6,000 Negroes were registered to vote . . . now we're saying that we, in Mississippi, want all the political power that political parties occupy in this country. We don't want any more, we don't want any less." With the exception of opposition to the war, all of these views matched the MFDP's support of the national Democratic Party's and President Johnson's Great Society legislation and opposed the avowed segregationist platform of the Democratic incumbents, who opposed any efforts to relieve Black poverty or expand political empowerment of the poor. Desegregation of public facilities and legislative reapportionment did not even represent "radical" views but instead merely called for compliance with the law, as the Civil Rights Act of 1964 rendered segregation illegal and the Supreme Court's recent rulings in *Baker v. Carr* and *Reynolds v. Sims* mandated reapportionment.[38]

Guyot's congressional race enlivened an otherwise dull Democratic primary contest. Khayat's challenge to Colmer forced the congressman to come home and campaign in the Fifth District, something the other Democratic incumbents did not do. Colmer attacked the MFDP in speeches on the House floor but did not mention it in his campaign appearances. Khayat positioned himself as a "moderate," attacking Colmer as a decrepit reactionary and Guyot as a radical. He avoided race-baiting the MFDP chairman but did attack his support for expanded welfare programs and his opposition to the Vietnam War. Guyot in turn drew on his labor background and spoke to the shipyard unions on the coast in his efforts to win white Democratic voters in the district.[39]

In early 1966, Guyot outlined the MFDP's political agenda in more detail in the journal *Freedomways*. The periodical, devoted to African American politics and culture, provided significant coverage of the civil rights movement. Guyot and Mike Thelwell, the director of the MFDP's Washington office, wrote an article for the spring issue titled "The Politics of Necessity and Survival in Mississippi." The two men opened by addressing the dismissive attitude the MFDP had received from mainstream politicians and the media, and even other civil rights leaders. They said that the political mainstream regarded the party as "an incongruous coalition of naïve idealists and unlettered sharecroppers without serious political intent or possibility—a kind of political oddity embodying simply a moral protest," or worse, a voice for "an intransigent and unreasonable 'militance.'" Rather, the authors said, "there is nothing inherently unique in the idea and operation of the MFDP. . . . Our purpose is gaining and utilizing the greatest possible measure of political power and influence in the interest of our constituency, *as that constituency expresses its interests*" (emphasis in original). Reflecting that desire to translate SNCC's ethos of participatory democracy into real political power, they said that "the entire community must be encouraged to participate in the decisions governing their lives and that vote must be used as an instrument of social change." Black Mississippians and the MFDP would need to take this power through the hard work of organizing themselves, as Guyot and Thelwell said they could not count on white liberals and the various components of the federal government to go against their own self-interests and aid Black Mississippians in any significant way.[40]

Guyot and Thelwell then laid out a political history of the Magnolia State, arguing that the state government made the subjugation of Blacks to white rule its central aim. This repressive nature originated under slavery with militias and slave patrols, and continued after emancipation with the Mississippi Plans of 1875 and 1890 to strip all power from the Black electorate, while at the same time preserving the majority-Black population as a servile labor force through denial of adequate funding for Black education and the use of debt sharecropping.[41]

The authors said that the state government enacted the new Mississippi Plan of "gradual genocide, the goal of which was to effect the dispersal or extinction of the Negro population." This included state funding for the White Citizens' Councils as a means to increase economic coercion of the Black population, such as cutting off welfare payments to unemployed sharecroppers. This plan worked in tandem with longer-term economic changes shaping the state, in particular the growing pool of surplus Black labor created by the mechanization of the cotton fields. State economic agencies, seeking to reduce the reliance upon Black labor, actively promoted mechanization. These factors all led to an organized eviction campaign waged by Delta planters against Black sharecropping families, of which 250 had already been expelled by early 1966.[42] Mechanization meant less dependence on unskilled labor, which fundamentally changed the nature of this new Mississippi Plan from earlier ones that had sought to deny rights but keep Black people as economic serfs. Now not even that was needed, and the white elite cast aside this thin veneer of planter paternalism in favor of a low-grade form of racial "cleansing."

The "genocidal" nature of this new plan, the authors argued, revealed itself in recent bills never before introduced in the state legislature. One bill authorized prison trustees to sterilize inmates after a third felony conviction, something that would heavily impact Black inmates disproportionately targeted by the state's police forces. It met external pressure and failed to pass. The second bill called for the imprisonment or sterilization of parents who had a second "illegitimate" child. The sterilization portion passed the House, but state senators removed it and reduced the "illegitimacy" penalty from a felony to a misdemeanor.[43] The mere consideration of these bills indicated a new direction in how the white power structure would deal with the state's Black population.

Guyot and Thelwell argued that due to the federalist structure of the government, in which governors approved and administered federal poverty programs—or, as they put it, "the right of the State government to conduct the affairs of its concentration camp as it sees fit," the only solution was to mobilize Black political power to wrest control from the segregationists. The Freedom Vote in 1963 represented the first step in that political mobilization, with the goal of awakening Black Mississippians statewide to their political rights guaranteed under the US Constitution but denied to them by the state government. The authors also included some self-criticism in how SNCC had administered the Freedom Vote, in the light of the bitter experience of Atlantic City. Reiterating their lack of faith in the federal government, they indicated that their initial plan to use the Freedom Vote to challenge the 1963 gubernatorial elections under the Civil Rights Act of 1957 and the older Reconstruction-era statutes failed, because they had naively thought that the federal government, once alerted to the injustice, would do the right thing—something Guyot and Thelwell likened to the misplaced faith that serfs and peasants in imperial Russia had put in the czar.[44] Black people needed to rely only on themselves, through the MFDP's own expression of Black Power through electoral politics, and this is why the MFDP waged the congressional challenge of 1965 and ran its slate for 1966.

The MFDP continued to use legal means to assist its electoral chances and political mobilizing as well—not just in the ongoing reapportionment suit but also in the fight against the remaining segregationist rules in the Mississippi Democratic Party. On 29 April the MFDP filed a suit challenging the constitutionality of the June primary on the grounds that state law required the primary candidates to support the principles of the state Democratic Party—in this case racial segregation—and support the nominees the party primary produced.

The MFDP also challenged rulings by the state attorney general disallowing those who had run in the primaries from filing and running as independents later. This legal challenge indicated that the MFDP knew it would lose the Democratic primary and looked ahead to an independent slate in November, an action that would further solidify its separateness from the state Democratic Party—and its separate course from the NAACP and AFL-CIO, whose leaders wanted to integrate the segregationist party. US District Court Judge Claude Clayton heard the suit from his bench in Oxford and dismissed it on 16 May.[45]

Less than a week later, the MFDP filed a second suit arguing that the ten-month period between the enactment of the Voting Rights Act and the June primary did not give enough time to allow "a substantial number of Negroes to register to vote." As evidence, the party indicated that the federal government had assigned registrars to less than 30 percent of the state's counties, and that those counties with registrars experienced higher registration increases than those without them. Judge Clayton, previously the city attorney for Tupelo and thus no friend of the movement, dismissed the suit on 17 May and a three-judge federal panel upheld his ruling days before the election.[46]

Shortly before the June primary elections, a new twist—or rather an old one—added to the election drama. James Meredith resurfaced in Mississippi. Since graduating from the University of Mississippi three years earlier, he largely stayed out of the movement, relocating to New York and enrolling in law school at Columbia University. He now decided, without consulting national or state civil rights leaders, to begin a one-man "March against Fear" from Memphis to Jackson to convince Black Mississippians that it was safe for them to register to vote. Although the number of Black voters registered under the Voting Rights Act had risen from 28,500 in 1964 to over 130,000 by April 1966, an uneven distribution across the state resulted from where the attorney general sent federal registrars. In some counties, like Panola on Meredith's planned march, white registration greatly outpaced Black registration, and the first Black candidates there faced insurmountable electoral odds.[47]

Meredith began his maverick 220-mile march on 4 June down Highway 51. On the second day, he crossed the Mississippi state line, accompanied by some reporters and friends. South of Hernando, a white man shot and injured him with a shotgun. Although the attack left Meredith only superficial wounds, the response—which included condemnation of the attack by President Johnson and the *New York Times*—guaranteed that Mississippi once again would receive the nation's unwanted attention.[48]

The MFDP showed little interest in Meredith's march, as its attention was focused on the primary elections. A. B. Britton, the chair of the Civil Rights

Committee in Jackson, visited Guyot before the march began and suggested he participate in it. Guyot refused, as he considered Meredith's march to be little more than a distraction. After Meredith's wounding, according to Ed King, MFDP members "cussed him coming and going," as they feared that the attack on Meredith would frighten Black voters away from the polls. MFDP attorneys then filed a motion to delay the primary elections, but the court denied the request.[49]

To no one's surprise, the MFDP lost all the elections the following day. With federal registrars in only fourteen counties, Black voter registration still lagged and white intimidation added to the Black electoral defeats. The candidates suffered high margins of defeat, with Ed King, the sole white candidate, running the closest race. He received 15,313 votes in the Third Congressional District around Jackson to John Bell Williams's 54,751. Guyot himself fared poorly, winning only 3,011 votes against the incumbent William Colmer, who won the primary with 40,762 votes, and Edward Khayat, who netted 24,193 votes. Not surprisingly, white Democrats who opposed Colmer chose the less conservative—and white—Khayat over Guyot, seen when Khayat received the AFL-CIO's endorsement over Guyot.[50]

The MFDP did well in some counties with heavy Black majorities. The most promising area for the potential power of the Black vote came from the Fourth District, where there was no Democratic incumbent. Prentiss Walker, the state's lone Republican congressman, was not running for reelection so he could instead challenge James Eastland for his Senate seat. The lack of a white Democratic incumbent in the primary election split the white vote and almost led to a runoff, as Rev. Clinton Collier of the MFDP won 7,404 votes, beating one of the three white candidates. Collier won Holmes County and came close in two other counties. G. V. Montgomery managed to edge out all his opponents and win the nomination, however.[51]

In the Senate primary, Rev. Clifton Whitley also did well, outpolling his white opponents in Claiborne and Jefferson Counties in southwest Mississippi. Yet the MFDP drew no solace from the results. The party's rival Charles Evers, with the help of the NAACP, organized these counties. The threat of white violence in the wake of Meredith's shooting appeared to have a detrimental effect as well. Although state voter registration rolls now listed 140,000 Black Mississippians—one-third of the total Black population of voting age—only about a fourth actually voted in the primary.[52]

The MFDP had little time to analyze the defeat. On 7 June, after the attempt on Meredith's life, national civil rights leaders held an emergency planning meeting at the Lorraine Motel in Memphis. There they decided to expand the march from Meredith's solo effort to one encompassing the major civil rights organizations. National civil rights leaders invited Guyot to the meeting, and he accepted, as did Holmes County MFDP chair Ralthus Hayes and local organizers Henry and Sue Lorenzi, whose county lay on the planned path of the Meredith March. Guyot reversed his earlier indifference to the March and now saw it as a way to expand voter registration and break the fear that Black Mississippians still had about voting. As he noted, "We instantly associated it with registering people," and he, Fannie Lou Hamer, R. L. T. Smith, and Clifton Whitley joined the other March leaders in Memphis.[53]

On 9 June, Guyot met with the other leaders at the Lorraine Hotel to plan the rest of the march. He brought a carload of MFDP members with him, and another group, workers from Collier's campaign in the Fourth District, joined them the next day from Lauderdale County. The march now became an extension of the MFDP's voter mobilization, with the goal of registering voters in some of the heavily Black counties along Highway 51.[54]

The presence of the MFDP and SNCC likely contributed to the change of attitude by Charles Evers. He had spoken in support of the march in Memphis at the first rally after the assassination attempt against Meredith, but now he reversed his position. He said that the Carmichael-penned manifesto that the organizations agreed to at the beginning of the march criticized President Johnson too severely. The NAACP and Urban League had already refused to participate in the march over the tone of the manifesto, and now Evers joined them and criticized the MFDP as Black separatists.[55]

Evers cannily raised his national profile among white liberals with his position, and mended his contentious relationship with Roy Wilkins of the NAACP. Wilkins had entertained firing Evers over his own public statements on armed self-defense and for endorsing political candidates, both actions contrary to NAACP policy. In addition to expanding his power base in the wake of the Natchez boycott, Evers enriched himself personally by aiming Black boycotts at his business competitors. He did little to conceal his self-interest from his rivals, once telling Guyot that he was "in this to make money," while Guyot was "in this to help people."[56]

Evers's stance underscored the tensons in the Meredith March among the various civil rights organizations, ones building since Atlantic City and Selma. While the NAACP considered Meredith's march too radical, many SNCC activists thought that Martin Luther King Jr., the most prominent figure in the march, exerted an unwanted conservative influence on the events. King and Carmichael had differences over nonviolence and even disagreed publicly on the march, but they also shared many goals. Other SNCC activists like Cleveland Sellers also developed a respect for King during the march, despite the public tensions.[57]

The presence of luminaries like Dr. King and the fiery rhetoric of Stokely Carmichael meant that Guyot and the MFDP largely labored in their shadows during the Meredith March. Local newspapers, when they covered the march, focused on the celebrity leaders. The *Greenwood Commonwealth* ran a front-page editorial that compared King to Joseph Stalin and Mao Zedong and called on the residents of Leflore County to ignore the march. The *Neshoba Democrat* also referenced King and asked whites to avoid the marchers, "who will go to any means to provoke incidents which the national press . . . will pick up to beat us over the heads with." The newspapers made little or no mention of the voter registration efforts, usually only to defend their own local records regarding Black access to voter registration.[58]

On 15 June, the marchers headed away from the original Highway 51 route and into the Delta to register and mobilize potential voters. James Meredith returned to the spotlight by holding a press conference in Pleasantsville, New York, with Guyot at his side. Meredith fed into the tensions within the movement by criticizing both the NAACP and the Johnson administration, and paradoxically said that the march was neither a "nonviolence demonstration" nor "an arena for experimentation in Black nationalism." He also expressed his support for the MFDP.[59]

MFDP members represented the organization during Guyot's brief absence. During the first week of the march, all the national leaders there took periods of absence to tend to other matters. The MFDP and Delta Ministry directed voter registration efforts in communities along the route of the march and registered more than 1,300 Black people in Grenada.[60]

The simmering tensions in the march erupted into the open in Greenwood, the next stop after Grenada as the march left Highway 51. Carmichael, after police arrested and then released him on bail for defying a city order regarding the marchers' pitching tents on public property, gave the famous rallying cry that defined him and his involvement in the movement. Before 600 supporters, he shouted, "We want Black power!" five times, with the crowd echoing his cry. As Carmichael biographer Peniel Joseph put it, his speech "instantly transformed the aesthetics of the Black freedom struggle and forever altered the course of the modern civil rights movement."[61]

The speech received nationwide attention due to the press following the march, and the coverage thrust Carmichael into the forefront of white media attention. The militant tone and anger of the speech frightened white people, and the phrase "Black Power" quickly overshadowed the work on voter registration. The phrase quickly became associated, thanks to biased media coverage rather than any actions by Black activists, with Black violence against white people.

It was not a well-defined phrase, and it came to represent the alienation SNCC activists felt from white liberals and integration into white society in general. This slogan clashed with the vision of Martin Luther King Jr., the SCLC, and NAACP, one of nonviolent direct action and an integrated society where Black people had full political participation.[62]

Yet "Black Power" attracted people on the Meredith March, and not just as a means to scare white people. Carmichael himself expressed frustration with media distortion of the phrase toward antiwhite sentiment and away from Black autonomy, his prime understanding of the slogan. And the MFDP liked the phrase as well. The MFDP represented the moderate integrationist vision of Black political participation in the electoral process, but the almost all-Black composition of the party meant it also symbolized Black self-reliance and independent Black control. Guyot and Thelwell's own writings in *Freedomways* spoke of the MFDP's efforts to create an independent Black political base in Mississippi. Guyot and Carmichael were not always synchronized in what Black power should look like, however. Guyot's commitment to the MFDP angered Carmichael and other SNCC activists, who wanted the Meredith March to be completely independent of party politics. These tensions carried over into the march, as Guyot remained on SNCC's staff.[63]

Guyot expressed his own vision of Black power during the Meredith March. He spoke at Jackson on 26 June at the end of the march, where he tapped into the growing militant mood normally associated with Carmichael. Guyot addressed the right of Black self-determination, and first mentioned "Black Power." His speech attacked neocolonialism and white supremacy as national issues that needed to be addressed and brought cheers from the crowd, prompting a nervous CBS to break away from his speech. Guyot, despite his clashes with Carmichael over the importance of electoral politics in Mississippi, reconciled the right of Black Mississippians to control their own political destiny with the fiery, often imprecise rhetoric that made the Meredith March famous.[64]

Even in the most controversial area of Black Power, the endorsement of armed self-defense, the MFDP expressed some support. All of the Meredith March activists had benefited from the protection of the Deacons for Defense, the armed self-defense group that originated in Louisiana. The Deacons had requested to join the march, and Carmichael pushed for their inclusion, persuading a reluctant King. The Deacons provided armed protection during the actual marching and while participants camped at night, protection needed since the federal and state governments refused to provide adequate security. The MFDP benefited directly from the presence of armed participants when Klansmen attacked the FDP headquarters in Philadelphia during the march.

Armed movement activists repulsed with gunfire four raids on the headquarters on 21 June, wounding at least one of the white assailants. And on 22 June, armed Blacks shot and wounded a white man in a group that attacked the Canton FDP office.[65]

The MFDP had already showed its transition toward an endorsement of armed self-defense by rejecting the pure nonviolence stance it had taken in Natchez the previous year. A campaign flyer for the 1966 congressional candidates depicted an illustration of a Black man holding a shotgun, with the image displayed directly above the party's name. The MFDP released the flyer in the spring, well before the Meredith March. Combined with the vigorous armed self-defense that members of the Deacons, SNCC, and the MFDP advocated, many of the rank-and-file members clearly did not embrace pure nonviolence. Although Guyot did not comment on these matters, the circulation of the campaign material indicated he at least tacitly accepted it. In this area he echoed the attitudes of Martin Luther King Jr., who expressed concerns about the Deacons but did not demand a strict adherence to nonviolence by participants in the march.[66]

Guyot's silence suggests that his attitudes shifted after his speech at the Bright Star Baptist Church that past December. Despite uttering "Black Power" at the Jackson rally, he expressed ambivalence about the slogan, even if he supported the idea of independent Black political power. Although Black Power resonated somewhat with an almost entirely Black political party like the MFDP, the lack of coherence in the new message went against the idea of a well-organized and disciplined party. Guyot said that after the 'Black Power' slogan gained steam, "everything was torn asunder in Mississippi. Even though they caused a stir, Black power zealots had difficulty organizing around a slogan."[67]

The Vietnam War increasingly consumed SNCC and Stokely Carmichael, as he urged young Black men by the summer of 1966 to refuse induction into military, a year after the MFDP flap over draft resistance.[68] Meanwhile, the MFDP labored at the grassroots to create Black political power, away from the attention-grabbing headlines of Vietnam and Black Power that became indelibly identified with SNCC. The MFDP focus on politics also contributed to further estrangement between SNCC and the MFDP, as the clash between a hierarchical organization versus the decentralized model that had emerged at Waveland in December 1964 continued. Carmichael came to increasingly personify and embody SNCC, since his fame after the Meredith March created a major demand for him as a speaker. His lecture and speaking fees became SNCC's main source of income, but local projects fell into disarray due to the lack of internal organization and discipline, and at an October 1966 meeting in Knoxville, members forced Carmichael to grant more control to the organization's central committee. Cleveland Sellers visited SNCC offices in Mississippi in the summer of 1966 and saw the obvious lack of a significant SNCC presence. He found few volunteers carrying out their duties, and he controversially ordered the Holly Springs office closed for using white volunteers on the staff. The director of the program countered that he had to use white volunteers since SNCC did not provide funds to hire Black staffers. By October, SNCC workers in Mississippi had no contact with the Atlanta office. Guyot himself charged that since SNCC now provided little support for the MFDP, it was necessary for the party to chart a separate course, something SNCC could not contest. Still, the problems with SNCC resembled a squabble between family members rather than a final divorce. At the Knoxville meeting, some organizers told the SNCC central committee that Guyot and the MFDP were open to SNCC's renewing its involvement in Mississippi, although SNCC never did recommit due to its internal problems.[69] These problems showed that the earlier complaints by Cleveland Sellers and James Foreman rang true when they unsuccessfully pushed SNCC to implement tighter control and discipline through a hierarchal structure. SNCC's growing dissolution, and specifically the lack of authority in the organization, made the MFDP's separate course into electoral politics necessary for it to have any relevance.

Guyot's leadership style balanced local grassroots organizing against the need for a certain amount of centralization to effectively run a political party. As early as the summer of 1965, white volunteers caught up in the "freedom high" leadership style of Bob Moses had derided Guyot as a political boss. Some volunteers had brought these criticisms to the state convention in 1965, criticizing the MFDP board for accepting Guyot's proposals without much discussion or debate. Of course, the party held the convention in the middle of the congressional challenge, and the MFDP ran it as a political convention, not a grassroots event organized by local FDPs.[70] Guyot's leadership never reached the autocratic and self-aggrandizing levels of Charles Evers's machine in southwestern Mississippi, making the volunteers' charges of his "bossism" a bit unfair.

Guyot maintained ties and communications with local FDPs, despite the criticism of the party's top-down nature. The Holmes County FDP, through its organizers Henry Lorenzi, a white activist, and Ralthus Hayes, a Black organizer, kept in regular communication with Guyot. By 1966 Guyot also maintained links with Howard Taft Bailey and Walter Bruce, two other local leaders in the county. Sue Lorenzi, Henry's wife, said that local leaders, especially Henry, would "inform Guyot of Holmes [sic] plans and needs and get advice and suggestions." Guyot himself said that "there was nothing like Holmes County's political organization in all of Mississippi; in fact there was nothing like it in the South." He credited much of this to the Lorenzis and their organizing ability.[71] When the Holmes County FDP decided to run an all-Black slate in the 1966 Democratic primary elections, Guyot gave his approval and did not interfere, despite the MFDP's preference for independent candidacies. As Sue Lorenzi recalled, "No party line was handed down; the decision to run as Democrats or as Independents was ultimately up to the community and the beat organizations."[72]

The Meredith March had added 4,000 new Black voters to the rolls in Mississippi, and on 13 July the federal district court in Jackson ruled in favor of the MFDP in its apportionment suit, further emboldening the party. Judge J. P. Coleman ordered the legislature to reapportion its legislative seats in accordance with the Supreme Court's rulings in *Baker v. Carr* and *Reynolds v. Sims*. The party also prepared for its next electoral campaign, a three-candidate independent slate in the November midterm elections chosen at a statewide meeting. They ran two of the June primary candidates—Clifton Whitley for Senate, against James Eastland, and Dock Drummond for the First District, both reprising their earlier campaigns. Emma Sanders, a Black activist and housewife from Jackson, replaced Ed King as the candidate in the Third District. Movement historian John Dittmer called her nomination, which removed the only white candidate from the slate, an unofficial "FDP nod in the direction of Black power." Or as MFDP historian Michael Sistrom put it, "The Freedom Party's political program for 1966 was essentially Black Power in practice, but without the violent, revolutionary, and separatist bent that the slogan took elsewhere in the country in the later 1960s." According to MFDP member Les McLemore, the FDP Executive Committee chose Sanders due to rumors that her opponent, John Bell Williams, planned to resign after the election due to poor health, which meant that if Sanders placed second in the vote count, she would automatically become the elected representative under the law.[73]

To increase their odds, the MFDP filed suit on 19 September against the state to extend the registration period, challenging a state law that did not allow anyone registered after 7 July to vote in the general election. They did so on the grounds that the July date differed from the 23 September cutoff date used by federal registrars. The federal district court rejected the MFDP's request for a temporary injunction to halt enforcement of the law. The State Election Commission also refused to certify the three candidates as independents, which led Guyot to file a federal suit against the commission. On 22 October, only days before the election, the federal court ordered the three candidates on the ballot, suspending a 1966 state law the state had used to exclude the independent candidates.[74]

Clifton Whitley opened his fall campaign with attacks on both Eastland and the Republican nominee, Representative Prentiss Walker, as candidates who "tried to out do one another in racism." Whitley ran on a job-creation platform aimed at sharecroppers laid off by the increasing mechanization of the Delta cotton plantations. He also pledged his support for the Child Development Group of Mississippi (CDGM), promising to consistently fund the antipoverty agency. All three FDP candidates ran on a pro-desegregation, pro–War on Poverty platform, and, in a nod to the growing opposition to the Vietnam War, a pledge to change the nation's "militaristic foreign policy."[75]

Walker gave Black Mississippians little incentive to vote for him or the newly emerged state GOP, echoing the full-throated racism of James Eastland. Eastland charged that Walker had appointed a Black Mississippian to the Air Force Academy, to which Walker responded by declaring that he did not know the man was Black when he made the recommendation. Walker in turn attacked the confirmation of Robert Weaver as the first Black US cabinet secretary, and Clarke Reed, head of the Republican State Executive Committee, called the MFDP "racist" and charged that national Democrats had pressured the MFDP to not run candidates against the state Democrats to maintain party unity. The rhetoric prompted the *Delta Democrat-Times* to comment that "neither party has any reason for pride."[76]

While the MFDP ran candidates for high-profile federal races, its NAACP rival focused on local and county ones. R. L. Whitaker, a Black minister, announced his candidacy for justice of the peace in Holmes County in a 27 September special election. Several other Black candidates emerged for the November election, all of them for school board positions in Holmes, Jefferson, Claiborne, and Wilkinson Counties, the last three counties being the center of Charles Evers's voter registration drive.[77]

Evers also made his opposition to the MFDP very clear in the press, in an apparent effort to increase his palatability to whites. In a favorable interview with the national magazine *The Reporter*, Evers criticized Stokely Carmichael and other Black Power advocates as advocating "Black supremacy." He also threw barbs at the MFDP. He explained away his support for the MFDP candidates in the June primary, describing them as obviously more palatable to Black voters than the white segregationist Democrats. He stressed that this was not a sign he supported the party or its use of independent candidacies, and he did not welcome MFDP organizing in his power base. "We're on the right road, and we're not going to let them in here," he said. "We're not going on some wild-goose chase trying to create a third party." To further distance himself from any charges that he wanted an all-Black government, he expressed his support for the state's biracial Young Democrats. As a final shaft to the MFDP, Evers endorsed Republican Prentiss Walker in the general election over Whitley. While he indicated this was because he felt Walker had a better chance of winning the race than Whitley, his dislike of the MFDP clearly played a role in his public backing of an archsegregationist.[78]

Some white Democrats apparently felt the MFDP congressional candidates posed a threat, especially with the presence of a GOP candidate adding to the risk of the white vote being split. Guyot claimed that he rejected a bribe from a Democratic state legislator to keep the three candidates off the November ballot. The campaigns of the three candidates also meant that in heavily Black counties, the MFDP forced white Democrats for the first time to solicit Black votes.[79]

Yet none of these developments could offset the pessimism that overtook the MFDP late in the election. The federal courts rejected the MFDP's urging to overturn the state legislature's division of the Delta into three separate congressional districts, a blow to MFDP organizing efforts in that region. And the MFDP continued to struggle financially. According to informants within the party, Guyot considered a merger with the SCLC due to the MFDP's lack of financial resources. The gloom really took hold during a meeting in late October, which resulted from Fannie Lou Hamer's calling fifty Mississippi activists to Jackson for a strategy meeting. At the meeting, Ed King conceded the effectiveness of the NAACP's top-down organizing strategy, since the political machine Evers created could deliver on federal programs and patronage. The MFDP could not compete with the NAACP, as it was losing members and could not even pay an office staff. The minutes described the congressional races as "not organized and may hurt the movement by showing its weaknesses." The best impact the MFDP could have would be on local elections in 1967, effectively copying the NAACP strategy. As for November, the party told activists to make their own decisions on whether or not to work on the elections.[80]

The MFDP had already diverted energies to other issues, such as the ongoing fight to preserve federal funding for the CDGM. On 8 October Guyot attended a rally in Jackson where Hamer spoke and demanded that the OEO restore funding to the CDGM. Guyot spoke before the crowd of 3,500 and said that the MFDP would support the CDGM with boycotts and picketing if it would help secure the funds. At a 21 October meeting, CDGM officials voted to accept a compromise that gave the antipoverty group less funds. When Guyot, Hunter Morey, and others spoke out against this "sellout," the officials present outvoted them, prompting the MFDP members to walk out in protest.[81]

The 8 November election saw a high Black voter turnout due to presence of thirteen MFDP- and NAACP-backed candidates on the ballot, but it still disappointed. All three MFDP congressional candidates lost resoundingly, and the five white Democrats won their races easily. In the Senate race, Evers's endorsement of Walker clearly undercut Whitley, as Black voters gave Walker a majority in Claiborne and Jefferson Counties, and almost delivered Wilkinson County to him. The shift to Walker from counties that had solidly supported Whitley in June showed the effective political control Evers enjoyed through his machine in the southwestern river counties. By contrast, MFDP stronghold Holmes County could not deliver enough Black votes to keep the county from going to Eastland, who won reelection. The only Black victory that year came in Jefferson County, where Robert Williams, an NAACP member, won an election in a majority-Black ward to the county board of education. The fact that Williams ran as an independent—the strategy that Evers had explicitly rejected—but belonged to the NAACP, not the MFDP—surely added another bitter dose to the MFDP's electoral medicine.[82]

John Dittmer called 1966 "a frustrating year" for the MFDP, with no electoral victories and little to show from the Meredith March and its activists' hard work registering voters. In its rivalry with the NAACP and Evers, the latter beat the MFDP in delivering and turning out Black voters. By 1966 Evers set up five districts in Jefferson and Claiborne Counties, each with a chairman who each had ten workers to canvass on Election Day and five cars to transport voters to the polls. His organization even enlisted Black ministers and teachers to rally and educate potential voters.[83] The MFDP, focused on high-profile and ultimately symbolic races, had not developed any such organization and likely would have faced significant resistance from some of its volunteers had it tried to do so.

In a quiet nod to the NAACP's tactics and successes, the MFDP went into 1967 with a new focus on local races. The election that became the focal point of MFDP efforts to win a sorely needed victory originated with a lawsuit filed by Fannie Lou Hamer. The Federal District Court in Oxford had ruled in April 1965 that Cecil Campbell, the registrar of Sunflower County, had systematically denied Black residents their right to vote. The court ordered a one-year "freeze" on these practices to allow sufficient numbers of Blacks to register. However, local officials successfully cited state laws regarding payment of poll taxes and early registration to shut these new voters out of the June 1965 municipal elections. In response, Hamer and four Black plaintiffs filed a class-action lawsuit on 23 April 1965 seeking to halt elections in six municipalities in Sunflower County. On 11 March 1966, a three-judge panel of the Fifth Circuit Court of Appeals ruled in favor of the plaintiffs but pared the ruling down to ordering new elections only in Sunflower City and Moorhead. The state of Mississippi appealed to the Supreme Court, which dismissed its claim in October, paving the way for the MFDP to run in the 1967 municipal elections.[84]

The MFDP also broadened its focus outside Sunflower County. Guyot planned races in Black-majority Delta counties in the 1967 November elections. A. L. Hopkins, an investigator with the SSC, spoke with Guyot as he visited Canton in the wake of the November 1966 election and then shadowed him as he traveled to Mileston, site of a Freedom House and headquarters for MFDP activities in Holmes County. Hopkins learned from informants that Guyot helped local leaders select a slate of Black candidates to run for county offices in 1967. The MFDP faced critical shortages of both material and manpower by the end of 1966, leaving it in poor shape to wage a campaign. Guyot communicated with the contacts he had made during his visit to Oberlin College. Bill Sherzer, chairman of Oberlin Action for Civil Rights, said that Guyot had told him that the party preferred Black volunteers but that "there is now a desperate need for workers of any color."[85]

At the same time the party organized for the 1967 elections, the MFDP continued to resist the Black nationalism that had overtaken SNCC. SNCC's Atlanta Project staff, under the direction of Bill Ware, pushed for the exclusion of whites from the organization. Ware, a native Mississippian who embraced Pan-Africanism after working for the Peace Corps in Ghana, led Black separatists in an increasingly militant and antiwhite direction, which included sharp criticism of Blacks in SNCC who did not share their views. At a December 1966 meeting in New York, Ware clashed with Carmichael, who argued that SNCC needed white financial support and white volunteers. Fannie Lou Hamer attended the meeting and opposed the expulsion of the remaining white members, which invited ridicule from the Atlanta separatists, who said that she "was no longer relevant." With most of the staff members abstaining, the SNCC members narrowly voted to expel the white members, but only after several days of bitter debate.[86]

Guyot shared Hamer's commitment to interracialism as SNCC abandoned it. To him, the antiwhite rhetoric of Ware and the Atlanta separatists would make the MFDP unpalatable. He said that "you couldn't sell it to Miss Jones, who's a Baptist lady, and believes in the Bible, which states that everyone should be treated equally." The party had to respect the deeply religious feelings of Black Mississippians, and he insisted that "you can't sell an anti-white thing to churches." In Sunflower County, Guyot tried to find local whites to run an integrated slate for the municipal elections, but he could not find any who would run with Black candidates. Black Power to the MFDP meant Black political and economic empowerment, broadly defined in a way to be used in elections, boycotts, and voter registration campaigns. The MFDP reflected that ethos in its close relationship with the integrated Delta Ministry, which fielded twenty-six staff members under the direction of Owen Brooks, a Black activist who focused on economic issues.[87]

Of course, Guyot also had deeply personal reasons for rejecting the separatists. As the SSC obsessively noted, Guyot lived with Monica Klein in a Jackson apartment. SNCC members radicalized by Black separatism ended their friendships and relationships with whites, no matter how intimate. Julius Lester, who played a key role in pushing SNCC toward militancy, left his white wife when he joined SNCC. But in 1967, Guyot went the opposite route, marrying Monica that year during a visit to Washington, DC.[88] Although the MFDP struggled to find white supporters among Mississippi's deeply racist white population, Guyot still led the party on both a professional and personal level toward the dream of an interracial democracy.

In addition to rejecting Black-only organizations, Guyot also rejected the sexist and misogynistic rhetoric and attitudes of some Black Power groups. Guyot worked extensively with women in SNCC and the MFDP, and he confessed that Ella Baker disabused him of notions that men should lead and women follow. As Steve Estes has noted, even pre–Black Power civil rights groups embraced "masculinism," a strategy that couched racial uplift with the idea that Black men headed households and worked as the primary breadwinners of their families, and also operated as the main authority over women and children—an idea they shared with white Americans. This attitude included rhetoric that feminized opponents, linking them to weakness. This masculinist rhetoric is best remembered as part of the ideology of groups like the Black Panther Party, but Guyot would on occasion use strongly gendered language as well, such as his reaction to the Sunflower County elections. Organizations like SNCC experienced this sexism, as some women volunteers protested male leaders' assigning them to secretarial tasks before and during Freedom Summer, and leaders often assigned women to teaching in Freedom Schools while men did the dangerous, "macho" work of voter canvassing and field organizing. This occurred even though SNCC organizers largely avoided masculinist rhetoric when recruiting volunteers. These kinds of attitudes led SNCC members Casey Hayden and Mary King to issue their famous *A Kind of Memo* on sexism, which became an influential document in the women's liberation movement that emerged in the late 1960s.[89]

Although the MFDP did apparently nod to "electability" and gender attitudes by nominating an all-male slate in 1966, the organization had a high level of participation by women, including runs for political office. Guyot himself worked extensively with women in leadership roles, including Hamer and others. Victoria Gray Adams's journal, for example, showed frequent communication and collaboration with him when they worked in Hattiesburg in 1963 and 1964.[90] The masculinist rhetoric and attitudes of some Black Power groups did not mesh with the participatory democracy ethos that Guyot and the MFDP carried over from their SNCC origins, a philosophy that included women's empowerment.

Other than his wife Monica, Guyot's immediate family did not play any active role in the civil rights movement. That changed at least briefly in February 1968, when the SSC reported that his younger brother, Jules Guyot, appeared in Jackson and Mt. Beulah. Aside from the February 1968 appearances, Jules Guyot—referred to as "Jewel" and "Juel" by the state director—does not appear in the state agency's records. In his numerous oral interviews given over the course of his life, Guyot did not mention his sibling's involvement in the civil rights struggle, and typically only discussed his brothers when he recalled his childhood.[91]

The tensions between SNCC and its growing racial nationalism and the political organizing of the MFDP created problems within the Mississippi movement, exacerbated by Guyot's earlier dismissal of the organization. In June 1967, SNCC sent ten Black workers into Holmes County, none of them native Mississippians. They resented the presence of Henry and Sue Lorenzi, who were white northern organizers for the county FDP. Henry Lorenzi, according to Guyot, wisely avoided engaging or getting in conflict with the "SNCC guys," as they were known. He interacted with Edgar Love, a local Black organizer, and Love's regard for and consulting of Lorenzi for advice drew the resentment of the SNCC volunteers, who saw Love as a puppet of Lorenzi's. To avoid confrontation, local Black MFDP leaders Walter Bruce and Ralthus Hayes became the points of contact for the SNCC men and the local FDP. Adding to the problems was the lack of respect and deference the "SNCC guys" showed to local Black leadership, such as calling for a boycott of white businesses in Durant without talking to local leader Bruce first. Despite the tensions, the county FDP managed to avoid a racial disturbance as it organized for the 1967 county elections. As Guyot recalled, "They [the SNCC members] were creatively contained. . . . Thank God they didn't cause any more trouble than they caused."[92]

The NAACP also saw 1967 as a promising year for Black political empowerment. That March, Evers called a meeting of the state's civil rights organizations and Black leaders to create a political committee that could unite and expand the Black electorate. Evers now sounded a note of unity, as he invited the MFDP,

SNCC, CORE, and the Delta Ministry, despite his past differences with them. The meeting led to the creation of a fifteen-member executive committee to coordinate Black political activity and voter registration statewide.[93]

The main source of external support for the MFDP came from outside the state, however. After the April 1966 ruling in *Hamer v. Campbell*, prominent civil rights supporters established the National Committee for Free Elections in Sunflower. Members included Stokely Carmichael, Julian Bond, Senator Eugene McCarthy (D-MN), Dick Gregory, and John Kenneth Galbraith. Eleanor Holmes Norton, who had played a key role in saving Guyot from death in the Winona city jail, coordinated the committee from New York City with Sandra Nystrom, a fellow former SNCC worker. McLemore called the committee "perhaps the best organized political campaign conducted in the Deep South." Aside from visits by some of the members, the committee also raised money for the campaign and conducted political workshops leading up to the election. All told, the committee spent almost $14,000 on the Sunflower elections, with over $8,000 going directly into election funds.[94]

The MFDP needed all the help it could get in Sunflower County. Home of Senator James Eastland's 5,800-acre plantation and the birthplace of the White Citizens' Councils, the county included some of the worst conditions of the Delta. In 1967, the county had 70 percent Black unemployment, and 40 percent subsisted on public relief. Of those employed, wages averaged $2.50 a day as a domestic, or thirty cents an hour for a laborer in the cotton fields. The county fared no better with education levels. Among its 67.8 percent Black population, students completed an average of seven years of school. The MFDP had to conduct sessions instructing locals on how to recognize the MFDP candidates due to the widespread illiteracy.[95]

With no whites willing to join the MFDP campaign, Guyot called in March for a "Black primary" in Sunflower County. The MFDP ran an all-Black slate, but because of white racism, not Black separatism. The MFDP contested all the races in the primary except for one, the Sunflower City mayoral race. Out of 154 Black votes cast, the MFDP selected a mayoral candidate and five aldermen candidates, a slate equally split between men and women. Reflecting the growing influence of youth activism in the county, young men headed both town slates. Otis Brown Jr., the twenty-one-year-old chairman of the Sunflower County FDP, headed the ticket. The former SNCC field secretary had attended the local Freedom Schools. Although Brown was young, Guyot called him "charismatic," "fearless," and a "true believer." In Moorhead, local delegates selected Jimmy Lee Douglass, a twenty-two-year-old employee at a grocery chain, to run for mayor with an all-male alderman slate.[96]

Guyot spent much of March and April in Sunflower County helping with the campaigns, but he also continued to raise funds and publicity out of state, such as when he spoke at a forum at Catholic University in Washington, DC. There he reminded the audience of the important of the party's SNCC-derived ethos. Instead of being the initiators of the change, he said, "the most important thing is to find out who the people look to when they have problems and approach this person with your program." He returned to the state after this trip, and on 14 April the MFDP held a convention at Baptist Grove Church in Sunflower City. Guyot sent a letter of invitation to all the candidates—white and Black—to attend and speak to the voters. Not surprisingly, the white candidates did not attend, but a crowd of 300 heard from the Black candidates, as well as from other speakers. Fannie Lou Hamer struck the defiant tone of the meeting when she declared that "you used to shoot us and we'd be singing. Now you shoot one, and 2,000 show up. . . . [The] FDP is alive, and we're going to be active all over this state."[97]

Sunflower City's election looked more promising for the MFDP, as there were 185 Blacks registered to 154 whites. In Moorhead, white registration barely outpaced Black with 418 whites registered to 412 Blacks registered, impossible odds to overcome given white refusal to support the MFDP. Reflecting the party's bottom-up ethos, the candidates wrote their own platforms focusing on local issues, and the MFDP executive committee dictated nothing to them. Brown, for example, promised to impose a youth curfew, seek economic development, and improve municipal services and antipoverty programs. Brown also tried to appeal to more conservative African Americans put off by Black Power. He admitted that Stokely Carmichael was a friend of his but that he "has his ideas and I have mine. . . . If we elect Blacks in Sunflower, I won't consider myself part of Black power." He also pledged to integrate the city departments, not make them all-Black. Even Lela Brooks, a candidate for alderman whom Les McLemore described as "the most vocal and perhaps militant" of the candidates, said that "we want our people to represent us, and we feel it wouldn't be equal if we didn't let the whites be represented by their own people."[98]

As a sign of how much this election mattered to the MFDP, the Executive Committee held the party's state convention on 16 April in Sunflower's community center. The candidates spoke at the convention, as did Guyot, Hamer, Whitley, and two attorneys, Morton Stavis, a lawyer for the MFDP, and Percy Sutton, who had served as Malcolm X's legal counsel. The MFDP ran a traditional election campaign, distributing flyers and holding mass meetings in local churches. It also held meetings in private homes for candidates to speak to supporters. This groundwork continued the previous year's work since the federal court ruling, as the party spent over $2,800 on a voter registration drive in the county the previous autumn, running a deficit in the process.[99]

Guyot expressed his hope that the Sunflower elections would energize Black political power throughout Mississippi. He told people at a rally for the candidates, "Look, if they can do it in the little town[s], we can do it here." If nothing else, the elections forced the white power structure in Sunflower City to finally solicit Black voters. W. L. Patterson, the incumbent mayor, publicly admitted as much and ran on his record, claiming that he had provided services to the town's Black citizens. The white candidates sent mailers to Black voters accusing the MFDP of harassing Black citizens and promised to "protect" them with the State Highway Patrol on Election Day, an unsubtle effort at intimidation. One of their political fliers attempted to link the MFDP to Black Power, calling them "racial agitators" and warning of dire economic consequences if the MFDP slate won. The flyer urged them to "vote for a sensible, sane government." The *Jackson Advocate*, as the mouthpiece of Black conservatism in the state, also criticized the MFDP candidates, likening them to Reconstruction-era carpetbaggers.[100]

As the flier's language indicated, whites in Sunflower used fear as their major tactic to hold onto power. But other factors hampered the MFDP. The state office only reported $800 in income during the summer of 1967, which meant that it relied on the Delta Ministry to do all of the voter registration and candidate support during the election. The MFDP operated a network of precinct and block captains in the county, who provided vital election information to Black voters. The federal government gave no help either, refusing to send registrars to avoid offending James Eastland in his home county, even though neighboring Bolivar and Leflore Counties had had them for months. This meant that that out of 14,000 African American residents of voting age, only 4,000 were registered. US attorney general Ramsey Clark finally sent observers, but not registrars, to the two towns just days before the election.[101]

The intimidation efforts continued on the day of the election. The chief of police in Sunflower stationed himself at the entrance to the courthouse—ostensibly to "greet" each voter—so every Black voter had to pass him as he or she entered and left the building. A white man took a photograph of each Black voter as well. The election officials also only allowed local whites to act as assistants to illiterate Black voters, which raised questions of them marking the ballots against the voter's wishes. The MFDP accused the white election commissioners of breaking a promise they gave to allow Joseph Harris, the election manager for the MFDP candidates, to work as one of the three election officials who would be able to assist illiterate voters. The city denied there was any such agreement, and said they rejected Harris since federal observers had arrived. As the Delta Ministry later reported, the presence of whites at the polls intimidated some first-time Black voters into voting for the white candidates.[102]

On Election Day, the MFDP candidates decisively lost. While the defeat in Moorhead was to be expected, the candidates also lost in Sunflower City. Otis Brown received the most votes of the defeated candidates—121 to Patterson's 190. But that was still less than all the other white candidates. In Sunflower, 38 ballots were thrown out and 27 Black voters were "assisted" by local whites in marking their ballots. That margin of 65 votes meant that there was enough of a statistical margin to call into question a couple of the aldermanic races—but not all of them.[103]

Clearly, some Black voters had voted for the white candidates, as the recorded Black voter turnout was twenty votes higher than white turnout. MFDP member Charles McLaurin charged that some white Democrats approached Black voters and urged them to stay loyal to the state party and had given them bribes to secure that loyalty. White charges that MFDP candidates lacked the qualifications for public office likely swayed some Black voters. Whatever the reason, as Rachel Reinhard noted in her study of the MFDP, "Black voters, courted by movement and establishment candidates, made personal decisions about which candidate could best meet their needs. That candidate was not always Black."[104]

Fear, or what she aptly called "the well-honed survival skills of Delta residents," still hampered the MFDP. Black people in the Delta, having lived under white terror and economic and physical coercion for their entire lives, did not vote strictly along racial lines. Guyot later recalled that "you can teach people how to organize, how to think, how to use information, but you can't teach courage." Or, as Les McLemore put it, "The Blacks of Sunflower and Moorhead were not apathetic; rather they were victims of fear and the caste system."[105]

Not surprisingly, the MFDP felt betrayed, and Guyot best expressed that feeling with bitter and emotional statements after the results. "We've been raped," he exclaimed, "and our dear white brother wasn't the only rapist." Lela Mae Brooks agreed, saying that "people split their tickets. Colored folks and white folks voted white folks. But white folks didn't vote for colored folks." Still, she expressed optimism, declaring, "We haven't lost. We've just started." The loss seemed to cement Guyot's steering the MFDP toward an independent course. "We've got to line up a Black slate for Sunflower County, to run as independents—and stay the hell out of the goddamn Democratic primaries," he told a large rally in Sunflower after the election. Reporters ran the quote slightly differently in another newspaper, New York's radical *National Guardian*, as well as in the Freedom Information Service. According to the reporter, Guyot said that "people in the Delta have got to decide how they're going to fight for the first time in their lives. We are going to run a complete slate of Black candidates in November. And we'll stay the hell out of the goddamn Democratic Party."[106]

Guyot, remembering his audience, then said he hoped he didn't offend anyone and knew "we're all very religious people," but he wanted them to understand what "the Democratic Party and the Republican Party (that all of us try to love) have done to us." He urged members to "fight for the right of Black people to eat and sweat and to live in the Delta" and register as many Blacks as possible before the statewide primaries that summer. The call for independent candidacies fell on the receptive ears of angry MFDP members. One Hinds County FDP member who volunteered during the elections called Guyot's speech "the most important one he has ever made." The volunteer said that "we've been fooling around with the Democratic and Republican parties so long 'til we don't know what freedom is anymore. . . . Like Mr. Guyot said, 'We have been raped,' by all the 'good people' who keep the poor people in chains. If the FDP can really get out of the 'we're-the-real-Democratic-Party-in-Mississippi' bag, and build a party of us, then I think we've got a chance to win."[107]

Charles McLaurin said that Guyot's reaction to Sunflower was one of "devastation," but he did not publicly show it. Within days after the election, the MFDP attorneys filed a lawsuit challenging the election results, but the effort came to naught as the federal observers reported no irregularities.[108]

Meanwhile, Charles Evers rubbed salt in the MFDP's wounds by publicly agreeing with whites who charged that the MFDP candidates lacked qualifications. He told reporters that the MFDP ran near-illiterate candidates who lacked the political skills to succeed. His comments echoed those of the *Jackson Advocate*, which said that the "qualified Negro voters in the two towns had refused to give total bloc support to the all-Negro list of candidates." Using language straight out of the Citizens' Council, the Black-run newspaper in the pay of the SSC falsely charged that the MFDP had "picked and designated" the slate and described the party as "under the control of non-resident whites, largely Jewish, with temporary residence in the state," and that it received funding "from contributors outside the state, and reported to be all shades of left-wing and communist persuasion."[109]

Pro-MFDP media outlets tried to paint as positive a picture as they could of the Sunflower loss. Eleanor Holmes Norton, in a coauthored piece in *New America*, said that "things will never be the same" in the county after the election. "There may be further delays, but things will never be the same in Sunflower." Mainstream news outlets struck a more pessimistic tone. The *Wall Street Journal* pointed out the obvious, that with some Black voters willing to vote for white candidates, only a wide majority of registered Black voters could guarantee victory. But the economic conditions of the Delta, which included a sharp decline in the demands for field labor due to mechanization, meant that the number of Black voters declined as Black outmigration increased. In Sunflower alone, the number of registered Black voters had dropped by thirty-one from the fall to the time of the election.[110] The changing economic nature of the Delta tempered the realities of local political organizing by the MFDP.

The summer of 1967, then, saw few gains for the MFDP even as it changed strategies. The high hopes for Sunflower and Moorhead instead became another year of defeat. This bitter medicine finally forced Guyot to recognize that the MFDP could not gain political access isolated from both the NAACP and the state Democratic Party. It simply did not have the numbers or access. What followed fundamentally altered the party forever.

# CHAPTER 6

# THAT'S AS CLOSE TO A MACHINE AS YOU CAN GET

## FUSION AND THE END OF THE MISSISSIPPI FREEDOM DEMOCRATIC PARTY

The bitterness of the losses in Sunflower and Moorhead finally forced Guyot and the Mississippi Freedom Democratic Party (MFDP) to reckon with political reality. The independent approach to state and local politics did not work, and significant numbers of Black Mississippians simply did not support the MFDP. The taint of radicalism from Black Power hurt the party, despite Guyot's avowed interracialism. The National Association for the Advancement of Colored People (NAACP), in contrast, made gains and would continue to do so under the leadership of Charles Evers, who ran the NAACP with a far more authoritarian bent than Guyot. His style clashed with the MFDP's ethos, but it yielded dividends. This realization prompted Guyot to begin a rapprochement with Evers in preparation for the 1967 statewide elections. This path ultimately led to fusion with the Loyalist Democrats, dominated by moderate civil rights activists like Evers and Aaron Henry. The MFDP settled for junior status and a loss of independence at the 1968 Democratic Convention as the price of political power and access, an action that would not endear Guyot to some of his more radical members under the influence of both Black Power and New Left ideologies. But the fusion brought the end of the MFDP's identity and independent existence, and the party lost Guyot's steady leadership as he departed the state after the convention. At the end of 1968, Guyot would leave Mississippi for a new chapter in his life.

Just a week after the Sunflower elections, Guyot found himself pulled into another racial crisis. On the night of 11 May, police officers in Jackson shot and killed Ben Brown, a Jackson State College student and civil rights activist, who was attending a protest of about 1,000 students demonstrating against the arrest of a student on campus the previous day for speeding. Police gunfire wounded several others as well. Guyot and Evers put aside their differences and joined Owen Brooks of the Delta Ministry and others at Brown's funeral at the Masonic Temple in Jackson, where they all spoke to the crowd of mourners. Evers denounced the Jackson police as "murderers" with "uniforms and badges," and Guyot said that "we must organize around one thing—survival." They joined calls for a boycott of white businesses in downtown Jackson, and local citizens at a community meeting elected Guyot to be the publicity chairman for the boycott. He said that if Black organizations did not join the boycott, he predicted "a bloody series of neighborhood-by-neighborhood uprisings" that summer.[1]

Guyot helped organize the summer boycott for the newly created Hinds County Citizens' Action Committee, and conducted operations through May and June. On 5 June, Jackson police arrested him on Capitol Street for disorderly conduct as he talked to people downtown about the boycott. His supporters quickly bailed him out, and he continued his efforts on the boycott, but as June dragged on, support waned. Despite receiving help from Stokely Carmichael, who knew Brown from his work in the Student Nonviolent Coordinating Committee (SNCC), Guyot could not secure broader support. In fact, the support from Carmichael may have been a factor in Evers's refusal to join the campaign in Jackson.[2]

By late June another event emerged to attract MFDP support, one that Guyot hoped would help with political organizing and voter registration. James Meredith returned to Mississippi on 24 June to recreate his march that had been cut short a year earlier. The MFDP lent strong support to the march and Guyot drove up and down Highway 51, seeking to raise support for the party, but little came from the effort. This time the state of Mississippi provided police protection for Meredith, and the event drew little attention as Meredith marched to Canton, with a crowd of 1,000 in Grenada the biggest highlight. Guyot also continued his support for welfare-related matters, such as a march for welfare rights that occurred toward the end of the Meredith March, and helped the CDGM secure funds to fight childhood hunger in Mississippi.[3]

Yet the summer months after the Sunflower elections passed quickly, and the August Democratic primaries approached, during a gubernatorial year. While Guyot declared that the MFDP would stay on its independent course, Charles Evers announced that the NAACP would sponsor over two dozen candidates in local races. Despite Guyot's statement, he still had the MFDP endorse all Black candidates, independent, Democrat, and NAACP-backed or not, indicating that even a Black officeholder who was not an MFDP supporter served Black interests better than a white Mississippian. The MFDP put aside its rivalry with the NAACP and worked together, in the spirit of the old Council of Federated Organizations (COFO), in groups like Mississippians United to Elect Negro Candidates. In a joint statement with the Delta Ministry, the MFDP said that "open and abrasive disunity must be avoided" and called for "an informal and articulated agreement" among Black organizations to coexist, at least for the election season. The MFDP backed about sixty candidates, and in all seventy-six Blacks in twenty-two counties ran in August primary, most of them in heavily Black counties.[4]

Representatives from fourteen Mississippi counties formed Mississippians United and channeled out-of-state funds to political groups in the county, not individual candidates. The group also conducted political education workshops for Black voters and selected Joseph Harris, the MFDP campaign manager from the Sunflower County elections, as its chairman and executive director. Guyot, Charles McLaurin, and Hollis Watkins also served on the steering committee, making MFDP members four-fifths of the panel (Owen Brooks was the fifth member). To add support, Guyot said that the MFDP lobbied county and state officials to appoint Black election managers to aid illiterate Black voters at the polls, something that had been denied in Sunflower County. Guyot publicly downplayed the MFDP-NAACP rivalry and declared that the distance between the two organizations "is certainly decreasing." He said he and Evers had met and agreed to "bury the interorganizational fight." To avoid a repeat of 1966, where Evers endorsed the Republican over the MFDP candidate, the two men agreed not to make any endorsements regarding the gubernatorial candidates.[5]

As John Dittmer has noted, the 1967 elections demonstrated the influence of the Voting Rights Act and became a turning point in the state. White candidates now sought Black votes, due to over 180,000 Black voters—over half the eligible Black electorate—casting votes that year. In heavily Black towns, such as Edwards and Bolton in Hinds County, white candidates even appeared at a local FDP convention. Yet the Black votes largely did not benefit the MFDP, and once again, the NAACP had more success with Black candidates. Sixteen Black candidates won posts outright and twenty-three others made it to runoff elections. Eleven of those sixteen won in the southwestern river counties— the center of NAACP support—while the other five came from the Delta. The NAACP successfully backed eleven of twenty-five candidates; the MFDP only successfully backed five out of a total number of sixty. The runoffs later that August also failed for the civil rights organizations, as a united white vote defeated the Black candidates who made it to the runoff elections.[6]

The return of collaboration among the various organizations extended beyond electoral politics. In July, Evers and Guyot responded to the shooting of a Black man in Jackson by a Black policeman. Guyot said that "we must forget organizational differences. We must demand the right to control not only election officials, but everything that goes on in the Black community, or these things will control us." In August, Charles Evers organized a march in Jackson to demand welfare and medical care for the poor. The MFDP and the Hinds County Welfare Rights Movement assisted the NAACP in organizing the rally. The rally speakers included moderate civil rights leaders like Aaron Henry and the Reverend R. L. T. Smith. The march organizers bused people from counties all over the state, and over 700 attended. Still, not everyone welcomed the influence of the moderates. One woman said that Evers "is too easily persuaded," while others objected to halting the march due to a police presence on the Capitol grounds. The *Mississippi Newsletter* said that "there was not the excitement of past demonstrations" and that the march left "mostly tired feet and confused minds."[7]

The ongoing financial woes of the MFDP likely motivated the collaboration. Guyot, Hamer, Ed King, and Joseph Harris, who all played a major organizing role in the Sunflower elections, proposed a six-month project for the latter half of 1967. It included political organizing in twenty counties to train 100 local leaders. But with a proposed price tag of $141,000, the party did not have the resources to carry it out. Expense statements from the autumn of 1967 show that the party had a balance of $2,400 by the end of November and was kept in the black largely by donations. But the party spent no money on major organizing projects, its resources largely consumed by day-to-day expenses.[8]

The MFDP also continued its relationship with and support for at least some of the ideas of Black Power during the 1967 election season. In July 1967, Guyot, along with Victoria Gray Adams, Owen Brooks, Frank Smith, and others, went to Newark, New Jersey, to attend the first Black Power conference. The conference members met only days after the urban rebellion in Newark, triggered by police brutality and creating the worst racial violence since Watts two years earlier. Not surprisingly, the State Sovereignty Commission (SSC) used this to try to tie Guyot to violence and extremism, falsely claiming that he visited Newark "at the height of the rioting there." It also tried to paint him as an ally of H. Rap Brown, the controversial new director of SNCC, who later endorsed violence as a means to achieve Black liberation, calling it "as American as cherry pie."[9]

While Guyot did not mention which workshops he attended, it is unlikely he enrolled in the ones on armed self-defense, given the positions he took at Natchez. The Newark conference went well beyond a singular focus on Black men and guns, which is how the media preferred to depict Black Power. Far more likely Guyot and his colleagues attended the workshops on community control and economic empowerment, and given their experience with the MFDP, they likely provided valuable input for the conference resolution that called for investigating the possibility of creating a political party.[10]

The MFDP also sent a delegation to the National Conference for New Politics, which took place over Labor Day weekend in Chicago. Activists hoped the conference could forge a coalition of antiwar liberals, New Left student radicals, and civil rights activists, particularly Black Power organizations. The conference seemed well-suited for the MFDP, as attendees debated whether to work within the two-party system, support third-party candidates, or focus on community organizing. Guyot and Victoria Gray had previously attended a meeting of the New Politics board in November 1966, where she presented the historical background of the MFDP and he spoke on political organizing and leadership. At the New Politics convention in 1967, the MFDP delegation, led by Victoria Gray, delivered a position paper endorsing the Black independent candidates running in the general election that fall. They declared that Mississippi Blacks "are faced with virtual genocide and are therefore fighting for their survival" and that the MFDP wanted to increase Black economic and political power—including self-defense—through community organizing. Gray delivered a speech outlining the local political organizing of the MFDP, carried out "right under the white man's nose." She connected the struggle in Mississippi to the North and, in a nod to Black Power, echoed Franz Fanon, declaring that "we in Mississippi are the wretched of the earth, but you are not so free yourselves. . . . Join our struggle, and we will join yours." The delegation used the national platform of the New Politics convention to appeal for funds and pressure on the federal government to send registrars. Their views on Vietnam fit well with the antiwar theme of the conference, as they called for an end to drafting Black Mississippi men and the implementation of job training programs instead. But the MFDP met only with disappointment in Chicago, as the conference failed to achieve anything constructive. The racial split between white radicals and moderates and Black Power activists proved insurmountable and fatally split the convention.[11]

The statement on the draft, which had caused problems for the MFDP in the past, meshed with the bottom-up pressures of Black Power in the party. Given the decentralized, grassroots ethos that the MFDP had inherited from SNCC, it seemed inevitable that local FDPs would do or say things that would undermine, intentionally or not, the MFDP's central agenda of electing Black officeholders and growing Black self-empowerment. The FDP in Hinds County became more radical than the central organization. Under the influence of activists like Henry Hatches, an organizer in the county FDP, the organization shifted toward Black militancy. By 1967, the *Hinds County FDP News* openly endorsed Black Power and ran speeches from prominent figures like Stokely Carmichael and H. Rap Brown. In July 1967, in the wake of the Newark and Detroit uprisings, a front-page editorial said that "violence may be the answer," expressing frustration about the media focus on Black rioting and not on white violence against Blacks. The Hinds County FDP leadership remained committed to Black electoral power, however, as Hatches himself entered local politics and ran for constable in Hinds County in 1967.[12]

The MFDP soon experienced a repeat of the McComb draft controversy of two years earlier. On 16 September, the *Hinds County FDP News* ran an editorial endorsing the FDP candidates but included on the front page the slogan "Burn, Baby, Burn!"—words reportedly chanted by Black rioters during the summer's urban uprisings—along with drawings of firearms and a Molotov cocktail. Inside the newsletter, the author of one of the articles endorsed Black people engaging in guerrilla warfare, which the author referred to as "self-defense warfare." "Take ten honkies with you," the author exhorted. "In this country, we have seen that four summers of riots or rebellions have brought more results than ten long years of non-violence." The paper included remarks from Guyot endorsing self-defense, a quote where he said that "nobody will protect Black folks but Black folks." It also made reference to his "goddamn Democratic Party" speech after Sunflower to rebut charges that Guyot wanted to "get into the white Democratic Party." The *Mississippi Newsletter*, published by the Freedom Information Service and edited by Jan Hillegas, ran similar editorials. Hillegas, a white female CORE volunteer from Syracuse, New York, had previously done voter registration work in Lowndes County, Mississippi, with COFO and began her work with the Freedom Information Service in 1967. In September, the paper displayed visual and written instructions on how to make a Molotov cocktail, over the caption "New Politics." The next page carried an article titled "Black Power Is Fire Power" and called for organizing shooting clubs "to train every Black man, woman and child how to protect our community with violence when necessary."[13]

One day after that article was published, Guyot announced that the executive committee of the MFDP had decided to challenge the white regular delegation at the Democratic Convention in Chicago the next year. The unanimous decision came after the Executive Committee met in Sunflower and marked the MFDP's abandonment of its independent course, which Guyot publicly committed the party to after the losses in Sunflower County. He correctly anticipated that some members would not agree with this decision. The *Mississippi Newsletter* ran an editorial critical of what it perceived as flip-flopping by Guyot. Hillegas, who attended the Sunflower meeting, contrasted his statement after the Sunflower elections with the decision to send delegates to the 1968 convention, and also highlighted his comments on self-defense. At a political workshop in September, Guyot told Black candidates that "everyone in the civil rights movement should carry a gun. We need to be prepared to defend those we're trying to organize. . . . There's a time to be nonviolent and there's a time to BE." Guyot's statements did not impress Hillegas, who declared that "many FDP members find it hard to know just where state chairman Lawrence Guyot stands on various issues."[14] While a significant departure from his stance in Natchez, Guyot still only advocated armed self-defense. In fact, the armed protection that the Deacons for Defense provided during the first Meredith March likely influenced him away from strict nonviolence—or the earlier stance may merely have been a tactical ploy.

Whatever the reason, the change in course caused, according to Les McLemore, "a great deal of debate and animosity within the Party's ranks." One militant hyperbolically declared that the MFDP sought "the blessings of the American Fuhrer" by going to the 1968 convention. The Hinds County FDP also opposed the move, favoring the independent electoral course. While some in the party saw the reversal as at best inconsistent and at worst treasonous, it represented pure pragmatism to Guyot. The independent course did not yield results, and the MFDP had tacitly acknowledged this reality during the summer, when it began cooperating again with the NAACP and Charles Evers. At the executive committee meeting that September, Guyot said that a "lack of progress that can be directly identified with the FDP" marked the party's recent efforts.[15]

Some grassroots civil rights workers harbored frustrations with Guyot, and had for some time. Some of the SNCC members working in Mississippi had always viewed the MFDP's focus on electoral politics as a sellout, especially since that approach meant working with whites within a white-dictated political and voting system. The SSC eagerly looked for any signs of discontent, no matter how improbable. In January 1967, the SSC quoted Susie Ruffin, a Black woman from Laurel who founded and ran the *MFDP News* from 1965 to 1967, as declaring that Guyot was no longer interested in the MFDP and may have been "paid off" by somebody. Guyot's activities in 1967 effectively counter this charge, but Ruffin's comments indicate a growing dissatisfaction in some quarters with his leadership.[16]

With the November elections approaching, the MFDP mobilized its support for the eleven Black candidates it had backed that won their August primary races. The MFDP focused its support on three legislative candidates and five candidates for county offices. As Evers had done with Prentiss Walker the previous year, the party also decided to back the Republican candidate for governor, Rubel Phillips. Phillips ran for governor in 1963 as a staunch segregationist, as Walker had done against Eastland. By 1967, Phillips had rebranded himself as somewhat of a racial moderate in his campaign against the archsegregationist John Bell Williams, and had publicly expressed doubts about the state's refusal to comply with federally ordered desegregation guidelines. This stance won him the support of the *Delta Democrat-Times* as well as the MFDP, but Phillips unequivocally rejected the latter's support, calling Guyot and other civil rights leaders "not responsible citizens."[17]

The MFDP endorsement of Phillips created controversy within the party. Some members opposed endorsing any white candidate, even if Phillips lacked the crude racism of Walker. Alfred Rhodes, a candidate for the state legislature in Hinds County, sent a letter to forty-five MFDP leaders asking them to oppose the endorsement. He called the support for Phillips "a step backwards" and said that endorsing a statewide white candidate would open the door to endorsing local white candidates. Guyot's attempt at pragmatism did not win him any moderate support either, as the administration of Jackson State College denied him a speaking engagement on 2 November. The white board of trustees allowed Evers to speak but denied a student body request to let Guyot give a speech on campus.[18]

The major success for the MFDP came in Holmes County, a part-Delta county that was also the fifth-poorest in the nation. The county's 800 Black-owned farms, 110 of which were in the fertile soil of the Delta (a historically whites-only preserve), made the county unique in Mississippi. These Delta farms resulted from a Farm Security Administration program during the Great Depression that sold subdivided land from bankrupted plantations to poor Black sharecroppers and tenant farmers with long-term, low-interest loans. These land sales produced a base of Black farmers freer from white control and influence than most other Black farmers, and directly stimulated the strong local movement in Holmes County that produced defiant activists like Hartman Turnbow, who had resisted the local authorities when he led a group of local Black residents to the Lexington County Courthouse in 1963 to register to vote.[19]

Independent Black farmers started Holmes County's freedom movement, and it was effectively inseparable from the local FDP. In 1967, the local FDP nominated four members, including Ralthus Hayes, as official candidates for countywide and beat positions. The local FDP recognized that it needed as much support as possible from even poorly organized beats, since a high Black voter turnout would help countywide candidates. Therefore, the party made an effort to recruit candidates in every beat in Holmes County. This recruiting effort led to more candidates being nominated, and the number rose to ten by April. Robert Clark, a schoolteacher who held degrees from Jackson State College and Michigan State University, emerged from the middle-class Black community. Clark hesitated at first to run as a candidate backed by the MFDP. He had no affiliation with its movement activists, not surprising given that he was a public schoolteacher and easily susceptible to white pressure. He had some contacts with FDP officials from his role as project director of the Migrant Farmers' Education Program, an adult education program in the county. Yet he drew suspicion from MFDP members, as he had been appointed by whites to the Community Action Program board in 1966 and beat FDP member Burrell Tate in an election for the seat. The real change for Clark came that same year, however, as he left the public school system and took over a federal program run through Saints Junior College in Lexington, a private Black institution. He had become disillusioned working with whites on the Community Action Program board, and the new program gave him more freedom from white influence. After that, he began attending FDP meetings and eventually declared, with FDP support, as a candidate for state representative.[20]

Although Guyot had indicated that the MFDP was moving back to the Democrats, he remained true to his grassroots ethos and did not try to impose this policy on local FDPs. The Holmes County FDP decided to skip the August Democratic primary and focus on the November election with independent candidates. The local factored in a number of considerations, including cost, increased voter registration time, and the hope to avoid a "moderate" white candidate soliciting Black voters in the Democratic primary. Sue Lorenzi, working in Holmes County at this time, recalled that the FDP explicitly rejected Evers's model of working with whites in favor of building a stronger Black organization along the model of the Lowndes County Freedom Organization in Alabama.[21]

Clark ran a campaign that McLemore called "part of, and yet separate from, the FDP; he went after and got the middle-class Black vote." The taint of radicalism and Black Power that still lingered about the MFDP meant that Clark straddled both worlds; the world of the grassroots activist and the world of the middle-class Black voter. Clark could do both, as a highly educated schoolteacher who by the time of his candidacy worked as both athletic director and business manager at Saints Junior College. His father, grandfather, and uncles had worked as teachers in the county, so his family had many community connections. Yet his stated reason for running—the refusal of the county school board to sponsor an adult education program—gave him appeal to the activists and meant he could not be dismissed as an "Uncle Tom." The school board's decision angered him. "The whites still had no feeling for the Negro," he said. "This was too much to stand." In one speech, he referenced the Black political power that existed during Reconstruction, mentioning his grandfather, who was chairman of the Hinds County Republican Party and used armed self-defense against white racists during the "redemption" of Mississippi.[22]

Clark ran what McLemore called "the most well-organized campaign since Sunflower," with the MFDP supporting his independent campaign committee. This committee organized rallies for the candidates, distributed campaign literature, used paid radio advertisements, and did traditional canvassing with block captains, like in Sunflower. The block captains in particular reached Black voters in the remotest parts of the rural county. All the candidates ran on platforms that promoted education, economic development, and health care. Clark used the MFDP organization to his advantage, but he never identified himself as a member of the party. In his radio ads, he called himself "your independent candidate for state representative." The NAACP and MFDP continued their détente, with local NAACP leaders serving on the Holmes County Independent Campaign Committee, an MFDP-dominated organization.[23]

Clark narrowly unseated his opponent, J. P. Love, by a margin of 116 votes, becoming the first Black state legislator in Mississippi since the nineteenth century. All the other county candidates lost, with the exception of Griffin McLaurin, a constable candidate. Both these men benefited from the extreme racism of their opponents, neither of whom attempted to solicit Black voters. All the other white candidates in Holmes County who had Black opponents did directly ask Black voters for their support, and they all won. Elsewhere in the state, the NAACP-backed Black candidates received the Democratic nominations, eleven in all, and won office. Statewide, Phillips lost to the segregationist Democrat John Bell Williams. Twenty-two Black candidates won office across the state, but only three won countywide offices, and only one—Clark's race—had intensive MFDP organizing.[24]

Clark's victory owed much to the MFDP campaign, with Guyot himself leading workshops on independent candidacies. Guyot told members to focus on community issues in their campaigning and when giving speeches, addressing issues like paving streets, school textbooks, and other matters. While the MFDP definitely helped, Clark's personal campaigning style also played a key role in his narrow victory that November. He stopped at every house in a neighborhood when he canvassed, and he suggested that other Black candidates may not have been successful because "not all of them got around to see people, [and] aren't as well known around the county." Still, it is doubtful that Clark would have won without the organizing efforts of the MFDP. Claude Ramsey, the head of the

AFL-CIO and a critic of the MFDP, later tried to take credit for Clark's victory. He claimed that he sent some organizers to Holmes County to help turn out Black voters and declared that "we broke the color barrier in the legislature," giving no credit to the MFDP. His boast, at odds with the bottom-up efforts of the MFDP, is not supported by the available evidence and is unlikely given Ramsey's hostility to the MFDP and its independent efforts. It also confirms Guyot's view of Ramsey as a "manipulative labor organizer who wanted the benefit of working with the Black vote but didn't want to be identified with it."[25]

Given that the NAACP elected a slate of successful candidates to office, the 1967 elections can easily be seen as another blow to the independent strategy for Black office seekers. But Robert Clark's victory gave Guyot and the MFDP a much-needed win after a long string of bitter electoral defeats. Les McLemore, in his assessment of the 1967 Sunflower and Holmes County elections, emphasized the role that fear still played on suppressing Black voting in Mississippi, which made the election of Clark that much more remarkable for the MFDP. Guyot himself emphasized the positive, and said any victories were important, because "look at what we are dealing with."[26]

After the election, Guyot joined with Clark, Owen Brooks, and Joseph Harris to congratulate the twenty-two successful Black candidates and hold a conference in Mileston to "seek ways to make Black officials a powerful force in Mississippi. . . . We must develop new ideas and programs to help out goals," the four stated in a joint letter, "[and] we must begin now." Guyot continued to lend financial help for this nascent Black political power, providing support to Clark for travel and to defend himself against J. P. Love, who unsuccessfully challenged Clark's election and seating in the state legislature. In anticipation of Clark's seating, the MFDP executive committee also helped Clark by establishing a committee to assist him in writing legislation. Guyot even met with his rival Claude Ramsey to discuss helping Clark secure his seat, and traveled to Atlanta to find supporters to demonstrate in Jackson for Clark, but these plans ended once Love withdrew his challenge.[27]

The MFDP-NAACP détente turned into a formal alliance after the election as they faced another challenge to the emerging Black political power in the state. Mississippi law required that public officials be bonded to protect them from lawsuits while exercising their official duties, but the state had no Black-owned bonding company. The bonding companies turned down the surety bond applications of all but two of the newly elected Black officials, which meant the elections of the declined officials would be voided.[28]

Guyot and Evers, with their hard-fought electoral gains threatened, held a joint press conference on 19 December in Jackson calling for a nationwide boycott of the bonding companies, some of whom were part of national insurance companies. The threat worked, as four days later several companies backed down, and additional legal action by the MFDP-affiliated Lawyers Committee for Civil Rights under Law led to all of the candidates being bonded.[29]

The real symbol of the renewed cooperation between the two civil rights organizations came with the onset of the new year. On 25 January 1968, Charles Evers announced his candidacy for the US House seat that Williams vacated so he could assume the office of governor. He sought election in the Third District, which covered six counties in the southwest as well as part of the Delta. In a sign of how far the MFDP-NAACP rapprochement had come, he named Guyot as his campaign manager and took a leave of absence from his NAACP field secretary position to campaign.[30]

Evers made a curious decision, given his preference for local races and building a political machine in southwestern Mississippi. The Third District had almost twice as many registered white voters as Black ones, so an Evers victory seemed impossible. In fact, the district makeup mirrored the high-profile races the MFDP had run in 1965 and 1966, races which brought little tangible success. He borrowed another MFDP tactic when he ran as an independent instead of a Democrat, since the special election did not require a party nomination.[31] Evers likely ran for the House seat to raise his statewide profile further, given his future political ambitions.

Evers brought other MFDP members besides Guyot into the campaign. Evers appointed Ed King to the position of coordinator for speaking engagements, while Alfred Rhodes received the post of publicity director. Other groups involved in the political coalition included the Prince Hall Masons and the Mississippi Teachers Association, but the NAACP and MFDP held the most clout. Yet white liberals and moderates like Claude Ramsey and the AFL-CIO did not support his candidacy or join his coalition.[32] White refusal likely pushed Evers toward the MFDP, as he had nothing to lose by bringing them aboard if he had already lost any meaningful white support.

The State Sovereignty Commission responded with concern about the NAACP-MFDP rapprochement, in particular the selection of Guyot as Evers's campaign manager. Director Erle Johnston Jr. wrote in a memorandum that "the entry of Charles Evers into the congressional race has more significance than merely having a Negro candidate. Evers and the NAACP have been at bitter odds with the Freedom Democratic Party. . . . It is extremely important that to note that Lawrence Guyot has agreed to be Charles Evers' campaign manager. . . . There have been many times in the past when Guyot and Evers would hardly speak much less collaborate." He thought Evers planned to bring all the civil rights groups together under his control, thus widening his power and influence. Ruben Anderson, a Black attorney who worked closely with Evers, indicated that the hiring of Guyot "to some degree" bridged the gap between the two sides, and said that Guyot was also a "great stump speaker" who was "one of the most influential guys with the younger group" of civil rights activists.[33]

The MFDP addressed the old conflict between the two organizations head-on. The party in its newsletter told its members that "voting for Evers is a blow against racism." The newsletter admitted that "there are and have been differences in policy and technique between the MFDP and the NAACP in the past but we are supporting the *candidate* not the state nor the national NAACP. . . . We believe Mr. Evers can be supported by FDP members in good conscience since he has fought on many local issues with us AND he has supported many programs the MFDP has fought for." But privately, Guyot did not succumb to Evers's charms. "He was a hustler," he said of Evers. "I wasn't a hustler."[34]

During his campaign, the NAACP-MFDP coalition experienced some of the problems directly related to Black Power advocates and their criticism of Guyot's new course for the MFDP. Evers spoke at a luncheon at Tougaloo College in February, shortly after filing his nominating petitions. Howard Spencer, chairman of the campus's Political Action Committee, challenged Evers's statement that he wanted to see the Federal Bureau of Investigation (FBI) and Central Intelligence Agency hire Black agents. Spencer called the two agencies "agents of the oppression of Black people in both the United States and in other countries." He said that "we don't want them integrated; we want them stopped, broken down, so Black people in Mississippi can have a decent existence." Spencer pulled no punches with Evers, telling him that "we know that way you dealt with the power structure in Natchez and about your personal empire in Fayette. You talk about reactionary Black power: That is, I'm Black, put me up in public office. We want revolutionary Black power: That is, get rid of the whole rotten system so that people can have a reasonable existence." He called for Evers to "get out of that [the Democratic] party." Evers thanked the student for his "frank opinion" but declared that he was an integrationist. Clearly, not all Black Mississippians embraced Guyot's newfound relationship with Evers, but Guyot did advocate for students who supported Evers, including appearing at a press conference for three Alcorn A&M students whom the administration suspended for pro-Evers activity on their campus.[35]

Evers campaigned extensively, repeatedly visiting every county in the district. He ran on a liberal platform calling for federal funding for rural housing, expansion of health and welfare services, and opposition to the Vietnam War. He cited discrimination against Black people at home for why he opposed the war. Evers received some acceptance as the "moderate" Black civil rights leader, including an invitation to speak at the all-white Mississippi College in Clinton. He led the field of candidates in the first round of voting but won only 30 percent of the total vote. In the March runoff, he faced Charles Griffin, a former congressional aide to John Bell Williams. Perhaps the most notable thing about the runoff was the lack of racist rhetoric from Griffin, who knew he could rely on a solid white majority to elect him. Griffin defeated Evers in the runoff by a more than two-to-one margin.[36]

The MFDP continued to aid local Black candidates in this period, even as it supported the high-profile Evers race. The executive committee sent $150 to Robert Miles, a farmer in Panola County who ran in February for a county supervisor position after the death of the white incumbent. Miles helped organize the Voters League in 1959 with other independent farmers and ministers, establishing himself as a longtime civil rights activist in the county. In 1964, delegates elected him to the MFDP state executive committee, and he went to Atlantic City as a member of the MFDP delegation (and voted against the compromise). He also served as Panola County's FDP chairman, ran the county Head Start program through the CDGM, and in 1965 one movement paper called him "perhaps Panola County's most revered freedom fighter." Miles led the voting in the first election but lost to the county's former sheriff in the runoff. Like in the congressional election, white voters united behind the white candidate in the runoff, and the presence of the county's first Black supervisor candidate in the twentieth century boosted both white and Black turnout.[37]

The NAACP-MFDP détente carried over into other local races as well. Annie Devine successfully convinced Flonzie Goodloe, the branch director of the Canton NAACP office, to run for an election commission post in Madison County. She ran as an independent since a federal antipoverty program employed her. In what the local paper called "a political upset," she unseated the white incumbent in November.[38]

As the events of 1968 unfolded, Martin Luther King Jr. continued his support for the MFDP. King visited Mississippi in February to raise support for his Poor Peoples' Campaign, which he was planning for April in Washington. He met with Guyot and other civil rights leaders at Mt. Beulah. Guyot, likely thinking of the experience of the congressional challenge, questioned the wisdom of aiming this campaign at Congress but said he would support it if it was a broad enough plan. Guyot also joined with King and other civil rights leaders in a statement defending H. Rap Brown, the outspoken SNCC chairman who was prosecuted by the federal government for violating terms of his bond when he traveled to California to attend a rally for Black Panther Party leader Huey Newton. The statement condemned the prosecution of Brown, who eventually received five years in prison for carrying a rifle while under indictment, as an effort to silence him politically.[39]

By late March, the State Sovereignty Commission reported that both Evers and Guyot threw their "whole-hearted support" behind the Poor People's March. The MFDP now belonged to a group called the Steering Committee against Repression (SCAR), formed to provide support for Black Power organizations and figures like Brown. SCAR included the MFDP, SNCC, CORE, the Southern Christian Leadership Conference (SCLC), the Southern Student Organizing Committee (SSOC), and the Delta Ministry—but notably not the NAACP, which likely wanted to avoid association with controversial figures like Brown. SCAR held meetings in support of King and the sanitation workers' union and against the city government of Memphis after riots swept the city when police shot a Black teenager during a demonstration. Guyot showed that despite his commitment to the Democratic Party, he could still make controversial statements, such as when he criticized the White House's attempts to "decide what we can do, who we can associate with, even what we think" by targeting people like Brown for prosecution. "If so," said Guyot, "then Johnson is no different than Hitler."[40]

Guyot also showed that despite his decision to stay in the party, he had no aversion to meeting with others more radical than him. He attended the National Black Government Convention in Detroit on 30 and 31 March, a meeting of about 500 Black nationalists, socialists, and other Black Power advocates. Many of them, like Guyot, had attended the Newark conference the previous year. While the conference may be best known for creating the provisional government of the Republic of New Afrika (RNA), an organization calling for an independent Black nation-state in the US South, attendees also discussed reparations and other issues related to Black freedom. While Guyot did not join the provisional government and never explicitly endorsed the RNA, his attendance is not surprising. He had pursued independent approaches to Black political power through the MFDP, and his commitment to the Democratic Party represented practicality rather than an abandonment of the idea of an independent Black political base. Just as Guyot had worked with his more conservative rival Charles Evers, he did not shy away from active connections and support from more radical Black activists. Indeed, the RNA, despite its goal of an independent Black homeland, endorsed Black political participation in the meantime. In 1971, the RNA even endorsed the gubernatorial race of

Charles Evers. Imari Obadele, leader of the RNA, called for his supporters to back Black candidates, whatever their ideology, viewing them as future leaders of the eventual Black homeland. Perhaps because of this, some Black politicians and civil rights activists maintained links with the RNA. Robert Clark backed out of attending the Detroit convention after unfavorable publicity about the conference in the Jackson newspapers, but he publicly defended the right of people to join the RNA. Fred Banks, an NAACP lawyer, provided legal services to the entire spectrum of civil rights activists, including the RNA. These overlaps resembled the earlier involvements of the Deacons of Defense with the NAACP during the Natchez movement, and indicated, along with MFDP-NAACP cooperation, how fluid the boundaries "separating" Black political activism were in the state.[41]

After King's assassination in Memphis on 4 April, Guyot joined other Black leaders and called for a boycott of all white businesses around the state. SCAR, which King had joined, issued a formal statement, signed by luminaries from Dr. Benjamin Spock to Bobby Seale to the Reverend Fred Shuttlesworth, calling for Brown's release and "amnesty to all those who have been arrested in the aftermath of Doctor King's assassination." The latter referred to the riots that swept the country after his murder. SCAR also called for the withdrawal of all federal troops from the cities and the "demilitarization of the police forces," and withdrawing US troops from Vietnam.[42]

On a more personal note, Guyot recalled that he visited his grandfather, who was dying, shortly after King's murder. His grandfather had played a large role in his life, as he often recalled in interviews. His grandfather asked him what Black people should do now after King's death, and Guyot replied, "Pa, we are going to do just fine. We are going to fight, we'll organize; he's done all he can now so it's up to us to do the rest."[43]

King's assassination briefly overshadowed the bitterly contested Democratic primary campaign for president, which took a dramatic turn on 31 March when President Johnson, facing the twin antiwar challenges of Senators Eugene McCarthy (D-MN) and Robert Kennedy (D-NY) and declining poll numbers, announced he would not to seek reelection. Guyot and the MFDP soon focused their energies on their earlier stated plan to challenge the regular Mississippi delegation at the 1968 Democratic convention. According to McLemore, the MFDP "vacillated from one position to another until at least May of 1968" in regards to its challenge.[44] Guyot's own statements on Johnson in defending Black Power activists like Brown indicated what McLemore referred to, as Guyot gave at least lip service to Black radicalism in the spring of 1968 as the domestic political situation in the country heated to a fever pitch.

Some movement activists still considered the convention challenge a betrayal of party principles. Jan Hillegas reprinted in the *Mississippi Newsletter* an article from the November 1967 issue of the New Orleans Movement for a Democratic Society's newsletter. The article, written by Ed Clark and titled "The Mississippi Freedom Democratic Party: The End of a Movement?" expressed his radical views clearly. Clark held a leadership post in the New Orleans Movement and membership in the Progressive Labor Party (PLP), a Maoist group that split off from the Communist Party of the United States in 1962. The Progressive Labor Party advocated armed revolution to overthrow the capitalist system, definitely outside the pale of MFDP politics. Clark charged that "a whole group of Black hustlers/hipsters" influenced the MFDP, and these outside influencers sought "like Adam Clayton Powell, to build Black political-economic machines to carry out the further exploitation of the Black people of Mississippi." He made this apparent reference to Evers clearer when he said that the influence came from the "growing power" of the NAACP within the MFDP, and he cited statements from Guyot in September 1967 endorsing legal suits on legislative apportionment and other issues as proof, actions more reformist than revolutionary.[45]

Clark, writing from a white Marxist perspective, then aimed at "the most important labor struggle in Mississippi in decades," the strike by Local 5543 of the International Woodworkers of America against the Masonite Corporation in Laurel. He criticized some (but not all) of the Black workers who he said had "scabbed on their striking brothers" for returning to work. The Black workers claimed this was due to Ku Klux Klan influence in the union. Clark admitted that some Klansmen had membership in the union, but he dismissed the Black strikers' concerns since the union had integrated after the Civil Rights Act of 1964 went into effect, an action that led to Klan retaliation and a highly publicized union battle against the Klan. He accused the MFDP of remaining "aloof" from the struggle and of supporting the Black scab workers, while at the same time focusing its energies on court cases and the upcoming Democratic convention. He also cited Guyot's inflammatory comments after Sunflower and contrasted them to the decision to now seek power within the Democratic Party. Clark harshly criticized Guyot's perceived policy reversals, citing the Hinds County FDP's statement defending armed self-defense, and Guyot's commenting that this stance was not MFDP policy but endorsing self-defense a week later. Clark said that due to Guyot's actions, the MFDP had become "a cog in the national Democratic Party machine" and said "such gross betrayal could only have succeeded with the active help of people inside the MFDP, inside the leadership of the MFDP." Clark saw the federally funded poverty program as the vehicle of this co-opting, using federal funds to buy off "whole chunks of this movement's best people." He also accused the party leaders of supporting the Vietnam War by affiliating with the national Democrats. He declared that the "radical people's movement" of the MFDP "may be coming to an end."[46]

Clark's inflammatory editorial said more about what he wanted the MFDP to be rather than what it actually had become. His focus on comments from 1967 on made it sound as if the Guyot and the party shifted radically after the Sunflower elections. They had not. The MFDP had always focused on legal action through the courts as part of its strategy. Clark did not once mention the congressional challenge, which the party carried out through traditional legalistic measures. Even as the MFDP encouraged independent candidacies, it still supported Black candidates who ran in the Democratic primaries. In short, the MFDP always worked within the political system, either as Democrats or independents, an approach that largely alienated it from SNCC. It was "radical" only in the sense that it defended the basic civil rights of Black Mississippians in the 1960s—which made it radical to most white Mississippians. And at no time did the party ever make a statement of support for the Vietnam War, instead defending the right of local FDPs to make antiwar and antidraft statements, and the party later endorsed antiwar Democrats in the 1968 primaries. Finally, the MFDP did endorse the Masonite strike and condemned Masonite's demonizing of the local as being Klan-affiliated, calling it an effort "to keep Black and white workers apart," and highlighting the integration of the local.[47] It is unclear whether the MFDP endorsement came in response to Clark's editorial or not.

Clark's criticism of the MFDP's perceived lack of support for the strikers in Laurel also reflects his white privilege and the traditional blind spot that American Marxism had regarding Black workers. He too readily dismissed the Klan influence in the local, admitting to some infiltration but putting more blame on the Black strikers who went back to work. A white man like Clark could easily make a scab charge, as he had not grown up with the constant threat of white supremacist violence. His criticism essentially minimized the racism of the white working class and suggested that Black workers should be the ones doing most of the accommodating, not white workers. Some Black workers also returned to work because the Mississippi Supreme Court had ordered the strikers to do so, and the Masonite Corporation hired both white and Black strikebreakers, but Clark only focused on the Black ones.[48] His comments showed that for many white Marxists, their skin color and privileged worldview blinded them to the realities of being an African American worker in the Deep South.

Guyot, at any rate, had little sympathy for the socialist politics of Clark. He favored liberal reform within a capitalist system, which put him at odds with both white Marxists and Marxist-influenced Black Power groups like the

Republic of New Africa and the Black Panther Party. He recalled a debate he had with Casey Hayden about socialism. She told him, "You answer all of the question right but you don't come to the final conclusion. I said, 'Honey, let me tell you just one thing. We just look at this differently.' She would say, 'Well, do you think labor people should be organized?' I said absolutely. 'Do you think they should own the factories?' I said, 'Yes, if they can afford it.'"[49]

In May, Charles Evers resigned temporarily from his NAACP office to work on the Kennedy campaign in Mississippi. He initially met with Vice President Hubert Humphrey in April at a breakfast at the University of Mississippi, a meeting also attended by Aaron Henry, the Reverend R. L. T. Smith, and Amzie Moore, but he ended up supporting the brother of the slain president instead. He cochaired the Kennedy campaign in Mississippi with Oscar Carr Jr., a white planter from Coahoma County. Carr, who ran his family's cotton and real estate business in Clarksdale, had gotten involved in the civil rights movement due to his association with Aaron Henry and Mississippi Action for Progress, the antipoverty group they founded to oppose the MFDP-backed Child Development Group of Mississippi.[50]

Guyot indicated that the MFDP would work with other groups on a joint challenge to the regular Democrats, and met with Henry, who cochaired the Young Democrats of Mississippi. Yet the MFDP had done little groundwork since its September 1967 announcement that it was going to Chicago. The party suffered severe financial strain—the *Mississippi Newsletter*, for example, had cut its publication from weekly to bimonthly in the spring of 1968—and Senator Eastland used his positions on the Judiciary Committee and Internal Security Subcommittee to investigate the MFDP and its connection to the National Conference for New Politics. Guyot remained publicly committed to the idea of a grassroots party of participatory democracy, declaring that the MFDP "will meet in convention in Jackson, and it will listen to its constituency in the writing of a platform, and then it will go to Chicago and say here is our plank, here is what your plank should be." This suggested that unlike the Young Democrats, the MFDP still favored an independent course rather than working within the state Democratic Party. Given that Henry himself reported that at least thirty-nine Mississippi counties in May 1968 denied Black participation in their precinct and county conventions, Guyot not surprisingly still had reservations about integrating the state party.[51]

As the MFDP held its own meeting, the Young Democrats and the NAACP organized around the Mississippi Voter Registration and Education League, an organization sponsored by those two groups and headed by Henry. The coalition included the Delta Ministry and civil rights leaders like Evers and Henry, as well as white moderates like Hodding Carter III and Claude Ramsey. The MFDP did not join, and the party's executive committee said publicly that it felt Black participation in the regular party's precinct and county conventions would "have little to no effect in shaping the already established policies of the reactionary and segregationist Mississippi Democratic Party." The new coalition pledged to work through the regular party, but prepared to send a delegation to Chicago to challenge the regulars if they refused integration. This group did manage to get the regulars to select three Black men, including Evers, to integrate the state delegation to Chicago. But Governor Williams confirmed Guyot's reluctance when the regulars, headed by Williams, rejected any cooperation with the league at their state convention. Evers and Dr. Matthew Page resigned as delegates, leaving Dr. Gilbert Mason as the sole Black delegate for the regular delegation.[52]

The regulars shut out the loyalists, but both groups shut out the MFDP. With this impasse, the MFDP leadership grudgingly accepted that the civil rights forces needed a coalition that included every progressive organization in the state to defeat the regulars, and that the ongoing division had to end. Guyot played a key role in persuading the other members of the executive committee to accept this reality. Despite his reluctance to participate in the regular party's local conventions, he knew the MFDP would gain nothing by maintaining its independent course. Additional help came from Senator Eugene McCarthy, who told the loyalists that he would not support their challenge unless the coalition included the MFDP, a statement that prodded reluctant white moderates into accepting the party. The party's executive committee voted to join with the other forces "in this political confrontation with Eastland's party." The Loyalist Democrats formally organized on 21 June in Jackson, in a coalition that included the MFDP, the Prince Hall Masons, the state AFL-CIO, the Young Democrats, the NAACP, and the Black Mississippi Teachers Association. As Les McLemore has noted, the MFDP's prior work on the Evers campaign paved the way for this alliance.[53]

The new alliance had its tensions. Guyot demanded 50 percent representation for the MFDP in the delegation, which the other groups quickly rejected. After several days of discussion, the MFDP managed to get ten delegates out of a forty-four-person delegation, as well as eight alternates out of twenty-four. This was disproportionately in the MFDP's favor, out of the six groups in the delegation. Les McLemore called it "clearly a victory" for the MFDP, and Guyot said that the party had entered the alliance "from a position of strength." Some MFDP activists still opposed cooperation with the likes of Evers and Ramsey, and Fannie Lou Hamer called them "these same folks in 1964 that were willing to sell us down the drain and tried to do it." But Guyot defended the compromise and said that it "is a mass challenge and the people support it."[54]

Despite the concessions to the MFDP, observers inside and outside the party begin to write its political epitaph. The State Sovereignty Commission reported that the MFDP "does not appear to have very much power or authority, certainly not that held by Evers and the NAACP." Buford Posey, a white civil rights activist from Philadelphia, Mississippi, who had given the FBI information about the murders of Chaney, Schwerner, and Goodman, wrote that summer that the MFDP has "more followers *outside* Mississippi than it does inside. . . . Its chairman, Lawrence Guyot, is a very capable leader but suffers from lack of finances and the general apathy of the poor Blacks he aspires to lead. Had it not been for the assistance of the Delta Ministry headed by Owen Brooks, the Mississippi Freedom Democratic Party would have ceased to exist long ago."[55]

The creation of a center-left coalition like the loyalists also meant that its members split over which Democrat to support. Initially, the coalition strongly favored Robert Kennedy, even though some members, like Aaron Henry, favored Humphrey. Although McCarthy envisioned a desegregated society and proposed active measures to achieve it, versus Kennedy's preference for encouraging private development in urban ghettos, Kennedy commanded the support of Black voters in the primaries. Kennedy's assassination after the California primary in June effectively fractured the MFDP's unity on a presidential candidate, with the more liberal and MFDP-affiliated members, like Representative Robert Clark, favoring McCarthy, while the more establishment Humphrey attracted the support of the moderates.[56]

McCarthy's staffers reportedly tried to get the MFDP to send a separate delegation to Chicago after Kennedy's death. Recollections here differ; Aaron Henry said that Jan Goodman, a McCarthy organizer and former MFDP staffer, had tried to get the MFDP and the loyalists to send separate delegations to Chicago with the plan to get both of them seated, which would aid McCarthy's chances of carrying Mississippi at the convention. Guyot denied that Goodman herself made such an offer but instead attributed the push to other people in McCarthy's campaign.[57]

The focus on creating the coalition to go to Chicago also overshadowed the 4 June primary elections. Black candidates ran against the white incumbent Democrats in three US House Districts—Thelma Barnes of Greenville in the First District, Clarence Hall of Issaquena County in the Fourth District, and the Reverend J. C. Killingsworth of Hattiesburg in the Fifth District. All three candidates participated in civil rights activities in their respective hometowns, and all had signed the call for a boycott of white businesses as a response to

Dr. King's assassination. Guyot, working with the Delta Ministry and Mississippians United to Elect Negro Candidates, solicited funds for the candidates, but otherwise the campaigns attracted little attention from the civil rights groups now looking ahead to the Democratic Convention. The MFDP had little to spare, at any rate, and with no congressional district possessing a Black majority, the Black candidates had no more of a chance of success than Evers did in the Third District. The lack of attention even carried over to the white electorate, as Governor Williams expressed concerns about low voter turnout and apathy, paired with his fears of a strong Black voter turnout. Despite his concerns, the white incumbents defeated their Black challengers in a landslide, with William Colmer beating Reverend Killingsworth by a more than ten-to-one margin in the Fifth District.[58]

The loyalists organized their own convention, with precinct and county meetings held over the summer of 1968. The tensions between the MFDP members and the NAACP centrists erupted in these meetings as well. The centrists—or "traditionalists," as Les McLemore called them—clashed with the MFDP members over the delegates and alternates for the state convention. The MFDP elected at least one member or sympathizer in each district caucus except the Second District, which the traditionalists completely controlled. Guyot himself ran for a delegate position at the Fourth Congressional District caucus, and Evers nominated a white centrist, Danny Cupit, to run against him. A political ally of Evers, Cupit had successfully sued the University of Mississippi's board of trustees (where he was enrolled as a law student) in 1968 for trying to block Evers from speaking on campus. Guyot lost the delegate race to Cupit.[59]

At the loyalist convention on 11 August at Jackson's Masonic Temple, where the MFDP had held its 1964 convention, the traditionalists reasserted control. Three thousand people attended, with approximately half that number being the delegates and alternates. Aaron Henry presided over the meeting as convention chairman, and dignitaries like Bayard Rustin and Joseph Rauh spoke in favor of seating the loyalists and promised to walk out of the Chicago convention if they were not. Representatives of the six groups in the loyalist coalition had agreed in advance to the slate of at-large delegates, effectively preventing any nominations from the convention floor. Guyot, along with other MFDP members or sympathizers such as Robert Clark, Ed King, and Clifton Whitley, attended as at-large delegates. During the negotiations, the traditionalists eroded the MFDP's status further as the convention settled on ten delegates and six alternates, five fewer alternates than originally offered. Ultimately, the MFDP had ten delegates in the sixty-eight-member delegation.[60]

The real showdown between the two opposing forces came over the post of national committeeman, which proved to be the most dramatic and contentious issue at the convention. The two nominees, Charles Evers and Robert Clark, clearly represented the continuing NAACP-MFDP division in the loyalist coalition. Clark won the initial vote by the nominating committee, 8–6. A defiant Evers declared that "you may wipe Evers today, but tomorrow will be a different ball game." None of this drama carried over to the national committeewoman's nomination, which went to Patricia Derian, a white civil rights activist who had supported school desegregation and worked for Mississippi Action for Progress.[61]

Les McLemore called the convention "largely free of controversy" and filled with many speeches and committee reports, enough to "test the patience of the most patient of mortals." Some of the MFDP resentment over the compromises required for entering the loyalist coalition surfaced, however. The convention rejected fourteen different at-large delegate nominations from the floor, and the MFDP's lack of support for these nominations led one member to ask Guyot, "What happened in that room?" when the six organizations agreed to the delegate slate. A Clay County delegate openly questioned why the MFDP participated in the Democratic Party, as he regarded both the state and national parties as corrupt. These events presaged the committeeman election. A member of the nominations committee filed a minority report nominating Evers for national committeeman, which created "pandemonium" on the convention floor. His supporters seconded and supported his nomination from the floor, and a band erupted in a "spontaneous" performance, accompanied by confetti from the hall balcony. This nomination—apparently staged entirely by Evers—soon turned ugly. Clark's supporters spoke up for his nomination, declaring the need to develop new leadership in the state. One Evers supporter then declared it to be "a sin before God for any man to run against Charles Evers!" Evers's supporters shouted down Clark supporters, including a young man named John Buffington, whom Evers's supporters manhandled when he tried to give a pro-Clark speech. He resigned as a delegate in protest. At the end of the speeches, Evers won the election to the post of national committeeman. As one observer said of the fracas, "That's as close to a machine as you can get."[62]

The national committeeman vote showed the price the MFDP paid for political access. Evers had planned his convention coup for weeks, garnering support from county delegations. As McLemore, who observed this all as an MFDP member, concluded, the party had been outfoxed by Evers and the NAACP traditionalists. "Political crudeness" on the part of the MFDP was how he characterized it, a lack of the careful planning that went into Sunflower County and Clark's election that left the party leadership "politically impotent." McLemore did not single Guyot out by name but the implication was clear—they had "spent too much time congratulating themselves" after Clark's nominations committee victory and had seriously underestimated Evers. Clark himself contributed to his defeat by erroneously assuming that Evers supporters would back him, since he was the state's lone Black state representative, a misstep that McLemore called "sentimentality" on Clark's part. Jan Hillegas in the *Mississippi Newsletter* blasted the convention events, lamenting the "blind-sheep actions of so many, and the silence of others."[63] True though that may be, Guyot and the MFDP leadership acquiesced as a price of staying in the coalition. The party achieved few tangible results as an outsider, but it would have to compromise to become a political insider. The events in Jackson showed that the MFDP's influence among the loyalists would be limited, at least if Evers—with the tacit support, most notably, of Aaron Henry—had anything to say about it.

The left-leaning forces shared the blame in this fiasco. Jan Goodman, the McCarthy field worker, "abrasively" pressured the delegates for commitments to McCarthy, according to Rowland Evans and Robert Novak—but these two columnists' hostility to the MFDP was well known, as they were still referring to "FDP Black extremists" in 1968. Goodman's own MFDP background apparently alienated some of the moderates, which made them wary of McCarthy's overtures. In addition, McCarthy himself persisted in referring to the entire loyalist faction as the MFDP, rather than acknowledging that the MFDP was now part of a broader coalition.[64]

Since all the major contenders for the Democratic nomination—Senators McCarthy and George McGovern and Vice President Hubert Humphrey—openly supported the loyalists, their seating was inevitable, unlike the 1964 Atlantic City convention. But the divisions in the coalition continued in Chicago. The MFDP continued to display its independent streak when the FDP delegates ignored a request from Henry and Evers to not attend a Black caucus called by Representative John Conyers Jr., the Black Detroit congressman. The MFDP also held its own press conferences and advocated for its own platform and programs, mostly notably land reform, economic justice, and an end to the Vietnam War.[65]

The question of the Democratic presidential nominee proved the bigger split between the two sides in the coalition. Guyot and the MFDP members favored McCarthy, the leading antiwar candidate after the assassination of Robert Kennedy. The MFDP opposed Humphrey, despite his strong civil rights record, since he was still supporting the Vietnam War. The loyalist coalition split about evenly between Humphrey and McCarthy, and SSC spies eagerly reported on the conflicts among Guyot and Evers and Henry. The latter two supported Humphrey.[66]

But not all the MFDP members supported McCarthy, and not all the moderates supported Humphrey. Some members favored George McGovern, and some delegates in Chicago tried a last-minute push to draft the sole remaining Kennedy brother, Edward, for president. Mayor Richard Daley of Chicago tried unsuccessfully to persuade the thirty-six-year-old Massachusetts senator to run, but Mississippi loyalists were involved in the effort. Fannie Lou Hamer joined the draft campaign, but Hodding Carter III managed to talk her into calling Kennedy before her plan to nominate him from the podium at the Chicago convention. She reached Steve Smith, his brother-in-law, who talked her out of the scheme. Ultimately, the MFDP delegates persuaded the loyalists to approve a plank opposing the Vietnam War, but the convention as a whole voted down this minority plank, and a plurality of the loyalist delegation endorsed Humphrey.[67]

The real drama in Chicago, of course, occurred outside the convention, as Mayor Daley's police engaged in a weeklong battle with antiwar protesters in the streets and parks along Lake Michigan. The violence famously spilled over into the convention floor, and even threatened the loyalist coalition. The highly emotional state of Chicago brought Guyot's combative nature to the forefront. No doubt recalling his own treatment by police at Winona, he argued forcefully that the state delegation should walk out in protest over the police violence, and he almost got into a fistfight with Carter when the latter insisted that the loyalists stay on the floor. He also clashed with Oscar Carr, the white planter who would soon head the "Planters for Humphrey/Muskie" organization in Mississippi. Carr, who founded the First National Bank of Clarksdale in the early 1960s to provide loans to Black farmers and businessmen and worked with Aaron Henry on Head Start, firmly supported the moderate camps. He had little enthusiasm for the MFDP, and at one point during the convention chaos declared in a memo that "Guyot is the problem." In a sign of compromise and pragmatism, Guyot settled for the Mississippi delegation's voting to condemn the police brutality and staying on the convention floor.[68]

Chicago left a bitter taste in the mouths of the MFDP members. Yet Guyot urged his party members to rally behind Humphrey and win in Mississippi. George Wallace, running as an independent segregationist and the darling son of the white South, opposed Humphrey in Mississippi, with the Republican candidate, former vice president Richard Nixon, a distant third. "The defeat of Wallace in Mississippi would be the beginning of a new day for the people of the South," Guyot declared in the MFDP newspaper. He also urged MFDP members to elect Black candidates on the ballot to local offices, in particular the election commissions and school boards, for which there were seventy-nine Black candidates running in 1968.[69]

Wallace won Mississippi, but nationally, Nixon made enough inroads in and out of the South to eke out a win over Humphrey in November. The end of a Democratic administration no doubt increased the bitterness of both the moderates and the MFDP members, but Guyot said little about that. The same could not be said of Hamer, who after the election called the Black loyalists "very middle-class people. . . . These were the same people who were willing to sell us down the drain and tried to do it. They talked about throwing people like me and Guyot out of the delegation." John Buffington, the MFDP supporter who was roughed up by Evers's supporters at the Jackson convention (and who did not go to Chicago), was even more blunt. "The FDP had no business in that delegation with people like Charles Evers and Claude Ramsey and Hodding Carter," he declared. He said that "too much effort and emphasis is placed on national politics" and that "the FDP is dead."[70]

It wasn't dead yet, but after Chicago the MFDP lived on borrowed time. Kenneth Fairly, a reporter for the *Clarion-Ledger*, speculated that the loyalists would purge Guyot, Hamer, and Ed King from the coalition after Chicago, likely wishful thinking on his part. Those expulsions did not happen, but the party effectively ceased to be an independent political force by becoming the junior partner to the NAACP. The party found itself more than $800 in debt as a result of Chicago. Donations returned the party to solvency, but only by the barest of margins, as the party treasury had only $3.13 by February 1969. By this point, almost all of its financial support came from the Delta Ministry. And due to its absorption into the loyalist coalition, the MFDP effectively ended its relationship with Black Power. As Leonard Moore has shown, the separatist course of Black Power met its end politically at the National Black Political Convention, also known as the Gary Convention, in 1972. The growth of Black political power led to the decline of Black Power separatism. As Moore notes, "Black nationalists did not evolve with the times," and "their narrow beliefs and outlook made it impossible for them to embrace the most basic form of electoral politics, since they considered voting to be a waste of time."[71]

Buffington called an MFDP meeting at Mt. Beulah on 10 November, where he aired these grievances against the moderates. With Guyot and Hamer present, the members agreed to a reorganization of the MFDP, with an eye toward future elections. Guyot effectively gave up leadership of the party at this meeting, as a planning committee headed by Joseph Harris assumed all the Executive Committee's responsibilities until a new chairman could be elected at the next state meeting on 5 January. If the MFDP went back into the course of independent

Black politics, it would do so without Guyot. While in Chicago, he visited a doctor who told him that if he returned to Mississippi, "you have about two months to live." At only twenty-nine years of age, Guyot's high blood pressure, heart trouble, and obesity took their toll, along with the physical trauma of the Winona beating and the stress of leading the MFDP. He announced in advance of the MFDP convention that he would not be seeking the chairmanship again.[72]

In December, 400 delegates attended the loyalist convention in Jackson, where they reelected Aaron Henry as chairman. The MFDP put up Robert Clark to run against Henry, but he lost and instead delegates named him to the state executive committee as its only MFDP-backed member. The absorption of the MFDP into the loyalists still rankled some its members. Fannie Lou Hamer blasted "house niggers" who were late arrivals to the loyalists and had skipped the hard and dangerous work of civil rights organizing. "As soon as the FDP walked through the valley of the shadow of death, they hopped on the bandwagon," she said bitterly. On 5 January 1969, the MFDP held its own convention, with 350 delegates from thirty-two counties. Guyot attended and gave a final address as chairman to the party. He urged members to continue to agitate and not simply exist as an extension of the national party, and to maintain an independent identity within the coalition. He said members should "continue to be unpopular and deal with the issues of poor people and attack every unacceptable institution." This meant continuing to use protest alongside political organizing, as members "must accept the responsibility to not allow dissent to become a relic of the past." Clark, who also attended, wondered if this would be the last time the MFDP held a state convention. The executive board voted in the Reverend Clifton Whitley as its new chairman, with Hamer as vice chair and Joseph Harris as treasurer. By the end of January, Lawrence and Monica Guyot had relocated to an apartment in Newark, New Jersey.[73]

The MFDP continued as best it could, but it had no financial resources of its own to organize programs. The Lawyers' Constitutional Defense Committee and the Lawyers Committee for Civil Rights under Law prepared a handbook for the party to organize for municipal elections in 1969, and Mississippians United to Elect Negro Candidates worked to solicit financial aid for candidates. MFDP and Delta Ministry members made up the membership of Mississippians United, with apparently no NAACP support. Clifton Whitley resigned only months into his chairmanship. This prompted Guyot to return to Mississippi for a meeting to give a report on party structure in Whitley's place. He also assisted with MFDP election efforts and on 8 May introduced Hamer at a Lexington rally to urge Black Mississippians to vote in the municipal elections. The party had sunk to a sad state by the time of its December 1969 Executive Committee meeting.

The Delta Ministry funded the entire party by this point, to the point of paying for its secretary, office rent, and utility bills. The party had not taken on any new programs, and its members could not even agree to support a Delta Ministry plan for the upcoming school board elections. Internal dissent and infighting rocked the party. Owen Brooks of the Delta Ministry called for a return to independent politics and running the MFDP as an all-Black party. He "exploded" at the assembled officers and upset some of them with his tone and rhetoric. Annie Devine and Joe Harris got into a heated exchange when she called him "a hired servant" who did not "get involved with the real problems of the party or the people." "I have tried to save this organization," Harris shot back.[74] But it seemed too late for that.

Guyot largely closed the door on his involvement in and leadership of the MFDP and for all intents and purposes started a new chapter in his life. He left a mixed legacy in Mississippi, as the party had not established itself as a successful alternative to the segregationist Democratic Party. Instead, it entered into a pragmatic collation with its rivals in the civil rights movement and effectively faded away as an independent entity. In counties like Sunflower, the MFDP continued to run candidates and work separately from the NAACP, and also did so in the 1971 elections when Charles Evers ran for governor. These efforts did not translate into success for the MFDP anymore than it did in earlier years, and Hamer herself lost her 1971 state senate race. Only the Holmes County FDP survived into the post–civil rights era.[75]

Guyot's move north reflected the same motivations of so many thousands of African Americans before him, like them looking for better opportunities. Mechanization and the resulting decline in demand by white planters for Black labor accelerated the economic decline of Black sharecroppers and hastened Black migration to northern cities for work. The Mississippi Delta alone saw double-digit population declines in most of its counties after 1950.[76] While he was not an impoverished sharecropper leaving the Delta for Chicago, Guyot's higher socioeconomic status in no way diminished the significance of his move. With his health seriously threatened by the stress of running the MFDP, no doubt compounded by the injuries he received at Winona, he moved for reasons more personal than economic. Adding to this was his desire to start a family, which he and Monica did in the coming years.

So did Guyot fail as a leader? The cynical answer may be yes, but the reality is far more nuanced and complex. The rank-and-file members of the MFDP, such as the Jackson FDP and Jan Hillegas, sniped at Guyot, calling him too quick to sell out, but as Charles Payne has noted, Guyot "never accepted the idea that cooperation with the regular Democratic party was evil. . . . The fight wasn't about being politically pure; it was a fight to get in and take over."[77] And then there is the back-and-forth nature of his focus on high-profile races for federal office, including the ones he personally ran in, versus the real groundwork of winning local races and community organization. While the MFDP mostly failed in its electoral campaigns, this had nothing to do with its local organizing or deviation from the loose structure of SNCC. Instead, the party's focus on symbolic congressional campaigns, at the expense of intensive local organizing, weakened it. The high-profile races had some symbolic effect, as the legal battles and presence of the MFDP candidates challenged the very notions of Black deference that white Mississippians expected in their social order. As Les McLemore wrote, despite the electoral losses "their presence, indeed, amply demonstrated to the white 'powers-that-be' that the FDP was in the state's political arena as a permanent fixture."[78] While his prediction of the MFDP's permanence proved overly optimistic (with the exception of Holmes County), McLemore's statement rings true. The intangible effects of the consciousness-raising of MFDP electoral contests cannot be quantitatively measured, but Guyot, Hamer, and others in the party clearly helped break the fear of the racial caste system for Black Mississippians.

While it is easy to criticize Guyot and the MFDP for the back-and-forth approach of independent candidacies versus working within the state Democratic Party, this proved an essential part of his complex relationship with the NAACP, most notably Charles Evers. His cooperation with Evers, as well as his conflict with him, reflected Guyot's experimental strategy of trying what worked. Simply put, Guyot had no hard ideological commitment to a specific set of tactics. Ultimately, his independent strategy, however laudable, failed. It produced few victories, so Guyot and the MFDP abandoned it. The fusion—or more accurately absorption—of the MFDP into the Loyalist Democrats came from the trend toward cooperation with the NAACP after the 1967 state elections and the MFDP's losses in Sunflower County. Of course, this angered some radicalized rank-and-file members, who sharply criticized Guyot for his practicality. But even a firebrand like Stokely Carmichael eventually had to deal with activists more radical than he, as seen when he and Cleveland Sellers fired Bill Ware and the other Atlanta separatists from SNCC.[79] Revolutions, even nonviolent ones, tend to eat their own children.

Guyot never expressed any reservations about joining the loyalist coalition in 1968, even if it meant a junior status for his party, and its eventual absorption. He recognized the costs of becoming a political insider, and he saw the loss of independence as an acceptable price. Even in 2012, the last year of his life, he stood by his decision. He specifically rejected the purist route that Black Power and SNCC activists wanted, saying that "if the MFDP was involved in a coalition with the loyalists, it would be seated. It was seated."[80]

The MFDP also never became a cult of personality around Guyot, unlike the political machine that Charles Evers constructed in Mississippi's southwestern river counties, in particular Jefferson County. Put another way, Guyot headed the party but never became a political boss like Evers, who freely flexed his muscle to intimidate local Black residents during the Port Gibson boycott in the 1960s.[81] He also never captured the kind of fame and attention of other civil rights figures of his generation. He mostly labored in the shadows of fellow activists like Stokely Carmichael, who experienced what his biographer called a "stratospheric ascent" after the publicity of the Meredith March, with major coverage in both the print and television media. Fueling this publicity for Carmichael were major disputes with mainstream civil rights leaders like Roy Wilkins of the NAACP, who criticized Carmichael's endorsement of Black Power as reverse racism and "Black death."[82] While Guyot clashed with other Mississippi civil rights leaders and the State Sovereignty Commission did what it could to highlight and exploit these fissures, they lacked the glamor and "sexiness" that Carmichael, the Black Panthers, and other Black Power militants developed, even though Guyot could on occasion indulge in the same inflammatory rhetoric of "Stokely Starmichael," as Ruby Doris Smith Robinson of SNCC labeled him for his ego and cult of personality.[83]

But with Guyot's move north, his role in the MFDP and the southern civil rights movement largely ended. He began a new chapter in his life—family, and eventually a return to political organizing in Washington, DC—one that built on his years of work with SNCC and the MFDP and would make him a political insider, something that, at least before 1968, had eluded him in Mississippi.

# CHAPTER 7
# YOU SHOULDN'T LET THEM USE YOU

THE WASHINGTON YEARS

Second-wave feminists in the 1960s said that "the personal is political," meaning that the political nature of society affected private matters and aspects of life commonly considered nonpolitical just as much as public affairs. Put more plainly, modern society contained no separation of life into public and private spheres.[1] Guyot's new life in Washington, DC, embodied this mantra. While it seemed at first that he abandoned politics for family life, he could never stay away from it for long, and likely never saw himself as leaving it. His years in Washington embodied the transition of his 1960s southern political organizing to the East Coast urban politics of the 1970s and beyond. Guyot's journey was another example of how the Student Nonviolent Coordinating Committee (SNCC) transformed its activists, creating grassroots leaders. But no grassroots organization, not even one run by former members of SNCC, changed Guyot into a DC activist. A political machine, run by the savvy Marion Barry, did that to Guyot. Unlike during his leadership years with the Mississippi Freedom Democratic Party (MFDP), Guyot now found himself to be a cog in such a machine, dispensing and benefiting from patronage. While he never lost his activist idealism and actively sought to mentor new leaders, the experience of being an insider meant that he now benefited from the status quo rather than battling it. This new realm of politics would create strange bedfellows.

While Guyot fit and seemed to personify the dominant narrative of the civil rights movement shifting from the 1960s South to the 1970s urban North, his story is more complex than that. Jacquelyn Dowd Hall has challenged that traditional narrative, as her analysis highlights civil rights struggles in the North, Midwest, and West that predated the mid-1960s. Guyot arrived in DC and joined an existing movement there that had already made political inroads, building on the work of Barry and earlier activists. Also, for Guyot the freedom struggle did not end even as he became involved in the Barry administration, which fits both with Hall's framework of studying areas outside the South and her point that an overemphasis on the South obfuscates Northern and Western racism. As someone who now had some access to political power, Guyot would also work to implement her fifth point, the use of civil rights laws and reforms to benefit the impoverished people of Washington, DC, and more broadly, poor people in the country as a whole.[2]

At their new residence in Newark, the Guyots entered the next stage of their lives. Guyot enrolled in the law school at Rutgers University, and Monica worked and supported Guyot while he attended classes. Arthur Kinoy, whom he worked closely with on the congressional challenge, had been on the faculty at Rutgers since 1964. Guyot received his law degree from Rutgers in 1971. Aside from education, Guyot also focused on raising a family for much of the 1970s. After his graduation, the Guyots moved to Washington, DC. He came to DC to continue his civil rights work, but in a less stressful way than with the MFDP. "I came here to work with the Lawyers Committee for Civil Rights under Law, to monitor the 1965 Voting Rights Act," he later recalled. In 1971, Monica gave birth to their first child, a daughter they named Julie. Three years later, Monica had their second and final child, a son they named Lawrence Guyot III. Lawrence Jr. and Monica rejected identifying their children as biracial. Although light-skinned, neither child could pass as a white person—one writer described Julie as "café-au-lait" in complexion with curly hair, and the younger Lawrence's facial features led people to mistake him for an Asian in his adult life. Guyot, mindful of raising mixed-race children in white America, told his children that they were Black since people would regard them as such, so they needed to be prepared to deal with racial prejudice. Guyot dismissed biracial identities as "escapism" and legitimate only "if we lived in a country purely devoid of racism." Both parents worked while raising the children, and Monica proved a devoted mother, at one point even pulling young Lawrence out of school temporarily when he suffered an allergic reaction to a bee sting. She did so since there was no nurse at the elementary school to administer the appropriate injections to counter future insect stings.[3]

But a legal career did not loom for Guyot. The impetus for him to enter big-city urban politics came from an old associate and fellow Mississippian from SNCC. Marion Barry, a native of Itta Bena in the Delta, served as the first chairman of SNCC. He did much of his civil rights work outside of Mississippi, and he supported the MFDP and Guyot during crucial campaigns like the Atlantic City challenge. He left the southern civil rights movement before Guyot, however. Raised in Memphis, Barry was drawn to urban politics, and he went to Atlanta to volunteer for Julian Bond's campaign for the Georgia legislature. That campaign inspired him to then move to Washington, DC, to organize there.[4]

Barry's community organizing in DC led to friction with the SNCC headquarters, in particular with Cleveland Sellers. Barry responded by resigning from SNCC in January 1967 and focused on building a political organization in the capital, a choice mirroring both Guyot's and Charles Evers's actions in Mississippi. That year he and other activists created Pride Inc., a youth employment program funded by the Department of Labor. It provided jobs to unemployed Black youth and focused on cleaning up the streets and controlling the rat population in the ghettos. The effort to keep Pride Inc. funded beyond its initial five-week period is what began Barry's ascent into DC politics, and he took control of the organization and procured a second federal grant of $2 million for it.[5]

Barry's Pride organization exemplified the transition from protest politics to electoral politics, but in an urban setting rather than the rural focus of Guyot's MFDP. Pride employed Black teenagers and young men, many of them with criminal records, so this and Barry's own brushes with the law drew criticism, and white conservatives lambasted the Black Power overtones. By the end of the 1960s, Barry and his wife Mary Treadwell had expanded Pride into entrepreneurship when they created Pride Economic Enterprises, an arm designed to harness public and private grants to promote Black business. Barry and Treadwell promoted Black capitalism and moved into real estate and business ventures, hardly radical activities. Their actions provided a clear example of the mainstreaming of the protests of the 1960s into existing government channels on the municipal and federal levels.[6]

Barry entered DC politics as an officeholder shortly after building his political organization with Pride. He did so as the city moved toward home rule. In 1967, President Johnson appointed a nine-member city council headed by a mayor/commissioner. Johnson named Walter Washington, a Black housing bureaucrat active in the Urban League, to head the Black-majority council. The council did little to quell Black citizens' anger over police brutality from the heavily white force, however. Its members held office for barely six months, and then the city erupted into devastating riots after the assassination of Dr. Martin Luther King Jr. in April 1968. Barry capitalized on the urban unrest through Pride, establishing food distribution centers in riot-torn areas and sending Pride workers to protect Giant Foods, a chain of grocery stores that employed Pride teenagers, from looters. Following the riots, he took part in efforts to oppose freeway construction through Black neighborhoods.[7]

In 1971, Barry ran for the school board, the only elected body in DC. He unseated Anita Ford Allen, the head of the school board, channeling the younger Black militancy and community organizing in low-income neighborhoods into his first electoral victory. That same year, Walter Fauntroy won the election to the new position of nonvoting congressional delegate for the city, then played a major role in helping unseat John McMillen, a segregationist South Carolina congressman who had long opposed DC self-government. His defeat led to Black Michigan representative Charles Diggs's becoming chair of the House District Committee. From this position Diggs pushed the DC Home Rule Act through the House, and President Nixon signed it into law in December 1973. The act established an elected government with a mayor and thirteen-member council, but one still subject to congressional review and veto.[8]

Despite these limitations, home rule opened the doors for Barry's ascension and Guyot's own entrance into DC politics. Walter Washington won his first elected term as mayor and Barry a seat on the city council during the 1974 elections. The city had a 71 percent Black population, and with the elected leadership, the city, in the words of one recent history of the capital, "reasserted itself as the capital of Black America."[9]

Barry entered the 1978 mayoral race after his term on the council, where he had chaired the Revenue and Finance Committee, which helped him build ties with the city's business community. He also enjoyed publicity from a hostage situation the previous year, where he was shot during a gunfight between police and a splinter sect from the Nation of Islam. Barry suffered only a superficial wound but received enormous press coverage. In a three-way race against Washington and council chairman Sterling Tucker, Barry's cultivation of white supporters paid off, as they favored him and his socially liberal positions. He narrowly won the primary and went on to easily defeat Arthur Fletcher, a Black Republican who had served in the Nixon administration. In a sign of the racial polarization that would mar DC politics for years to come, many of Barry's white primary supporters voted Republican in the general election.[10]

The Guyots became Washington, DC, residents in 1973, and appear to have spent much of the 1970s raising their young children and staying out of local politics. But when Barry became mayor, he brought civil rights activists from his SNCC days into his administration. Ivanhoe Donaldson, Courtland Cox, Frank Smith, and others soon found jobs with the city, with Donaldson serving as Barry's most important adviser. Before becoming mayor, Barry had tapped Guyot to work with Pride Inc., and by the early 1970s Guyot was directing social services for the organization. By the end of the 1970s, Barry hired Guyot as director of training and education of youth at Pride, on the recommendations of Ivanhoe Donaldson and Mary Treadwell. No longer head of a political organization, Guyot now labored as one of many bureaucrats in the vast municipal apparatus of Washington, DC. He oversaw job training for youth offenders, as an alternative to sending them to prison. He also worked with Black youth through the Afro-Academic Cultural, Technological, and Scientific Olympics, a program created by the National Association for the Advancement of Colored People (NAACP) to promote academic and cultural achievement among Black high school students. He organized the program and promoted it on local public broadcasting, declaring that that the community needed the program "to acclaim and recognize the talents of our city's young people." Guyot kept the teenagers focused on the political events of that day, such as the social service cuts of the Reagan administration and the debate over renewal of the Voting Rights Act, as they traveled in 1981 to the NAACP's national convention in Denver.[11]

In 1979, the *Washington Post* ran a series of articles on Pride that proved the undoing of the organization, which by then had received more than $20 million from the federal government. By 1982, Pride no longer operated and was facing a federal corruption investigation because of the actions of Mary Treadwell, now Barry's ex-wife. In 1983, in an early sign of the coming troubles for the Barry administration, federal prosecutors convicted Treadwell for conspiring to defraud the federal government while operating the Clifton Terrace Apartments, one of the complexes previously managed by Pride. She was sentenced to three years in prison for pocketing low-income housing funds for her personal use, but the scandal did not affect Barry, who no longer had any connections to Pride when the fraud occurred (and had divorced Treadwell in 1977). The scandal also did not affect Guyot, whom prosecutors never indicted for any Pride-related work.[12]

Homelessness, one of the major issues of the Reagan era, consumed much of Guyot's prodigious energy in the 1980s. A new generation of activists now borrowed the protest tactics of the civil rights movement. In DC, the Community for Creative Nonviolence (CCNV) represented much of that activism. Founded in DC in 1970 by Ed Guinan, a white Catholic activist, the CCNV began as an antiwar organization but soon shifted to fighting poverty in the city. By 1975, a new branch of the CCNV known as Euclid House focused on direct action protest. Mitch Snyder, a charismatic activist who favored confrontational tactics over Guinan's emphasis on serving the poor, headed Euclid House, located in Columbia Heights. Originally a middle-class Black neighborhood, Columbia Heights had deteriorated rapidly into a drug-infested slum after the 1968 riots. It contained numerous vacant homes held by speculators, while homelessness rose among the city's working poor. The city also lacked an adult homeless shelter, leaving that burden to faith-based nonprofits that could not meet the demand.[13]

Snyder and his Euclid House activists lobbied Walter Washington's administration to provide adult shelters, but the system the city created in the 1970s degraded and penalized any people who sought help. Euclid House built a working relationship with Barry after his electoral victory in 1978, and he openly embraced the CCNV program by 1979. The CCNV honeymoon with the Barry administration proved brief, however. The city deficit had reached $115 million by 1981, which prompted Barry to introduce spending cuts and other austerity measures in his budget. He dissolved the Mayor's Commission on the Homeless (which he had just created after taking office) and declared the closure of two emergency shelters. Using pro bono attorneys, the CCNV obtained an injunction that required the city to keep the shelters open. The cuts splintered Barry's political coalition, angering activists and labor unions while improving his relations with the white business community, who favored reductions in social services.[14]

Guyot moved into homelessness advocacy in 1984, when he won election to the Coalition for the Homeless, a nonprofit organization of religious and private providers of aid to the homeless. The coalition formed in 1979 and in 1984 opened a 600-bed shelter in Southeast DC. Guyot's work on the city's homelessness problem brought back some of the activist in him, as the issue, like so many others in DC, divided on racial and class lines. But at times the activist now advocated *against* the interests of social justice. In the summer of 1984, Guyot and other coalition board members campaigned against Initiative 17, a ballot item supported by the CCNV mandating that the city guarantee shelter for the homeless. The former head of the MFDP, which once had a platform calling for the government to remedy social and economic justice for the poor and disadvantaged, now campaigned against such a government mandate. Voters approved Initiative 17 by a majority of 73 percent, the first such homeless shelter mandate in the country. But Barry, two weeks after the election, challenged the initiative in court and won a ruling revoking the measure.[15]

Seeking to do something about the pressing issue, the Georgetown Clergy Association opened a shelter in its neighborhood on 17 January 1985. This created friction almost immediately in the area. Once run-down and working-class, Georgetown had been transformed by white gentrification in the 1920s and 1930s into one of DC's most exclusive neighborhoods. The DC Board of Education leased two vacant buildings to the clergy association, but problems at the shelter—which included numerous police calls for disorderly conduct, public drunkenness, and other crimes—led the school system to revoke the lease after only a month of operation. Guyot called the closing "unconscionable," and city officials backed his criticism. He clashed with local residents, telling the *Washington Post* that the predominately white neighborhood apparently felt that "the boundaries of Georgetown are too good for the homeless."[16] Guyot again crossed swords with the white power structure, but now he did so from a position of some influence himself, navigating the various different bureaucracies and constituencies in DC that often found themselves in conflict.

The not-in-my-backyard reaction to homeless shelters came up frequently in DC neighborhoods. The CCNV stepped up its clash with city officials, demanding more shelter space after a federal judge sided with federal officials who closed down the city's largest homeless shelter after inspectors condemned it as unfit for habitation. Later that year the coalition opened a shelter in Anacostia, in the city's Southeast quadrant, part of a planned disbursement of smaller shelters around the city. A news conference about the planned shelter erupted in acrimony, as local residents said no one had consulted them about the shelter's location, which the federal government, not the coalition, selected. At the press conference a reporter witnessed a "heated exchange" between Guyot and a member of the Advisory Neighborhood Commission (ANC). Guyot, ever combative, reminded local residents that "this is federal property, [and] if anyone thinks they can move us, we dare them to try." Yet Anacostia had a predominately Black population. Nadine Winter, a Black city councilwoman who represented the area, supported the residents' opposition to the shelter.[17]

Even some residents of Guyot's own LeDroit Park neighborhood opposed the actions of the Coalition for the Homeless. Theresa Brown, president of the LeDroit Park Preservation Society, wrote a letter to Patricia Makin, the coalition's executive director, and expressed concern that the coalition was locating shelters exclusively in Black residential neighborhoods. Emphasizing that she supported homeless shelters, she asked that the coalition cooperate with Snyder and the CCNV on using federal grant money to rehabilitate an already existing shelter. She said that "the Coalition in its zeal to out-do and embarrass Mitch Snyder is undermining the goodwill of the homeless by acting in an arrogant, reckless and unlawful manner by locating homeless shelters exclusively in Black neighborhoods . . . and unfortunately the homeless have become your pawns in the sad battle you are waging against the CCNV and Mitch Snyder."[18]

Snyder's activism with the CCNV and his protesting city inaction on the homeless meant that he and the coalition soon locked horns in a bitter dispute over who would lead the way on the issue. The coalition could count on city resources like buses and service programs, which the CCNV did not have. To activists like Snyder, the coalition and its board members like Guyot provided cover for the Barry administration on the issue. Snyder charged that the coalition could not raise enough funds as its end of its partnership with the US Department of Health and Human Services and charged that its plan required shelter residents to work without pay. Guyot denied the charge, declaring that the coalition would compensate for labor and that "there is nothing sinister about this." In a sign of his embeddedness in the Washington power structure, he pointed to one of the coalition's prominent and powerful fundraisers as proof it would meet its goals. The fundraiser was Susan Baker, wife of James Baker, Ronald Reagan's secretary of the treasury.[19]

Scandal soon plagued the Coalition for the Homeless, however. The federal government increased its scrutiny of the Barry administration after Mary Treadwell's conviction. In March 1986, DC police and the Federal Bureau of Investigation (FBI), responding to a request from the city's human services department, investigated allegations that the coalition had diverted federal funds to coalition members or spent them improperly. DC police reported that the coalition had "inadequate controls and recordkeeping" regarding federal grants for the emergency shelter in Anacostia that the coalition opened the previous year. The coalition's efforts to purchase real estate for homeless shelters fueled allegations of graft, in particular a $21,000 payment to DC police officer Vernell Tanner, an advance payment for rent on a building that Tanner intended to purchase. It appeared that the coalition acted in good faith, as Guyot, serving as the coalition's treasurer, told the *Washington Post* that Tanner had a contract to buy the property. He said that "there was no possible . . . fiscal irresponsibility" and that he did not know that Tanner would be unable to close the deal. He trusted Tanner enough to propose to the board another $10,000 to assist Tanner in closing the deal, but the board rejected that proposal. The coalition ended up purchasing the building itself in April 1986.[20]

In addition to the financial allegations, the Coalition for the Homeless did not screen its employees for criminal records. After police arrested an employee with what the *Post* called a "lengthy criminal record" after he attacked a shelter resident with a baseball bat, the authorities began to investigate other reported assaults by staff members on shelter residents. The board fired the employee, and coalition president Elisabeth Huguenin called it an "isolated event." She ordered an internal investigation after the police investigation became public but claimed no knowledge of any other assaults.[21]

Mitch Snyder and the CCNV used the scandals to attack the Coalition for the Homeless publicly and escalate Snyder's long-running feud with the organization. Snyder had just waged a successful campaign in his crusade to end homelessness, with the CCNV managing to keep its shelter open through the winter of 1985–86. Snyder and several supporters launched a hunger strike in early 1986 to protest the lack of federal funds for needed renovations at the shelter. The hunger strike continued for a month, and the publicity forced the Reagan administration to agree to provide $5 million to renovate the shelter. Snyder said that the assaults and the misuse of federal funds showed that the coalition could not adequately deal with homelessness in the nation's capital. He asked federal officials to block the coalition from spending the remaining $2 million of a $3.7 million grant it received the previous fall. "A mess has been created. . . . The taxpayers' money is being squandered." Huguenin, who had recently claimed that the two groups were moving closer together, said that "it really saddens me that he said that."[22]

The Vernell Tanner affair proved to be an ongoing headache for Guyot. He told the *Post* that the police accused him of acting improperly in his handling of real estate transactions. "There's an attempt by the [police] to make this look underhanded between Mr. Tanner and myself," he said. "I've got nothing to hide." His troubles became part of a broader problem of corruption in the city that rocked the Barry administration by the mid-1980s. In August 1986, the *Washington Post* ran a feature called "The District Corruption Issue," detailing fifteen different DC officials under investigation for financial issues or violations of ethics rules, including Vernell Tanner. The article mentioned his financial dealings with Guyot. The high-profile convictions of Treadwell in 1984, and then in 1985 of Ivanhoe Donaldson, Barry's longtime confidant and "the shadow power" behind the mayor, prompted the heavy media scrutiny of the municipal government. Donaldson, who oversaw Barry's 1982 reelection, confessed to embezzling $190,000 from the city government and received a seven-year prison sentence. Deputy Mayor for Finance Al Hill resigned in March 1986 after confessing to accepting kickbacks for diverting city contracts to friends. Unlike the Tanner case, however, Guyot had no connection to these corruption investigations and convictions. Ultimately, investigators placed Tanner on administrative leave for his role in this affair, but prosecutors never indicted him and he kept his job on the police force.[23] All in all, it was a time of significant investigation of the governance of the Black-run city.

Or was it harassment? The prosecutions in Washington presaged an official corruption crackdown by the Department of Justice during Reagan's second term, and one that disproportionately affected Black elected officials. In 1987 and 1988, the Justice Department carried out highly publicized prosecutions in Baltimore, Tennessee, Atlanta, and Washington, DC, where prosecutors targeted both Walter Fauntroy (now serving as the nonvoting delegate in the House for the District of Columbia) and the Barry administration. Overall, Black elected officials in the mid-1980s were suspects in 14 percent of federal corruption investigations but only made up 3 percent of all elected officials. The Barry raids, which targeted city officials and Black businesses with city contracts, led to numerous arrests but then a long period of inactivity as prosecutors built their cases. The delay in prosecutions led Barry and many in the Black community to speculate that the entire affair was a setup. It was easy for Barry to imply this, as his sizable reelection victory in 1986 made him the political kingpin of DC, dubbed by the *Post* "Boss Barry." US attorney Joseph diGenova became Barry's nemesis, as the federal government first investigated the mayor in 1984 over allegations of drug use. DiGenova expanded this probe into broader corruption investigations, which led to the prosecutions of Treadwell and Donaldson and the 1987 raids. His use of highly publicized raids and selective leaks sparked allegations of racism, since white contractors received two-thirds of the city's business, which gave an appearance of disproportionate targeting of Black business owners and officials. But reality of Barry's drug addiction and the corruption scandals led to his eventual downfall.[24]

While prosecutors never indicted Guyot in these cases and no evidence exists of him engaging in any wrongdoing, he still had his own problems. The dispute between the Coalition for the Homeless and the Community for Creative Nonviolence became a nasty and personal one between Guyot and Snyder. In November 1985, the two men appeared on *Capital City Magazine*, a local news show. They also appeared on *Evening Exchange*, a public-access program, where they clashed sharply over homelessness in the wake of the CCNV's opening an illegal shelter in an old building. At a roundtable discussion, Guyot accused Snyder of blocking the opening of coalition homeless shelters in the city. Snyder denied this, and said that his objection was that the coalition was ignoring local residents and opening them "in a heavy-handed way and getting everyone pissed off." Opening a shelter successfully in a neighborhood is an "art," he said, and "you cannot trample the neighbors whether it is Georgetown or Anacostia." "I wish you were committed to that, Mitch," Guyot interrupted, when Snyder said that the priority was saving the lives of the homeless. "I live in a shelter, Larry," he responded wearily. On TV, Guyot became his usual combative and confrontational self, as he had been back in his SNCC and MFDP days. Visibly angry, he frequently interrupted Snyder, who remained calm during the exchange. Host Kojo Nnamdi asked Snyder about the CCNV, and Guyot interrupted and said, emphatically jabbing his finger at Snyder, "That's the man. That's the power right there. He runs that." Snyder replied, "Tell the other forty-five to fifty people that work twelve hours a day that I'm the entire community; they will eat you alive." Guyot continued to try to portray Snyder as the sole power in the organization, even accusing him of brainwashing the homeless. "If he really concerned about the homeless, he would release those people from the potential Jim Jones situation that he, individually, because he's a cult leader, is putting them in." Guyot then complained that Snyder's opposition to the coalition forced them to get federal funds—a disingenuous claim, given that the Barry administration had cut homeless shelter funding to balance the budget. Snyder in turn said that the CCNV's activism is what got them that money from the Reagan administration, and that Guyot and the coalition were "being used as a wedge between us and the administration; you're gonna have to moveout of the way and when you do, we're gonna face the administration head-on and then let me tell you, brother, we're gonna push them right out of this damn city because they are the most vile, vulgar, insensitive, inhuman human beings that we have ever seen and you shouldn't let them use you."[25]

The roles now seemed reversed from the 1960s. Guyot, the combative organizer who once had no reservations about using inflammatory language to describe the institutional power of the government—a man who said that the MFDP needed to "stay the hell out of the goddamn Democratic Party"—now stood inside the power structure, arguing with the confrontational activist and denigrating his intentions. Republicans even joined Guyot in his attacks on Snyder. C. McClain Haddow, an official in Reagan's Department of Health and Human Services, publicly painted Snyder as a violent extremist, suggesting that the CCNV stored weapons and explosives at its shelter, so that some of the homeless, namely the Vietnam veterans among them, could engage in armed struggle. Guyot's actions largely came from his willingness to be a loyal and able soldier for Barry. This reflected Guyot's political mainstreaming and ability to do dirty work for the Barry political machine, as he defamed Snyder on behalf of the mayor, since the Barry administration could not co-opt him.[26]

Barry did not always reciprocate the loyalty. The *Washington Post*, which extensively covered the feud between the Coalition for the Homeless and the Community for Creative Nonviolence, noted that the relationship among the two organizations and the federal government shifted from 1984 to 1986, with Mayor Barry initially siding with the coalition against the CCNV, and then backing the CCNV against the federal government. When the Reagan administration granted funds to Snyder after his highly publicized hunger strikes, Barry again supported the CCNV and distanced himself from the coalition, especially it came under investigation. Barry joined Snyder in criticizing the coalition's Anacostia plan, even though Guyot held a seat on its board, because he feared that if the federal government completely cut its ties to Snyder, the city would have the burden of taking care of the homeless in the CCNV shelter. The federal government, meanwhile, thought that the coalition would be a manageable alternative to Snyder and the CCNV, but it proved not up to the task.[27]

Guyot blamed the US Court of Appeals, where Snyder sued and won a ruling in late 1985, for giving the coalition only "a matter of days" to develop a viable shelter program. That led Guyot to make the ill-fated financial deal with Tanner for a new shelter. Despite his clashes with Guyot, Snyder expressed sympathy for the coalition's perils. Reiterating his statement on television, he said that the coalition "has been dumped on a number of times and has been used a number of times by people. That is the nature of Washington. That is the nature of politics. It makes for strange bedfellows." An unnamed DC official provided a less charitable assessment, telling the *Post* that the coalition's board members "weren't promised a marriage, just an evening of fun."[28]

Guyot earned an annual salary of $24,316 a year ($70,034 in 2024 dollars) working for the DC Department of Human Services. He received $630 in compensation for negotiating the coalition's grant with the federal government, but waited eight months to collect the fee since he said he "didn't need it immediately." But a June *Post* story on city employees profiting from finder's fees and other questionable payouts reported on his fee, so the press coverage created guilt by association.[29]

By April 1986, the US Department of Health and Human Services suspended the remainder of the $3.7 million grant from the previous fall, citing the financial improprieties and lack of screening of coalition employees. It then quickly revised its position, allowing the coalition to spend the federal money but requiring prior approval of all future expenditures. By then Guyot had had enough. He submitted his resignation on 15 April and told the *Post* that it was partly in protest over recent negotiations between the coalition and Snyder. Politics made for strange bedfellows once again, as the two organizations appeared to be "moving toward an agreement of mutual support," according to reporter Arthur Brisbane. Guyot, apparently motivated in part by his personal dislike of Snyder, showed no interest in being part of this rapprochement and ended his involvement in homelessness with his resignation.[30]

The feud between Guyot and Snyder, which Guyot took quite personally, recalled the broader feud between the white New Left and Black activists that went back to the 1960s. Guyot experienced this personally when the MFDP attended the National Conference for New Politics in Chicago in 1967. That conference fell apart over splits between white and Black delegates, with the former focusing on opposing the Vietnam War and the latter wanting to dismantle institutionalized white supremacy. Black and white activists in the 1960s often clashed over intractable issues, such as the demands of Black activists at the New Politics convention to get half of the seats, which white activists, heavily motivated by white guilt, agreed to do. White radicals, speaking from the comfort of their white privilege, in turn often made condescending remarks about Black activists not revolutionary enough for their taste, such as when Ed Clark of the Progressive Labor Party criticized the MFDP for not allying with racist working-class whites in Mississippi. Although some white radical and Black Power alliances did occur—notably the Black Panthers' work with organizations like the Peace and Freedom Party—resentment tended to be the norm.[31]

Mitch Snyder represented much of that radical white New Left tradition, albeit from a religious standpoint rather than a secular Marxist one. Born Jewish in Brooklyn, he had converted to a radical antiwar strain of Roman Catholicism while in prison serving time on a fraud conviction. Sharing the same faith with Guyot did little to improve their relationship, however. Snyder's nonviolent direct activism and hunger strikes carried on directly from 1960s Black civil rights activism, but since Snyder now opposed in part former civil rights activists who had created a Black political power structure in DC, his actions drew their resentment and echoed the 1960s tensions.[32]

Guyot also faced off against another white constituency in Washington, this time over the issue of recycling. Recycling first emerged in the city in the 1970s with the DuPont Circle Neighborhood Ecology Corporation drop-off recycling program. This program arose from a series of recycling drop-off centers in Mount Pleasant, Adams Morgan, and DuPont Circle. The first two neighborhoods experienced a rapid increase in home prices in that decade, as landlords evicted low-income tenants to convert apartment blocks into condominiums. Dupont Circle, meanwhile, experienced an influx of gay and lesbian residents in the 1970s.[33]

These early recycling efforts, like much of the environmental movement, had an association with higher-income white populations in gentrifying neighborhoods. Yet one environmental solution involved reusing instead of recycling. The growing problem of solid waste accumulation, particularly in the form of nonreturnable beverage containers, bedeviled states and local communities. The shift of soft drink manufacturers to one-way (nonreturnable) containers in the 1960s created a massive increase in solid waste, which built on earlier waste created by beer companies also abandoning returnable bottles. Oregon and Vermont passed the nation's first state-level bottle-deposit laws in 1972, and seven more states followed. But bottle-bill advocates won their last victories in Michigan and New York in 1982, and the well-funded beverage industry blocked several subsequent ballot initiatives around the country.[34]

In April 1987, some deposit advocates got a bottle-deposit law approved for the November ballot in Washington, DC. Known as Initiative 28, the proposed law would place a minimum deposit of five cents on beer and soft drink cans and bottles. Local organizations like Environmental Action Foundation and the Bottle Initiative Committee campaigned for the bill. Their funding could not equal that of the Clean Capital City Committee (CCCC), an organization headed and funded by a Coca-Cola executive and bankrolled by major soft drink and beer corporations. By October, the CCCC raised and spent over $1 million—fifteen times what pro-deposit forces had spent—and was running radio and television ads against the initiative. The beverage companies argued in their ads that recycling, not a bottle-deposit law, solved the waste issue, and that a deposit law would hurt the recycling industry. Their approach came from a deliberate program adopted by companies like Coca-Cola and Pepsi beginning in the 1970s to undercut the bottle-deposit movement while appearing to address the solid waste issue (but in reality doing little about it). In DC in 1987, recycling had little support. The DuPont Circle Neighborhood Ecology Corporation reported that nonprofit volunteer groups did almost all the recycling in the city, and the chief of waste management policy in the city's Department of Public Works said the recycling effort was "just at its initial stages." The community recycling groups did not even recycle glass, one of the key materials in the debate over Initiative 28.[35] In short, the local recycling industry would not lose any jobs because it had no jobs to begin with.

Class soon became a dividing line in the battle over the bottles, as DC's homelessness crisis overlapped with the election campaign. Opponents raised social class issues, charging that the bill would lead to DC's homeless population scavenging for bottles and cans and invading grocery stores to return the containers. That lurid image and the costs of handling the returned containers led DC's grocers to overwhelmingly oppose the measure. But race as an issue proved a far more effective means for the corporations to kill the initiative. The beverage companies rallied opposition to the initiative in the Black community and recruited ministers to oppose the bottle-deposit law. About 130 ministers joined Clergy against Initiative 28, and Ed Arnold, a spokesman for the CCCC, reached out to the Council of Churches of Greater Washington about creating a recycling program in the District—but only after supporters of Initiative 28 began gathering signatures to put it on the ballot.[36]

Guyot himself became part of these efforts to kill the bill. The industry's opposition campaign hired him to coordinate its efforts in Ward 1, where they provided him with a van with a two-way radio so he could travel from precinct to precinct, where he communicated developments to the campaign's phonebanks.

Other prominent Black community members hired by the campaign include Lenneal Henderson, a Howard University economics professor, who testified in commercials that the initiative would raise beverage prices for DC residents. The question of costs passed on to consumers resonated with Black voters, but opponents of the bill tapped into homophobia as well, with the nation in the midst of hysteria over the AIDS crisis. H. R. Crawford, a Democratic councilman for Ward 7 and an initiative opponent, enraged gay activists when he raised the unfounded issue of contracting HIV from dirty containers during a television debate. Doll Fitzgerald, a community activist hired by the industry campaign, acknowledged encouraging these fears at church meetings in the final days of the campaign.[37]

The white corporate executives "cleverly and cynically" exploited race, according to *Washington Post* columnist Marc Fisher. Newspaper ads aimed at Black residents said, "You can tell a lot about an issue by who supports it and who opposes it," and then listed the organizations from white neighborhoods that supported the initiative, such as the Citizens Association of Georgetown, and then listed numerous Black organizations—including the NAACP and Operation PUSH—that opposed it. Kathryn Pearson-West, president of the North Michigan Park Civic Association, said that Black residents in her Northeast neighborhood opposed it and that the initiative "appeared to be more of a white issue" that "was almost like something they were trying to impose on us."[38]

DC voters soundly rejected Initiative 28 in November, after the beverage industry coalition broke city election spending records by investing $2 million in the campaign. It failed by 55 percent to 45 percent, and voters in the middle-class Black neighborhoods of Wards 4, 5, and 7 soundly rejected it. Integrated areas saw closer results, and in predominately white, upper-income areas the bill received heavy support. Even Ward 4, which contained many well-to-do Black voters, rejected the measure by more than 2-to-1.[39]

Guyot's employment by a major corporation may seem surprising, but it, too represented his increased mainstreaming into the DC power structure. It was also consistent with his politics throughout his career: he had never been an anti-capitalist or a Marxist. The MFDP, while it espoused a liberal platform of expanded welfare benefits and other measures in the 1960s, did not endorse policy any different from Lyndon Johnson's Great Society, legislation firmly in the tradition of postwar American liberalism. The MFDP wanted the federal government to address Black inequality and poverty through the traditional state apparatus. It never embraced the socialist program of more radical Black Power organizations like the Republic of New Africa (RNA), a 1960s group based in Jackson that advocated for collective Black ownership of the land for a Black homeland. Guyot did not become the only former 1960s civil rights movement figure to embrace corporate America. Andrew Young of the Southern Christian Leadership Conference (SCLC) went in a considerably more conservative direction than Guyot when he later took up paid advocacy work for Nike and Wal-Mart and defended both companies' controversial labor practices, including Nike's factories in Vietnam. This corporate advocacy drew considerable criticism from some of Young's former allies for social justice, who said he defended companies that exploited impoverished laborers.[40]

None of this should be construed to mean that Guyot embraced the rightward shift of the United States in the 1980s under Ronald Reagan, with his program of color-blind conservatism and supply-side economics. Guyot supported Barry's affirmative action programs, minority set-asides, rent control, and, above all, vigorous support for federal voting rights protection, all measures opposed by the Reagan and Bush administrations to varying degrees. His willingness to take support from corporate America did not mean he supported antiwelfarism or neoliberal economics. As he put it, he was "the most radical, poorest capitalist there is. But I think there is enough flexibility in capitalism for us to do what we want to do."[41]

Guyot did not let his stint with corporate America draw him out of DC politics. While he never aspired to high political office like Barry, he remained active in city politics. He did so through the Ward 1 Democrats, the same ward where SNCC veteran Frank Smith won election to the school board and then the city council.[42] Regarding the corruption of Barry and Donaldson and other Black DC politicians, Guyot kept any criticism private. And if he was angry at Barry over his shifting support of the Coalition for the Homeless, he did not say so in public or on the record. More than likely, he knew it was not personal on Barry's part and just part of the political nature of the District. This was an echo of Guyot's MFDP days, when he did not publicly air his conflicts with Bob Moses, Aaron Henry, or other Mississippi civil rights leaders outside of movement circles. He was also in a role he had not been accustomed to given his MFDP experience—he was a follower now, not a leader, occupying various roles that Barry needed him to fill. Guyot gave no indication that he chafed at or resented his new subordinate position or his place in the Barry administration. He never reached the level of influence with Barry that fellow SNCC veterans like Ivanhoe Donaldson achieved, even though he regularly played poker with them on Saturday nights. Barry, in fact, never mentioned Guyot in his autobiography, which he published after Guyot's death. As the *Washington City Paper* put it, in comparison to his fellow Mississippi civil rights activists, "Guyot is the one who never quite made it."[43] Of course, another way of reading this is that after years heading the MFDP, Guyot was glad to let someone else take control; as he never made any bids for higher office in DC, Guyot and Barry also remained close friends through Barry's tenure.

Guyot by the 1980s now filled the roles of loving husband, devoted father, and respectable member of the Black bourgeoisie in the nation's capital, rather than the political outsider he had been when he headed the MFDP. He had vacillated then between working inside or outside of the Democratic Party, but this was in relation to the segregationist Democratic Party of 1960s Mississippi, not the urban Black political machine of 1980s Washington, DC. Marion Barry, not Ross Barnett, ran this party. Under Barry's political organization, the Democratic Party in the city became a Black-majority political party that held all the city offices and had only minimal input from white voters. This was the kind of unified Black electoral bloc Guyot fought for but failed to achieve in Mississippi, outside of areas like Holmes County. Even the Republican Party, once an organization with significant influence in DC's Black middle class, had atrophied in the city as the national GOP abandoned its loyal Black voters and shifted to the right.[44] For Guyot, these events settled the question of whom to support and how to participate in the political process.

Guyot's fierce loyalty to Barry often appeared racially charged, but few white residents of the city supported the mayor. In January 1988, ten members of the DC city council sponsored a bill which would limit future mayors after 1990 to two terms. If enacted, it would have allowed Barry to run for a fourth term in 1990, but then bar him from running again in 1994. Guyot, now working in the mayor's office as a general assistant, appeared at a heavily pro-Barry public hearing. When some of the councilmembers said the debate should avoid focusing on Barry himself, Guyot said that "it's impossible to separate the two." Given that the bill would only apply to the mayor and not to city councilmembers, Guyot seemed correct that this bill fired a salvo at the "Mayor for Life." While term limits did not become explicitly racial, as the majority of the city council was Black, the bill—which did not pass—showed Guyot's loyalty to the mayor. He organized Barry supporters at a Ward 1 meeting to appear at the Council meeting, and used that meeting to mobilize supporters in other wards.[45]

Guyot involved himself in almost every facet of DC politics, from homelessness to the bottle bill to education. On that latter issue, he lobbied extensively for Andrew Jenkins, hired to be the DC school superintendent in 1988. Jenkins, serving as acting superintendent after Superintendent Floretta McKenzie resigned earlier that year, benefited from an intense lobbying campaign aimed at the board members. Guyot said he "made a lot of calls" because "Jenkins is someone we know"—an insider favored by local residents and politicians over outside candidates being considered by the board. The hiring of Jenkins showed that Guyot readily used his clout, which stemmed from both his association with the Barry regime and old civil rights ability to mobilize grassroots support, to influence elections and city government hiring. But he sometimes backed losing candidates and issues, and he did not become a kingmaker. He backed Jerry Moore, a Black Republican councilman who lost his seat in the primary in 1984 and ran for his old seat in 1988. While he was able to pull the support of Guyot and numerous local ministers (Moore was himself a Baptist minister), the moderate Republican lost in a crowded field. The winner, William Lightfoot, an independent Black attorney who ran as a liberal, drew support from organized labor and tenant groups and won 27 percent of the vote for the at-large seat. Guyot, who once headed an independent political party with a liberal record, now backed a moderate Republican over a liberal, prolabor, and prohousing candidate, a stance that perhaps best represented his move into the mainstream political hierarchy. Still frustrated with the Democratic Party at times, Guyot sometimes flirted with the GOP. In a 1987 interview, he said he supported Jesse Jackson for the presidency, but that if Jackson did not get the Democratic nomination then he would support Robert Dole, the conservative Republican from Kansas, partly over his support for the Voting Rights Act. Guyot said, "The Democratic Party can't deal with Jesse Jackson. They want Black folks with no demands."[46]

Despite his loyalty to Barry, Guyot did not always see eye to eye with him. They differed on gay rights. Both men supported gay rights, and Barry consistently backed LGBT rights early in his career. This support, going back to his days on the DC school board in the 1970s and including attendance at some of the first DC Pride parades, had led LGBT voters to back him consistently since his 1978 election as mayor. But in the years after Barry's terms as mayor—when he served as a councilman for Ward 8—he opposed same-sex marriage. In 2009, when the DC city council considered a measure to legalize same-sex marriage in the city, Barry appeared at a rally with a Christian pastor and said, "We have to say no to same-sex marriage in DC." He later cited his constituents' opposition as the reason for his vote against the bill, which passed that year with only Barry and Councilwoman Yvette Alexander from Ward 7 voting against it. He stressed that he supported civil unions and other LGBT rights, just not same-sex marriage. He later said he regretted his vote.[47]

Barry's acknowledging his constituents' opposition to same-sex marriage is not surprising, since as a ward politician he no longer required the LGBT vote like he did in his narrow 1978 election. Tensions existed in DC between DC's LGBT and Black communities, especially with Black churches and their religiously motivated opposition to homosexuality. In 2005, some Black pastors protested the opening of a gay bar by two gay white businessmen in the Shaw/U Street neighborhood. Other civil rights activists also opposed same-sex marriage. Walter Fauntroy, an old SCLC ally of Martin Luther King Jr. who co-organized the March on Washington and served as the nonvoting DC House delegate until his defeat in 1990, adamantly opposed same-sex marriage. Unlike Barry, he opposed LGBT rights in general, and called sexual orientation a "behavior, something that can be changed."[48]

Guyot dismissed these views, and in 2009 said, "You either want liberty for everyone, or you want liberty for nongays." He likened opposition to same-sex marriage to opposing interracial marriage, and cited the illegality of his own marriage to Monica in a number of states before the *Loving* decision. While he had been raised Catholic and said that he was a "man who carried out his religious beliefs by his political activity," that did not mean he felt his beliefs should be imposed on law and society. Reflecting on his long relationship with Monica, he said, "Can I really accept all of this and deny it to two other people of the same sex who are in love with one another? I couldn't." He reminded Christians that they should be nonjudgmental, and said, "All my politics has been based on my religious beliefs . . . [and] when you're told religiously to feed the hungry, clothe the naked, those who are bound, it doesn't tell you to find out what the charges are." He shared this support for LGBT rights with Julian Bond, who interviewed him for the Civil Rights History Project in 2010.[49]

Guyot's acceptance homosexuality is not surprising considering that he worked alongside a number of gay and bisexual people in the civil rights movement. Aaron Henry, leader of the Council of Federated Organizations (COFO), married and had a family but engaged in relationships with men, something known and noticed—but not commented on—by fellow movement activists and the Black community. White supremacists drove Bill Higgs, one of the white attorneys assisting the Mississippi movement, out of the state after a conviction involving sex with a male teenage runaway, a story that at least one historian deemed credible given Higgs's sexuality. Guyot also worked closely with R. Hunter Morey in the Mississippi movement. In 1984 Morey, a white gay man, coauthored a teacher's guide on homosexuality.[50]

Barry, unlike Guyot, had his personal demons. As early as 1981, DC police received reports that Barry used drugs, a habit that overlapped with his already extensive womanizing, information that soon made its way to federal prosecutors. He also made little effort to conceal this behavior, engaging in it at various disreputable establishments around the city. Joseph DiGenova's 1987 corruption raids grew out of his investigation of Barry for suspected drug use. The George

H. W. Bush administration's "War on Drugs" increased the focus on DC and the Barry administration. Barry's behavior finally caught up with him when he met up with a former girlfriend, Hazel Diana "Rasheeda" Moore. A former model-turned-drug-addict, she left DC after an affair with Barry, but the FBI convinced her to return to the city to take part in a sting operation. On 18 January 1990, Barry met her in her hotel room in the hope of having sex. She insisted that they smoke crack cocaine first. After some initial hesitation, Barry complied. Federal agents and local police burst in and arrested him, with a stunned Barry uttering the now-famous line, "That goddamn bitch set me up."[51]

Yet the arrest did not knock Barry out of the political game in DC. He refused to resign and courted public sympathy by checking into a rehabilitation center and attending church regularly. His political future uncertain, he retained a core of loyalists, bolstered by polls that showed 59 percent of Black DC residents held him blameless or only partially responsible for his arrest, given that federal authorities had long been targeting him.[52]

The mayor's arrest did not shake Guyot's faith in him. "Most of the support-ers I know," he said, "we've been spending our time trying to make sure that he has the option" of running for reelection. By the time of Barry's arrest, Guyot was working as an activity coordinator in the mayor's office and serving as the advisory neighborhood commissioner for LeDroit Park. He, like many other loyalists in Barry's political machine, followed a wait-and-see approach with the mayor. Guyot indicated that if Barry did not seek reelection, many of his followers would rally behind his designated successor, "as a way of maintaining what he stands for." But Barry missed the filing deadline for the Democratic primary as he prepared for his trial, and members of Barry's campaign team, including Guyot, drifted toward Charlene Drew Jarvis, a DC city council mem-ber representing Ward 4. Guyot had spoken highly of her, even though she had once challenged Barry in the mayoral race in 1982. He said she "is the closest person to Marion Barry in terms of style, strength, and commitment. Because I believe in Barry so strongly, I support Charlene Drew Jarvis."[53]

Sharon Pratt Dixon eventually won the race and became Washington, DC's first woman mayor. Eleanor Holmes Norton, who had been instrumental in saving Guyot's life in the Winona city jail so many years ago, defeated Walter Fauntroy to become DC's nonvoting delegate in the House of Representatives. Meanwhile, Barry's political career seemed over. He ended up jumping into the election campaign as an independent candidate for an at-large council seat, switching his party affiliation so he could bypass the Democratic primary and appear on the November ballot. Guyot supported his effort—the *Washington Post* called him one of Barry's "staunch supporters"—and circulated petitions on his behalf. Barry lost the race but enjoyed more success with the jury during his trial, as they only convicted him of a misdemeanor. The judge handed down a harsh sentence of six months in prison.[54]

Guyot did not limit himself to working in the mayor's race, but he never succeeded in turning himself into a political powerbroker. In an at-large council race (not the post Barry ran for), he endorsed Terry Lynch, a thirty-one-year-old white man who had worked as a homeless advocate in the city, then as executive director of the Downtown Cluster of Congregations, a coalition of twenty-seven churches that worked to protect housing and small businesses in downtown DC. Guyot served as his campaign manager, but could not produce a winning campaign. It was Lynch's first bid for public office, and he lost.[55]

Guyot soon found himself in a new position in Washington, DC—opposing the mayor's office. In May 1991, riots erupted in Mount Pleasant, a diverse neighborhood with a growing population of Latinos, especially refugees from the civil war in El Salvador. The lack of legal status for the Salvadorans, mostly young impoverished men (and nonvoters), meant that they competed with African Americans for the lowest-paying jobs but had no voice in city government. The predominantly Black police who expelled the Salvadorans from city parks and street corners for loitering and other public disturbances only added to the tensions. On 5 May, when police shot and wounded a Salvadoran man for resisting an arrest for public intoxication, angry Latino residents destroyed property and looted businesses in the neighborhood. The DC police quickly contained the riot with minimal violence, and Mayor Dixon's conscious efforts to avoid a heavy-handed approach won her wide praise in the city.[56]

The Mount Pleasant riots exposed Latinos' lack of access to city services, a situation Dixon pledged to improve. Guyot joined a meeting of Black and Latino community leaders the week following the riots, and he warned the mayor afterward that she needed to improve summer employment opportunities for local youths. Echoing what Barry had done with Pride Inc., he called for reversing city budget cuts, otherwise "it could drive more people into the streets." But a spokesman for the mayor said the recession would likely curtail any restoration of funding. Guyot worked to bridge racial divisions in the city and build coalitions, much like his support for other marginalized groups like gays and lesbians. Others present echoed Guyot's concerns, such as Antonio Montez, an aide to DC delegate Eleanor Holmes Norton, who organized the interracial meeting and said that "we don't want anyone to turn this into a racial thing. This is much more a poor folks problem." But it already had turned into a racial matter, as the riots had exposed deep fissures between Black and Latino residents. Dixon's efforts to improve Latino access ran up against Black opposition, including from elected officials like Councilman H. R. Crawford and William Lightfoot, who feared increased services for Latinos meant fewer for African Americans.[57]

Guyot tempered some of his comments when the police department investigated its officers for their behavior during the riot, showing that he was still firmly in the political mainstream of city politics. When some Latinos complained that police harassment was endemic in their neighborhood, he warned that "the worst thing we can do is make the police the scapegoat, because that is simply another form of polarization."[58] This comment indicated that he focused his criticism of the city more on individuals like Dixon rather than any institutional problems—since Black civil servants and bureaucrats now controlled many of those city institutions, and Guyot likely did not want to criticize a predominately Black police department. Guyot's comments instead became part of a broader criticism he had of the new mayor.

Although he worked for the city in the Youth Services Administration, Guyot, still true to his nature, did not hesitate to speak up. As the city government planned to lay off up to 2,000 employees due to budget shortfalls, Dixon proposed suspending seniority rights, which led Guyot and others to fear that she would purge the bureaucracy of Barry loyalists. "I know a lot of city employees who are frightened to death," said Guyot, adding that the "level of fear throughout the government would be unbelievable to anyone outside the government." Budget woes and layoffs plagued Dixon throughout the rest of her term as mayor, as would the frustrations of Latino residents, who received from the city the appointment of a DC Latino Civil Rights Task Force. Little came from it or the newly created Office of Latino Affairs or the Commission on Latino Development, which hired older Latino activists—and muted their criticism by providing them with city jobs. Guyot said the fault lay with the population's inability to deal with racial issues, and blamed "white racism, the powerlessness of Hispanics and the tensions between Hispanics and Blacks." He expressed his frustration, declaring that "we can't deal in this city with race."[59]

The Board of Education ward where the Guyots lived possessed a significant Latino population, and a Guyot ran for office in 1992—but not Lawrence Guyot. His wife Monica made a bid for the Ward 1 seat on the DC Board of Education in 1992. She worked as director of a child care center, the GAP Community Child-Care Center for preschoolers, which she cofounded in 1982. Ward 1 had some of the lowest test scores in the city, the highest dropout rate of any ward, and the highest enrollment of Latinos. She challenged, along with two other candidates, incumbent Wilma Harvey, a Black woman and former teacher first elected to the position in 1986. Monica ran on a platform to reduce the dropout rate and increase parental and community involvement, which did little to set her apart from her three opponents. She charged that Harvey had not been "an effective leader with parent outreach or the dropout rate," and said that "a lot more things could have been done." Although Monica trailed in fundraising—raising less than $1,000 by the end of September, while another challenger, Beatriz Otero, raised about $8,000 by then—she did secure the endorsement of a Teamsters Union local. Her husband, not surprisingly, worked as her campaign consultant.[60]

While Monica Guyot had worked in organizations like the LeDroit Park Civic Association, she had never run for elected office. With her children now adults, she had additional time for public life. The four-way Ward 1 race became heated, with the *Washington Post* calling it one of the "feistier" races that fall. Harvey defeated her opponents, but only with a plurality of 42 percent; Monica placed third with 17 percent of the vote, trailing both Harvey and Otero. Guyot's influence here fell short, as with his earlier backing of Terry Lynch, indicating that he while he worked within the city government and political system, he did not have the skills of a political kingmaker.[61]

Those same elections marked the political comeback of Marion Barry. Three months after his release from prison in April 1992, he announced his candidacy for the city council seat in Ward 8 in Southeast DC. More than 80 percent Black, Ward 8 had the highest infant mortality rate in the city, and 22 percent of its residents living below the poverty line. Barry wrapped himself in a mantle of political redemption, which appealed to the residents of the crime-ridden ward—half the Black men in Ward 8 had experienced the criminal justice system in some capacity, primarily for drug crimes. He campaigned against mass incarceration, even though he had presided over many of those policies as mayor. His own stint in prison struck a chord with voters, many themselves victims of the War on Drugs. He defeated Wilhelmina Rolark, a former Barry ally in the seat since 1976, with 70 percent of the vote in the September Democratic primary, then swept aside his Republican and independent challengers with 90 percent of the vote that November.[62]

Guyot stayed loyal to Barry throughout his trials, both personal and legal. Guyot met with Barry weeks after his arrest, and then made a public statement that Jesse Jackson would run for mayor to replace Barry when he decided not to run for a fourth term. But Jackson changed his mind, and Barry lost his bid for city council and went to prison. But Guyot knew that Barry craved power and would return. In the meantime, Guyot stayed heavily involved in civic affairs through the local Advisory Neighborhood Commission (ANC), a volunteer board of thirty-seven commissions throughout the city representing individual neighborhoods. The ANCs, a system of local governance not utilized or replicated in any other US city, advised the DC government on planning, streets, recreation, sanitation, safety, sanitation, and social services. Guyot served on the ANC for LeDroit Park, where he addressed issues of drug-related crime that plagued the neighborhood. Voters elected him to the unpaid position from 1988 to 2004 for two different seats, the only elective office he sought and won in DC.[63]

For a time, Guyot wavered in his support for Barry's political comeback. In May 1993 at a public hearing on DC statehood, he mentioned six candidates for mayor in the 1994 election, including Kevin Chavous, a community activist who in 1992 had scored an upset over a three-term incumbent in the Democratic primary for the Ward 7 city council seat and beat his Republican opponent with 96 percent of the vote. Chavous spoke up at the meeting and denied he was a mayoral candidate, which prompted Guyot to reply that he "didn't say that you are," but that "you are considered by people in this city in that high regard." The *Washington Post* noted that Guyot did not mention Barry as a possible candidate.[64]

The city's deepening debt, fueled by a declining tax base as Black families who could afford to left for the suburbs, coupled with police corruption and a skyrocketing murder rate (over 440 murders annually between 1990 and 1993), greatly eroded Sharon Pratt Kelly's popularity as mayor. Guyot said he had "written off" any chance of Kelly's reelection but then gave her some rare praise when in October 1993 she called on the National Guard to help fight crime in the city, an action that Guyot said "captured the dialogue" and "convinced John Q. Public she is serious about that issue." But his initial views proved correct. One of the candidates that Guyot named at the public hearing did run for mayor in 1994. He was John Ray, an at-large city councilman with a strong personal dislike of Barry that he had difficulty concealing. Although Black himself, Ray suffered from Barry's attacks painting him as the white man's candidate. Barry easily won the Democratic primary, and then the election that fall. Despite the scandal associated with him, many middle-class Blacks supported Barry. As Guyot pointed out, the government contracts during Barry's three terms and the growth of the city bureaucracy played a significant role in expanding DC's Black middle class. "Marion intensified it, accelerated it, and protected it in its economic growth," Guyot said, referring to the Black middle class in Maryland's neighboring Prince George's County. Barry may have expanded the city's debt, but that spending created a bloc of loyalist Black voters. Racial polarization added to his strong Black support as most white voters abandoned Barry to vote for Carol Schwartz, the Republican nominee whom Barry beat in November.[65]

The Republican Party secured majorities in both houses of Congress in the 1994 midterm elections, and the House leadership of Newt Gingrich and Tom DeLay became hostile toward the District and its spending. With the city $722 million in debt shortly after Barry took office, Congress rejected Barry's calls for the federal government to assume control of nonessential services and instead passed legislation in April 1995 creating a Financial Control Board that oversaw the city budget and severely cut into the home rule of the municipal government, as the board had veto power over local legislation and management authority over city agencies. President Bill Clinton, sensing the new conservative mood and stinging over Democratic losses in Congress, signed the legislation into law. Andre Brimmer, a Black economist who had served for fourteen years on the Federal Reserve Board, headed the Control Board, officially known as the DC Financial Responsibility and Management Assistance Authority. He possessed civil rights credentials as well, previously preparing testimony at the Department of Commerce for the Supreme Court on the negative effects of racial segregation on interstate commerce. The Court cited his research when it upheld the Civil Rights Act of 1964's Public Accommodations Section. He won praise from activists like Jesse Jackson but represented the more conservative approach of past Black leaders like Booker T. Washington rather than the fiery confrontation of Barry's 1960s activism. Joyce Ladner, the SNCC veteran whom Guyot first met at Tougaloo College and who had recently served as the interim president of Howard University, also sat on the board. But the board also included Vice Chair Stephen Harlan, a real estate mogul. A registered Republican and the board's only white member, he would become an outspoken opponent of Barry. Two other Black members rounded out the five-member board, but then Brimmer selected John Hill, a former General Accounting Office employee, to be the board's executive director. Hill previously oversaw the District's finances at the behest of Congress in 1994, and the Barry administration had hired him three times before to conduct studies of the city's financial status. Guyot predicted that Hill would be "the primary power" on the board.[66]

Guyot hated the Control Board with a passion, referring to it as "the slave board." The metaphor of DC as a plantation under the white Republicans in Congress resonated with DC Black politicians and activists, as Barry himself called the city "a territory, half slave and half free," and one Black resident spoke admiringly of Barry's "refusing to be the overseer" for the GOP. By implication, then, the Control Board's members were the overseers. At its first public meeting with DC residents in July 1995, Guyot assailed the board for its role in the "nullification" of the District's home rule, declaring that he "saw no way for this board and local self-government to exist simultaneously."

He appeared to be right, as the board unanimously approved eliminating 5,600 positions in the city government, which would necessitate laying off 2,000 city employees. The board also shifted from public meetings to closed-door session and limited public input at future public meetings, all at the cost of citizen input.[67]

Under the legislation creating the Control Board, Barry and the city council retained many of their executive and legislative abilities. Speaker of the House Gingrich hoped to win over the Black professional and middle class to GOP economic policies, and that prompted him to accept the idea of the Control Board—which had initially been suggested by DC delegate Eleanor Holmes Norton to stave off more punitive Republican proposals for the city. She had recommended Brimmer and the other local residents to President Clinton when he appointed the board members.[68]

Norton's role in establishing the Control Board, and her and Ladner's efforts to get Barry to cooperate with it, led Barry to feign cooperation before launching an offensive against its austerity measures. Like Guyot, the two women navigated the political waters and made compromises. That did not spare them, especially Norton, from Guyot's criticism. When community activists mobilized to oppose the Control Board and defend home rule, Guyot led the way. Norton defended her role in establishing the board, insisting that its establishment did not significantly undermine home rule. Guyot in turn accused Norton of being under the sway of the Chamber of Commerce and other corporate-driven entities, and compared the struggle to his Mississippi years. "Everything we fought for in Mississippi is being taken away," he said. "In Mississippi, the strategy was to prevent us from voting; the strategy now is to render our votes worthless." David Clarke, chairman of the DC City Council, raised similar concerns with Norton—albeit more diplomatically than Guyot.[69]

Guyot's rhetoric clearly indicated that he saw the fights against the Control Board and for home rule as an extension of his civil rights activism, and he returned to some of the independent political course he followed in the 1960s. Just as he fought for access to the ballot and political power for poor Black Mississippians with the MFDP, he now fought to keep that access in Washington, DC. And his actions in DC, like his activism in Mississippi, interconnected with economic rights, specifically the Black middle class that Barry helped create with government jobs and contracts for minority-owned businesses. "Who is going to suffer the most when we fire 10,000 people?" he said at an April meeting about the board. "We can collaborate with the board or we can do everything to fight it. I intend to fight it. There is no middle ground." Other activists echoed his strident opposition.[70]

But Republicans and their perceived Black collaborators, not southern Democrats, represented his new enemies. A southern Republican in particular replaced James Eastland as a focus of his ire. Speaker of the House Newt Gingrich of Georgia, who played a major role in curtailing the elected government of the city, led the budget impasse in Congress against President Clinton that resulted in the government shutdown of November 1995. Guyot added his name to a petition with numerous labor, civil rights, religious and political leaders, including some Mississippi state legislators, opposing the shutdown and supporting Clinton. The petition included a statement titled "Defeat Newt Gingrich! Defend the U.S. Constitution!" The petition focused on economic concerns, as Clinton vetoed the budget due to cuts in education and environmental protections and Medicare premium increases that the congressional Republicans had added to it. Republican insistence on these cuts only fortified Guyot's desire to work within the Democratic Party. He joined Kathryn Pearson-West, an at-large member of the DC Democratic State Committee, in asking the local party to support dissolving the board. The committee, which had no legal authority over the board or Congress, approved the resolution.[71]

To Guyot, the Black members of the board collaborated with the enemy, like the more conservative African Americans who resisted the civil rights movement in the 1960s. He said that the residents of DC "are now being disenfranchised by a predominately Black group operating under the banner of the Republican wing of the federal government." The board and its Republican enablers intended to "humiliate, abuse and co-opt the local government." The comment may have been overly harsh, given the civil rights credentials of some of the Black members, but when the Control Board moved in November 1996 from budget-cutting to taking control of the public schools away from the elected school board, even some previous allies became concerned, as Stephen Harlan, the board's only white member, then shifted to focus to the city police department, while Brimmer conducted a review of the financially troubled University of the District of Columbia. Kevin Chavous, a city councilman who had previously been friendly to the board, worried that the Control Board was trying "to ensnare themselves as a fixture in the bureaucracy."[72]

Guyot's criticism of alleged Black collaborators mirrored his criticism of the overall DC population. He voiced his frustrations as he fought against the Control Board and for home rule. He complained in interview that the slow pace of change in the city resulted from "a conformist mentality in DC, to a degree that's not found anyplace else." He said that "a large degree of acceptance by the population" accounted for the status quo, that many residents "did not know what was going on," and that "a lot of people who should be involved in this fight are not."[73]

While Guyot and Norton worked within the Democratic Party, the two civil rights activists still clashed, with the Control Board their central disagreement. When Norton secured Gingrich's endorsement of a reduction of federal income tax rates for city residents to a flat 15 percent rate, Guyot quickly linked it to the Control Board's budget-cutting measures, calling it "another piece of legislation to drive poor people from the city." When both of them attended the Democratic National Convention in Chicago in the summer of 1996, Norton, as the chair of the delegation, lobbied for DC statehood. Not even this satisfied Guyot, as he grumbled that the DC delegation was "an entourage, not a delegation. All the decisions were made by Ms. Norton." He aimed his most inflammatory attack during the convention at the Control Board, when he bluntly stated that "Norton tells us lies" and is "worse than an Uncle Tom." Norton, by contrast, avoided any public comment or criticism of Guyot.[74]

Barry, now back as mayor, mobilized his core supporters by confronting the Control Board. This pleased Guyot, who felt that Barry had waited too long to confront the board, especially after its members rejected a city contract that Barry tried to give to a longtime political ally. Yet Barry played the political game as well, maintaining a close relationship with Gingrich, which, like Norton's initial approval of the Control Board, had the effect of staving off more damaging GOP policies for DC. At the same time, Norton and Joyce Ladner both advised him to cooperate with the board, which he did, at least superficially. Yet political realities forced Barry to cut 700 jobs in the Department of Public Housing from his 1996 budget, so his opposition resembled political theater more than actual mobilization.[75]

The Control Board's expanding authority coincided with Barry's decline, as rumors of a drug-related relapse circulated among reporters. Barry left the city in April 1996 for an undefined period to recuperate from "physical exhaustion" but refused to resign as mayor. Pressured by Republicans in Congress, Brimmer announced his support for an unelected city manager to run the city directly, an effective end to home rule and self-government for the city's residents. Senator Lauch Faircloth (R-NC) proposed the idea as a counter to a Gingrich-Norton proposal to assume the city's debt and turn over some of its operations to the federal government. Norton blocked the city manager idea, and the resulting legislation—the National Capital Revitalization Act of 1997—covered the city's debt burden. But the cost of the bailout suspended home rule, as the Control Board now administered the city's nine largest agencies and tasked a chief management officer to run the city and report directly to the board. The Control Board could now veto the city council, and Barry lost most of his power as well. He protested the new law vigorously but declined to run for reelection in 1998. The Barry era came to an undignified end.[76]

Despite the opposition of Guyot and other activists, the poor state of the city, with lackluster services and a high crime rate, muted residents' opposition to the new order. Anthony Williams, the city's chief financial officer, won the mayor's office in 1998 on a platform of good governance. Meanwhile, Norton broke with the Control Board over Williams's support for ending home rule the previous year. She persuaded President Clinton to appoint a new chair when Williams's three-year term ended, and he did, naming Alice Rivlin, a white woman serving as director of the Office of Management and Budget. Williams also pursued unpopular polices of privatization in the city, such as closing DC General Hospital. When voters rejected the closing, the Control Board overruled the popular will in its most aggressive action against majority rule to date. Yet the board at times won majority approval in the city. In another education issue, Guyot opposed the School Governance Charter Amendment Act of 2000, which passed the DC City Council and now faced a voter referendum. This amendment proposed changing the Board of Education from an eleven-member elected body to a nine-member board that was split into five elected members and four members appointed by the mayor. Guyot successfully rallied his ANC to oppose the referendum, seeing this as a further erosion of the city's independence under Rivlin and the Control Board. "Disfranchisement of the voters must not be tolerated," he said. But on 27 June 2000, voters approved the amendment. The Control Board itself finally disbanded in September 2001 after six years, having worked to balance the city budgets under Williams. Local residents deeply opposed the policies, as austerity came at the cost of firing hundreds of city workers, most of them Black. Williams only narrowly won reelection in 2002 as home rule effectively returned to the city, but now in a post-Barry era.[77]

Guyot remained loyal, and even defended Barry cronies like former deputy mayor Ivanhoe Donaldson, who after serving a prison term for stealing $180,000 from the city quietly returned to serve as an unofficial adviser to the mayor in mid-1990s. But Guyot did not view Barry through rose-colored glasses. He spoke more openly about the former mayor in 2004, in an interview with two Mississippi authors. He told them that he hoped that Barry would lose in his race that year, citing concerns about Barry's health. He said he unsuccessfully tried to convince Barry to not to run for office on those grounds. Reflecting on Barry and his troubles, he said, "Everything he did, he did to himself . . . but he's still my hero."[78]

Yet politics is a dirty business, and being a man on the inside and his vigorous defense of the Barry administration meant that some of the taint of the numerous scandals fell on Guyot, even though investigators never implicated him in any wrongdoing. Mary Treadwell, Barry's ex-wife, had another run-in with the law after her 1983 conviction. In 1998, she plead guilty and was sentenced to four months in federal prison for improperly diverting over $10,000 from a Columbia Heights neighborhood group. Guyot rushed to the defense of the woman who once recommended him for a job in the Barry administration. While Guyot had no involvement in the scandal, he felt it necessary to defend her based on their long friendship. "Within the realm of law and politics, when my friends are under attack, I consider myself under attack," he said. Investigators uncovered the scandal in a city audit of ANC 1B's finances, which forced her out of her position in the ANC. Guyot attacked ANC commissioner Glenn Melcher and Gary Imhoff, a former commissioner and president of *DCWatch*, a local political affairs magazine, for steering the FBI toward Treadwell after the audit. Guyot said that she should not have been "treated like a common thief" and that their involvement with the FBI "was a break in thought, temperament and action." Melcher, a white commissioner who had a history of clashes with Black institutions in the city, said that Guyot "constantly made it a racial issue" regarding Treadwell and that Guyot and his allies paralyzed the ANC for more than a year by making "that point each and every time they got a chance."[79] While honest himself, Guyot's loyalty to his friends could at times lead him to excuse their corruption.

Another matter that Guyot closely identified with the civil rights movement also attracted his prodigious energies. By the 1990s, he had become involved with Howard University, one of the major institutions of higher education in the city. The historically Black university, founded in 1867 and long famous for its stellar alumni—such as Supreme Court Justice Thurgood Marshall and SCLC leader Andrew Young—had long served as one of the most popular schools among America's Black elite. Yet the school had a history rife with colorism, dominated by light-skinned upper-class African Americans and possessing a conservative reputation that avoided activism and instead concentrated on being the "Black Harvard." That changed in 1969, with the appointment of James Cheek as president, after two years of student activism against conditions on the campus. The school's student body continued its activist direction in the post–civil rights era, shutting down the campus for five days in 1989 to protest Cheek's appointment of Lee Atwater to the university's board. Black students opposed Atwater, who had worked on Vice President George Herbert Walker Bush's successful presidential election campaign in 1988, for his race-baiting

"Willie Horton" ad campaign from that election. The publicity from the student protests forced both Atwater and Cheek out of the university.[80]

But the administration of Howard University had a chilly relationship with neighboring LeDroit Park, where the Guyots lived. This hostility had existed for over a century as LeDroit Park, founded as an exclusive white suburb in 1873, had clashed with its Black neighbors in Howardtown, the area of Black-owned businesses and homes around the university. By the early 1900s LeDroit Park had integrated and become home for much of the city's Black elite. But like other Black neighborhoods in the city, it suffered an economic downturn after the 1968 riots. In 1994, one resident said that the neighborhood had "liquor stores on almost every corner," but it also had numerous churches, indicating that a still-vibrant community existed. So, in 1990, when Howard University won permission from the city to turn a small park on its edge into a multilevel parking garage for its employees, local residents protested. Local residents utilized the park, the only green space in a twelve-block radius from the campus, and Howard had pledged in 1981 to preserve the park for community use. University officials in turn complained about the burden of picking up trash in the park, and university official Angella Ferguson testified at public hearings that criminal elements created security issues for the community and campus. Guyot, one of two ANC commissioners to vote against the garage, criticized the campus leadership, declaring that "the undesirables she's talking about are the residents of LeDroit Park. You're talking about a neighborhood of low-income individuals and seniors." The university still pursued the garage, as Guyot publicly complained again about the project four years later, when he and several city council members objected to the contractors' pumping water from an aquifer and creating a sinkhole risk in the neighborhood.[81]

Guyot's advocacy for his neighborhood as an ANC commissioner made him popular with his neighbors, as he frequently ran unopposed for the seat. The neighborhood lay on the boundaries of Ward 1, which fellow SNCC veteran Frank Smith represented. The ward had a linguistically and ethnically diverse population, with a population 60 percent Black (including Ethiopian and Caribbean immigrants), 30 percent white, and 18 percent Latino. Or, as Guyot put it with his characteristic bluntness, "If you're not comfortable with diversity, you don't belong here." Diversity sometimes led to tensions, however, as it had during the 1991 Mount Pleasant riots. And residents differed politically on even basic civic issues like public safety. Nonviolent crime like burglary worried the upper-income—and white—residents of the Sheridan-Kalorama area, but the Black residents of Adams-Morgan welcomed the drop in violent crime in the same reports. And in the area of affordable housing, Guyot fell clearly on the side of the poor, as gentrification increased rents in the city. Only 25 percent of residents in Ward 1 owned their homes, a figure below the 35 percent average for the city. Thirty-one percent of homes already exceeded $200,000 in value by 1996, although the prevalence of vacant lots depressed the average housing price in the District, which ranged from $85,000 to $130,000 that same year. When Manna Inc., a nonprofit affordable housing developer in the city, proposed two-unit condominiums on U Street in some of the vacant lots, some residents wanted the new homes to resemble the brick-facade homes of the neighborhood—what the Preservation Society in LeDroit Park called "architectural integrity." Guyot, likely concerned that this would raise the cost of the homes for buyers, supported Manna Inc.'s initial plans to build stucco-style condos. He declared that the proposed housing would boost the low rate of homeownership in the ward. For Guyot, affordable housing was another social and economic justice issue, more than simply advocacy for his constituents. He won the George H. Richardson Civil Rights Award in 1996 for his work through the LeDroit Park Civic Association. He continued his advocacy for affordable housing into the next decade, as the city continued to become richer and whiter.[82]

Guyot returned to involvement with Howard University in the 1990s, but this time as a mentor to a new generation of civil rights activists. The school's activist reputation had also not subsided in the 1990s, and Jonathan Hutto emerged as one of those new leaders. Hutto first met Guyot in October 1996 when the young man ran for an ANC seat in Pleasant Plains, a neighborhood in Northwest Washington. Guyot, running for reelection to the ANC, quickly recognized a fellow activist. "I'm a SNCC veteran, so I must support progressive students," he told Hutto. The distrust between the community and Howard University became a liability for Hutto, as he said that local residents saw him as a pawn of the university.[83]

The ANC elections marked the beginning of what Hutto called "a bond of love and deep admiration" between him and Guyot. Hutto saw Guyot as "an elder who actually embraced what I was doing not simply from a patronizing or idealistic position, but at the standpoint of being right there in the thick of it with you. Here stood an elder I considered a mentor. On that day, I met an elder who related to me as a comrade which was an extension of the intergenerational principles he internalized as a young freedom fighter working alongside movement veterans such as Ella Baker and Bayard Rustin." Despite the number of Howard students he and his friends had helped register, some in the community challenged their credentials. Guyot intervened and said, "Let the students vote!" and Monica Guyot loaned Hutto her car to ferry students to the polls. Hutto won by only eleven votes, indicating the importance of the support.[84]

Guyot with Jonathan Hutto,
November 1997. Photo courtesy
of Jonathan Hutto.

Hutto said that Guyot was "always backing up young people," and that he enjoyed the company of youth activists. Despite his years of working as a Washington insider, Guyot, in Hutto's words, still "preferred the grassroots," the 1960s-style activism of SNCC and the MFDP. Hutto appreciated the support of the elder activist. "My relationship to Lawrence Guyot was critical to my political survival," he recalled. Hutto needed that support when he took office as an ANC commissioner. Following his election to the ANC board, the students elected Hutto student body president of Howard University. The community's distrust of him surfaced quickly, and some area residents wondered if Hutto was overextending himself. Some told the campus newspaper that they had not been able to get in touch with him since his election. Guyot rushed to his defense, calling him "a natural leader" who could perform in both positions simultaneously. "He has the qualities needed to be a leader of the students and the residents, so I don't see why he wouldn't be able to do the things he has committed to do." He also backed another Howard student, Nik Eames, for the ANC and also supported his eventual transition to board chairman.[85]

Guyot continued to openly criticize the university administration. One long-running issue between the university and LeDroit Park concerned the state of disrepair of university-owned abandoned houses, now havens for the homeless and drug dealers. In 1997, Howard University began the LeDroit Park Initiative, a university partnership with Fannie Mae to renovate vacant homes and open them back up for family use. Yet community pressure also shaped the program. Guyot said that the university was "not advancing its interpersonal relationship with people in the community other than people in those houses." The LeDroit Park Civic Association mobilized to stop Howard from demolishing historic property in the community and stopped the university from using substandard materials in the renovation of the houses. Guyot said that the university needed to show residents "mutual concern or mutual respect."[86]

Guyot, Hutto, and Eames also opposed an effort at street privatization, another initiative from Howard. In the summer of 1997, the university administration asked the DC City Council to allow the campus to close several on-campus streets. Both Barry and Frank Smith favored the plan, and the mayor even introduced it to the council on behalf of the Howard administration. Guyot opposed it, which pitted him against his two former SNCC colleagues. Guyot said the university could exclude the residents of LeDroit Park from the streets in the name of security, as some students proposed erecting barriers around campus due to violent crime in the area. But Guyot and most of the students thought this a cure worse than the disease. "Why should a wall be built between neighbors?" he asked. The editorial board of the campus newspaper also opposed it, arguing that a barrier would close off any cooperation with the community over crime prevention or other issues. Maybelle Bennett, the campus community liaison, admitted that she could not verify that the university contacted the ANC about the plan, meaning that the administration did not solicit any community input. Hutto, who chaired the General Assembly—the student governing body at Howard—also opposed the plan. He and Eames brought it before the ANC in July and, with Guyot and all other members of the commission, voted against it.[87]

Howard student journalist—and future author on race relations—Ta-Nehisi Coates summarized the entire street privatization affair as an example of the university's historic elitism and classism, as it sat in the midst of a working-class Black community. He acknowledged the crime problem that threatened the students, many of whom were from suburban neighborhoods, but he criticized the university's approach and lack of communication with area residents. He said that "whatever its fine points, the plan has all the makings of a community powder keg: a relatively rich university of middle-class students annexing property from a city that is famously touchy about its sovereignty." Community leaders complained about the condescending attitude Howard displayed toward them. The president of a civic association put it bluntly, declaring that "the community doesn't trust Howard." This opposition persuaded the project's backers to abandon it. Frank Smith, facing a tough reelection battle for his council seat, came around in September after DC residents and Howard students participated in a Stand Up for Democracy rally at the Capitol, organized to demonstrate for full democracy in the District. The following day, Smith called Hutto and asked him, "What do you need me to do?" At Hutto's request, he sent a letter to Howard University president H. Patrick Swygert asking him to withdraw the privatization proposal, citing the "extensive and intensive community opposition," and made specific reference to Hutto's and Eames's role in that opposition. Meanwhile, Hutto persuaded the General Assembly at the university to vote down the street plan, telling the members that Howard "must choose interdependency with its neighbors." Out of thirty-one members, only three voted for the street privatization. The growing opposition prompted Mayor Barry to reverse course, effectively killing the plan. He requested that the city council withdraw Howard's application, citing requests from Howard students and indicating that the proposal had "severely divided the surrounding neighborhood and campus community, pitting students against students, neighbors against neighbors and the community against the University." While Barry apparently did so at the request of Howard's vice president for administration, Harry Robinson, whose office oversaw the proposal, Hutto said the real reason emerged from a meeting in Barry's office. Hutto, Guyot, Nik Eames, and another

Howard student met with Barry in his office — at Barry's request — to discuss the matter. Hutto said they asked him to drop the bill, and Barry agreed without hesitation. Hutto credited Guyot and Barry's SNCC relationship as a key factor, indicating that Guyot still had influence with the mayor even if he was not one of his closest advisers. Hutto said that "in spite of Barry being the Mayor, he had more solidarity with us than Howard University's administration. Barry and Guyot turned that meeting into a training historical school on advocacy and student activism."[88]

Guyot's opposition to the street privatization plan reflected these "town versus gown" class divisions. In response to a student question about the plan at an on-campus forum, he said that he did "not support apartheid in the name of safety." Hutto said that the apartheid comment "lit a match where you could visibly see where people in the room stood . . . the difference between students on federal work study versus those driving cars and living off campus." Hutto recalled years later that he could "still remember the nearly thirty seconds of deafening silence due to Guyot utilizing the word 'apartheid' to describe the administration's position." But despite his clashes with Howard, he also advocated for the campus at other times, helping it secure tax-exempt bonds for campus development and other matters, which won him the gratitude of the Howard University Community Association.[89]

Guyot's support for the students and his aligning with them from the beginning against the proposal did not mean a break with Barry. Instead, it showed that for all his insider status, Guyot, in Hutto's words, "ALWAYS put his constituency first." The elitist background of Howard University didn't fall into Guyot's ANC constituency. In addition to mentoring and inspiring these new student activists, he retained a commitment to representing the poorer Black residents of his community, like he had in Mississippi in the 1960s. The dynamism of student activists like Hutto also motivated him. Guyot himself said that he "got and continue to get my energy from people. I like people. People stimulate. Ideas, different ways people react to the same thing. That fascinates me, it energizes me."[90]

While Guyot clearly got things done as commissioner, he made his share of enemies. His overbearing style, which could be authoritarian in meetings, rankled many people. At a community forum in 2001 about development in the Columbia Heights neighborhood, he met with residents concerned about gentrification and displacement. This was a hot-button issue in the area, where the previous year the city government had served eviction notices to residents of decrepit properties but taken no action against the landlords, raising fears of the city's colluding with developers to displace the low-income population.

He told the residents that he would, in the words of a local reporter, act as "a benevolent dictator" for the session, which upset some of the residents and prompted two of the invited speakers to leave the event. He unapologetically declared that he would "rather do an effective job in a meeting than make one friend in a meeting," and that he "wanted to send a message of immediacy, of danger." Tom Coumaris, another ANC commissioner who worked with Guyot for eight years, left the commission over his authoritarian ways, specifically when Guyot ignored the commission's practice of deferring to individual commissioners guiding project decisions in their neighborhoods—what was called single-member deference. He saw it as usurpation of power from individual members. Even a staunch Guyot ally like Hutto attested to this style, citing a 1998 vote on a new ANC chair. Tom Porter, a Black commissioner, sought to replace Guyot, and Glenn Melcher, the white city commissioner who had a history of confrontation with Guyot, lent Porter his support. When one commissioner abstained and the commission deadlocked in a tie, Guyot used Robert's Rules of Order to halt any new business until the tie was broken. After hours of inaction, the abstaining commissioner, who had business she wanted the commission to address that night, gave in and voted for Guyot. Coumaris called it "the most high-handed pressure tactic imaginable." Hutto simply called it "classic ole school shit."[91] In many ways Guyot's approach mirrored the old problems that plagued SNCC in the 1960s, with the clash between the "freedom high" volunteers and the "authoritarians" who wanted a more efficient organization. Guyot, who attempted a more efficient model in the MFDP, continued these efforts, however heavy-handed, in urban politics.

Guyot's invoking of racial bias also rankled his white political rivals and some in the press. Erik Wemple of the *Washington City Paper* criticized Guyot, saying that for all of his activism, he "has little to show for his efforts except soundbites," but "if playing the race card and smearing elected officials qualify as progress, Guyot's movement is chugging along." He uncharitably called Guyot's activism "a list of causes . . . as long as it is unspectacular." Glenn Melcher complained that Guyot "is the first person to throw the race card out there." Melcher previously clashed with Guyot over the Treadwell affair and also had a history of legal action against Black institutions in the city. The animosity between the two men led to a power struggle, as Melcher replaced Guyot as chairman of their Ward 1 commission in January 2001, after serving for five years with Guyot. He unseated him after winning over some of Guyot's supporters on the commission, but the power shift also showed the growing political clout of white residents as the city's Black neighborhoods gentrified. But both men recognized that they only clashed politically, not personally, as Melcher said he still had a good working relationship with him, and described Guyot as a tough political opponent. And that same focus on race helped Guyot, too. He said that "race is the pervasive issue in the District of Columbia" as well as in the entire country. His record as a civil rights activist in Mississippi gave him immense credibility with Black voters, noted Maybelle Taylor Bennett, director of Howard University's Community Association, who frequently interacted with Guyot. "He's not just any resident," she said. "He is a resident who put his life on the line." And Guyot even inspired young white activists, despite alienating older whites. In 2004, Nate Matthews, a white history major at Howard, won election to the ANC. He told the student newspaper that his "goals and ambitions are to be a community activist, like Lawrence Guyot. People respect his name because of his work in the community and that's where I want to be and what I want to do."[92]

The replacement of Guyot by Melcher indicated that his political power, especially with Barry out of office, declined as the new millennium opened. Indeed, as the city whitened, including his own LeDroit Park neighborhood, his political career—so tied to Marion Barry and the majority-Black DC electorate—faded. Rising rents, driven by the gentrification of the city in the early twenty-first century, changed the character of the city and heightened racial tensions, as many of the new affluent white residents expressed disdain for their lower-income Black neighbors. Mayor Williams did little to change this course, and even hastened it with his prodevelopment policies, such as pushing through the city council a deal to build a new stadium for a Major League Baseball team. He belatedly backed additional public housing in response to residents' concerns, but only after prioritizing the sports stadium.[93]

Guyot did not lose his interest in city politics, even if he ceased to be a political insider. When Williams opted to not run for reelection, the mayor's race became one between veteran councilwoman Linda Cropp and Adrian Fenty, who, like Guyot, had risen in DC politics through his ANC. Fenty eventually won a seat on the city council, upending twenty-year incumbent Charlene Drew Davis in 2000. Fenty won the primary and general election overwhelmingly, and his ability to attract white votes seemed to put him beyond the racialized politics of the Barry years. Yet the thirty-five-year-old mayor was not the kind of Black politician that Guyot appreciated. Fenty said that he didn't think much about race, citing his own mixed-race heritage of a Black father and Italian American mother. During the election, he said that he "always heard politicians talk about race, but not the people. They were just talking about making sure every neighborhood gets the same attention." Fenty's colorblind focus clashed with the older Guyot's lifelong activism. Still, Guyot endorsed Fenty in the 2006

Democratic primary, likely due to his reputation as the political outsider against the veteran Cropp.[94]

Fenty is perhaps best remembered for his appointment of the controversial education reformer Michelle Rhee as the schools chancellor, where her proposal to close numerous schools in low-income Black neighborhoods for underperformance and low enrollment triggered a strong backlash from local residents. Like Fenty, she made heavy use of white appointees and experts to dictate changes to nonwhite residents, and solicited little input from parents and teachers. Her approach to white parents was the opposite, often personally soliciting them to keep their children in the District. When she—with Fenty's support—pushed through a mass firing of predominately older Black staff and Black teachers in the District, both her and Fenty's approval ratings tumbled. During Fenty's administration, Black teachers ceased being a majority in DC schools, and the number of low-income housing units continued to decline as he did little to addressing affordable housing. Reversing his earlier support for Fenty, Guyot summed up the feelings of many Black residents when he said that the mayor "treated white folks with deference and Black folks with diffidence." Unsurprisingly, Fenty lost the Democratic primary in 2011 to Vincent Gray, the chairman of the city council, who then won the general election that fall. The race went back to the racially polarized elections of earlier years, as 80 percent of Black voters voted for Gray, while an equal number of whites supported Fenty.[95]

While Guyot's political star rose and fell in DC, he did not forget his origins in the civil rights movement. Indeed, he saw his activism in the nation's capital, and his mentoring of young students like Hutto, as a continuation of that struggle. But as he left Mississippi, he remained connected to the memory of the movement, even as the mass organizing of the 1960s declined. Early on, he cultivated an interest in preserving the movement's history. In 1973, Guyot encouraged the writer Kay Mills, who had just completed her first trip to Mississippi, to write a biography of Fannie Lou Hamer. He provided many contacts and let Mills interview him for what he called "our book."[96] These interviews he did with Mills, and those he did before and after, would be the closest Guyot would come to writing his own memoir. The demands of DC politics and his family apparently kept him from penning his own recollections, or perhaps he simply had no interest in doing so. He told his story through interviews and conversations, not the written word.

Movement veterans eventually returned to commemorate the campaigns and battles of the 1960s. One of the first major postmovement gatherings of Mississippi civil rights figures occurred under the cloud of tragedy. In 1977, Fannie Lou Hamer died of heart failure. Her funeral in Ruleville attracted many movement figures, including Stokely Carmichael, Ed King, Ella Baker, Charles Evers, and Andrew Young (then serving as President Carter's ambassador to the United Nations). Guyot was not on the program as a speaker, so it seems unlikely he attended. This was just as well, because Charles Payne said that some of the old SNCC and COFO activists saw her funeral as "an embarrassment, a media event with dignitaries from around the country competing with one another to be seen on camera, pushing her neighbors into the background. It seemed the perfect contradiction of the values she tried to live by."[97]

Guyot returned to Mississippi in the fall of 1979, as movement veterans commemorated the fifteenth anniversary of Freedom Summer. In late October of that year, Tougaloo and Millsaps Colleges hosted a symposium, "Mississippi Freedom Summer—A Fifteen Year Perspective on Progress in Race Relations 1964–1979," with panels on various topics. The event showed that even at this early date, veteran activists clashed with historians over how the movement should be remembered. Clayborne Carson, later one of the movement's foremost scholars, served as moderator. In 1979, Carson was an assistant professor in the Department of History at Stanford University. Two years later he published his landmark book *In Struggle*, the first in-depth study of SNCC.[98]

Controversy erupted on 30 October at a panel at Tougaloo moderated by Carson that included movement veterans Willie Peacock and Sam Block, Guyot's fellow SNCC veterans from their days in Greenwood. The two activists got into an argument with Carson over the lack of movement people at the conference, in particular the absence of prominent organizers Bob Moses and Stokely Carmichael. Carson told them that he had invited or attempted to invite them, but that they did not show or could not be reached, an answer which did not satisfy Block and Peacock. The two activists in particular objected to Al Lowenstein's attending as a panelist. The presence of Lowenstein and not the others implied to them that Lowenstein organized Freedom Summer, something they hotly disputed.[99]

Guyot attended the conference, but not as a panelist. In the midst of the contentious debate, he stood up and identified himself, and made his point clear in typical Guyot fashion. "I want to identify with what Willie Peacock and Sam Block are saying." Carson then invited him up onto the stage to join the panel, to which Guyot bluntly said "no." He took aim directly at Lowenstein, then sitting on the stage. "Let's let this program proceed as organized, and we will create a forum, we know who we are, to mute the rewriting of history," he said. He then declared that "Al Lowenstein, under no set of circumstances known to man, can ever speak for me." This last statement brought a round of applause from the audience. Although Guyot had never liked Lowenstein, he did show the man respect, as he continued and said, "But he has a right. He has a right as does every member of that panel. Let's let his get through. I urge your cooperation on this." He then sat down as the audience applauded again.[100]

Mike Thelwell, who had collaborated with Guyot on earlier civil rights writings, continued the pressure and brought up Lowenstein's connections to the Central Intelligence Agency (CIA), which came from his association with the National Student Association (NSA). Thelwell in particular objected to Lowenstein's condescending comment on Freedom Summer: "I want to say in retrospect that Mississippi was a very important contribution to the process of learning what the difficulties were in working across racial differences." The statement suggested that Black distrust of whites was as large of a factor as white racism in hindering an interracial movement, and this did not sit well with Thelwell. He stood up and said, "To hear you talk[,] the Summer Project [Freedom Summer] was conceived as some kind of encounter group to teach Black people and white people how to work together across racial lines. That's bullshit Al Lowenstein!" Lowenstein denied that was what he meant, but to no avail. "You're answering like you're a clown," Thelwell replied.[101]

Lowenstein may have been the epitome of white liberal paternalism, but his role in the CIA's involvement with the NSA appears marginal at best. While a vocal anticommunist in regards to Soviet influence in international student organizations, Lowenstein does not appear to have been drawn in as an insider to the CIA's funding of the NSA, which began in the early 1950s. Indeed, some associates viewed him as reckless and unable to keep a secret, and the CIA completely circumvented him. However, his biographer William Chafe thinks it is likely he knew of a CIA connection and almost certainly knew it by the 1960s. This reinforces in particular Lowenstein's anticommunist liberalism, which oriented him toward more conservative approaches to the civil rights movement, like voter registration and making Black Mississippians part of the national Democratic Party. Lowenstein did not like the idea of the MFDP, which caused friction with Guyot. Lowenstein also clashed with Bob Moses during the summer of 1965 over Moses's increasing rejection of working within the electoral system to facilitate meaningful change. Guyot recalled that Lowenstein "was very talented, very energetic, but most suspect."[102]

The following day, Guyot attended a panel titled "Race Relations in Mississippi before 1964," this one held at Millsaps College. He gave a far warmer reception to the historian on this panel, Neil McMillen of the University of Southern Mississippi, than he had given Lowenstein. McMillen established his reputation as a scholar of white resistance in Mississippi with his 1971 book *The Citizens' Councils: Organized Resistance to the Second Reconstruction, 1954–64.*

Guyot, speaking during the audience comments time, praised McMillen's scholarly work but expressed concerns about the predominately white audience. Referencing the audience members, he said, "I hope some of them are from Mississippi. And the frightening thing about this meeting is that the less you understand that the state, it was active in every detail that Professor McMillen described, could happen again in this state tomorrow." This connection of the recent past to the present drew a rebuke from some whites in the audience. Some shook their heads, while others shouted at him that "you've got political power and this will never happen again." Guyot, knowing all too well how little the hearts of white Mississippians had changed without federal action, said he was speaking directly to white Mississippians and that "the answer to that question lies in your heads."[103] His comments also show that he regarded an accurate history of the movement as essential to preventing historical regression and a resurgent white supremacy—in short, he believed in historical writing providing a useable past for present-day activists and citizens. But his criticism of Lowenstein also points to something else—he wanted to "mute the rewriting of history." To Guyot, activists like Lowenstein, who had opposed the MFDP, had the right to make their voices heard, but he resisted any efforts by the more conservative side of the movement to shape the historical narrative to minimize the contributions of grassroots activists and Black Mississippians.

As historians began to compile interviews of movement activists, Guyot did not appear in many of the early accounts. Howell Raines, a reporter, conducted two interviews of Guyot for the Mississippi chapter in his 1977 book *My Soul Is Rested*, an early oral history of the movement. His old SNCC colleague Joyce Ladner also interviewed him when he was still working with Pride Inc. in Washington, DC. By the 1980s, Guyot played a more direct role in civil rights movement reunions and commemorations. In 1985, Henry Hampton, a Black filmmaker who participated in "Bloody Sunday" march on the Edmund Pettus Bridge in Selma, Alabama, began production of a documentary film series on the civil rights movement, from extensive footage he and his coproducer, Jon Else, had complied. Titled *Eyes on the Prize* and using interviews and archive newsreel footage, the fourteen-episode series became the defining documentary on the history of the movement. Hampton and Else started filming interviews for the series in 1979, beginning with major movement events like the Montgomery Bus Boycott and Emmet Till's lynching. When they reached Freedom Summer and the founding of the MFDP, the filmmakers focused more on Bob Moses and the women of the MFDP, in particular Victoria Gray Adams and Unita Blackwell. Annie Devine, by then suffering from Alzheimer's, was unable to provide anything of value. But the filmmakers largely overlooked Guyot's

MFDP leadership. He only appeared on-camera once for less than a minute in the series, commenting on the difficulties Black Mississippians faced from white voting registrars in the early 1960s.[104] The *Eyes on the Prize* documentary series, which heavily shaped how the movement was remembered due to its frequent airings on public television, relegated Guyot to a secondary, almost invisible role. But he did not seek the limelight.

Guyot continued to participate in movement events, never showing any resentment over a lack of attention to his activism and sacrifices. He joined old movement friends and colleagues at reunions and academic conferences, including a 1988 symposium on SNCC at Trinity College in Hartford, Connecticut. There he appeared with SNCC veterans Hollis Watkins, Victoria Gray Adams, and Mendy Samstein on a panel on the Mississippi movement. Eventually, civil rights scholars sought him with more regularity, and Guyot generously provided his recollections. In 1989, for the twenty-fifth anniversary of Freedom Summer, *People* magazine ran a recollection piece he penned. In 1993, he took part in a forum at Howard with Adams and Joyce Ladner, then the university's vice president of academic affairs. In 1996, the Mississippi Oral History Project at the University of Southern Mississippi interviewed him for its civil rights collection.[105]

Guyot played probably his most important role in civil rights commemoration by aiding the documentary series that all but ignored him. *Eyes on the Prize*, after its initial success, fell on hard times. Due to fears of lawsuits from corporations that held copyright to some of the archival material, PBS ceased its annual broadcast of the series in 1994, with video rental outlets following suit and withdrawing videocassettes of the series from purchase or rental. Changes in copyright law hamstrung efforts to get it relicensed. The entire series went out of print in 1997, and by 2004, only bootleg copies or expensive original sets on internet auction sites existed.[106]

Guyot took action to preserve this important movement record. He said that the disappearance of *Eyes* from television screens "is analogous to stopping the circulation of all the books about Martin Luther King, stopping circulation of all the books about Malcolm X, stopping the circulation of books about the founding of America. I would call upon everyone who has access to *Eyes on the Prize* to openly violate any and all laws regarding its showing." For Guyot, this was a new era of civil disobedience, and a new technology—the internet—aided him in his campaign. He partnered with Downhill Battle, an online activist collective, and digitized the entire series from VHS tapes. It became known as the "Eyes on the Screen" project, which was distributed over the internet in defiance of copyright law. Guyot and his allies went further with their civil disobedience, arranging for nationwide public community screenings in seventy cities of the entire fourteen-episode series during Black History Month in 2005. But then the estate of Henry Hampton, who had died 1998, threatened legal action, which forced Downhill Battle to cease streaming and Guyot to apologize. But the publicity paid off: the Ford Foundation, one of the original funders of the series, delivered a grant to secure the rights to release the entire series on DVD and broadcast it again on PBS in 2007.[107]

In his interviews, Guyot candidly recalled the Mississippi civil rights movement, but he avoided overly negative comments about movement people he had clashed with, like Bob Moses, James Foreman, and others. But he spared no criticism of Charles Evers, his old rival from organizing in Mississippi in the 1960s. Despite their brief alliance in late 1967 and 1968, he had little positive to say about Evers and his activities, which included not just their 1960s clashes but Evers's later political career as mayor of Fayette and controversial role as an independent spoiler in the 1978 US Senate race in Mississippi. Guyot minced no words in a 2004 interview. "I think he was a disgrace," Guyot said bluntly, "a man who destroyed a lot of dreams and lot of expectations about people." He said Evers was "at best a sellout" and lamented that it was "just such a waste of how he stopped believing change and empowerment was possible and started thinking about how to make money."[108]

As movement veterans got older, their numbers inevitably thinned. Sadly, funerals became another method of civil rights reunion and commemoration. In November 1998, Stokely Carmichael, who had long since changed his name to Kwame Ture and moved to Conakry, the capital of the West African nation of Guinea, died of prostate cancer. He had visited his alma mater, Howard University, in February of that year. While the two men had parted ways politically over Black Power, they had remained close. Guyot told the student newspaper that Ture "stood for what he believed in. I feel I have lost a good friend. He and I differed on some issues, but whenever you risk your life for something you believe in, you are bonded for life." In 2006, his old MFDP colleague Victoria Gray Adams died. At her memorial service in Palmers Crossing, Mississippi, Guyot gave a brief tribute, as did SNCC and CORE veterans Hollis Watkins, Dave Dennis, and Peggy Connor, among others.[109]

Guyot retired in 2006 from his city job but continued his speaker engagements. He also took his message to audiences that rarely heard it. In October 2004, he appeared on the highly rated Fox News TV show *The O'Reilly Factor*. He discussed an ongoing IRS investigation of the NAACP, launched after Julian Bond, as host Bill O'Reilly put it, "viciously attacked" the George W. Bush administration. Bond had accused Bush of lying about the Iraq War. The show followed a typical format on Fox News, putting a liberal opposite a conservative, with O'Reilly joining the conservative to team up against the liberal. Guyot was on with Robert Woodson, a Black conservative from the National Center for Neighborhood Enterprise. O'Reilly and Woodson attacked Bond's statement and voter registration work as activism on behalf of the Democratic Party, in violation of the organization's tax-exempt status. Or as O'Reilly said memorably, "I'm all for free speech, but I don't want to pay for it." Guyot countered by bringing up that Bond had invited Bush to speak before the organization, and compared the IRS action to Alabama in 1957, when the segregationist state government tried to secure the membership lists of the organization to target members. Woodson and O'Reilly focused on issues like NAACP volunteers handing out Democratic campaign literature, while Guyot pointed out that the NAACP Executive Board had never endorsed a political candidate, and was not endorsing John Kerry, the Democratic nominee, in the election—which Guyot incorrectly predicted Kerry would win.[110]

The following year, he appeared again on the show in the wake of Hurricane Katrina. O'Reilly severely criticized Louisiana governor Kathleen Blanco's response to the disaster, using it as part of a broader critique of "the government"—he made no distinction made between state and federal—allegedly being unreliable. His contradicted himself, simultaneously saying that "no government can protect you from danger or provide you with a decent living," while at the same time criticizing Blanco for not calling the federal government sooner to get help. Guyot protested the media coverage of the disaster, in particular the racialized way the media called Black New Orleanians "looters" and "refugees." "If the victims were white, the response would have been quicker," he declared. Unsurprisingly, O'Reilly disputed this, saying that "people who are taking television sets are being called looters. I haven't heard any overt racial reporting at all."[111]

Guyot did not just spend his time sparring with Black conservatives and Fox News hosts. He strongly endorsed Barack Obama's presidential campaign in 2008, and traveled with old civil rights friends to campaign for him. He said that the Illinois senator "is carrying on our tradition of organizing from the ground up in order to encourage the broadest possible participation in the democratic political process especially among women, young people, African Americans and Hispanics." After Obama's victory, Guyot published a self-titled newsletter addressing civil rights issues, including health care policy and the memory of the movement. His health problems had necessitated a kidney transplant in 1987, and a reaction to the kidney medicine affected his eyesight, requiring implants in both his eyes. His weight continued to be a problem, and he suffered from hypertension. Rather than let this sideline him, Guyot, always indefatigable, made his health issues part of his activism. He championed organ donation and transplants, specifically for hospitals in the District. He also used *Guyot's Newsletter* as a platform to encourage voter registration for Obama's reelection, and met Obama in 2010 at a White House function honoring the civil rights movement. He linked his activism directly to the Mississippi movement and declared that "we cannot fall into the mean trap that the Republican Party is a real choice for those who fought to make this country great." He also reprinted newspaper stories on racial issues in the newsletter.[112]

Guyot attended the fiftieth anniversary of the founding of SNCC in 2010 at Shaw University in Raleigh, North Carolina, one of the last gatherings he attended in his life. There he served as a panelist for two sessions, one covering SNCC organizing in Mississippi and the other on the MFDP. At the Mississippi panel, an enthusiastic Guyot interrupted his old friend Owen Brooks and called himself a "resident of Washington" but acknowledged his Mississippi origins and heritage. He gestured emphatically throughout his passionate speech. But never one to hog the spotlight, he recognized several past and current activists in the audience. He opened his presentation by addressing current politics and the importance of organizing for the 2010 midterms. He specifically warned about the GOP and the Tea Party and their actions in the wake of Obama's election, and also advised against voting outside the two-party system. He was unapologetic here, acknowledged that some of his "more purist friends" said, "There you go again, trying to bring us into the Democratic Party. Well, I'm guilty as hell." He gave credit to his old partner Bob Moses, saying he did the right thing in not taking him on after Atlantic City when some SNCC members wanted to "straighten out" the MFDP. By avoiding conflict, Guyot said Moses allowed the MFDP to accomplish its work, which he felt would not have happened had Moses challenged him. Yet he emphasized SNCC's importance, declaring that "the Student Nonviolent Coordinating Committee made Mississippi, and Mississippi made the Student Nonviolent Coordinating Committee." And ever the teacher, Guyot lectured people in the audience on the importance of the movement, telling them, "If you don't write when I'm talking, I'll stop talking. Because I'm here to teach, I'm not here to amuse." He dropped the names of authors, citing David Garrow's book on Selma and crediting the Mississippi movement with helping with the passage of the Voting Rights Act. Brooks eventually had to interrupt Guyot's monologue, as he dominated the panel and went over his allotted time.[113]

At the MFDP panel, Guyot arrived late, making a dramatic applause-greeted entrance about seven minutes into the meeting, when Mike Thelwell was still giving an introduction on the history of the MFDP. Guyot began his talk by promoting Michael Paul Sistrom's dissertation on the party, calling it "the most dynamic portrayal of the history of the Mississippi Freedom Democratic Party that can be expected to come out." Unlike many civil rights veterans, who remained reticent to talk to historians, Guyot showed his support for scholars of the civil rights movement. SNCC historian Wesley Hogan indicated that Guyot had personally invited her to be on the panel. He gave her book a shout-out to the audience, calling it "excellent." Guyot then went on to discuss the familiar ground of Atlantic City, calling SNCC "the best group of organizers ever assembled in America." He cited the extensive scholarly coverage of SNCC by Hogan, John Dittmer, Taylor Branch, and Charles Payne, calling their collective works "a luxury of literary stupendomonium." Thelwell good-naturedly pointed out that Guyot had neglected to mention Stokely Carmichael's *Ready for Revolution* (coauthored with Thelwell), which prompted Guyot to shake with laughter, saying, "How could I [forget]?" Like on the Mississippi panel, he warned of the need to keep organizing and to be vigilant against voter suppression, in particular voter ID laws. MFDP attorney Armand Defner added to this, mentioning the recent *Citizens United* ruling as a threat to democracy with its easing of limitations on campaign finance spending. Guyot closed by invoking his enthusiasm for youth activism and organizing when he declared that "there should be no age differential between people who are organizing for change. If you're old enough to be oppressed, you're old enough to fight oppression."[114]

He also continued to assist historians in compiling a historical record of the movement. In 2010, Julian Bond interviewed him for the Civil Rights History Project at the National Museum of African American History and Culture. Joshua Moore and Diana Dombrowski from the University of Florida interviewed him in 2011. That year he also participated in a conference related to his interview by the University of Florida researchers. At a conference at Delta State University in Cleveland, Mississippi, Guyot recollected movement events like the congressional challenge but also made it clear how he felt about the current state of American politics. Foreshadowing of the rise of Donald Trump and authoritarian politics, Guyot said, "We have to come to the realization, brothers and sisters, that we now face the greatest danger we've ever faced in America. And by 'we' I mean non-Republicans. This university is bipartisan—I ain't. I have not made the intellectual mistake of assuming that the Republican Party is an ethical alternative to the Democratic Party; it is not." He first focused on the threats to collective bargaining, Social Security, and the rest of the social and economic safety net presented by the GOP. But he then shifted to the obstacles to voting presented by voter ID laws in Republican-led states, and the

Guyot in Hattiesburg,
Mississippi, recalling the
movement, 22 October 2010.
Associated Press Photo/
Rogelio V. Solis.

calls of some GOP politicians to change the Fourteenth Amendment to eliminate birthright citizenship. To Guyot, these trends reminded him of the 1960s Jim Crow barriers to voting he had organized against in SNCC and the MFDP and represented an existential threat to American democracy. His solution to this? "Organize," he said.[115]

At the conference, Guyot reiterated what he told Julian Bond the year before, that he was "astounded that the political commentators look at a sense of equivalence between the Republican Party and the Democratic Party. There is none." Warning of dark years ahead—and, without realizing it, predicting the rise of Donald Trump, he said that if progressives did not organize, then "not only will it be lost, it will be irretrievable. It's not a question of waiting another ten years and there'll be a flip."[116]

Guyot's involvement with oral historians and conferences sets him apart from some other movement veterans, who were often reluctant to speak to professional historians chronicling the civil rights movement. Bob Moses voiced his distrust of historians and in particular how popular culture began to portray the movement. The 1988 film *Mississippi Burning*, in the words of SNCC veteran Bob Zellner, "incensed" Moses. The relegation of grassroots activists and Black Mississippians to passive bystanders while two white FBI agents were made the heroes of Freedom Summer was "turning history on its head," according to Zellner. Zellner recalled that at the thirtieth anniversary of SNCC in 1990, Moses urged movement veterans to "start writing our own stories, because history and the historians will either not tell about it or get it wrong."[117]

Moses had a point, as some academics and authors also replicated the top-down, white savior narrative that Hollywood portrayed in film and television. Charles Payne, in *I've Got The Light of Freedom*, his bibliographic essay at the end of his landmark study on Mississippi organizing, singled out authors like Seth Cagin and Philip Dray, who wrote about the Schwerner, Chaney, and Goodman murders in *We Are Not Afraid*, and Nicolaus Mills, who, in *Like a Holy Crusade*, minimized or outright ignored the indigenous Mississippi movement, presenting it as being rescued by brave white volunteers. Although these authors are not professional historians, their 1980s-era works shaped the early movement historiography.[118]

Guyot did not support this kind of scholarship, but he did seem content to let others tell the stories. He broke with Moses again, as he had years earlier in Mississippi, over Moses's disdain for professional historians. Guyot had criticized and clashed with historians he did not agree with, such as Carson at the 1979 panel. But he had a long history of endorsing historians who covered the fight against white supremacy, such as Neil McMillen, Kay Hogan, Charles Payne, and others. To Guyot, young activists like Hutto needed to be mentored and encouraged—but not controlled—and those activists, as well as society at-large needed a historical interpretation of the past to help fight white supremacy and continue the struggle. As Guyot had told both white and Black attendees at the 1979 conference, it "could happen again."

Some ominous political signs emerged late in Guyot's life. The proliferation of voter ID laws in many states in the early twenty-first century particularly alarmed him. To some, there seemed reason for optimism. In 2005 an overwhelming bipartisan majority in Congress renewed the Voting Rights Act for another twenty-five years, and President George W. Bush signed the renewal into law. In 2009, the Supreme Court gave its approval when it rejected a Texas challenge to Section 5 preclearance in the act, in *Northwest Austin Municipal Utility District No. 1 v. Holder*. Frank Parker, an attorney with the Lawyers Committee for Civil Rights under Law who had represented Black plaintiffs in numerous cases out of Mississippi, called it the "national consensus on voting rights," arguing that Americans across all races now saw voting as a fundamental right and did not view it with the same hostility as many whites did busing or affirmative action.[119]

J. Morgan Kousser, an academic and expert witness in nineteen federal voting rights cases, did not share Parker's optimism. Kousser pointed out that since the 1990s the Supreme Court applied a double standard to majority-Black versus majority-white electoral districts. In *Shaw v. Reno* in 1993 and *Bush v. Vera* in 1996, the Court struck down majority-Black districts in North Carolina and Texas, respectively, based on their unusually gerrymandered shapes to elect Black candidates. But in the latter case, the Court upheld a white-majority Republican district of similar shape. Kousser warned that these cases would help undo the hard-fought gains of the civil rights movement, much as the Court had unraveled Reconstruction electoral gains in the nineteenth century.[120]

As the twenty-first century progressed, the Court validated Kousser's fears of regression. Both Parker and Kousser wrote their views before the Supreme Court's decision in 2008 in *Crawford v. Marion County Election Board*, where it upheld a Republican-backed voter ID law in Indiana that had been approved purely along party lines. The legislature passed the law to fight voter fraud, a familiar Republican charge, even though the state of Indiana admitted it knew of no cases of such fraud. While voter ID laws existed in some states prior to this ruling, the Court ruling allowed for the passage of more, and by 2013 more than two dozen states had them, with eleven alone since 2010, when the Republicans won majorities in both houses of Congress.[121]

Guyot feared that these restrictions would lead to President Barack Obama's defeat in 2012. By early that year, Guyot's health worsened. The last of his line, he had outlived three younger brothers. He suffered from heart problems and diabetes over the years, and on 13 April 2012, he had a heart attack. The doctors diagnosed him with kidney failure and predicted a quick death. But he defied the odds. His daughter said that he "spent the next eight months confusing his doctors with his sheer willfulness, his determination to see things through." He continued to speak, giving one of his last interviews in July 2012 to Paul Murray, a professor at Siena College. He also cooperated with Davis Houck and Maegan Parker Brooks of Florida State University, who used his insight in editing a collection of Fannie Lou Hamer's speeches. They interviewed him while he lay in an intensive care unit. Brooks said that "between rough coughs and occasional gasps for air, the memories he shared with me were incisive and crystal clear." He continued to urge people to register to vote, in particular to reelect Barack Obama that November. He lived long enough to see that historic event, and in the words of Avis Thomas-Lester, editor of the Washington, DC, newspaper the *Afro*, Guyot was "elated" that the GOP voter suppression efforts failed to defeat Obama. His daughter Julie said that Guyot "left when he was ready to do so." That day came on 22 November, when he died at his home. He was seventy-three years old.[122]

The passing of the civil rights veteran, who often labored out of the limelight that followed higher-profile activists, triggered an outpouring of sympathy and memories from the civil rights community and Washington, DC's political class. His family buried him on 8 December at Our Mother of Mercy Catholic Church in Pass Christian, his childhood church. Two memorial services followed, on 10 December at Woodworth Chapel at Tougaloo College and on 15 December in Washington, DC, at the Goodwill Baptist Church and the African American Civil War Memorial. In Washington, DC, Mayor Vincent Gray, DC US House delegate Eleanor Holmes Norton, and former mayor and now city councilman Marion Barry all paid tribute to him from the pulpit, before a crowd of hundreds. Barry called him "an unsung hero among thousands of unsung heroes who were not looking for anything." Gray admitted he did not know Guyot from his Mississippi days, but "if he was half the person in Mississippi that he was in the District, I wouldn't want to tangle with Guyot. He was resolute, he was clear, he was eloquent and he was brilliant." His old SNCC colleague and Tougaloo classmate Joyce Ladner said he "gave far more than he received," and Dick Gregory, the comedian who had long supported the civil rights movement, also eulogized him.[123]

In time, the public commemorated Guyot in other ways, from naming a street for him in Washington, DC, to his hometown of Pass Christian and the Mississippi Freedom Trail honoring him with a historical marker and rock garden in July 2023. At the latter dedication, his family members and local officials met with the press to celebrate his memory. His daughter Julie told the media that Pass Christian "nourished his activism, his journey, as a man, as a politician." John Spann, the outreach officer for the Mississippi Humanities Council, praised Guyot for his efforts "to change voting rights for Mississippians throughout the state and then also push for a more inclusive and equal Democratic Party to represent the state in Washington."[124] Yet that legacy of voting rights also became enmeshed in the web of historical memory.

# CONCLUSION

Even in death, Guyot stoked controversy. In the immediate aftermath of his passing, the press highlighted Guyot's civil rights legacy, in particular his near-death ordeal at the Winona city jail. The Constitutional Accountability Center, a progressive think tank in Washington, DC, memorialized Guyot in a post urging the Supreme Court to consider his legacy in its upcoming review of the Voting Rights Act, in a case out of Shelby County, Alabama, the soon-to-be landmark *Shelby County v. Holder*. Doug Kendall and Emily Phelps of the center said that Guyot's death "reminds us just how little time has passed since it took genuine, physical courage even to seek the right to vote in certain parts of the United States." They said that "Mr. Guyot will not be in the courtroom as the Supreme Court takes up Shelby County, but his story should loom over the Court's deliberations and should lead the Court to affirm, rather than strike down, this iconic and still essential law." The invoking of the tribulations Guyot suffered in the 1960s did not sit well with James Taranto, a conservative columnist with the *Wall Street Journal*. He called the center a "left-liberal outfit" that made its argument "based on little more than an appeal to emotion—specifically, on nostalgia for the heroism of the civil rights movement half a century ago." Taranto said that "paying tribute to the heroes of the past is entirely fitting, but clinging to the policies of the past is reactionary." He cited the success of the Voting Rights Act and outlined the arguments made by the plaintiffs in the Alabama case, namely that the act's preclearance provisions had not been updated with renewal in 2006. While Taranto did not explicitly say if he favored the repeal of Section 5, he did not seem troubled by that possibility, as he said that Section 2 of the act, which prohibited discrimination based on race, color, or language, would still protect minority voters.[1]

If Justice Anthony Kennedy knew of Guyot's sacrifices, they made no impact on him. Considered the swing vote on the Court in 2013, he cast the deciding vote in *Shelby County v. Holder*, agreeing with the plaintiffs and ruling Section 4(b) of the act unconstitutional, on the grounds that it was outdated and had not been updated by Congress in 2006. Justice Ruth Bader Ginsburg delivered a stinging rebuttal, declaring that "throwing out preclearance when it has worked and is continuing to work to stop discriminatory changes is like throwing away your umbrella in a rainstorm because you are not getting wet." Without Section 4(b), Section 5 preclearance became unenforceable, barring new legislation by Congress—which did not materialize. In the five years since the ruling, twenty-three states advanced new restrictions, ranging from voter ID laws to reducing early voting to purging voter rolls. The Justice Department of the Trump administration had little interest in filing challenges to these state laws, which were overwhelmingly pushed by Republicans. In the summer of 2021 in an Arizona case, the Supreme Court—bolstered by three conservative Trump appointees—then effectively limited the scope of Section 2 (the part of the act Taranto had defended), by upholding that state's new voting restrictions, despite the suppressive effect they had on minority voters.[2] The decision provided a depressing coda to the act that Guyot and his fellow members of the Mississippi Freedom Democratic Party (MFDP) had played a key role in creating.

Things did not improve. The years 2021 and 2022 saw a new wave of voter suppression efforts in Republican-controlled states, after Joseph Biden's defeat of incumbent Donald Trump for the presidency and the historic flipping of the two Senate seats in Georgia to the Democrats. With the continued stalling of the John Lewis Voting Rights Advancement Act in the Senate, the voting rights consensus that Frank Parker described over twenty years ago now seems to be in ruins, if it ever really existed in the hearts of the GOP. Only one Republican senator, Lisa Murkowski of Alaska, voted for the bill, which could not overcome a GOP filibuster. The GOP, having lost due to record turnout among Democratic voters that overcame its own impressive turnout for Trump, seems to have fundamentally retreated from the bipartisan efforts of its congressional predecessors of the 1960s who overcame the white South's opposition to landmark civil rights legislation. The only bright spot came in the summer of 2023, when a brazen effort by white Republicans in Alabama to destroy the rest of the Voting Rights Act backfired on them, when in *Allen v. Milligan* the Court preserved Section 2 of the act and ruled that the state discriminated against Black voters when it racially gerrymandered its congressional map.[3]

This state of affairs can easily demoralize individuals, but this is where Guyot's call—to organize—is critically important. Were he alive today, he no doubt would call on activists to continue to organize and agitate. Indeed, he would only point at the years of work that grassroots organizers did in Georgia and Arizona to flip those states to the Democratic column for the first time in decades, as well as Georgia's two Senate seats.[4] Organizing is hard work, not glamorous and typically done below the radar. But, short of armed revolution, it is how to achieve change in a society.

Lawrence Thomas Guyot Jr. wanted a revolution, but a nonviolent one, in the spirt of Dr. Martin Luther King Jr. and others from the civil rights movement. He grew up on the segregated Gulf Coast but in relative isolation from the experiences of the Delta and elsewhere that Fannie Lou Hamer, Amzie Moore, and other fellow activists endured. Not your typical Mississippi civil rights activist and born from the labor organizing and Catholic traditions of the coast, he then experienced an intellectual awakening at Tougaloo College. But as a Black man, he still knew racism and that drove him into the movement.

Guyot's time in the Student Nonviolent Coordinating Committee (SNCC) honed his skills as an organizer. Braving white violence in the Delta and later in Hattiesburg, he saw the true brutality of Jim Crow, physically and psychologically, on Black Mississippians. He dropped old preconceptions and embraced a democracy for all and worked toward that end. And he did so at almost the cost of his own life. But the sadistic beatings he received in a Winona jail did not deter him, any more than his incarceration at Parchman did.

From his start as SNCC field secretary, Guyot rose to help organize and lead the Mississippi Freedom Democratic Party, born of SNCC's grassroots organizing and determination to integrate the state's political establishment. Loyal to the national Democrats and opposed to the state ones, the MFDP labored with little federal recognition or assistance. Even old SNCC allies were wary, considering this political organizing to be dangerously close to sleeping with the enemy. While old allies like Bob Moses drifted away, Guyot and his allies—in particular the women of the party—organized, ran for office, and lobbied legislators. They ran Black candidates for office to raise awareness and give a voice to Black Mississippians, even if the powers that be in Washington, DC, did not want to hear that voice.

The high-profile efforts of the congressional challenge won them publicity, but not victory, as the House continued to seat the white segregationist Democrats. But the efforts highlighted the voter suppression of Black Mississippians, and contributed to the passage of the Voting Rights Act. Guyot recognized that battles could be lost but the war could be won. That realization, that politics is the art of the possible, led him to break from the idealism of SNCC and focus on the realities of building a political organization to gain access to power and patronage. Yet the old activist remained, and Guyot alternated between the Freedom Democrats working as an independent party and working within the

Democratic Party. While Stokely Carmichael and others preached Black Power and racial separatism, Guyot accepted the former and rejected the latter. Black Power meant votes, political office, federal patronage to aid the local people of Mississippi. The shift to local elections and organizing did not bring success either, bitterly seen in Sunflower County. Outflanked by his rivals in the National Association for the Advancement of Colored People (NAACP), he finally reconciled with them and saw a broad coalition of activists as the only way to integrate the political establishment of the Magnolia State and gain power. But the price, a loss of independence, proved a bitter pill to swallow.

Guyot's life encompassed more than Mississippi, however. A transitional figure, his life represented the shift in Black political activism and power from the rural grassroots organizing of the 1960s South to the new urban politics of northern cities. With the close of the 1960s, Guyot moved on to Washington, DC, to restore his health and raise a family. But politics remained in his blood, and he was soon working in it again, with fellow Mississippian Marion Barry in the DC mayor's office. Now a member of the organization rather than a leader, he dutifully followed orders and, after so long a wait, enjoyed some of the benefits that came from a community controlled and organized by Black politicians. A loyal follower of Barry, he defended him even as Barry became increasingly hard to defend. Being in the circle of power meant that sometimes he confronted the very activists whose side he once would have joined, as seen in his clashes with Mitch Snyder. Access to power also made him an institutional figure, closer to the rich and powerful, and perhaps the inevitable consequence of gaining access to the political mainstream. He still mentored young activists in the city, inspiring them to organize and continue the struggle for equality. He faded from the political scene with the end of the Barry years, but he remained active in politics and in particular in preserving the memory of the civil rights years for future generations, to inspire and lead future activists to continue the struggle for change. Even as his health failed him, he never gave up on that. He lived to see the election and reelection of the first Black president, events that brought him great joy. And he warned of the constant need to be vigilant to keep the gains of the movement, which so many had fought and died for, from regressing to the darkness of the past.

In this present era of the rollback of hard-fought civil rights gains, perhaps the best postscript for Lawrence Guyot came from the obituary published by the funeral home that handled his burial. The Guyot family made this simple request, asking that "in lieu of flowers, the family asks that you register to vote and aid others in doing the same."[5] It was a fitting epitaph.

# NOTES

## INTRODUCTION

1. Minutes of the LeDroit Park Civic Association meeting on 26 February 2013, LeDroit Park Civic Association, 8 March 2013, www.ledroitparkdc.org/2013/03 /ledroit-park-civic-association-february-26-2013/.

2. Mills, *This Little Light of Mine*; Lee, *For Freedom's Sake*; Larson, *Walk with Me*; Bracey, *Fannie Lou Hamer*; Brooks, *Fannie Lou Hamer*; Blain, *Until I Am Free*; Asch, *Senator and the Sharecropper*; Brooks, *Voice That Could Stir an Army*; Brooks and Houck, *Speeches of Fannie Lou Hamer*; Burner, *And Gently He Shall Lead Them*; Visser-Maessen, *Robert Parris Moses*; Williams, *Medgar Evers*; Joseph, *Stokely*; Beito and Beito, *Black Maverick*.

3. Blackwell with Morris, *Barefootin'*.

4. Brown interview by Murray, 6. This transcript was graciously given to me by Paul Murray.

5. For unpublished manuscripts, see Sistrom, "'Authors of the Liberation'"; and Davis, "'Sisters and Brothers All.'" Examples of typical coverage of the MFDP in SNCC histories include Carson, *In Struggle*, and, more recently, Hogan, *Many Minds, One Heart*. The MFDP monograph is Reinhard, *Politics of Change*. Leslie Burl McLemore, who served as an officer in the MFDP, has written what is still the best source on the party in his PhD dissertation, "The Mississippi Freedom Democratic Party."

6. Hall, "Long Civil Rights Movement," 1239; Asch and Musgrove, *Chocolate City*, 3.

7. Morrison, *Aaron Henry of Mississippi*.

8. Brodie, *Thomas Jefferson*.

## CHAPTER 1

1. For example, Fannie Lou Hamer, who was raised in the Delta town of Ruleville, was not even aware that she could register to vote when SNCC workers arrived there to canvass for applicants in 1962. Marsh, *God's Long Summer*, 12.

2. "Louis Joseph Piernas"—Harrison County, Works Progress Administration (WPA) Slave Narratives, MSGenWeb Library Slave Narrative Project, msgw.org/slaves /piernas-xslave.htm; Our Lady of the Gulf Baptismal Record for Louis Joseph Piernas, Hancock County Historical Society.

3. "Louis Joseph Piernas," WPA Slave Narratives; Fitzgerald, *Urban Emancipation*, 10–14. Some studies argue that New Orleans had less discrimination based on skin color between lighter- and darker-skinned Blacks; see, e.g., Hirsch and Logsdon, *Creole New Orleans*, 193–95, 197. Yet Arnold Hirsch admits that such attitudes existed and were eroded by Jim Crow, forcing the lighter-skinned elite to accept commonalities with other African Americans. Hirsch, "Simply a Matter of Black and White," 263.

4. "Louis Joseph Piernas," WPA Slave Narratives; Caire and Caire, *History of Pass Christian*, 51–52.

5. Foner, *Reconstruction*, 62–66, 262–63, 355–56, 362; Rankin, "Politics of Caste," 110–11, 122, 133–38. David Rankin has a less positive view than Arnold Hirsch and Joseph Logsdon about the divisions of skin color in New Orleans before and during emancipation, even though the community in general came to support universal Black male suffrage. Rankin, "Politics of Caste," 130–31, 133–34.

6. Foner, *Reconstruction*, 558–62; McMillen, *Dark Journey*, 41–44, 47, 60.

7. McMillen, *Dark Journey*, 39, 60; Kirwan, *Revolt of the Rednecks*, 16–17; Piernas, WPA Slave Narratives; Hancock County Obituary Record for Louis Joseph Piernas, unknown newspaper, 25 July 1954, Hancock County Historical Society; 1880 US Census, Harrison County, Mississippi, population schedule 1, Pass Christian, p. 26B, dwelling 252, family 268, Eliza Williams, Romain Morgan, and Armand Morgan, digital image, ancestry.com. Guyot claimed in a 2011 interview that Morgan had been mayor of Pass Christian, but the only evidence is an "R. Morgan" who served as a councilman in the 1880s. "City Officials, Pass Christian, Mississippi," Billy Bourdin Historical Collections; Guyot interview by Rachal, 1; Guyot interview by Moore and Dombrowski, 1, 2. C. Vann Woodward first argued this in *The Strange Career of Jim Crow*.

8. McMillen, *Dark Journey*, 60; Kirwan, *Revolt of the Rednecks*, 59; Hancock County Obituary Record for Louis Joseph Piernas, *Sea Coast Echo*, 29 July 1954, Hancock County Historical Society; Alphabet File, p. 297, Hancock County Historical Society.

9. McMillen, *Dark Journey*, 61–62; Plessy v. Ferguson, 163 US 537 (1896).

10. McMillen, *Dark Journey*, 62–63; Hancock County Obituary Record for Louis Joseph Piernas; Caire and Caire, *History of Pass Christian*, 54, 109.

11. For the Delta planters and their post-Reconstruction practice of fusion, as well as their abandonment of it, see Cobb, *Most Southern Place on Earth*, 84–90.

12. Lang, *History of Harrison County*, 1–2; Pillar, "Religious and Cultural Life," 387–89.

13. Kahrl, *This Land Was Ours*, 54; Lang, *History of Harrison County*, 25–27, 29, 33, 79, 188; Jackson, *Dixie's Italians*, 66–69 (for the murders in Erwin) and chapter 4 (for the attempts at school segregation of Italian children).

14. Kahrl, *This Land Was Ours*, 55–57.

15. Lang, *History of Harrison County*, 17, 19, 102; Sanford and Caire, *Past at the Pass*, 12.

16. Lang, *History of Harrison County*, 109; McMillen, *Dark Journey*, 88.

17. Joseph Guillot, Louisiana, Statewide Death Index, 1819–1964, ancestry.com; Joseph Guillott, 1830 US Census, New Orleans, Orleans, Louisiana; series M19, roll 45, page 210, Family History Library Film: 0009688, ancestry.com; Auguste Guillot, 1870 US Census, New Orleans Ward 7, Orleans, Louisiana; Roll: M593_522; Page: 392B;

Family History Library Film: 552021; Monique Guyot to Chris Danielson, email, 28 August 2018 and 7 May 2021.

18. 1900 US Census, Harrison County, Mississippi, population schedule, Pass Christian Ward 2, 5A, dwelling 86, family 89, Armand A., Mary L., Leonard W., Elvina A., Thomas E. and Arthur A. C. Guyot; digital image, ancestry.com; 1910 US Census, Harrison County, Mississippi, population schedule, Pass Christian Ward 2, p. 9A, dwelling 187, family 192, Armand A., Evelina, Elvina, Thomas, and Caesar Guyot; digital image, ancestry.com; Orleans Death Indices, 1877–1895, vol. 87, p. 568 (1885), Armantine Eveline Guyot; digital image, ancestry.com; Orleans Death Indices, 1877–1895, vol. 93, p. 1037 (1888), Armand Guyot; digital image, ancestry.com; 1920 US Census, Orleans Parish, Louisiana, population schedule, New Orleans Ward 11, p. 18B, dwelling 440, family 487, Leonard, Alice, Leonard and Inez Guyot; digital image, ancestry.com; Caire and Caire, *History of Pass Christian*, 109; Glatthaar, *Forged in Battle*, 124; Military Service Record of August[e] Guillot, 73rd US Colored Infantry, *Carded Records Showing Military Service of Soldiers Who Fought in Volunteer Organizations during the American Civil War, 1890–1912*, War Department, Adjutant General's Office, National Archives Identifier 84419597, National Archives and Records Administration; Military Service Record of Arthur Guillot, 73rd US Colored Infantry, *Carded Records Showing Military Service of Soldiers Who Fought in Volunteer Organizations during the American Civil War, 1890–1912*, War Department, Adjutant General's Office, National Archives Identifier 84403395, National Archives and Record Administration; "Arthur Guillotte/Guillot/Guyot," Guyot/Prudeaux combined family tree, Monique Guyot to Chris Danielson, email, 7 May 2021; "Ernest Guillott," *U.S. Civil War Soldier Records and Profiles, 1861–1865*, ancestry.com. I am grateful to Monique Guyot for these references to the Guillots' military service.

19. 1920 US Census, Orleans Parish, Louisiana, population schedule, New Orleans Ward 5, p. 9A, dwelling 180, family 181, Evilina, John, and Evilia Guyot, Elvina, Myrtle, and Cecilia Benoit; digital image, ancestry.com; Orleans Death Indices, 1918–1928, vol. 174, p. 354 (1918), Armant A. Guyot; digital image, ancestry.com; 1930 US Census, Harrison County, Mississippi, population schedule, Pass Christian, p. 1B, dwelling 15, family 16, Elvina, John, Amelia, Myrtle, Cecilia, Olivia, and Madeline Benoit, and Evelina Guyot; digital image, ancestry.com; Orleans Death Indices, 1929–1936, vol. 207, p. 1853 (1935), Evaline Biamie Guyot; digital image, ancestry.com. The death certificate for Armand Guyot contradicts other census data, on not only the spelling of his name but also his age, listing him dying at age fifty-four rather than sixty.

20. Draft Registration Card for Thomas Eugene Guyot, Harrison County, Mississippi, *World War I Selective Service System Draft Registration Cards, 1917–1918*, National Archives and Records Administration, roll 1682922; digital image, ancestry.com; 1920 US Census, Harrison County, Mississippi, population schedule, Pass Christian, p. 11B, dwelling 241, family 241, Thomas, Elinore, Rosie, and Lawrence Guyot; digital image, ancestry.com; 1930 US Census, Harrison County, Mississippi, population schedule, Pass Christian, roll 1146, p. 4A, dwelling 74, family 76, Thomas, Elinore, Rose, Lawrence, Thomas Jr., and Edith Guyot; digital image, ancestry.com.

21. Sitkoff, *New Deal for Blacks*, 35–36.

22. 1940 US Census, Harrison County, Mississippi, population schedule, Pass Christian, roll T627_2025, p. 4A, dwelling 71, Jules, Mathilda, Aurora, Roman, Lucien,

O. Juliette, and Rosamond Piernas, Lawrence Sr. and Lawrence Jr. Guyot, Lawrence, Thomas Jr., and Edith Guyot; digital image, ancestry.com; 1940 US Census, Hancock County, Mississippi, population schedule, Bay St. Louis Ward 2, roll 808, p. 1B, dwelling 207, family 207, Henri S. Piernas; digital image, ancestry.com; 1939 Gulfport City Directory, 379, *U.S. City Directories, 1821–1989*, digital image, ancestry.com; McMillen, *Dark Journey*, 76, 89.

23. 1940 US Census, Harrison County, Mississippi, population schedule, Pass Christian, roll T627_2025, p. 4A, dwelling 71, Jules, Mathilda, Aurora, Roman, Lucien, O. Juliette, and Rosamond Piernas, Lawrence Sr. and Lawrence Jr. Guyot, Lawrence, Thomas Jr., and Edith Guyot; digital image, ancestry.com; Sitkoff, *New Deal for Blacks*, 66–67, 70, 72–73, 75; Guyot interview by Moore and Dombrowski.

24. Guyot interview by Rachal, 1; Nelson, "Organized Labor and the Struggle for Black Equality," 958, 972–73, 976–77; Cobb, "World War II and the Mind of the Modern South," 5; Crouch, "Ingalls Story in Mississippi," 194–95.

25. Mosley, "Labor Union Movement," 253–54, 257; Russell, *Men along the Shore*, 84–85, 88; Kimeldorf, *Reds or Rackets?*, 56, 144–45. Guyot interview by Rachal, 5.

26. 1940 US Census, Harrison County, Mississippi, population schedule, Pass Christian, roll T627_2025, p. 4A, dwelling 71, Jules, Mathilda, Aurora, Roman, Lucien, O. Juliette, and Rosamond Piernas, Lawrence Sr. and Lawrence Jr. Guyot, Lawrence, Thomas Jr., and Edith Guyot; digital image, ancestry.com; "Lawrence T. Guyot," *U.S. Social Security Death Index, 1935–Current*, ancestry.com; US Census Bureau, Census of Population: 1950, vol. 1, Number of Inhabitants, 24-7, 24-8, 24-10, www.census.gov/prod/www/decennial.html.

27. Strickland, "Remembering Hattiesburg," 151–54; "Lawrence T. Guyot," *U.S. World War II Army Enlistment Records, 1938–1946*, National Archives and Records Administration, ancestry.com; "Jules Guyot," *U.S. Social Security Death Index, 1935–Current*, ancestry.com.

28. Dittmer, *Local People*, 16–17, 20, 25–27; Caire and Caire, *History of Pass Christian*, 55.

29. 1953–54 City Directory, Gulfport, Mississippi, 515, *U.S. City Directories, 1821–1989*, digital image, ancestry.com; Dittmer, *Local People*, 45, 46, 70–71, 179–80; Douglas Martin, "Lawrence Guyot, Civil Rights Activist Who Bore the Fight's Scars, Dies at 73," *New York Times*, 26 November 2012, www.nytimes.com/2012/11/27/us/lawrence-guyot-civil-rights-activist-who-bore-the-fights-scars-dies-at-73.html; Guyot interview by Rachal, 1; Dunn interview by Smith, 144–47; "Council Is Organized at Gulfport," *Jackson Clarion-Ledger*, 1 July 1960, digital image, SCR ID# 10-34-0-20-1-1-1, Mississippi State Sovereignty Commission Online, https://da.mdah.ms.gov/sovcom (hereafter MSSCO); Smith, "Local Leadership," 212, 214; Guyot interview by Ladner, 23.

30. Mason and Smith, *Beaches, Blood, and Ballots*, 39; Dittmer, *Local People*, 53–54.

31. Dunn interview by Smith, 136–38.

32. Guyot interview by Rachal, 6.

33. Guyot interview by Moore and Dombrowski, 2; Caire and Caire, *History of Pass Christian*, 53, 55.

34. McMillen, *Dark Journey*, 229–31; Guyot interview by Moore and Dombrowski, 3.

35. Lang, *History of Harrison County*, 132–34; Finnegan, *Deed So Accursed*, 17–18, 33. In the Yazoo Delta region, there were 148 lynching incidents from 1881 to 1940, comprising 25.9 percent of all Mississippi lynching incidents in that period. Finnegan, *Deed So Accursed*, 28.

36. Finnegan, *Deed So Accursed*, 252; McMillen, "Fighting for What We Didn't Have," 104; Dittmer, *Local People*, 21–22; McGuire, *At the Dark End of the Street*, 48–50.

37. Dittmer, *Local People*, 55–57; Moody, *Coming of Age of Mississippi*, 132. For extensive coverage of the Emmett Till murder, see Whitfield, *Death in the Delta*.

38. Guyot interview by Moore and Dombrowski, 3; Guyot interview by Ladner, 3; Guyot interview by Bond, 8; "St. Philomena Catholic," in *Pass Christian School History*, www.school.passchristian.net.

39. Davis, *History of Black Catholics in the United States*, 255–56; Newman, *Desegregating Dixie*, 15, 31–32, 94, 162.

40. Nash and Taggart, *Mississippi Politics*, 182–83; Guyot interview by Nash and Taggart; Anderson interview by Nash.

41. For white Mississippi evangelicals' reaction to *Brown*, see DuPont, *Mississippi Praying*, chap. 3.

42. DuPont, *Mississippi Praying*, 98–99.

43. "St. Philomena Catholic," www.school.passchristian.net; Harold B. Hinton, "Officials Confirm Negro Vote Block," *New York Times*, 4 December 1946, 64; "Bilbo Asks Other Candidates to Help Bar Negro Voting," *Jackson Daily News*, 6 June 1946, 1; Lawson, *Black Ballots*, 100, 105–12; US Senate, *Testimony of Rev. George T. J. Strype*, 149, 150, 154; "Election Held Tuesday July 2nd," *Sea Coast Echo*, 5 July 1946, 1; "Colmer Announces," *Sea Coast Echo*, 31 May 1946, 1; Guyot interview by Murray, 1.

44. "St. Philomena Catholic," www.school.passchristian.net; Guyot interview by Moore and Dombrowski, 2–3.

45. Guyot interview by Rachal, 1. For information on Evers's activities in Mississippi in this period, see Williams, *Medgar Evers*, chap. 4.

46. "Sammy Davis Jr. Weds," *New York Times*, 13 November 1960, 61; Perez v. Sharp, 32 Cal. 2d 711, 198 P. 2d 17 (1948); Allyn, *Make Love, Not War*, 86–87; Guyot interview by Ladner, 23–24.

47. Guyot interview by Ladner, 23–24.

48. Sistrom, "'Authors of the Liberation,'" 38; Guyot interview by Bond, 3–4; Lang, *History of Harrison County*, 156; Guyot interview by Nash and Taggart; Guyot interview by Blackside Inc.

49. Sistrom, "'Authors of the Liberation,'" 38–39. Guyot did not work much out of the local in that year, logging only twenty-eight hours. Confirmation of Guyot's work out of the ILA is from Victor Walsh, Administrator, GSC-ILA Plans and GSA-ILA Plans, International Longshoremen's Association #1752, Pascagoula, MS.

50. Guyot interview by Bond, 15; Guyot interview by Moore and Dombrowski, 3; Guyot interview by Rachal, 2; Williamson, "Black Colleges and Civil Rights," 117–18, 121–22; Mc-Millen, *Dark Journey*, 101–2, 291; Lowe, "'Sowing the Seeds of Discontent,'" 869–71. Mangram is also sometimes credited as "John Mangrum." Dittmer, *Local People*, 89.

51. Campbell and Rogers, *Mississippi*, 168; Graham, *Our Kind of People*, 10; McMillen, *Dark Journey*, 20–21; Moody, *Coming of Age in Mississippi*, 261–63.

52. "Biographies of the Candidates" (pamphlet), series S.4, box 3, folder 29, Rims Barber Collection, Mississippi Department of Archives and History, Jackson; Dittmer, *Local People*, 78–79; Payne, *I've Got the Light of Freedom*, 60; Guyot interview by Sinsheimer, 16.

53. Payne, *I've Got the Light of Freedom*, 60.

54. Dittmer, *Local People*, 83–85. For more on the Parker lynching, see Smead, *Blood Justice*.

55. Butler, "Mississippi State Sovereignty Commission," 107, 114, 125–29; Dittmer, *Local People*, 85–86.

56. Dittmer, *Local People*, 85–87; Payne, *I've Got the Light of Freedom*, 57–58.

57. Williamson, "Black Colleges and Civil Rights," 119–20, 122.

58. Williamson, "Black Colleges and Civil Rights," 123; Salter, *Jackson*, 4–5.

59. Williamson, "Black Colleges and Civil Rights," 124–25.

60. *The Eaglet*, 1958, 1959, and 1960 editions, published by Tougaloo Southern Christian College, Tougaloo, MS; Guyot interview by Bond, 20–21; Ross, *The Divine Nine*, 74–77, 86; Harris, "Lobbying Congress for Civil Rights," 212, 220; MacKenzie, "Community Service and Social Action," 32–34. Guyot was listed (but not photographed) in the 1957–58 varsity football lineup but was not mentioned in the 1959 edition of *The Eaglet*.

61. Parks and Brown, "'In the Fell Clutch of Circumstance,'" 442; Branch, "Variegated Roots," 327–28, 333; McCoy, "Calls," 297–98, 306; Kimbrough, *Black Greek 101*, 49.

62. These hours provided by Victor Walsh.

63. Lowe, "'Sowing the Seeds of Discontent,'" 871, 873–74, 877.

64. Guyot interview by Rachal, 5; Hunter Gray to Chris Danielson, email, 24 April 2014; Hunter Gray (John Salter) to Chris Danielson, email, 26 April 2014.

65. Gray to Danielson, 24 April 2014; Gray to Danielson, 26 April 2014; Salter, *Jackson*, 60, 89–90; Guyot interview by Rachal, 3, emphasis in original.

66. Gray to Danielson, 24 April 2014.

67. Williamson, *Radicalizing the Ebony Tower*, 66–67; Guyot interview by Rachal, 3; Sistrom, "Authors of the Liberation," 65.

68. Guyot interview by Murray, 1.

69. Branch, *Parting the Waters*, 577–78; Garrow, *Bearing the Cross*, 194; Guyot interview by Rachal, 3; Carson, *In Struggle*, 19–21. For Baker and her role in founding SNCC, see also Ransby, *Ella Baker and the Black Freedom Movement*, chap. 8.

70. Carson, *In Struggle*, 31–36, 45–50.

71. Carson, *In Struggle*, 77–78; Moody, *Coming of Age in Mississippi*, 276.

72. Williamson, "Black Colleges and Civil Rights," 128.

73. Dittmer, *Local People*, 88; Guyot interview by Rachal, 5.

74. Zinn, *SNCC*, 107.


CHAPTER 2

1. Guyot interview by Rachal, 8; Arsenault, *Freedom Riders*, 478–79; Dittmer, *Local People*, 96–97.

2. Dittmer, *Local People*, 118–19; Payne, *I've Got the Light of Freedom*, 62, 130; Hamlin, *Crossroads at Clarksdale*, 102–3; Danielson, *After Freedom Summer*, 12–13; Henry with Curry, *Aaron Henry*, 114–15.

3. For details on this division in the early years of SNCC, see Carson, *In Struggle*, 38–42.

4. Brown interview by Murray, 2; Guyot interview by Rachal, 11–12 (emphasis in original); Payne, *I've Got the Light of Freedom*, 62; Dittmer, *Local People*, 199–120; Sitkoff, *Struggle for Black Equality*, 104.

5. Guyot interview by Sinsheimer, 13.

6. Guyot interview by Rachal, 9 (emphasis in original); Guyot interview by Sinsheimer, 2.

7. Guyot interview by Rachal, 9–10; Payne, *I've Got the Light of Freedom*, 119–20, 334–35; Carson, *In Struggle*, 20; Ransby, *Ella Baker and the Black Freedom Movement*, 188.

8. Marsh, *God's Long Summer*, 12–13.

9. Dittmer, *Local People*, 32, 49; McMillen, *Dark Journey*, 89; Hamlin, *Crossroads at Clarksdale*, 11, 16.

10. Guyot interview by Rachal, 6; Dittmer, *Local People*, 49.

11. Hogan, *Many Minds, One Heart*, 3.

12. Carson, *In Struggle*, 77–78.

13. Payne, *I've Got the Light of Freedom*, 133–35, 136–41.

14. Payne, *I've Got the Light of Freedom*, 141–46, 150; Brown interview by Murray, 2; Guyot interview by Sinsheimer, 2.

15. Payne, *I've Got the Light of Freedom*, 146–48, 150–51; Brown interview by Murray, 2; Dittmer, *Local People*, 132; Forman, *Making of Black Revolutionaries*, 283–84.

16. Forman, *Making of Black Revolutionaries*, 285–86; Zinn, *SNCC*, 84–85.

17. Forman, *Making of Black Revolutionaries*, 285, 286; Payne, *I've Got the Light of Freedom*, 151; "Negroes Say Armed Men Routed Them," *Greenwood Commonwealth*, 17 August 1962, 1.

18. Guyot interview by Sinsheimer, 3.

19. "Negroes Say Armed Men Routed Them," *Greenwood Commonwealth*, 17 August 1962, 1; "They Sow, But We Must Reap," *Greenwood Commonwealth*, 17 August 1962, 1; Forman, *Making of Black Revolutionaries*, 286–87.

20. "31 Leflore Negroes Take Voter Tests," *Jackson Daily News*, 25 August 1962, SCR ID# 10-52-0-23-1-1-1, Mississippi State Sovereignty Commission Online, https://da .mdah.ms.gov/sovcom (hereafter MSSCO); Lawrence Guyot Jr. to Chief Lary, 17 August 1962, SCR ID# 2-38-1-44-1-1-1, MSSCO; Zinn, *SNCC*, 85–86; Dittmer, *Local People*, 134; King, *Freedom Song*, 141; Brown interview by Murray, 3.

21. Foreman, *Making of Black Revolutionaries*, 287; Dittmer, *Local People*, 134; Payne, *I've Got the Light of Freedom*, 151–52; "County Citizens Told of Rights by Bar Group," *Enterprise-Tocsin*, 6 September 1962, 1.

22. Tom Scarbrough, Sunflower County Report, 11 September 1962, SCR ID# 2-38-1-45-2-1-1; Tom Scarbrough, Sunflower County Report, 26 September 1962, SCR ID# 2-38-1-47-1-1-1; untitled list, 6 April 1965, SCR ID# 98-7-5-140-1-1-1, all MSSCO.

23. Tom Scarbrough, Leflore County Report, 4 April 1963, SCR ID# 2-45-1-71-3-1-1; Tom Scarbrough, Leflore County Report, 19 April 1963, SCR ID# 2-45-1-72-1-1-1; Tom Scarbrough, Holmes County Report, 14 May 1963, SCR ID# 2-54-2-5-4-1-1; Tom Scarbrough, Leflore County Report, 14 May 1963, SCR ID# 2-45-1-75-1-1-1, all MSSCO; Katagiri, *Mississippi State Sovereignty Commission*, 41–42, 69.

24. Carson, *In Struggle*, 21, 24; Dittmer, *Local People*, 107; Sokol, *There Goes My Everything*, 44, 59.

25. Bolton, "Mississippi's School Equalization Program," 782–83; McMillen, *Dark Journey*, 72, 90.

26. Dailey, "Sex, Segregation, and the Sacred after *Brown*"; McMillen, *Citizens' Councils*, 184–86; Clune, "From Light Copper to the Blackest and Lowest Type," 292–94.

27. Cobb, *This Nonviolent Stuff'll Get You Killed*, 20–21; Guyot interview by Murray, 2.

28. Payne, *I've Got the Light of Freedom*, 62–63; Raines, *My Soul Is Rested*, 239 (quote).

29. Hogan, *Many Minds, One Heart*, 58; Raines, *My Soul Is Rested*, 239–40 (quote).

30. Quoted in Raines, *My Soul Is Rested*, 240.

31. Raines, *My Soul Is Rested*, 241–42 (quote on 241); Zinn, *SNCC*, 86; Guyot interview by Sinsheimer, 3, 4; "Hardy Lott, Retired Attorney, Dies at Age 86," *Greenwood Commonwealth*, 1 August 1995, 1.

32. Guyot interview by Sinsheimer, 7, 9.

33. Zinn, *SNCC*, 86–87; Burner, *And Gently He Shall Lead Them*, 85; Payne, *I've Got the Light of Freedom*, 167.

34. Burner, *And Gently He Shall Lead Them*, 85–86; Zinn, *SNCC*, 88–91; Tom Scarbrough, Leflore County Report, 4 April 1963, SCR ID# 2-45-1-71-3-1-1 and 2-45-1-71-2-1-1, MSSCO.

35. Guyot interview by Sinsheimer, 5.

36. Zinn, *SNCC*, 91–92; "Fire Chief Nips Negro Arson Talk," *Greenwood Commonwealth*, 25 March 1963, 1; "Police Probe Shooting in City," *Greenwood Commonwealth*, 27 March 1963, 1; "Negro March Leaders Jailed," *Greenwood Commonwealth*, 27 March 1963, 1; Raines, *My Soul Is Rested*, 268.

37. "Judge Jails Negro, Charges Contempt," *Greenwood Commonwealth*, 28 March 1963, 1; "Prisoners Removed to County Jail," *Greenwood Commonwealth*, 30 March 1963, 1; Carson, *In Struggle*, 86.

38. Dittmer, *Local People*, 147–48; "Barnett Pledges City Support," *Greenwood Commonwealth*, 1 April 1963, 1; "Sen. Stennis Blasts Outside Troublemakers in Floor Speech," *Greenwood Commonwealth*, 2 April 1963, 1; Payne, *I've Got the Light of Freedom*, 171–72;

39. Payne, *I've Got the Light of Freedom*, 171, 175; Guyot interview by Sinsheimer, 6.

40. "Justice Officials, City Reach Pact," *Greenwood Commonwealth*, 4 April 1963, 1; "Reasonable Accord," *Greenwood Commonwealth*, 4 April 1963, 1; Payne, *I've Got the Light of Freedom*, 173; Carson, *In Struggle*, 87.

41. Payne, *I've Got the Light of Freedom*, 174–75.

42. Tom Scarbrough, Leflore County Report, 19 April 1963, SCR ID# 2-45-1-72-1-1-1 and 2-45-1-72-2-1-1; Tom Scarbrough, Leflore County Report, 14 May 1963, SCR ID# 2-45-1-75-1-1-1 and 2-45-1-75-2-1-1; Tom Scarbrough, Holmes County Report, 14 May 1963, SCR ID# 2-54-2-5-4-1-1 and 2-45-1-75-2-1-1, all MSSCO; Dittmer, *Local People*, 191–93; Burner, *And Gently He Shall Lead Them*, 106–7; Sojourner with Reitan, *Thunder of Freedom*, 32–33.

43. Campbell and Rogers, *Mississippi*, 199, and Addendum, Class of 1963; *New York Times*, 26 November 2012, www.nytimes.com/2012/11/27/us/lawrence-guyot-civil -rights-activist-who-bore-the-fights-scars-dies-at-73.html?_r=0.

44. Carson, *In Struggle*, 21, 24; Moses interview by Romaine; Zinn, *SNCC*, 107; "Lawrence Guyot," Stanford University Project, S, 25.

45. Brown interview by Murray, 3; Marsh, *God's Long Summer*, 18–19; Zinn, *SNCC*, 94; Dittmer, *Local People*, 170–72.

46. Marsh, *God's Long Summer*, 19; Dittmer, *Local People*, 172.

47. Dittmer, *Local People*, 172; Raines, *My Soul Is Rested*, 269; Mills, *This Little Light of Mine*, 62–63; US v. Earl Wayne Patridge, Thomas J. Herrod, William Surrell, John L. Basinger and Charles Thomas Perkins, US District Court for the Northern District of Mississippi, Western Division, 2–6 December 1963, C. Action No. WCR 6343, 394, 397–99.

48. Over the years, Guyot's recollections of his arrest included some discrepancies. Milton Hancock said that Basinger struck Guyot, and Guyot himself later confirmed that during the criminal trial against the policemen, but in interviews years later he seems to have conflated the policemen in his mind, something understandable given that they all took part in beating him. In a 1977 oral history, he said that the sheriff, not Basinger, had followed him out and struck him. In that version, Patridge followed the SNCC workers to their car, walked up to Guyot and said, "Nigger, what you causing all these problems for?" He then hit Guyot in the mouth without waiting for a reply. Patridge then reached for his gun, and Guyot avoided any sudden moves, since he said he "didn't want no mistakes to be made." Raines, *My Soul Is Rested*, 268–69, Zinn, *SNCC*, 95; Lee, *For Freedom's Sake*, 54; Guyot interview by Rachal, 29–30; "Movement History: Mississippi Contested Elections—The Historic 1965 Testimony of Lawrence Guyot," 5, www.crmvet.org/nars/guyot_1965.pdf; *U.S. v. Patridge et al.*, 400.

49. Raines, *My Soul Is Rested*, 268–70; Lee, *For Freedom's Sake*, 54, 57; Marsh, *God's Long Summer*, 22.

50. Dittmer, *Local People*, 172; Raines, *My Soul Is Rested*, 269; Lee, *For Freedom's Sake*, 53; *U.S. v. Patridge et al.*, 404, 426; Statement of Lawrence Guyot Jr., 2 August 1963, in Report of Special Agent Orville V. Johnson, Memphis FBI Office, Field Office File No. 44-1063, US Department of Justice, 7 August 1963, 18–19; Report of Special Agent Joseph A. Canale, Memphis FBI Office, Field Office File No. 44-1063, US Department of Justice, 19 November 1963, 48; Statement of Lawrence Guyot Jr., 11 June 1963, in Report of Special Agent Timothy M. Casey, Memphis FBI Office, Field Office File No. 44-1063, US Department of Justice, 17 June 1963, 10–11.

51. Lee, *For Freedom's Sake*, 53–54; Tom Scarbrough, Montgomery County Report, 18 June 1963, SCR ID# 2-65-0-99-2-1-1, MSSCO. Charles Payne also suggested that the

phone calls "may have made his captors nervous." Payne, *I've Got the Light of Freedom*, 285; "The Historic 1965 Testimony of Lawrence Guyot," 6; FBI Director to SAC Memphis, "Unsubs, Fannie Hummer [*sic*], et al Dash Victims, CR," FBI, US Department of Justice, Communications Section, 10 June 1963.

52. *U.S. v. Patridge et al.*, 427–30, 497, 501–2.

53. Watters and Cleghorn, *Climbing Jacob's Ladder*, 374; Report of Special Agent Joseph A. Canale, 19 November 1963, 99.

54. Lester, *Fire in My Soul*, 112–13.

55. Raines, *My Soul Is Rested*, 270; Branch, *Parting the Waters*, 821; *U.S. v. Patridge et al.*, 424; FBI Director to SAC Memphis, 10 June 1963, 1; C. L. McGowan to Mr. Rosen, "Unknown Subjects: Fannie Lou Hummer [*sic*], et al.—Victims Civil Rights," FBI, US Department of Justice, Communications Section, 11 June 1963; C. L. McGowan to Mr. Rosen, "Unknown Subjects; Lawrence Guyot, et al.—Victims Civil Rights," FBI, US Department of Justice, Communications Section, 13 June 1963.

56. Raines, *My Soul Is Rested*, 270; Lee, *For Freedom's Sake*, 55–56; Watters and Cleghorn, *Climbing Jacob's Ladder*, 368 (quote); "Six Negroes Fined Here," *Winona Times*, 13 June 1963, 1; "The Historic 1965 Testimony of Lawrence Guyot," 4–5; FBI Director to SAC Memphis, "Unsubs, Fannie Hummer [*sic*], et al Dash Victims, CR," FBI, US Department of Justice, Communications Section, 11 June 1963.

57. Young, *An Easy Burden*, 257; Lester, *Fire in My Soul*; 113; Dittmer, *Local People*, 173; Raines, *My Soul Is Rested*, 270; Payne, *I've Got the Light of Freedom*, 285–88; Guyot interview by Rachal, 30. Whether the FBI agent was a real agent or the fake one that Guyot met is unclear.

58. Hamil R. Harris and Matt Schundel, "Lawrence Guyot, Civil Rights Leader and Community Activist, Dies at 73," *Washington Post*, 23 November 2012, www .washingtonpost.com/local/obituaries/lawrence-guyot-civil-rights-leader-and -community-activist-dies-at-73/2012/11/23/93fc754a-35af-11e2-bb9b-288a310849 ee_story.html; Douglas Martin, "Lawrence Guyot, Civil Rights Activist Who Bore the Fight's Scars, Dies at 73," *New York Times*, 26 November 2012, www.nytimes .com/2012/11/27/us/lawrence-guyot-civil-rights-activist-who-bore-the-fights-scars -dies-at-73.html?_r=0; Lester, *Fire in My Soul*, 113; "The Historic 1965 Testimony of Lawrence Guyot," 6; *U.S. v. Patridge et al.*, 405; FBI Director to SAC Memphis, FBI, 10 June 1963, 1; SAC Memphis to FBI Director, "Unsubs, Fannie Hummer [*sic*], et al Dash Victims, CR," 3–4.

59. "Negro Voter Aides Held in Mississippi," *New York Times*, 11 June 1963, A19; E. W. Kenworthy, "U.S. Acts to Block New Trial of Six Negros in Mississippi," *New York Times*, 18 June 1963, A23; "Six Negroes Fined Here," *Winona Times*, 13 June 1963, 1; Mills, *This Little Light of Mine*, 61–62; M. W. Newman, "Rugged, Ragged 'Snick': What It Is and What It Does," *Chicago Daily News*, 20 July 1963, SCR ID# 2-150-1-11-1-1-1, MSSCO.

60. Marsh, *God's Long Summer*, 20–21.

61. Jordan, *White over Black*, 34–35, 150–51, 158–59, 398–99; Cobb, *Most Southern Place on Earth*, 156–57, 238; White, *Ar'n't I a Woman?*, 27–61.

62. Jordan, *White over Black*, 154–57. For the "Lynching Era" in Mississippi, see McMillen, *Dark Journey*, chap. 7.

63. Dittmer, *Local People*, 17; Branch, *Parting the Waters*, 826; "U.S. Accuses Sheriff, Police of Race Brutality," *Washington Post*, 10 September 1963, A4; "Winona Defendant in Federal Action," *Winona Times*, 20 June 1963, 1; "Let Us Do the Job!," *Winona Times*, 20 June 1963, 1.

64. "The Historic 1965 Testimony of Lawrence Guyot," 6; "Federal Suit Filed to Free Negros," *Greenwood Commonwealth*, 29 June 1963, 1; Guyot interview by Rachal, 26; Tom Scarbrough, Leflore County Report, 2 July 1963, SCR ID# 2-45-1-85-1-1-1, MSSCO; Dittmer, *Local People*, 173–74.

65. Dittmer, *Local People*, 174; Zinn, *SNCC*, 96.

66. Oshinsky, *"Worse Than Slavery,"* 231–35.

67. Dittmer, *Local People*, 174; Tom Scarbrough, Leflore County Report, 2 July 1963, SCR ID# 2-45-1-85-2-1-1, MSSCO; "Federal Suit Filed to Free Negroes," *Greenwood Commonwealth*, 29 June 1963, 1.

68. Guyot interview by Rachal, 25–26; Zinn, *SNCC*, 96–97; Newman, "Rugged, Ragged 'Snick'"; "Prisoners Carried to Parchman," *Greenwood Commonwealth*, 1 July 1963, 1; Guyot interview by Ladner; Joseph, *Stokely*, 57; Carmichael with Thelwell, *Ready for Revolution*, 337; Branch, *Pillar of Fire*, 116–17.

69. SAC Memphis to FBI Director, "Earl Wayne Patridge, et al, Fannie Lou Hamer etal [*sic*], Dash Victims, CR," FBI, US Department of Justice, Communications Section, 30 July 1963; SAC Memphis to FBI Director, "Earl Wayne Patridge, et al, Fannie Lou Hamer et al, Dash Victims, CR," FBI, US Department of Justice, Communications Section, 31 July 1963, 3; SAC Memphis to FBI Director, "Earl Wayne Patridge, et al, Fannie Lou Hamer et al, Dash Victims, CR," FBI, US Department of Justice, Communications Section, 2 August 1963, 1–2; Statement of Lawrence Guyot Jr., in Report of Special Agent Timothy M. Casey Jr., 3.

70. SAC Memphis to FBI Director, "Unsubs, Fannie Lou Hummer [*sic*], et al dash Victims, CR," 3–4; A. Rosen to Mr. Belmont, "Earl Wayne Patridge, et al, Fannie Lou Hamer, et al.—Victims, Civil Rights," FBI, US Department of Justice, Communications Section, 8 July 1963, 1–2; Report of Special Agent Samuel N. Jennings, New Orleans FBI Office, Field Office File No. 44-1810, US Department of Justice, 17 July 1963, 8–9; Report of Special Agent Orville V. Johnson, Memphis FBI Office, Field Office File No. 44-1063, US Department of Justice, 7 August 1963, 15.

CHAPTER 3

1. Dittmer, *Local People*, 200; Chafe, *Never Stop Running*, 180.

2. Mills, *This Little Light of Mine*, 92; Guyot interview, Tougaloo College.

3. Dittmer, *Local People*, 202; Marshall, *Student Activism*, 67–68; Danielson, *After Freedom Summer*, 14–15.

4. Henry with Curry, *Aaron Henry*, 158.

5. King, *Freedom Song*, 238.

6. Marshall, *Student Activism*, 70–71; Dittmer, *Local People*, 203–6; Guyot interview by Moore and Dombrowski, 1, 7; "Negro Mock Election Rally Is Held Here," *Greenwood Commonwealth*, 23 October 1963, 1; Sistrom, "Authors of the Liberation," 90.

7. Marshall, *Student Activism*, 71–72; Dittmer, *Local People*, 201; Reinhard, *Politics of Change*, 43; Lawson, *No Small Thing*, 171.

8. Dittmer, *Local People*, 207–8; Zinn, *SNCC*, 186–87; "Yale Students Here for Rally Tuesday," *Hattiesburg American*, 28 October 1963, 1; Winfred Moncrief, "Yale Student Defends Self Well but Is Fined," *Hattiesburg American*, 29 October 1963.

9. Dittmer, *Local People*, 208–9; Zinn, *SNCC*, 187.

10. Quoted in Chafe, *Never Stop Running*, 188–89, 204–5.

11. Zinn, *SNCC*, 187–88; Dittmer, *Local People*, 209.

12. Dittmer, *Local People*, 209–11; Guyot interview by Rachal, 17.

13. Mills, *This Little Light of Mine*, 69.

14. Mills, *This Little Light of Mine*, 70–77.

15. Raines, *My Soul Is Rested*, 270 (Guyot quote); Mills, *This Little Light of Mine*, 71; *U.S. v. Patridge, et al.*, 404, 406–14, 431–32, 497–98 ("falling" quote); Branch, *Pillar of Fire*, 193 (Baker quote).

16. David Dennis to Shaner Bonding Company, 28 January 1964, SCR ID# 2-166-1-41-1-1-1, Mississippi State Sovereignty Commission Online, https://da.mdah.ms.gov/sovcom (hereafter MSSCO); Dittmer, *Local People*, 179–80.

17. Dittmer, *Local People*, 180–84; Zinn, *SNCC*, 104–5; Guyot interview by Sinsheimer, 18.

18. Zinn, *SNCC*, 102–3; Guyot interview by Rachal, 12; Summary of the Minutes of the COFO Staff Executive Committee Meeting, 10 January 1964, SNCC Papers, reel 65; Guyot interview by Sinsheimer, 17, 19.

19. Dittmer, *Local People*, 219–20; COFO staff meeting notes, Hattiesburg, 18 January 1964, series 2, box 1, folder 12, T/14, Charles Horowitz Collection.

20. Summary of the Minutes of the COFO Staff Executive Committee Meeting, 10 January 1964, SNCC Papers, reel 65; Zinn, *SNCC*, 104–6.

21. Zinn, *SNCC*, 106.

22. Guyot interview by Rachal, 13; Zinn, *SNCC*, 105; Findlay, *Church People in the Struggle*, 82–84.

23. Sistrom, "'Authors of the Liberation,'" 85. For King's sermons and rhetoric, see Miller, *Voice of Deliverance*. For King's writings and the citing of philosophers and other intellectuals instead of the Bible, see King, *Stride toward Freedom*.

24. COFO staff meeting notes, Hattiesburg, 18 January 1964, Charles Horowitz Collection; Zinn, *SNCC*, 243; Dittmer, *Local People*, 220.

25. "Agitators Seek to Whip Up Demonstration Here Wednesday," *Hattiesburg American*, 20 January 1964, 1.

26. Dittmer, *Local People*, 220–21; Zinn, *SNCC*, 109–12; Elliot Chaze, "Voter Registration Drive Begins Here," *Hattiesburg American*, 22 January 1964, 1.

27. Zinn, *SNCC*, 111–12, 121; Dittmer, *Local People*, 221; Chaze, "Voter Registration Drive"; "Pickets Resume Damp Trap," *Hattiesburg American*, 23 January 1964, 1; Elliot Chaze, "Quiet Demonstrations Move into Third Day," *Hattiesburg American*, 24 January 1964; "Pickets and Rain Return Together," *Hattiesburg American*, 27 January 1964.

28. Elliot Chaze, "Anti-picketing Injunction Issued after Nine Ministers Arrested," *Hattiesburg American*, 29 January 1964; Tom Scarbrough and Virgil Downing, Supplemental Report—Forrest County—Hattiesburg Voter Registration Demonstrations, 31 January 1964, SCR ID# 2-64-1-63-1-1-1, MSSCO; Dittmer, *Local People*, 221; "Negro Leader Charged with Contributing to Delinquency," *Hattiesburg American*, 28 January

1964, 1; "Guyot's Trial Set for Friday," *Hattiesburg American*, 29 January 1964, 1; Buzard -Boyett, "Race and Justice," 278.

29. COFO Hattiesburg Report, January 1964, SNCC Papers, reel 42; Tom Scarbrough and Virgil Downing, Supplemental Report—Forrest County—Hattiesburg Voter Registration Demonstrations, 31 January 1964, SCR ID# 2-64-1-63-3-1-1, MSSCO; Blackwell with Morris, *Barefootin'*, 79, 107; Blackwell interview by Garvey, 17–18.

30. Zinn, *SNCC*, 118; Buzard-Boyett, "Race and Justice," 279; Elliot Chaze, "Negro Convicted in Delinquency Case," *Hattiesburg American*, 31 January 1964, 1, 5; "Pickets Parade Peacefully," *Hattiesburg American*, 30 January 1964, 1; Tom Scarbrough and Virgil Downing, Hattiesburg Demonstrations (continuation), 13 February 1964, SCR ID# 2-64-1-65-1-1-1, MSSCO.

31. Buzard-Boyett, "Race and Justice," 279–84; COFO Hattiesburg Report, January 1964, SNCC Papers, reel 42; Arrests-General, 1964, SNCC Papers, reel 64; Report of SNCC Worker Pete Stoner on Experiences in Hattiesburg from January 7 to May 21, 1964, SNCC Papers, reel 65.

32. Buzard-Boyett, "Race and Justice," 281–82, 297–98, 300–301; Tom Scarbrough and Virgil Downing, Hattiesburg Demonstrations (continuation), 13 February 1964, SCR ID# 2-64-1-65-2-1-1, MSSCO; Guyot interview by Rachal, 22.

33. Betty Garman, "Mid-West Speaking Tour, SNCC Mississippi Summer Project," undated flyer, SNCC Papers, reel 40; "Guyot to Address Freedom Meeting," *Daily Egyptian*, 8 April 1964, 2; Minnijean Brown, "Race Problem Is National, Integration Leader Says," *Daily Egyptian*, 14 April 1964, 2; "Minnijean Brown Trickery," *Encyclopedia of Arkansas*, https://encyclopediaofarkansas.net/entries/minnijean-brown-trickey-720/. The colleges included Southern Illinois University, Oberlin, Denison, Ohio Wesleyan, and Wooster, but only SIU gave any coverage of his visit, so it is not clear if he visited all the campuses. Bill Higgs, a white lawyer from Mississippi active in the movement, spoke at Oberlin on 15 April, and the newspapers covered other civil rights issues. White students and faculty from Oberlin and Wooster were active in both local (Ohio) and Mississippi civil rights actions. Dick Berkman, "Civil Rights Leader Discusses Violence of Negro in South," *Oberlin Review*, 17 April 1964, 1; "Students to Teach in Freedom Schools during Strike Period," *Oberlin Review*, 17 April 1964, 1; "Tait Joins Hattiesburg Picket Line with Ministers' Project to Register Negroes," *Wooster Voice*, 17 April 1964, 1; Dittmer, *Local People*, 229.

34. McLemore, "Mississippi Freedom Democratic Party," 106–7; Resolution by the California Democratic Council, Long Beach, California, 21–23 February 1964, SNCC Papers, reel 65; Dittmer, *Local People*, 237.

35. Holt, *Summer That Didn't End*, 158–59.

36. McLemore, "Mississippi Freedom Democratic Party," 107–8.

37. Raines, *My Soul Is Rested*, 290 (quotes); Holt, *Summer That Didn't End*, 158; Dittmer, *Good Doctors*, 52.

38. McLemore, "Mississippi Freedom Democratic Party," 108–9; Forman, *Making of Black Revolutionaries*, 377; Dittmer, *Local People*, 236; McLemore interview by Nash.

39. Application of Lawrence T. Guyot for the appointment of at least five additional federal judges for the state of Mississippi during the months of June, July, August, and September 1964, Fifth Circuit Court of Appeals, 18 May 1964, SNCC Papers, reel 68;

Dittmer, *Local People*, 180; McAdam, *Freedom Summer*, 66–67; Belfrage, *Freedom Summer*, 22–23.

40. Sue Cronk, "They've Already Lost Election," *Washington Post*, 8 April 1964, F2; "Hattiesburg—Firing of Mrs. Victoria Jackson Gray's Husband," 4 May 1964, SNCC Papers, reel 65; Holt, *Summer That Didn't End*, 159; unidentified writer to J. Edgar Hoover, 7 June 1964, FBI, US Department of Justice. The letter-writer's name was redacted in the 2015 Freedom of Information Act request.

41. Charlie Cobb, Staff Executive Committee Meeting, 15 May 1964, SNCC Papers, reel 64; "COFO Sets Up Freedom Democratic Party," *NOW! The Voice of Freedom*, 4 May 1964, SNCC Papers, reel 42.

42. Mills, *This Little Light of Mine*, 94–96.

43. Mills, *This Little Light of Mine*, 94; Dittmer, *Local People*, 280; McLemore, "Mississippi Freedom Democratic Party," 112–16.

44. Dittmer, *Local People*, 280–81; Incident Summary, 25 July 1964, SNCC Papers, reel 42; Minutes, Leflore County Convention, 27 July 1964, SNCC Papers, reel 65; Willie Marie Johnson, Lafayette County Convention of Mississippi Freedom Democratic Party Minutes, 31 July 1964, SNCC Papers, reel 65.

45. Bob Moses and the FDP Coordinators, Emergency Memorandum, 19 July 1964, Council of Federated Organizations, Panola County Office: Records, 1963–1965, box 1, folder 15—MFDP—General State Papers, 1964–65, Wisconsin Historical Society, Madison.

46. Charlie Cobb, Staff Executive Committee Meeting.

47. Tentative Project Assignment, SNCC Papers, reel 64; Holt, *Summer That Didn't End*, 127–41; Marshall, *Student Activism*, 128–30. For populism and its attempts to solicit Black voters, see Goodwyn, *Populist Moment*, 118–23; and Woodward, *Tom Watson*, chap. 13.

48. Marshall, *Student Activism*, 128; Sutherland, *Letters from Mississippi*, 120–21.

49. Young, *An Easy Burden*, 257; Payne, *I've Got the Light of Freedom*, 335; Dittmer, *Local People*, 110–11, 321; Bob Zellner, "The Wrong Side of Murder Creek," 15–16, box 1, folder 19—Drafts and Edits of "The Wrong Side of Murder Creek," II, Bob Zellner Papers, 1968–2009, Wisconsin Historical Society, Madison.

50. Rushing and Orris interview by Danielson.

51. Rushing and Orris interview by Danielson.

52. Watson, *Freedom Summer*, 78–80, 205–6; McAdam, *Freedom Summer*, 96; Carson, *In Struggle*, 117.

53. Garrow, *Bearing the Cross*, 340, 341–42.

54. Garrow, *Bearing the Cross*, 341; Ortiz, *"I Never Will Forget,"* 33 (quotes).

55. Carson, *In Struggle*, 123; McLemore, "Mississippi Freedom Democratic Party," 119, Todd, *For a Voice and the Vote*, 197–201; Marshall, *Student Activism*, 134.

56. Sistrom, "'Authors of the Liberation,'" 125–26, 128–29; Guyot interview by Sinsheimer, 10, 33.

57. McLemore, "Mississippi Freedom Democratic Party," 119–22; Kinoy, *Rights on Trial*, 258. For the origins of the War on Poverty in the Kennedy administration, see Matusow, *Unraveling of America*, chap. 4. For the Supreme Court rulings on reapportionment and their impact, see Cortner, *Apportionment Cases*.

58. Davis, "'Sisters and Brothers All,'" 89–90; Sistrom, "'Authors of the Liberation,'" 218.

59. McLemore, "Mississippi Freedom Democratic Party," 132; Marsh, *God's Long Summer*, 38.

60. Dittmer, *Local People*, 283; Carson, *In Struggle*, 123–24; McCord, *Mississippi*, 116; McLemore, "Mississippi Freedom Democratic Party," 131; Todd, *For a Voice and the Vote*, 218; Lawrence Guyot interview by Blackside Inc.

61. Carson, *In Struggle*, 124–28 (quote on 126); Marsh, *God's Long Summer*, 37–42.

62. Davis, "'Sisters and Brothers All,'" 93–94.

63. Marsh, *God's Long Summer*, 43; Burner, *And Gently He Shall Lead Them*, 200; Carson, *In Struggle*, 128; McLemore, "Mississippi Freedom Democratic Party," 152–55.

64. McLemore, "Mississippi Freedom Democratic Party," 155–57.

65. Todd, *For a Voice and the Vote*, 340–42; Dittmer, *Local People*, 320.

66. Lynd interview by Danielson; Guyot interview by Sinsheimer, 22.

67. Marshall, *Mississippi Civil Rights Movement*, 302–04. Kenyatta, as president of Kenya from 1964 to 1978, actually pursued economic policies that favored capitalism. His independence struggle even inspired nonviolent civil rights leaders like Medgar Evers, who seriously considered a Mau-Mau style rebellion in the Mississippi Delta in the 1950s and even named his son Darrell Kenyatta Evers. Fage, *History of Africa*, 487, 526; Payne, *I've Got the Light of Freedom*, 49–50.

68. Dittmer, *Local People*, 320–22; Guyot interview by Moore and Dombrowski, 6.

69. Carmichael with Thelwell, *Ready for Revolution*, 412–13.

70. Joseph, *Stokely*, 77.

71. Joseph, *Stokely*, 414–15; Dittmer, *Local People*, 321, 336; Memorandum from William M. Kunstler to Lawrence Guyot, 14 October 1964, SNCC Papers, reel 68; Carson, *In Struggle*, 150.

72. Dittmer, *Local People*, 315–17; Rough Minutes of a Meeting Called by the National Council of Churches to Discuss the Mississippi Project, 18 September 1964, SNCC Papers, reel 41; Chafe, *Never Stop Running*, 192.

73. Dittmer, *Local People*, 316–17; NCC Minutes, 18 September 1964; Chafe, *Never Stop Running*, 192.

74. Forman, *Making of Black Revolutionaries*, 381–82.

75. Forman, *Making of Black Revolutionaries*, 416–18; Carson, *In Struggle*, 138–39.

76. Forman, *Making of Black Revolutionaries*, 418.

77. Lawrence Guyot to Fellow Mississippian, MFDP mailing, 27 October 1964, SNCC Papers, reel 63; "Freedom Vote Is Open to All," *Student Voice*, 28 October 1964, 1, 4, SNCC Papers, reel 68; Lawson, *Black Ballots*, 285.

78. Marshall, *Student Activism*, 165.

79. "Freedom Democratic Party Protests Campaign Intimidation in Telegram to Democratic National Chairman," press release from MFDP, 30 October 1964, SNCC Papers, reel 42; Lawrence Guyot to All County Chairmen, FDP Executive Committee Members, and Project Directors, undated memorandum, SCR ID# 2-165-1-93-1-1-1, MSSCO; "Freedom Party Files Petition," *Memphis Commercial Appeal*, 30 October 1964, SCR ID# 2-165-2-10-1-1-1, MSSCO.

80. Marshall, *Student Activism*, 168.

81. Running Summary of Incidents during the Freedom Vote Campaign, 18 October–2 November 1964, 95, SCR ID# 2-165-4-5-8-1-1, MSSCO; Statement by Lawrence Guyot, 5 November 1964, SNCC Papers, reel 63; S. T. Roebuck to Earl Johnston, 16 November 1964, SCR ID# 2-32-0-45-1-1-1, MSSCO.

## CHAPTER 4

1. Carson, *In Struggle*, 133, 140–41, 143.
2. Forman, *Making of Black Revolutionaries*, 422–23.
3. Forman, *Making of Black Revolutionaries*, 423.
4. Ortiz, *"I Never Will Forget,"* 73–74; Draper, "Class and Politics in the Mississippi Movement," 277–82, 284.
5. Carson, *In Struggle*, 149; Dittmer, *Local People*, 324; Lynd interview by Danielson.
6. Guyot interview by Murray, 4; King, *Freedom Song*, 491–93.
7. Brown interview by Murray, 5.
8. McAdam, *Freedom Summer*, 5, 168–69; Carson, *In Struggle*, 176; Rushing and Orris interview by Danielson.
9. McLemore, "Mississippi Freedom Democratic Party," 174–77.
10. Arthur Kinoy, *Rights on Trial: The Odyssey of a People's Lawyer* (Cambridge, MA: Harvard University Press, 1983), 266–68.
11. Kinoy, *Rights on Trial*, 268–69.
12. Dittmer, *Local People*, 338; McLemore, "Mississippi Freedom Democratic Party," 177–78; Report on Meeting of 13 November, Washington, DC, SNCC Papers, reel 63; Kinoy, *Rights on Trial*, 270–71.
13. Dittmer, *Local People*, 329–31; R. Hunter Morey, "Cross Roads in COFO," 3 December 1964, box 3, folder 1, Hunter Morey Papers (hereafter RHM Papers).
14. Dittmer, *Local People*, 330–31; Staff Meeting, Jackson COFO, 23 November 1964, SNCC Papers, reel 63, 2–5.
15. Staff Meeting, 23 November 1964, 3; Dittmer, *Local People*, 326; Brown interview by Murray, 5.
16. Morrison, *Aaron Henry of Mississippi*, 135; McLemore, "Mississippi Freedom Democratic Party," 178; Langum, *William M. Kunstler*, 66, 70–76.
17. "Mississippi Legislator Denounces Two-Party Government," SNCC NEW Release, 29 November 1964, SNCC Papers, reel 41; Lawrence Guyot to Chicago Friend of Freedom, 30 November 1964, SNCC Papers, reel 41; "MFDP Contests Miss. Seating," *Student Voice*, December 1964, 2, SNCC Papers, reel 63; Lawrence Guyot to All Staff and FDP County Chairmans [*sic*], 24 December 1964, SNCC Papers, reel 63; Kunstler and Isenberg, *My Life as a Radical Lawyer*, 144.
18. "'Negro Delegation' Visits U.S. Offices," undated clipping, SNCC Papers, reel 63; "Area Colleges to Run Civil Rights Seminar," *Greenfield Recorder-Gazette*, 28 January 1965, SCR ID# 1-76-0-62-1-1-1, Mississippi State Sovereignty Commission Online, https://da.mdah.ms.gov/sovcom (hereafter MSSCO); "Civil Rights Conference Schedule," *Massachusetts Collegian*, 8 February 1965, 3; Tom Donovan, "Davis Talk Defines Main Rights Factions," *Massachusetts Collegian*, 15 February 1965, 1; Roxana Adams, "OAU Delegate Accuses U.S. of Violence," *Massachusetts Collegian*, 15 February 1965, 5;

Raymond Abbott," "Supporter of Freedom Movement Voices Opinions on Civil Rights," *Massachusetts Collegian*, 15 February 1965, 5; Dittmer, *Local People*, 459n5; Peter Hendrickson, "UM Student Reaction Varied on Recent Civil Rights Conference," *Massachusetts Collegian*, 26 February 1965, 10. Dittmer reported that the MFDP consciously kept the number of summer volunteers from out of state small for the 1965 summer organizing. Dittmer, *Local People*, 344.

19. McLemore, "Mississippi Freedom Democratic Party," 180–82, 184, 185–86; Dittmer, *Local People*, 338; Statement by Martin Luther King, MFDP, 17 December 1964, SNCC Papers, reel 41; Jean Belle to Don Chandler, 21 December 1964, SNCC Papers, reel 64; Lawrence Guyot to unnamed donor, undated letter, SNCC Papers, reel 63.

20. McLemore, "Mississippi Freedom Democratic Party," 187–89; "Tentative Outline of MFDP Challenge Schedule," SNCC Papers, reel 63; Carson, *In Struggle*, 93–94; Alice Bleeckwell, "Trip to Washington," SNCC Papers, reel 63; Susanna McBee, "Goal Is Misunderstood, Say Miss. Challengers," *Washington Post*, 4 January 1965, SNCC Papers, reel 63; Dittmer, *Local People*, 340; Kinoy, *Rights on Trial*, 272.

21. McLemore, "Mississippi Freedom Democratic Party," 193–96; William L. Chaze, "Freedom Democrats Trying to Make Farce of Congress," *Jackson Clarion-Ledger*, 3 January 1965, SNCC Papers, reel 64; Kinoy, *Rights on Trial*, 275–76 (quote on 275).

22. "Greet U.S. Hearing Feb. 10 on Mississippi Vote Curbs," *The Worker*, 10 January 1965, 8, SNCC Papers, reel 68; FDP to All Ministers and Sunday School Superintendents, undated letter, SNCC Papers, reel 65; William L. Chaze, "FDP 'Purchases' Coffee for Sovereignty Group," *Jackson Clarion-Ledger*, 5 February 1965, SNCC Papers, reel 63; McLemore, "Mississippi Freedom Democratic Party," 206; Dittmer, *Local People*, 340–41; *Benton County Freedom Train*, 28 February 1965, 3, SCR ID# 2-23-0-26-3-1-1-1, MSSCO.

23. Lawrence Guyot, "Reply to Lawyers for Congressmen," SNCC Papers, reel 64.

24. Dittmer, *Local People*, 339.

25. Kinoy, *Rights on Trial*, 286.

26. Kinoy, *Rights on Trial*; McLemore, "Mississippi Freedom Democratic Party," 207.

27. Zwiers, *Senator James Eastland*, 228; Dittmer, *Local People*, 341–42; Carson, *In Struggle*, 181–82.

28. Kinoy, *Rights on Trial*, 260–61.

29. Lawrence Guyot to Friend, 2 March 1965, SNCC Papers, reel 41; Victoria J. Gray, Testimony on Proposed Voting Legislation in 89th Congress, House Committee on the Judiciary, 25 March 1965, SNCC Papers, reel 68; "Statement by Lawrence Guyot, Executive Chairman of the MFDP, on Rebuttal Hearings," 26 March 1965, SNCC Papers, reel 63.

30. Congressional Challenge Progress Report, undated, SNCC Papers, reel 63; MFDP press release, 1 April 1965, SNCC Papers, reel 63; Dittmer, *Local People*, 223; "Movement History: Mississippi Contested Elections—The Historic 1965 Testimony of Lawrence Guyot," 1–9, www.crmvet.org/nars/guyot_1965.pdf.

31. Garrow, *Protest at Selma*, chaps. 2–3.

32. Untitled press release from James Farmer, Lawrence Guyot, and John Lewis, 16 March 1965, SNCC Papers, reel 41; Rev. Leroy Johnson to Lawrence Guyot, Fannie Lou Hamer, Victoria Gray, and Annie Devine, 4 April 1965, SNCC Papers, reel 41; Fifth

District COFO Staff Meeting, 14–17 April 1965, Waveland, Mississippi, SNCC Papers, reel 42.

33. Fifth District COFO Meeting, April 14–17, 1965; Fifth District COFO Staff to Freedom Democratic Party, 14–16 April 1965, SNCC Papers, reel 42.

34. Mills, *This Little Light of Mine*, 160; William Strickland to Members of the New York Ad Hoc Committee for the Support of the Mississippi Freedom Democratic Party, Report on the MFDP National Conference, 29 April 1965, SNCC Papers, reel 41, 1–3.

35. Kinoy, *Rights on Trial*, 215–17, 283–84; Dombrowski v. Pfister, 380 US 479 (1965).

36. McLemore, "Mississippi Freedom Democratic Party," 207–8; Statement by Lawrence Guyot, Chairman, MFDP press release, 17 May 1965, SNCC Papers, reel 41; Statement by Dr. Martin Luther King, SCLC press release, 17 May 1965, SNCC Papers, reel 41; Statement by John Lewis, Chairman SNCC press release, 17 May 1965, SNCC Papers, reel 41.

37. Lawrence Guyot to FDP Staff, Affiliates, Friends, 17 May 1965, SNCC Papers, reel 41; Dittmer, *Local People*, 344.

38. Dittmer, *Local People*, 345; "Mass Arrests Mark MFDP Challenge," *National Guardian*, 26 June 1965, SCR ID# 2-165-4-40-1-1-1, MSSCO; "Mean Policemen and Nasty Jails in Jackson," *Voice of the Movement*, 17 June 1965, SNCC Papers, reel 65; Statement by Mrs. Victoria Gray, Executive Committee, MFDP, "Arrests and Beatings of Peaceful Marchers in Jackson, Mississippi," 15 June 1965, SNCC Papers, reel 65.

39. Kinoy, *Rights on Trial*, 285.

40. Kinoy, *Rights on Trial*; Dittmer, *Local People*, 345–46 (quote); "Jackson Demonstrations," 4, SNCC Papers, reel 65; MFDP Letter, 21 June 1965, SNCC Papers, reel 65; McLemore, "Mississippi Freedom Democratic Party," 212.

41. Zwiers, *Senator James Eastland*, 231; Dittmer, *Local People*, 189; Drew Pearson, "Johnson's Fifth Circuit Challenge," *Washington Post*, 15 June 1965, SNCC Papers, reel 41.

42. Statement of Victoria Gray, MFDP press release, undated, SNCC Papers, reel 41; Dittmer, *Local People*, 79–83; Statement of Victoria Gray, MFDP press release, 29 June 1965, SNCC papers, reel 41; Statement of Aaron Henry, Mississippi NAACP press release, 29 June 1965, SNCC Papers, reel 42; Zweirs, *Senator James Eastland*, 231–32.

43. McLemore, "Mississippi Freedom Democratic Party," 219–21.

44. Herring, *America's Longest War*, 133–55.

45. Herring, *America's Longest War*, 147; Kinoy, *Rights on Trial*, 286–87; Dittmer, *Local People*, 349–50; McLemore, "Mississippi Freedom Democratic Party," 234–36.

46. Kinoy, *Rights on Trial*, 287; Dittmer, *Local People*, 350; McLemore, "Mississippi Freedom Democratic Party," 236–37 (quote on 236); Andrew J. Reese Jr., "Draft Evasion Note May Kill FD Party," *Jackson Clarion-Ledger*, 8 August 1965, A7, SCR ID# 2-36-2-57-1-1-1, MSSCO.

47. McLemore, "Mississippi Freedom Democratic Party," 237, 241–42; Blain, *Until I Am Free*, 103–4.

48. Kinoy, *Rights on Trial*, 287; Dittmer, *Local People*, 350–51; McLemore, "Mississippi Freedom Democratic Party," 234, 239–40.

49. Kinoy, *Rights on Trial*, 292; McLemore, "Mississippi Freedom Democratic Party," 221–23.

50. McLemore, "Mississippi Freedom Democratic Party," 223–24; Press statement by Lawrence Guyot, September 1965, SNCC Papers, reel 41, 1.

51. McLemore, "Mississippi Freedom Democratic Party," 224; Kinoy, *Rights on Trial*, 295; "Congressional Challenge Defeated," undated, 3, box 4, folder 4, RHM Papers; Press statement by Lawrence Guyot, 2.

52. Reinhard, *Politics of Change*, 143–44; Memorandum on Congressional Challenge to FDP Members, Staff and Interested Person, from the State Office FDP, undated, SNCC Papers, reel 68; Monica Klein to Albertia Johnson, 4 August 1965, SNCC Papers, reel 65; Lawrence Guyot to Friend, 12 August 1965, SNCC Papers, reel 41; "Mississippi Challenge Killed 228–143," *Movement*, October 1965, 1–2, Michigan State University, series: Campus Underground.

53. Walton, *Black Political Parties*, 112.

54. "Carroll County, Mississippi," *Movement*, October 1965, 1.

55. Robert E. Baker, "Unusual Boss Directs Freedom Democratic Party," *Washington Post*, 29 August 1965, K5.

56. "Lawrence Guyot," Stanford University Project, chap. 30, 1–2, 7.

57. Dittmer, *Local People*, 346–47; Draper, *Conflicts of Interest*, 124–25, 137–41, 148.

58. Dittmer, *Local People*, 347.

59. Draper, "Class and Politics in the Mississippi Movement," 281–83, 297.

60. Dittmer, *Local People*, 348; Draper, *Conflicts of Interest*, 151–53; John Brown, "The Mississippi Democratic Conference Joins the Race for the Future Negro Vote but Gets Off to a Bad Start," *Mississippi Freedom Democratic Party Newsletter*, 28 July 1965, 2–3, Michael Davis Papers, 1965–1970, box 1, folder 2, Wisconsin Historical Society, University of Wisconsin, Madison; McLemore, "Mississippi Freedom Democratic Party," 412.

61. Draper, *Conflicts of Interest*, 148; "Young Democratic Clubs of Mississippi State Convention," 14 August 1965, 2, SCR ID# 6-47-0-14-1-1-1, MSSCO; Dittmer, *Local People*, 348; McLemore, "Mississippi Freedom Democratic Party," 414.

62. Hogan, *Many Minds, One Heart*, 224; Dittmer, *Local People*, 174, 335; "Young Democratic Clubs of Mississippi State Convention," 14 August 1965, 2, SCR ID# 6-47-0-14-1-1-1, MSSCO; R. Hunter Morey to B. Frank Deford, *Daily Princetonian*, 11 March 1960, 2.

63. Draper, *Conflicts of Interest*, 148; R. Hunter Morey to Claude Ramsey, 3 May 1965, box 4, folder 12, RHM Papers; Claude Ramsey to R. Hunter Morey, 6 May 1965, box 4, folder 12, RHM Papers; Ruby Doris Smith Robinson to R. Hunter Morey, 1 May 1965, box 4, folder 12, RHM Papers; R. Hunter Morey to Ruby Doris Smith Robinson, undated, box 4, folder 12, RHM Papers; R. Hunter Morey to Hubert Humphrey, 3 May 1965, box 4, folder 12, RHM Papers.

64. Roland Evans and Robert Novak, "Inside Report: Black-White Politics, 7 May 1965, RHM Papers, box 4, folder 12; John Sexton to Hunter Morey, 21 May 1965, box 4, folder 12, RHM Papers; Melvin Whitfield to Hunter Morey, 9 May 1965, box 4, folder 12, RHM Papers; Hogan, *Many Minds, One Heart*, 224.

65. R. Hunter Morey, "A Call for Support of the Young Democratic Clubs of Mississippi," undated, 2, box 5, folder 4, RHM Papers; R. Hunter Morey to the National Convention of the Young Democratic Clubs of America, 1–3, box 4, folder 12, RHM Papers;

Robert Oswald to R. Hunter Morey, 22 June 1965, box 4, folder 12, RHM Papers; R. Hunter Morey to Robert Oswald, 24 June 1965, box 4, folder 16, RHM Papers; Edwin C. Kruse to R. Hunter Morey, August 1965, box 4, folder 16, RHM Papers.

66. "The Mississippi Democratic Conference Is a Fraud," COFO special report, COFO Communications Department, undated, 2–4, box 4, folder 12, RHM Papers; Sovereignty Commission report, 12 April 1965, SCR ID # 6-47-0-2-1-1-1; untitled report on Jackson, 5–6 July 1965, SCR ID# 9-31-4-13-1-1-1; and untitled report on Jackson, 4 July 1965, SCR ID 9-31-4-17-1-1-1, all MSSCO.

67. Dittmer, *Local People*, 34–44; Meeting of Civil Rights Workers, Tougaloo College, 27 July 1965, 1–3, SCR ID# 2-1-6-4-28-1-1-1, MSSCO.

68. Susie Ruffin, Minutes of the MFDP Executive Committee Meeting, Washington, DC, 18 September 1965, 4, box 4, folder 4, RHM Papers; Sovereignty Commission report, 12 April 1965, SCR ID # 6-47-0-2-1-1-1, MSSCO; YDCM newsletter, April 1965, no. 1, no. 2, 2, box 5, folder 4, RHM Papers (first quote); Jack Sexton, "Report on Mississippi," undated, 2, box 5, folder 4, RHM Papers; unauthored memo, 13 July 1965, box 4, folder 16, RHM Papers; "This Week in Mississippi," COFO Communications Department, 25 July 1965, box 4, folder 16, RHM Papers; Morey, "A Call for Support," 5, box 5, folder 4, RHM Papers (second quote).

69. Dittmer, *Local People*, 364–65; Sistrom, "'Authors of the Liberation,'" 300, 315. For a detailed coverage of the MFLU strike, see Sistrom, "'Authors of the Liberation,'" 294–301.

70. Morey, "A Call for Support," 1, box 5, folder 4, RHM Papers; Dittmer, *Local People*, 349; "Young Democrat Meeting 'Fiasco,'" *Jackson Daily News*, 16 August 1965, box 5, folder 5, RHM Papers.

71. Sistrom, "'Authors of the Liberation,'" 292–94 (Guyot quote on 293; Wynn quote on 294); Carson, *In Struggle*, 125; Dittmer, *Local People*, 348.

72. Bayard Rustin, "From Protest to Politics: The Future of the Civil Rights Movement," *Commentary*, February 1965. For a detailed analysis of his editorial, see D'Emilio, *Lost Prophet*, 398–403.

73. "SNCC Conference on Jobs and Food," form letter, November 1963, Civil Rights Movement Archive, www.crmvet.org; Guyot interview by Sinsheimer, 39; Forman, *Making of Black Revolutionaries*, 358–59.

74. Dittmer, *Local People*, 353–54; Umoja, *We Will Shoot Back*, 128.

75. Dittmer, *Local People*, 354–55.

76. Umoja, *We Will Shoot Back*, 126–29; Wendt, *Spirit and the Shotgun*, 126–27 (quote).

77. Cobb, *This Nonviolent Stuff'll Get You Killed*, 183–84. Academic studies of armed self-defense in the movement have proliferated in recent civil rights historiography. The best ones are Umoja, *We Will Shoot Back*, and Wendt, *Spirit and the Shotgun*.

78. Wendt, *Spirit and the Shotgun*, 67–68; Umoja, *We Will Shoot Back*, 130–31, 133; Sovereignty Commission report, 29 August 1965, SCR ID# 9-31-4-32-1-1-1, MSSCO.

79. Sovereignty Commission report, 7 September 1965, SCR ID# 9-165-5-38-1-1-1; and Sovereignty Commission report, 8 September 1965; SCR ID# 9-31-4-30-1-1-1, both MSSCO; Garrow, *Bearing the Cross*, 446–47, 450.

80. Dittmer, *Local People*, 355–61.

81. Hill, *Deacons for Defense*, 196–97; Pincus and Neuman, *Black Natchez* (quotes).

82. Branch, *Pillar of Fire*, 331; Guyot interview by Bond, 23 ("the Black community"), 49 ("very proud"); King, *Freedom Song*, 324 ("Don't you see?").

83. Guyot interview by Bond, 9–10; Wirt, *Politics of Southern Equality:* 260–61.

84. Dittmer, *Local People*, 74; Minutes of the meeting of the MFDP Executive Committee, Washington, DC, 18 September 1965, 4; box 4, folder 4, RHM Papers; "The Dismissal of the Freedom Democratic Party Challenge to the State's Members of Congress," *Jackson Advocate*, 25 September 1965, SCR ID# 9-1-2-114-1-1-1, MSSCO. For the boycott enforcers, see Umoja, *We Will Shoot Back*, 136–39.

85. Gentine, "Mississippi Freedom Democratic Party's Congressional Challenge," 83; Carmichael with Thelwell, *Ready for Revolution*, 424; Todd, *For a Voice and the Vote*, 13, 353–54; King, *Freedom Song*, 355–56.

86. Todd, *For a Voice and the Vote*, 354; Garrow, *Protest at Selma*, 40, 68–69; Langum, *William Kunstler*, 66; Pratt, *Selma's Bloody Sunday*; Street and Lozano, *Shadow of Selma*.

87. McLemore, "Mississippi Freedom Democratic Party," 166, 220, 233, 246–47; Carson, *In Struggle*, 126–29.

88. Dittmer, *Local People*, 352; Gentine, "Mississippi Freedom Democratic Party's Congressional Challenge," 83; Califano, *Triumph and Tragedy of Lyndon Johnson*, 55–59.

89. Press statement by Lawrence Guyot, September 1965, 1; Lawrence Guyot to Friend, 28 September 1965, SNCC Papers, reel 41, 2.

CHAPTER 5

1. Susie Ruffin, Minutes of the MFDP Executive Committee Meeting, Washington, DC, 18 September 1965, 3, box 4, folder 4, RHM Papers; "Co-chairman Plans to Focus OACR Activities in Oberlin," *Oberlin Review*, 21 September 1965, 4; Lee Cooprider, "Freedom Democratic Party Head Asks More Political Involvement," *Oberlin Review*, 23 November 1965, 1; "Freedom Fast Launches Week of Civil Rights Activity," *Oberlin Review*, 16 November 1965, 1; Ray Mullineaux, "Campus Supports Fast for Freedom," *Oberlin Review*, 2 November 1965, 1; *Liberty Bell*, 10 October 1965, SCR ID# 2-165-5-1-1-1-1, Mississippi State Sovereignty Commission Online, https://da.mdah.ms.gov/sovcom (hereafter MSSCO); "Freedom Democrats Launch Massive Drive," MFDP press release, 28 October 1965, SNCC Papers, reel 63.

2. "Remarks by Lawrence Guyot, Chairman before the Special Equal Rights Committee of the Democratic National Committee—October 6, 1965," SCR ID# 2-165-4-109-1-1-1, MSSCO; William Leon Higgs, "LBJ and the Negro Vote: Case of the Missing Registrars," *The Nation*, 13 December 1965, 2, SCR ID# 1-176-0-66-3-1-1, MSSCO (quote).

3. Guyot, Stanford University Project, chapter 30, 5; "Address by Lawrence Guyot on Strategy of F.D.P. at Mississippi Staff Meeting, October 19, 1965, Greenwood, Miss.," SCR ID# 6-45-2-19-1-1-1 to 6-45-2-19-8-1-1, MSSCO; and FDP County Reports, 6–19 November 1965, 4, SCR ID# 6-61-0-9-4-1-1, MSSCO.

4. Minutes of Meeting of Civil Rights Workers, Tougaloo College, 27 July 1965, 3, SNCC Papers, reel 40.

5. Guyot interview by Murray, 3.

6. Dittmer, *Local People*, 333.

7. Dittmer, *Local People*, 334; Unita Blackwell and Annie Devine, "Congressman Resnick's Visit to Mississippi," undated MFDP press release, SNCC Papers, reel 41; James Saggus, "Resnick Says State Victimizes Negroes," *Jackson Clarion-Ledger*, 2 December 1965, SCR ID# 6-61-0-8-1-1-1, MSSCO (quote); Daniel, *Dispossession*, 86.

8. FDP County Reports, 6–19 November 1965, SCR ID# 6-61-0-9-5-1-1 and 6-61-0-9-2-1-1, MSSCO; Grim, "Black Participation in the Farmers Home Administration," 329–30; Student Nonviolent Coordinating Committee (US). Agricultural Stabilization and Conservation Service elections: News release, 1965. Gloria Xifaras Clark Papers (MS 865). Special Collections and University Archives, University of Massachusetts Amherst Libraries, credo.library.umass.edu/view/full/mums865-b001-f002-i002; Agricultural Stabilization and Conservation Service elections: Marshall County (Miss.) Candidates, 1965. Gloria Xifaras Clark Papers (MS 865). Special Collections and University Archives, University of Massachusetts Amherst Libraries, credo.library.umass.edu/view/full/mums865-b001-f002-i007.

9. Danielson, *After Freedom Summer*, 110, 112–14. For a comprehensive study of the Supreme Court's rulings on reapportionment, see Cortner, *Apportionment Cases*.

10. Cortner, *Apportionment Cases*, 160–25; Danielson, *After Freedom Summer*, 114; Connor interview by Nash.

11. Danielson, *After Freedom Summer*, 115–16.

12. Sistrom, "'Authors of the Liberation,'" 339 (quote); Walton, *Black Political Parties*, 118; McLemore, "Mississippi Freedom Democratic Party," 299–301.

13. Minutes of the Statewide Convention, 2 January 1966, Jackson, Mississippi, SCR ID# 2-165-5-7-1-1-1; and untitled SSC report, 2 January 1966, SCR ID# 9-31-4-74-1-1-1, both MSSCO.

14. Dittmer, *Local People*, 191. For the class backgrounds of the Atlantic City delegation, see Draper, "Class and Politics in the Mississippi Movement."

15. Robnett, *How Long? How Long?*, 18–19.

16. Evans, *Personal Politics*, chap. 4; Payne, *I've Got the Light of Freedom*, 70–71; Carson, *In Struggle*, 147–48; Dittmer, *Local People*, 331–32. Mary King complained later that Sara Evans had oversimplified and misinterpreted the memo. Dittmer, *Local People*, 332.

17. Payne, *I've Got the Light of Freedom*, 270–71; Ransby, *Ella Baker and the Black Freedom Movement*, 296.

18. Reinhard, *Politics of Change*, 46–47 (quote on 47); Daily planner of Victoria Gray Adams, weeks beginning 13 October 1963, 16 December 1963, 23 March 1964, 8 June 1964, 31 August 1964, box 7, folder 18, Victoria Gray Adams Papers.

19. Hogan, *Many Minds, One Heart*, 151, 163; "Jean Wheeler," SNCC Digital Gateway, accessed 3 January 2019, https://snccdigital.org/people/jean-wheeler.

20. Rothschild, *Case of Black and White*, 128, 137–39; untitled memo from the State Sovereignty Commission, 20 December 1965, SCR ID# 9-31-4-68-1-1-1, MSSCO; Guyot interview by Bond, 60; Monica Klein to Albertia Johnson, 4 August 1965, SNCC Papers, reel 65. For reactions to Selma, see Dailey, "Sex, Segregation, and the Sacred after *Brown*."

21. Newbeck, *Virginia Hasn't Always Been for Lovers*, 35–36, 44; untitled memo from the State Sovereignty Commission, 2 November 1966, SCR ID# 99-37-0-68-1-1-1, MSSCO.

22. Newbeck, *Virginia Hasn't Always Been for Lovers*, 186–88, 197–203, 205; Danielson, *After Freedom Summer*, 58; Loving v. Virginia, 388 US 1 (1967).

23. Untitled memo from the State Sovereignty Commission, 18 November 1965, SCR ID# 2-156-0-21-1-1-1, MSSCO.

24. McAdam, *Freedom Summer*, 195–96. Forty-seven percent of the movement marriages led to divorce by 1979. McAdam, *Freedom Summer*, 208.

25. Dittmer, *Local People*, 180–81, 391; Boyett, *Right to Revolt*, 143–45.

26. Boyett, *Right to Revolt*, 146–50, 158 (quote on 147); A. L. Hopkins, "Observation and Investigation in Hattiesburg, Forrest County, Mississippi," 20 January 1966, SCR ID# 2-64-1-94-2-1-1, MSSCO.

27. Untitled memorandum from the State Sovereignty Commission, 8 January 1966, SCR ID# 9-31-4-77-1-1-1; Mary Ann Pardue, "Eastland Brands FDP 'Red Stooge' Group," *Jackson Clarion-Ledger*, 20 January 1966, SCR ID# 2-165-3-21-1-1-1; Sen. James Eastland, "Freedom Democratic Party," *Congressional Record—Senate*, 19 January 1966, 617–18, SCR ID# 13-0-5-42-2-1-1; Memorandum by Erle Johnston Jr., 14 January 1966, SCR ID# 2-165-5-25-1-1-1; and "Proposed Statement to Be Made by Senator James O. Eastland," SCR ID# 2-165-6-118-1-1-1 and 2-165-6-118-2-1-1, all MSSCO.

28. Dittmer, *Local People*, 369–70, Sanders, *Chance for Change*, 82–83.

29. Sanders, *Chance for Change*, 82–84, 86–87, 185; Dittmer, *Local People*, 370–82; untitled Sovereignty Commission report, Jackson, 20 February 1966, SCR ID# 9-31-4-100-1-1-1 and 93-31-4-100-2-1-1, MSSCO. For an in-depth study of the CDGM funding battle, see Sanders, *Chance for Change*, chaps. 4 and 5.

30. Lawrence Guyot, Rev. Arthur Thomas, and Isaac Foster to President Lyndon Baines Johnson, 29 January 1966, SCR ID# 2-44-1-113-1-1-1; and untitled memorandum from the State Sovereignty Commission, 28–30 January 1966, SCR ID# 2-44-1-112-1-1-1, both MSSCO; Cobb, "'Somebody Done Nailed Us on the Cross,'" 928–29; Dittmer, *Local People*, 367–68.

31. Erle Johnston Jr. to James O. Eastland, 1 February 1966, SCR ID# 3-18A-0-125-1-1-1; and William Colmer, "Attack on Mississippi Is Communist-Inspired," *Congressional Record—House*, 16 February 1966, 3050, SCR ID# 2-165-6-4-1-1-1, both MSSCO.

32. Cobb, *Most Southern Place on Earth*, 253–59, 261–62, 270–73.

33. "New Law Required Filing by School Trustee Candidates" and "Moore Named Trustee in South Panola," *Panolian*, 24 February and 10 March 1966, 1; Wirt, *Politics of Southern Equality*, 148; "Merigold Man Is Named to Board," *Bolivar Commercial*, 10 March 1966, 1; "Look Who Drew the Race Line" and "Waide Re-elected to School Board," *Daily Times Leader*, 4 March 1966, 4, and 7 March 1966, 1; Walton, *Black Political Parties*, 119, 141.

34. James Bonney, "FDP Gives Slate for '66 Races," *Jackson Daily News*, 6 January 1966, SCR ID# 2-165-5-26-1-1-1; MFDP State Executive Committee Meeting, 19 February 1966, SCR ID# 2-165-6-10-6-1-1; untitled Sovereignty Commission report, 1 April 1966, SCR ID# 6-45-2-53-1-1-1; and "FDP Candidates Are Qualified," *Memphis Commercial Appeal*, 5 April 1966, SCR ID# 2-165-6-31-1-1-1, all MSSCO; Sistrom, "'Authors of the

Liberation,'" 321. For an example of the coverage of the antiwar rallies at UC Berkeley, see "Speeches on the Memo," *Daily Californian*, March 1966, 1; and *Berkeley Barb*, 22 April 1966, 12.

35. MFDP Key List Mailing, 14 April 1966, SCR ID# 2-1-165-6-16-1-1-1; undated MFDP Mailing, "Campaign Activity," SCR ID# 2-165-6-18-2-1-1; and undated memorandum, "Some Campaign Dates," SCR ID# 2-165-6-36-1-1-1, all MSSCO; McLemore, "Mississippi Freedom Democratic Party," 309.

36. Untitled Sovereignty Commission report, Jackson, 24 April 1966.

37. Sistrom, "'Authors of the Liberation,'" 327; "Civil Righters, Labor Join in Ballot Battle," *Greenwood Commonwealth*, 30 May 1966, 1.

38. McLemore, "Mississippi Freedom Democratic Party," 307–8; United States, *Civil Rights Act of 1964* (Washington, DC: US Government Printing Office, 1969). Baker v. Carr, 369 US 186 (1962); Reynolds v. Sims, 377 US 533 (1964); MFDP Summer 1966 campaign flyer, box 2, folder 5, Fannie Lou Hamer Collection (hereafter Hamer Collection).

39. Sistrom, "'Authors of the Liberation,'" 342–44.

40. Dittmer, *Local People*, 352; Jackson, *Freedomways Reader*; Carmichael with Thelwell, *Ready for Revolution*, 120–22 (quotes).

41. Carmichael with Thelwell, *Ready for Revolution*, 122–25.

42. Carmichael with Thelwell, *Ready for Revolution*, 125–28.

43. Carmichael with Thelwell, *Ready for Revolution*, 129–30.

44. Carmichael with Thelwell, *Ready for Revolution*, 130–32.

45. McLemore, "Mississippi Freedom Democratic Party," 301–4.

46. McLemore, "Mississippi Freedom Democratic Party," 304–6; biographical entry for Claude Feemster Clayton, Federal Judicial Center, www.fjc.gov/node/1379211.

47. Goudsouzian, *Down to the Crossroads*, 64–65; Dittmer, *Local People*, 389.

48. Dittmer, *Local People*, 389, 392.

49. Goudsouzian, *Down to the Crossroads*, 67–68.

50. Goudsouzian, *Down to the Crossroads*, 68; McLemore, "Mississippi Freedom Democratic Party," 312–13; Sistrom, "'Authors of the Liberation,'" 345.

51. McLemore, "Mississippi Freedom Democratic Party," 310, 312: Sistrom, "'Authors of the Liberation,'" 345.

52. McLemore, "Mississippi Freedom Democratic Party," 314; Dittmer, *Local People*, 394.

53. Sojourner with Reitan, *Thunder of Freedom*, 174; Goudsouzian, *Down to the Crossroads*, 69.

54. Untitled State Sovereignty Commission report, 9 June 1966, SCR ID# 1-103-0-6-1-1-1, MSSCO; Goudsouzian, *Down to the Crossroads*, 69.

55. Goudsouzian, *Down to the Crossroads*, 39–40, 73–74 (quote on 73).

56. Goudsouzian, *Down to the Crossroads*, 72–73; Dittmer, *Local People*, 355.

57. Goudsouzian, *Down to the Crossroads*, 82–84; Joseph, *Stokely*, 110.

58. "King and Followers Should Be Ignored," *Greenwood Commonwealth*, 16 June 1966, 1; "Let's Hold Our Tempers," *Neshoba Democrat*, 23 June 1966, 1.

59. Goudsouzian, *Down to the Crossroads*, 122.

60. Dittmer, *Local People*, 395.

61. Dittmer, *Local People*, 396; Goudsouzian, *Down to the Crossroads*, 114–15.

62. Dittmer, *Local People*, 397.

63. Goudsouzian, *Down to the Crossroads*, 68, 135.

64. Joseph, *Stokely*, 119–21.

65. Umoja, *We Will Shoot Back*, 146–47, 154–57.

66. Untitled MFDP flyer, SCR ID# 2-165-6-25-1-1-1, MSSCO. The flyer is undated but references a campaign event for the candidates on 24 April 1966.

67. Sojourner with Reitan, *Thunder of Freedom*, 242.

68. Joseph, *Stokely*, 135.

69. Joseph, *Stokely*, 153–55; Carson, *In Struggle*, 232–33; Dittmer, *Local People*, 408.

70. Reinhard, *Politics of Change*, 148.

71. Sojourner with Reitan, *Thunder of Freedom*.

72. Sojourner with Reitan, *Thunder of Freedom*, 232.

73. Dittmer, *Local People*, 402, 409; Walton, *Black Political Parties*, 121; Sistrom, "'Authors of the Liberation,'" 318; McLemore, "Mississippi Freedom Democratic Party," 317.

74. McLemore, "Mississippi Freedom Democratic Party," 317–25; Whitley v. Johnson, 260 F. Supp. 630 (S.D. Miss. 1966).

75. McLemore, "Mississippi Freedom Democratic Party," 327–29.

76. McLemore, "Mississippi Freedom Democratic Party," 329–31.

77. Walton, *Black Political Parties*, 121.

78. Henry Hurt, "Boycott and Ballot," *Reporter*, 11 August 1966, SCR ID# 10-42-0-1-25-1-1, MSSCO (quotes); McLemore, "Mississippi Freedom Democratic Party," 334.

79. McLemore, "Mississippi Freedom Democratic Party," 331–32.

80. Walton, *Black Political Parties*, 121–22; untitled SSC memo, 22 September 1966, SCR ID# 9-31-6-1-1-1-1, MSSCO; Dittmer, *Local People*, 409; Sue Lorenzi and Alex Shimkin, "Report of a Meeting of Community Organizers in Mississippi, Jackson, Miss.," 29 October 1966, SCR ID# 9-31-6-19-1-1-1 and 9-31-6-19-2-1-1, MSSCO.

81. Dittmer, *Local People*, 378; untitled SSC report, 8 October 1966, SCR ID# 9-31-6-10-1-1-1; and untitled SSC report, 24 October 1966, SCR ID# 6-45-4-96-1-1-1, both MSSCO.

82. McLemore, "Mississippi Freedom Democratic Party," 333–37; Dittmer, *Local People*, 410; Danielson, *After Freedom Summer*, 25.

83. Dittmer, *Local People*, 408; Walton, *Black Political Parties*, 126–27.

84. Hamer v. Campbell, 358 F.2d 215 (1966); McLemore, "Mississippi Freedom Democratic Party," 350–53.

85. A. L. Hopkins, "Continued Investigation in Madison County, Mississippi," 17 November 1966, SCR ID# 2-24-4-443-2-1-1, MSSCO; "OACR Considers Project in South for Christmas or Inter-semester," *Oberlin Review*, 2 December 1966, 1.

86. Carson, *In Struggle*, 193, 236–41.

87. Carson, *In Struggle*, 237–38; Dittmer, *Local People*, 411; McLemore, "Mississippi Freedom Democratic Party," 354.

88. "Mississippi Freedom Democratic Party," 20 December 1966, SCR ID# 2-165-6-69-1-1-1, MSSCO; Guyot interview by Bond, 60.

89. Estes, *I Am a Man!*, 7–8, 70, 74–75, 82–83. See chapter 7 of Estes's book for an in-depth analysis of the Black Panthers and masculinist liberation.

90. Adams journal, 14 October 1963, 16 December 1963, 23 March 1964, 4 May 1963, 8 June 1964, 31 August 1964, box 7, folder 18, Victoria Gray Adams Papers.

91. Erle Johnston Jr. memorandum, "The Ink Well," 13 February 1968, SCR ID# 1-89-0-10-1-1-1; and Erle Johnston Jr. memorandum, "Martin Luther King and Mt. Beulah," 19 February 1968, SCR ID# 2-152-0-42-1-1-1, both MSSCO.

92. Sojourner with Reitan, *Thunder of Freedom*, 243–48.

93. Walton, *Black Political Parties*, 123; Earl Johnston to Gov. Paul Johnson, "Civil Rights Situation on Mississippi," 13 March 1967, SCR ID# 4-0-4-55-1-1-1, MSSCO.

94. McLemore, "Mississippi Freedom Democratic Party," 353–54; Financial statement, National Committee for Free Elections in Sunflower, 12 May 1967, box 2, folder 1, Hamer Collection.

95. McLemore, "Mississippi Freedom Democratic Party," 347–49, 354.

96. McLemore, "Mississippi Freedom Democratic Party," 354–55, 362; Reinhard, *Politics of Change*, 253 (quote); Moye, *Let the People Decide*, 162.

97. "Sunflower," *Mississippi Newsletter*, Freedom Information Service (FIS), 7 April 1967, 3; "State Convention on Elections," *Mississippi Newsletter*, 21 April 1967, 1; Lawrence Guyot to J. H. Henry, 14 April 1967, File: Correspondence-1967, February–April, Fannie Lou Hamer Papers; "Mississippi Rights Leader Urges Political Change," *Washington Post*, 10 April 1967, B3.

98. McLemore, "Mississippi Freedom Democratic Party," 358, 360–63, 364–65.

99. Sunflower election flyer, box 2, folder 5, Hamer Collection; Flyer advertisement for mass meeting at the Church of God in Christ in Moorhead, Mississippi, 22 March 1967, box 2, folder 5, Hamer Collection; FDP State Convention Program, 16 April 1967, box 2, folder 5, Hamer Collection; untitled memorandum, 7 May 1966, box 2, folder 3, Hamer Collection; Expense Statement of Sunflower County MFDP Voter Registration Drive, 8 August 1966 to 19 October 1966, box 2, folder 6, Hamer Collection.

100. McLemore, "Mississippi Freedom Democratic Party," 364; Moye, *Let the People Decide*, 163; Sistrom, "'Authors of the Liberation,'" 373; Reinhard, *Politics of Change*, 250–51.

101. Sistrom, "'Authors of the Liberation,'" 374–75, 376; McLemore, "Mississippi Freedom Democratic Party," 366–67.

102. McLemore, "Mississippi Freedom Democratic Party," 371–72; Moye, *Let the People Decide*, 164; "Situation Normal at Sunflower, Moorhead," *Enterprise-Tocsin*, 4 May 1967, 1.

103. McLemore, "Mississippi Freedom Democratic Party," 369–70, 372.

104. Moye, *Let the People Decide*, 165; Reinhard, *Politics of Change*, 257.

105. Reinhard, *Politics of Change*, 260 (quote); McLemore, "Mississippi Freedom Democratic Party," 317.

106. Mertis Rubin, "Sunflower People Wonder Why Negro Candidates Lost," *Southern Courier*, 6–7 May 1967, 1; Robert Analavage, "Bitter Defeat in Sunflower," *National Guardian*, 13 May 1967, 9; McLemore, "Mississippi Freedom Democratic Party," 374; "Guyot: Run Independent," *Mississippi Newsletter*, FIS, 5 May 1967, 1.

107. "Guyot: Run Independent," 5 May 1967, 1.

108. Reinhard, *Politics of Change*, 261; "Sunflower: Back to Court," *Mississippi Newsletter*, FIS, 5 May 1967, 3; Walton, *Black Political Parties*, 124.

109. Reinhard, *Politics of Change*, 260; "Mississippi Freedom Democrat Party Fails in Attempt to Use Negro Voters to Gain Political Control Sunflower County," *Jackson Advocate*, 6 May 1967, SCR ID# 10-77-0-18-1-1-1, MSSCO.

110. Sandra Nystrom and Eleanor Holmes Norton, "Times Changing in Sunflower," *New America*, 18 June 1967, box 2, folder 1, Hamer Collection; Roger Rapoport, "Anatomy of a Mississippi Election," *Wall Street Journal*, 8 May 1967, box 2, folder 5, Hamer Collection.


CHAPTER 6

1. Dittmer, *Local People*, 413–14 (quote on 414); "Burial and Boycott in Jackson," *Mississippi Newsletter*, FIS, 19 May 1967, 1; James Bonney, "Negro Leaders Call for Capital Boycott," *Jackson Clarion-Ledger*, 20 May 1967, SCR ID# 2-135-0-29-1-1-1, Mississippi State Sovereignty Commission Online, https://da.mdah.ms.gov/sovcom (hereafter MSSCO); "Negro Groups Pick Targets for Boycott," *Jackson Clarion-Ledger*, 22 May 1967, SCR ID# 2-135-0-29-1-1-1; and "Jackson Police Kill Ben Brown," *Southern Patriot*, June 1967, SCR ID# 13-59-0-56-8-1-1, both MSSCO.

2. Untitled SSC reports, 27 May 1967, SCR ID# 99-47-0-17-1-1-1; 24 May 1967, SCR ID# 9-31-6-89-1-1-1; 30 May 1967, SCR ID# 9-31-6-90-1-1-1; 5 June 1967, SCR ID# 9-31-6-91-1-1-1; 8 June 1967, SCR ID# 99-47-0-14-1-1-1; 14 June 1967, SCR ID# 99-48-0-293-1-1-1; 22 June 1967, SCR ID# 9-31-6-96-1-1-1; and "Police Arrest Negro Leader," *Jackson Clarion-Ledger*, 7 June 1967, SCR ID# 2-165-6-94-1-1-1, all MSSCO; Joseph, *Stokely*, 193.

3. Goudsouzian, *Down to the Crossroads*, 249–51; untitled SSC memo, 27 June 1967, SR ID# 9-31-7-2-1-1-1; untitled SSC memo, 5 July 1967, SCR ID# 9-31-6-97-1-1-1; and Erle Johnston to Roland Kennedy, 6 July 1967, SCR ID# 99-48-0-270-1-1-1, all MSSCO.

4. Walton, *Black Political Parties*, 124–25; Danielson, *After Freedom Summer*, 27, 29; Dittmer, *Local People*, 414 (quote).

5. "Funds to Help Elect Negroes," *Memphis Commercial Appeal*, 20 July 1967, box 9, folder 26, Delta Ministry Collection; "Mississippians United to Elect Negro Candidates," *Mississippi Freedom Democratic Party Newsletter*, 1 October 1967, 1, box 3, folder 20, Virginia Gray Adams Papers.

6. Dittmer, *Local People*, 415; Walton, *Black Political Parties*, 125; "Big FDP Beat 2 Election May 13," *Hinds County FDP News*, 6 May 1967, 1, box 6, folder 84, Delta Ministry Collection.

7. "Poor People Ask State Help," *Mississippi Newsletter*, 18 August 1967; "Around the State," *Mississippi Newsletter*, 28 July 1967, 3, box 3, folder 21, Virginia Gray Adams Papers.

8. Guyot et al., "Proposal for Six-Month Project for Mississippi Freedom Democratic Party," box 2, folder 3, Fannie Lou Hamer Collection (hereafter Hamer Collection); Expense statement, MFDP, 10 October 1967 to 25 November 1967, box 2, folder 4, Hamer Collection.

9. *Mississippi Newsletter*, Freedom Information Service, 21 July 1967, 2, SCR ID# 2-163-0-11-2-1-1; and untitled SSC memo, 31 July 1967, SCR ID# 9-31-7-5-2-1-1, both MSSCO; Joseph, *Waiting 'til the Midnight Hour*, 183–85, 190.

10. Joseph, *Waiting 'til the Midnight Hour*, 185.

11. *Welfare Rights News*, Hinds County Welfare Rights Movement, 13 September 1967, 4–5; Minutes NCNP Board Meeting: 11/12–11/13, 1966, 4, box 3, folder 7, Virginia Gray Adams Papers; Victoria Gray, "Black Politics in Mississippi," 2 September 1967, Hamer Collection, box 2, folder 3. The history of the National Conference for New Politics and its failure is outlined in Hall, "On the Tail of the Panther," 59–78.

12. Umoja, *We Will Shoot Back*, 192; "Race Riots," *Hinds County FDP News*, 28 July 1967, 1, box 6, folder 84, Delta Ministry Collection.

13. *Hinds County FDP News*, 16 September 1967, box 1, folder 26, Segregation-Integration Miscellaneous Collection, Mississippi State University Special Collections; *Mississippi Newsletter*, 22 September 1967, 2–3, SCR ID# 6-46-0-22-3-1-1 and 6-46-0-22-4-1-1, MSSCO; Hillegas v. Sams, 349 F.2nd 859 (5th Cir. 1965); "Jan Hillegas," *Veterans of the Civil Rights Movement*, www.crmvet.org/vet/hillegas.htm.

14. Dittmer, *Local People*, 418; "FDP: In or Out?," *Mississippi Newsletter*, 29 September 1967; "Leader or Changing Wind?," *Mississippi Newsletter*, 29 September 1967; McLemore, "Mississippi Freedom Democratic Party," 415–16.

15. McLemore, "Mississippi Freedom Democratic Party," 415–16; Dittmer, *Local People*, 418 (Fuhrer quote); MFDP Executive Committee Minutes, 17 Sept. 1967, Sunflower, Miss., 2, box 2, folder 4, Hamer Collection (Guyot quote).

16. Memorandum from Erle Johnston Sr., SSC, 24 January 1967, SCR ID# 2-165-6-74-1-1-1, MSSCO; "Susie B. Ruffin," *Mississippi Encyclopedia*, https://mississippi encyclopedia.org/entries/ruffin-susie-b/.

17. Walton, *Black Political Parties*, 125–26; Hathorn, "Challenging the Status Quo," 245–53, 261.

18. "Around the State," *Mississippi Newsletter*, 3 November 1967 (quote); "NAACP," *Mississippi Newsletter*, 10 November 1967, 4, series 2, box 1, folder 24, Charles Horowitz Collection.

19. McLemore, "Mississippi Freedom Democratic Party," 378–79; Andrews, *Freedom Is a Constant Struggle*, 79, 115–16. For more on the FSA program, see Saloman, "Time Dimension in Policy Evaluation."

20. McLemore, "Mississippi Freedom Democratic Party," 380–83; Sojourner with Reitan, *Thunder of Freedom*, 228–31.

21. Sojourner with Reitan, *Thunder of Freedom*, 232–35.

22. Sojourner with Reitan, *Thunder of Freedom*; McLemore, "Mississippi Freedom Democratic Party," 382–83 (quote on 383).

23. McLemore, "Mississippi Freedom Democratic Party," 383–85; Sojourner with Reitan, *Thunder of Freedom*, 261; Dittmer, *Local People*, 416.

24. Danielson, *After Freedom Summer*, 32; Walton, *Black Political Parties*, 125–26; Dittmer, *Local People*, 416–17; McLemore, "Mississippi Freedom Democratic Party," 388.

25. "Independents May Be Out If," *Mississippi Newsletter*, 15 September 1967, SCR ID# 2-163-0-9-1-1-1, MSSCO; "Around the State," *Mississippi Newsletter*, 13 October

1967, 3, series 2, box 1, folder 24, Charles Horowitz Collection; Danielson, *After Freedom Summer*, 30; McLemore, "Mississippi Freedom Democratic Party," 386 (quote); Ramsey interview by Caudill, 186–87; Guyot interview by Nash and Taggart.

26. McLemore, "Mississippi Freedom Democratic Party," 387–90; Guyot interview by Sinsheimer, 25.

27. Robert Clark et al. letter, 15 November 1967, FLH Papers, File: Correspondence —1967, Sept.–Nov.; Joseph Harris to Robert G. Clark, 6 December 1967, FLH Papers, File: Correspondence—1966–69, RE: Financial Matters; Joseph Harris to Robert G. Clark, 19 January 1968, FLH Papers, File: Correspondence—1966–69, RE: Financial Matters; McLemore, "Mississippi Freedom Democratic Party," 386–87; untitled SSC report, 13 December 1967, SCR ID# 9-31-7-58-1-1-1, MSSCO; "News from Mississippi," *Mississippi Newsletter*, 1 December 1967, 1, series 2, box 1, folder 24, Charles Horowitz Collection; untitled SSC report, 2 January 1968, SCR ID# 9-31-7-61-1-1-1, MSSCO.

28. Walton, *Black Political Parties*, 126.

29. Walton, *Black Political Parties*, 126–27.

30. Walton, *Black Political Parties*, 127.

31. Walton, *Black Political Parties*; Danielson, *After Freedom Summer*, 39.

32. McLemore, "Mississippi Freedom Democratic Party," 396, 397.

33. Erle Johnston Jr. memorandum, "Charles Evers and Lawrence Guyot," 29 January 1968, SCR ID# 1-72-1-79-1-1-1, MSSCO; Anderson interview by Nash, 17 June 2004.

34. McLemore, "Mississippi Freedom Democratic Party," 396–97; Reinhard, "Politics of Change," 294 (quote).

35. "Evers Criticized by Students," *Mississippi Newsletter*, 9 February 1968; "Alcorn Students Speak," *Mississippi Newsletter*, 23 February 1968, 1, series 2, box 1, folder 24, Charles Horowitz Collection.

36. McLemore, "Mississippi Freedom Democratic Party," 399–401; Danielson, *After Freedom Summer*, 39–40.

37. "Twelve Qualify for District 5 Supervisor," *Panolian*, 8 February 1968, 1; Nancy and Gene Turitz, "The Pioneering Days Are Over—Freedom Is Still Ahead," *Movement*, August 1965, 4; "Miles, Travis Will Run-Off Supervisor Post," *Panolian*, 15 February 1968, 1; "Travis Wins Supervisor Post," *Panolian*, 29 February 1968; Wirt, *Politics of Southern Equality*, 118–19, 141.

38. Wright-Brown, *Looking Back to Move Ahead*, 78–81.

39. Garrow, *Bearing the Cross*, 597–98; Erle Johnston Jr., untitled memorandum, 19 February 1968, SCR ID# 2-152-0-42-1-1-1, MSSCO; Don McKee, "King Seeks Mississippi Help for Poor," *Jackson Clarion-Ledger*, 16 February 1968, SCR ID # 1-85-0-76-1-1-1, MSSCO; Carson, *In Struggle*, 288–89; "Southerners Back Brown's Right to Speak," *Southern Patriot*, 5, SCR ID# 13-59-0-114-1-1-1, MSSCO.

40. Untitled SSC report, 27 March 1968, SCR ID# 9-31-7-95-1-1-1, MSSCO; Waldschmidt-Nelson, *Dreams and Nightmares*, 149–51; Lee Cole, memorandum, 4 April 1968, SCR ID# 1-95-0-17-1-1-1; "Around the State," *Mississippi Newsletter*, 5 April 1968, 6, SCR ID# 2-163-0-19-6-1-1 (quote); and Joanne Gavin, "Rap Loses 40 Pounds," *Southern Courier*, 6–7 April 1968, SCR ID# 2-150-2-47-1-1-1, all MSSCO.

41. Onaci, *Free the Land*, 1, 26–27; Danielson, *After Freedom Summer*, 47–48, 63–64.

42. Waldschmidt-Nelson, *Dreams and Nightmares*, 151; untitled SSC memorandum, 5 April 1968, SCR ID# 9-31-7-102-1-1-1, MSSCO; "Black Response to King's Murder," *Mississippi Newsletter*, 5 April 1968, 1; Lee Cole, memorandum, 5 April 1968, SCR ID# 9-31-7-103-1-1-1, MSSCO; "Steering Committee: Appeal for Justice," *New Left Notes*, 15 April 1968, series: Campus Underground, Michigan State University.

43. Guyot interview by Nash and Taggart.

44. Matusow, *Unravelling of America*, 389–94, 406; McLemore, "Mississippi Freedom Democratic Party," 416.

45. Michel, *Struggle for a Better South*, 201, 203; Ed Clark, "The Mississippi Freedom Democratic Party: The End of a Movement?," *Mississippi Newsletter*, 3 November 1967, 3, series 2, box 1, folder 24, Charles Horowitz Collection.

46. Clark, "Mississippi Freedom Democratic Party," 4–6; Boyett, *Right to Revolt*, 124, 167.

47. "MFDP Looks at Laurel Strike," *Mississippi Freedom Democratic Party Newsletter*, undated, box 3, folder 20, Virginia Gray Adams Papers.

48. Boyett, *Right to Revolt*, 167.

49. Guyot interview by Sinsheimer, 42.

50. Untitled SSC memorandum, 29 May 1968, SCR ID# 9-31-8-24-1-1-1, MSSCO; "Around the State," *Mississippi Newsletter*, 26 April 1968; "Oscar Carr, Jr. Dies; Active in Civil Rights," *New York Times*, 7 November 1977, 26.

51. "Many Say "We Want IN" to National Democrats," *Mississippi Newsletter*, 24 May 1968, 1; untitled memorandum, 29 May 1968, SCR ID# 9-31-8-24-1-1-1, MSSCO; McLemore, "Mississippi Freedom Democratic Party," 416–18.

52. Lee Cole Jr., untitled memorandum, 31 May 1968, SCR ID# 2-165-6-127-1-1-1, MSSCO; McLemore, "Mississippi Freedom Democratic Party," 419–20, 426–27; Dittmer, *Local People*, 420–21.

53. McLemore, "Mississippi Freedom Democratic Party," 421, 438, 440–41; Dittmer, *Local People*, 421.

54. McLemore, "Mississippi Freedom Democratic Party," 441–42; Dittmer, *Local People*, 421.

55. Untitled memorandum, 23 July 1968, SCR ID# 9-31-8-46-1-1-1, MSSCO; Buford Posey, "The Movement in Mississippi," *Liberation News Service*, 19 July 1968, 18; Olivia Bethany Moore, "Buford Posey," *Mississippi Encyclopedia*, https://mississippi encyclopedia.org/entries/posey-buford/.

56. McLemore, "Mississippi Freedom Democratic Party," 443–44; Matusow, *Unravelling of America*, 408–10.

57. McLemore, "Mississippi Freedom Democratic Party," 444–45.

58. MUENC to the Rev. Arthur Warmsley, 17 April 1968, box 2, folder 2, Hamer Collection; "Black People Boycott Mississippi!!!!," 5 April 1968, box 3, folder 40, Hamer Collection; "Constitution Changes before Voters Today," *Jackson Clarion-Ledger*, 4 June 1968, 1; First Primary Election Results, 4 June 1968, *Mississippi Official and Statistical Register, 1968–1972* (Jackson: Mississippi Secretary of State), 467.

59. McLemore, "Mississippi Freedom Democratic Party," 445–46, 448–50; Dittmer, *Local People*, 421; "Happenings among the Loyalists," *Mississippi Newsletter*, 2 August 1968, 1; Danielson, *After Freedom Summer*, 140; Cupit interview by Nash.

60. Dittmer, *Local People*, 421–22; McLemore, "Mississippi Freedom Democratic Party," 451–52; "Loyalists Stage Convention," *Mississippi Newsletter*, 16 August 1968, 1–3; untitled delegate slate, SCR ID# 3-17A-2-46-1-1-1 and 3-17A-2-46-2-1-1, MSSCO.

61. McLemore, "Mississippi Freedom Democratic Party," 452–53; John Damico, "Patricia Derian," *Mississippi Encyclopedia*, https://mississippiencyclopedia.org/entries/patricia-derian/.

62. McLemore, "Mississippi Freedom Democratic Party," 455, 458, 459–61; "Loyalists Stage Convention," *Mississippi Newsletter*, 16 August 1968, 2.

63. McLemore, "Mississippi Freedom Democratic Party," 461–62; "Loyalists Stage Convention," 3.

64. Rowland Evans and Robert Novak, "Turmoil Erupts in Nixon's Camp; McCarthy Backer Angers 'Loyalists,'" *Delta Democrat-Times*, 19 August 1968, box 8, folder 6, Delta Ministry Collection.

65. Dittmer, *Local People*, 422; McLemore, "Mississippi Freedom Democratic Party," 482–83.

66. McLemore, "Mississippi Freedom Democratic Party," 481; untitled SSC memo, 5 September 1968, SCR ID# 9-31-8-62-1-1-1, MSSCO.

67. McLemore, 483; Matusow, *Unraveling of America*, 417; Dittmer, *Local People*, 422; Brooks, *Fannie Lou Hamer*, 136.

68. Matusow, *Unraveling of America*, 416; Dittmer, *Local People*, 422; McLemore, "Mississippi Freedom Democratic Party," 483–84; Lemann, *Promised Land*, 314; "Democrats of Mississippi for Humphrey-Muskie," Special Collections, Mississippi State University; untitled memo, Special Collections, Mississippi State University (quote).

69. Lawrence Guyot, "Smash Wallace," *Mississippi Freedom Democratic Party Newsletter*, 5 November 1968, SCR ID# 2-165-6-128-1-1-1; and "79 Black Candidates Running; Miss. Disqualifies 8," *Mississippi Freedom Democratic Party Newsletter*, 5 November 1968, SCR ID# 2-165-6-128-1-1-1, both MSSCO. For Wallace's campaign, see Matusow, *Unraveling of America*, 422–26.

70. Matusow, *Unraveling of America*, 437; Robert Analavage, "Mississippi—Splits Beset Movement," *Mississippi Newsletter*, 8 November 1968, 2, SCR ID# 9-31-8-80-2-1-1, MSSCO.

71. Joseph Harris to Friend, 10 October 1965, box 2, folder 4, Hamer Collection; MFDP Expense Statement, 23 February 1968 to 8 November 1968, box 4, Hamer Collection; MFDP Expense Statement, 9 November 1969 to 7 February 1969, box 2, folder 4, Hamer Collection; Moore, *Defeat of Black Power*, 151; Kenneth Fairly, "Loyalist May Purge Radicals," undated, box 2, folder 3, Hamer Collection.

72. Untitled SSC memo, 13 November 1968, SCR ID# 9-31-8-81-1-1-1, MSSCO; Raines, *My Soul Is Rested*, 290; untitled SSC memo, 19 November 1968, SCR ID# 1-117-0-8-1-1-1, MSSCO; untitled memo, 10 November 1968, box 2, folder 3, Hamer Collection; MFDP News Release, 18 November 1968, box 2, folder 4, Hamer Collection.

73. Untitled SSC memo, 7 January 1969, SCR ID# 2-165-6-134-1-1-1, MSSCO; Joseph Harris to Lawrence Guyot, 29 January 1969, folder: Corresp. 1969, January–June, FLH Papers; Chesteen, "Change and Reaction," 484–85; Program for MFDP State Convention, 5 January 1969, box 2, folder 3, Hamer Collection; "FDP Shadowed by Doubts," *Delta Democrat-Times*, 6 January 1969, 1 (quote).

74. James A. Lewis and Robert Fitzpatrick, "Municipal Handbook 1969," box 2, folder 3, Hamer Collection; MUENC to Friends, 10 April 1969, box 2, folder 2, Hamer Collection; Minutes of the MFDP Executive Committee Meeting, 14 December 1969, 1–3, box 2, folder 4, Hamer Collection; Brooks and Houck, *Speeches of Fannie Lou Hamer*, 87.

75. Chesteen, "Change and Reaction," 513–16; Andrews, *Freedom Is a Constant Struggle*, 227; Constance Iona Slaughter, "The 1971 Mississippi Elections Manual," box 2, folder 3, Hamer Collection. In Sunflower County, the NAACP organization was much stronger than the MFDP presence, and when a Black man finally won a city alderman race in Indianola in December 1973, it was James Robinson, a Black businessman with no apparent MFDP connection and extensive connections to the white business community in the city. Chesteen, "Change and Reaction," 513, 536–37, 539–40.

76. Cobb, *Most Southern Place on Earth*, 254–55.

77. Payne, *I've Got The Light of Freedom*, 359.

78. McLemore, "Mississippi Freedom Democratic Party," 344–45.

79. Carson, *In Struggle*, 241.

80. Guyot interview by Murray, 5.

81. For Evers and the use of "boycott enforcers" in Port Gibson, see Crosby, *Little Taste of Freedom*, 139–47.

82. Joseph, *Stokely*, 125–27, 138–39.

83. Joseph, *Stokeley*, 138.

## CHAPTER 7

1. Rosen, *World Split Open*, 196–97.

2. Hall, "Long Civil Rights Movement," 1239, 1254.

3. Guyot interview by Bond; Campbell, *Mississippi*, 251; Kinoy, *Rights on Trial*, 264–66; Wendy Melillio, "Keeping D.C. Workers in D.C.," *Washington Post*, 18 November 1993, DC4; "Julie V. Guyot," US Public Records Index, 1950–1993, vol. 1, Ancestry.com; "Lawrence T. Guyot I," ancestry.com. US Public Records Index, 1950–1993, vol. 2, ancestry.com; Blake, *Children of the Movement*, 77–79; William Raspberry, "For Want of a Nurse . . ." *Washington Post*, 7 November 1979, A19.

4. Carson, *In Struggle*, 21, 24, 123, 166–68.

5. Jaffe and Sherwood, *Dream City*, 46–47, 49–52, 57–58; "Civil Rights Tour: Employment—Pride, Inc. Youth Empowerment," 1536 U Street NW, https://historicsites.dcpreservation.org/items/show/962; Barry and Tyree, *Mayor for Life*, 73.

6. Jaffe and Sherwood, *Dream City*, 92–93; Asch and Musgrove, *Chocolate City*, 350–51.

7. Asch and Musgrove, *Chocolate City*, 351–54, 358–59, 363; Jaffe and Sherwood, *Dream City*, 77–78.

8. Asch and Musgrove, *Chocolate City*, 376–80.

9. Asch and Musgrove, *Chocolate City*, 380–81.

10. Asch and Musgrove, *Chocolate City*, 384–88; Jaffe and Sherwood, *Dream City*, 116–19.

11. Sari Horowitz, "Ward 1 School Board Race Reflects Diversity at City's Core," *Washington Post*, 1 October 1992, DC 5; Jaffe and Sherwood, *Dream City*, 91; Bill

Alexander, "D.C.'s Juanita Bright Honored as 'Outstanding Young Woman,'" *Washington Post*, 2 January 1982, DC2; Joann Stevens, "Scared Straight: Exploring Ways to Discourage Juvenile Crime," *Washington Post*, 15 March 1979, DC1; "This Week," *Washington Post*, 7 May 1981, DC; John Carmody, "The TV Column," *Washington Post*, 8 May 1981, F11; Bill Alexander, "Brains, Not Brawn, Honored at D.C. 'Olympics of the Mind,'" 14 May 1981, *Washington Post*, DC2; Bill Alexander, "Olympics That Took Brains," *Washington Post*, 9 July 1981, DC5; www.naacp.org/act-so/; Guyot interview by Nash and Taggart.

12. Alexander, "D.C.'s Juanita Bright"; Bart Barnes, "Mary M. Treadwell, 71, Dies; Ex-wife of Marion Barry Served Prison Time for Defrauding the Federal Government," *Washington Post*, 25 July 2012; Halberstam, *Children*, 624.

13. Asch and Musgrove, *Chocolate City*, 390–92.

14. Asch and Musgrove, *Chocolate City*, 392, 396.

15. "People," *Washington Post*, 14 June 1984, DC3; "History of the Coalition for the Homeless," https://dccfh.org/about/history/; Arthur S. Brisbane and Joe Pichirallo, "Homeless Issue Alliances Shift," *Washington Post*, 16 April 1986, C9; Rader, *Signal through the Flames*, 231.

16. Asch and Musgrove, *Chocolate City*, 382; John Ward Anderson, "Closing of Shelter Sparks Verbal Battle," *Washington Post*, 25 February 1985, E1–2 (quote).

17. Ed Burke, "Moving of Homeless to Anacostia Protested," *Washington Post*, 1 October 1985, D1, D5; "Anacostia Historic District," www.nps.gov/nr/travel/wash/dc90.htm. Anacostia had once been predominately white, but the end of school desegregation accelerated its white flight to the suburbs. Asch and Musgrove, *Chocolate City*, 315, 330.

18. Theresa Brown to Pat Mackin, 19 November 1985, Lawrence Guyot Jr. Papers, box 11, folder 28, Collection no. 130, DC Public Library, Special Collections Department (hereafter LG Papers).

19. Burke, "Moving of Homeless to Anacostia Protested," D5; Arthur S. Brisbane, "D.C. Homeless Plan Criticized as Stopgap," *Washington Post*, 3 October 1985, B8 (quote).

20. Arthur S. Brisbane and Joe Pichirallo, "Police, FBI Investigate Spending by D.C. Coalition for Homeless," *Washington Post*, 13 April 1986, B1, B4 (quote).

21. Brisbane and Pichirallo, "Police, FBI Investigate Spending"; Joe Pichirallo and Chris Spolar, "Coalition Defends Shelter Operation," *Washington Post*, 14 April 1986, D1, D3.

22. Brisbane and Pichirallo, "Police, FBI Investigate Spending," D3; Pichirallo and Spolar, "Coalition Defends Shelter," D1 (Huguenin quote), D3 (Snyder quote).

23. Pichirallo and Spolar, "Coalition Defends Shelter," D3 (quote); "Questions about Conduct," *Washington Post*, 3 August 1986, A14; Martin Weil, "Ivanhoe Donaldson, Civil Rights Organizer, Confidant of Marion Barry, Dies at 74," *Washington Post*, 5 April 2016; Asch and Musgrove, *Chocolate City*, 407; Ruben Castaneda, "D.C. Police Officer Kills Teen after Car Chase," *Washington Post*, 16 May 1995, www.washingtonpost.com /archive/local/1995/05/16/dc-police-officer-kills-teen-after-car-chase /cdd42821-440b-4a6e-8879-c0bfbff9369d/.

24. Musgrove, *Rumor, Repression, and Racial Politics*, 129–33; Asch and Musgrove, *Chocolate City*, 400, 407–8.

25. "The TV Column," *Washington Post*, 23 November 1985, G6; Durrin, *Promises to Keep* (quotes).

26. Asch and Musgrove, *Chocolate City*, 400; Rader, *Signal through the Flames*, 232, 236, 241.

27. Brisbane and Pichirallo, "Homeless Issue Alliances Shift," C1, C9.

28. Brisbane and Pichirallo, "Homeless Issue Alliances Shift."

29. Brisbane and Pichirallo, "Police, FBI Investigate Spending," B4; www.usinflation calculator.com/; Arthur Brisbane, "Some D.C. Workers Profit from Grant for Homeless," *Washington Post*, 9 June 1986, B1, B10.

30. Brisbane, "Some D.C. Workers Profit," C1; Arthur S. Brisbane, "HHS Modifies Suspension of Homeless Coalition Grant," *Washington Post*, 17 April 1986, D1, D4.

31. Hall, "On the Tail of the Panther," 73, 76; Matusow, *Unraveling of America*, 371. See also chapter 4.

32. Asch and Musgrove, *Chocolate City*, 390–91. Special thanks to George Derek Musgrove for providing suggestions on this analysis.

33. Asch and Musgrove, *Chocolate City*, 383; Neil Seldman, "A Brief History of Solid Waste Management and Recycling in Washington, D.C.," *Institute for Local Self -Reliance*, 2 August 2017, https://ilsr.org/brief-history-of-solid-waste-management -and-recycling-in-washington-dc/; "Dupont Circle/Sheridan-Kalorama," www .culturaltourismdc.org/information2550/information.htm?area=2522; archived at https://web.archive.org/web/20080618021052/www.culturaltourismdc.org /information2550/information.htm?area=2522.

34. Elmore, "American Beverage Industry," 486–87, 490; Gwen Ifill, "More than Nickels at Stake in D.C. Bottle Bill Campaign," *Washington Post*, 9 August 1987, B1.

35. Ifill, "More than Nickels"; Ed Bruske, "Bottle Bill Opponents en Route to D.C. Spending Record," *Washington Post*, 19 October 1987, D1; Elmore, "American Beverage Industry," 492–94; Ed Bruske, "Bottle Bill Foes' Recycling Claim Disputed," *Washington Post*, 25 October 1987, B1.

36. Bruske, "Bottle Bill Foes' Recycling Claim Disputed"; "The Bottle Battle," *Washington Post*, 28 October 1987, A13; John Mintz, "D.C. Retailers Denounce Bottle Bill; Impact Seen as Costly, Unsanitary; Supporters Decry Scare Tactics," *Washington Post*, 30 October 1987, C1.

37. Ed Bruske, "Bottle Bill Is Rejected in District," *Washington Post*, 4 November 1987, A1, A27; Bruske, "Bottle Bill Opponents en Route to D.C. Spending Record."

38. Marc Fisher, "Raw Fisher," *Washington Post*, 1 June 2007, voices.washingtonpost .com/rawfisher/2007/06/random_friday_question.html?itid=lk_inline_manual_13; Ed Bruske and Eric Pianin, "Race, Economic Lines Seen in Bottle Vote; 'Whites and Blacks View the City Totally Differently,' Pollster Says," *Washington Post*, 5 November 1987, A1 (Pearson-West quote).

39. Bruske, "Bottle Bill Is Rejected"; Bruske and Pianin, "Race, Economic Lines Seen."

40. "Andrew Young Criticized for Wal-Mart PR Work," NBC News, 23 March 2006, www.nbcnews.com/id/11980467/ns/us_news-life/t/andrew-young-criticized-wal -mart-pr-work/#.XyL4yShKjcs. For more on the RNA's call for socialism based on the

Tanzanian concept of *ujamaa*, see Rickford, "We Can't Grow Food on All This Concrete," 956–80.

41. Hall, "Long Civil Rights Movement," 1237–38; Guyot interview by Sinsheimer, 42.

42. Ronald D. White and Judith Valente, "D.C. School Board Votes to Pick Ward 1 Member," *Washington Post*, 19 May 1983, B5.

43. Barras, *Last of the Black Emperors*, 80; Erik Wemple, "Lawrence Guyot," *Washington City Paper*, 16 February 1996, https://washingtoncitypaper.com/article/289210/lawrence-guyot/?fbclid=IwAR2CW-V97albJOPIigSWfsDM35MwnJu4VlmKIFUVCk1A-RIniDdzTja3JeA.

44. Asch and Musgrove, *Chocolate City*, 400.

45. Athelina Knight, "Barry Backers Hit Bill to Limit Mayoral Terms," *Washington Post*, 29 January 1988, C9.

46. Marc Fisher, "Politics, Push for Continuity Sealed Jenkins as Superintendent," *Washington Post*, 26 May 1988, B1, B12; Athelia Knight, "D.C. At-Large Race May Hinge on 'New Blood,'" *Washington Post*, 10 October 1988, C1; "District of Columbia Results," *Washington Post*, 10 November 1988, D10; Guyot interview by Sinsheimer, 44–45.

47. Lou Chibbaro Jr., "LGBT Activists Turn Out for Barry Statue Unveiling," *Washington Blade*, 6 March 2018, www.washingtonblade.com/2018/03/06/lgbt-activists-marion-barry-statue-unveiling/; Martin Austermuhle, "On Gay Rights, Barry Remembered for Long History of Support—and One Vote," 5 December 2014, https://wamu.org/story/14/12/05/on_gay_rights_barry_remembered_for_long_history_of_support_and_one_vote/.

48. Hyra, *Race, Class, and Politics in the Cappuccino City*, 113–17; Branch, *Parting the Waters*, 705, 835; Asch and Musgrove, *Chocolate City*, 338, 413; Michael Long, "From Black to Gay: Julian Bond on Civil Rights and Gay Rights," *HuffPost*, 11 January 2013, www.huffpost.com/entry/from-black-to-gay-julian-bond-on-civil-rights-and-gay-rights_b_2450090.

49. Aaron Morrissey, "Guyot, Lawrence," *Washington City Paper*, 21 December 2012, https://washingtoncitypaper.com/article/211005/guyot-lawrence-the-civil-rights-veteran-became-dcs-own-legendary/; "Civil Rights Leader Lawrence Guyot Dies at 73," *USA Today*, 25 November 2012, www.usatoday.com/story/news/nation/2012/11/25/civil-rights-lawrence-guyot/1725265/; Long, "From Black to Gay"; Guyot interview by Julian Bond, 60–61, 83.

50. For an in-depth discussion of Henry's sexuality, see Howard, *Men Like That*, 158–66. For Higgs, see Howard, *Men Like That*, 150–58. Françoise Hamlin refers to the tacit but unspoken acknowledgement of Henry's sexuality as "a complicity of silence" in the Black community enacted to protect the important civil rights leader. Hamlin, *Crossroads to Clarksdale*, 99–101; Human Rights Foundation and Morey, *Demystifying Sexuality*.

51. Halberstam, *Children*, 622–24; Asch and Musgrove, *Chocolate City*, 409–10 (quote on 410); Musgrove, *Rumor, Repression, and Racial Politics*, 140–41.

52. Asch and Musgrove, *Chocolate City*, 410.

53. R. H. Melton, "Barry Still Setting the Pace in D.C. Politics," *Washington Post*, 18 February 1990, A1, A20–21 ("Most of his supporters" on A20). "ANC Members to Go on

TV," *Washington Post*, 29 March 1990, DC10; Michael Abramowitz, "Barry Reportedly Trying to Keep Campaign Forces Intact," *Washington Post*, 28 January 1990, D1, D4 ("as a way"); Asch and Musgrove, *Chocolate City*, 411; Michael Abramowitz and Nathan McCall, "Barry's Resilience to Be Tested against Crowded Field of Challengers," *Washington Post*, 2 January 1990, B1–2; Michael Abramowitz, "Jarvis Gets Backing of Key Union," *Washington Post*, 14 July 1990, B1 ("is the closest").

54. Asch and Musgrove, *Chocolate City*, 411–13; Mary Ann French, "Barry Files Petitions for Council Race," *Washington Post*, 30 August 1990, A10.

55. Rene Sanchez, "Candidates Keep Mum on the Old, Accent New," *Washington Post*, 26 July 1990, DC3; Paul Schwartzman, "Is Terry Lynch Washington's Most Annoying Man?," *Washington Post*, 17 June 2012, A1.

56. Asch and Musgrove, *Chocolate City*, 413–15.

57. Asch and Musgrove, *Chocolate City*, 416; Rene Sanchez, "Community Leaders Assess Mt. Pleasant," *Washington Post*, 15 May 1991, C3.

58. Nathan McCall, "Mt. Pleasant Incident Probed," *Washington Post*, 1 June 1991, C3 (quote); Nell Henderson, "Fear of Personal, Political Firings Rises as Dixon Pushes to Cut Jobs," *Washington Post*, 24 June 1991, D1.

59. Henderson, "Fear of Personal, Political Firings," 24 June 1991, D1, D6 ("I know a lot"); Asch and Musgrove, *Chocolate City*, 416–17; Nell Henderson, "Power at Ballot Box Eludes D.C. Hispanics," *Washington Post*, 5 May 1992, A1, A16–17 ("white racism" on A17).

60. Sari Horwitz, "Ward 1 School Board Race Reflects Diversity at City's Core," *Washington Post*, 1 October 1992, DC 1, 5.

61. Horwitz, "Ward 1 School Board Race Reflects Diversity," DC1, 5; Sari Horwitz, "Intimidating Backlog of Problems Awaits the 6 Winning Candidates," *Washington Post*, 29 October 1992, DC9; Neil Henderson, "D.C. Vote Favors the Familiar," *Washington Post*, 4 November 1992, EA35.

62. Asch and Musgrove, *Chocolate City*, 220–21; Henderson, "D.C. Vote Favors the Familiar."

63. Barras, *Last of the Black Emperors*, 13–14, 43; Shaun Sutner, "New ANC Borders Spark Fierce Fights for Unpaid Posts," *Washington Post*, 29 October 1992, DC7; Brian Mooar and Gabriel Escobar, "Jackson's Wife Witnesses Slaying near Their Home," *Washington Post*, 16 May 1992, D2; Shaun Sutner, "267 ANC Seats Filled in Vote, but 32 Remain Open," *Washington Post*, 19 November 1992, DC4; Advisory Neighborhood Commissioner Historical List, District of Columbia Board of Elections, Washington, DC, 6–7, www.dcboe.org/dcboe/media/PDFFiles/nr_849.pdf; Garrison, "District of Columbia's Elected Advisory Neighborhood Commissions," 159.

64. Henderson, "D.C. Vote Favors the Familiar"; Sari Horwitz and James Ragland, "Fulwood Accepts the Pepsi Challenge," *Washington Post*, 6 May 1993, DC3.

65. Horwitz and Ragland, "Fulwood Accepts the Pepsi Challenge"; Asch and Musgrove, *Chocolate City*, 421–22; James Ragland, "Winds of Discontent May Blow Kelly Over," *Washington Post*, 6 November 1993, B1, B5 ("written off . . ."); Barras, *Last of the Black Emperors*, 81–83, 158 ("Marion intensified").

66. Asch and Musgrove, *Chocolate City*, 422–23, 430; Barras, *Last of the Black Emperors*, 179–84 (quote on 182).

67. Asch and Musgrove, *Chocolate City*, 423 ("a territory" and "refusing"); Barras, *Last of the Black Emperors*, 179, 183 ("slave board"); Aaron Morrissey, "Guyot, Lawrence," *Washington City Paper*, 21 December 2012, https://washingtoncitypaper.com/article/211005/guyot-lawrence-the-civil-rights-veteran-became-dcs-own-legendary/.

68. Asch and Musgrove, *Chocolate City*, 430–31.

69. Barras, *Last of the Black Emperors*, 184–85; Hamil R. Harris, "City Activists Condemn Control Board," *Washington Post*, 30 March 1995, DC7 (quote).

70. Yolanda Woodlee and DeNeen L. Brown, "Control Board Foes Strategize," *Washington Post*, 20 April 1995, 3.

71. "Defeat Newt Gingrich! Defend the U.S. Constitution!," *Washington Post*, 12 December 1995, A4; Yolanda Woodlee, "D.C. Democrat Says Control Board Has Got to Go," *Washington Post*, 7 March 1996, DC1; Yolanda Woodlee and DeNeen L. Brown, "Democrats Pick Convention Delegates," *Washington Post*, 30 May 1996, DC3.

72. David A. Vise, "Police Department, UDC Are Next on Control Board's List," *Washington Post*, 17 November 1996, A1, A10.

73. Guyot interview by BB. The transcript lists only the interviewer's initials, but the summary typed by the interviewer at the end of the transcript suggests the interview was conducted for a high school or university assignment.

74. Yolanda Woodlee and Hamil R. Harris," "Is Norton's Tax Plan 'the Plan'?," *Washington Post*, 8 August 1996, DC3; Hamil R. Harris and Vanessa Williams, "Former Activists Convene," *Washington Post*, 5 September 1996, DC11 ("another piece"); Wemple, "Lawrence Guyot" ("Norton tells us").

75. Yolanda Woodlee and Michael A. Fletcher, "Financial Crisis Clouds Barry's First Year Back," *Washington Post*, 4 January 1996, DC1–2; Barras, *Last of the Black Emperors*, 184–85, 188–89.

76. Asch and Musgrove, *Chocolate City*, 432–34.

77. Asch and Musgrove, *Chocolate City*, 434–38; "Resolution Regarding Proposed Charter Amendment," box 17, folder 42, LG Papers; Flyer from Just Vote No! Committee, box 17, folder 42, LG Papers; Eugene Boyd, "District of Columbia School Reform Proposals: Congress's Possible Role in the Legislative Process," 13 March 2007, Congressional Research Service, 4, https://crsreports.congress.gov/product/pdf/RS/RS22613/6.

78. Yolanda Woodlee, "Barry Aide Who Stole from City Regains Influence," *Washington Post*, 27 October 1996, B1, 8; Guyot interview by Nash and Taggart.

79. Kate Alexander, "A Provocative Figure," *Common Denominator*, 23 April 2001, www.thecommondenominator.com (quotes); Bart Barnes, "Mary Treadwell, 71, Dies; Ex-wife of Marion Barry Served Prison Time for Defrauding the Federal Government," *Washington Post*, 25 July 2012, www.washingtonpost.com/local/obituaries/mary-m-treadwell-71-dies-ex-wife-of-marion-barry-served-prison-time-for-defrauding-the-federal-government/2012/07/25/gJQAz5Qz9W_story.html; www.dcwatch.com; Courtland Milloy, "The Right Way to Take Over the City," *Washington Post*, 2 October 1999, www.washingtonpost.com/archive/local/1999/10/03/the-right-way-to-take-over-the-city/c30a5e54-43c8-42d4-8984-f8be6f3d4f91/.

80. Graham, *Our Kind of People*, 66–67, 69–70; Douglas Martin, "James E. Cheek, Forceful University President, Dies at 77," *New York Times*, 21 January 2010. For more

on Lee Atwater and his role in the Willie Horton ad and other racial "dirty tricks," see Brady, *Bad Boy*.

81. Asch and Musgrove, *Chocolate City*, 185–87; Paige Osburn, "Mapping Segregation: A Walking Tour of LeDroit Park," 17 April 2017, American University Radio, https://wamu.org/story/17/04/17/mapping-segregation-walking-tour-ledroit-park/; Margaret K. Webb, "LeDroit Fights to Keep Park," *Washington Post*, 13 December 1990, DC1, 10 (quote); Hamil R. Harris, "City Failed to Evaluate Risks at Excavation Site, Leaders Say," *Washington Post*, 6 January 1994, DC2.

82. "Advisory Neighborhood Commission Results," *Washington Post*, 24 November 1994, DC7; Neil Henderson, "Dealing with Diversity in Ward 1," 7 July 1994, *Washington Post*, DC1, 3 (quote); Angela E. Couloumbis, "LeDroit Park: Marriage of Past, Present," *Washington Post*, 6 January 1996, E1; Hamil R. Harris, "Barney Circle Freeway Controversy Flares Anew," *Washington Post*, 7 November 1996, DC9; Lawrence Guyot to *Washington Post*, "Close to Home" letters, 10 March 2003, box 17, folder 22, LG Papers.

83. Jonathan Hutto, "Remembering Lawrence Guyot," *Washington Post*, 28 November 2012, www.washingtonpost.com/blogs/therootdc/post/lawrence-guyot-soldier-of-the-people-mentor-for-the-youth/2012/11/28/aca397fc-396c-11e2-a263-foebffed2f15_blog.html?utm_term=.ba465e0a4873; Hutto interview by Danielson.

84. Jonathan Hutto, "A Child of the Student Non-violent Coordinating Committee (SNCC)," *Peace Chronicle*, Winter 2023, www.peacejusticestudies.org/chronicle/a-child-of-the-student-non-violent-coordinating-committee-sncc/.

85. Hutto interview by Danielson; Kacee Wilkerson, "Run-Off Seals Victories for Nation Time, Classic Slates," *Hilltop*, 4 April 1997, A1; Lolly Bowean, "ANC Residents—Wonder if HUSA President-Elect Hutto Can Still Represent," *Hilltop*, 18 April 1997, A1 (quote); Rafiah David, "After Two Years in Office, Eames to Head ANC 1," *Hilltop*, 15 January 1999, A1.

86. Enjoli Francis and Rafiah Davis, "Howard University Works to Heal Wounds with LeDroit Park Community," *Hilltop*, 5 March 1999, A6 (quotes); Hutto interview by Danielson.

87. Ta-Nehisi Coates, "Plans to Privatize On-Campus Streets Meet Community Opposition," *Hilltop*, 12 September 1997, A1 (quote); "A Bad First Step," *Hilltop*, 12 September 1997, A8; Jonathan Hutto to Chris Danielson, email, 20 November 2021; Ta-Nehisi Coates, "Cul-de-Sacking the Community," *Washington City Paper*, 24 October 1997; Minutes of 17 July Meeting of Commission 1B.

88. Coates, "Cul-de-Sacking"; Hutto to Danielson, email, 20 November 2021; Keva Graves, "D.C. Residents, Howard Students Rally at Capital [*sic*]," *Hilltop*, 5 September 1997, A5; Charles Coleman Jr., "General Assembly Votes Down Street Privatization," *Hilltop*, 3 September 1999; Frank Smith to H. Patrick Swygert, 16 September 1997; Hutto to Danielson, email, 22 November 2021; Ta-Nehisi Coates, "General Assembly Reaches Quorum, Votes on Campus Street Privatization," *Hilltop*, 19 September 1997, A1; Marion Barry to Linda W. Cropp, 30 September 1997; Ta-Nehisi Coates, "University Withdraws Campus Street Privatization Proposal," *Hilltop*, 3 October 1997, A1; Hutto, "Child of the Student Non-violent Coordinating Committee."

89. Hutto to Danielson, email, 27 November 2021 ("lit a match"); Natalie P. McNeal, "Howard, Neighbors Clash," *Community News*, 18 September 1997, 1; Maybelle Taylor Bennett to Lawrence Guyot, 21 October 2002, box 17, folder 22, LG Papers; Hutto, "Child of the Student Non-violent Coordinating Committee" ("still remember").

90. Hutto to Danielson, email, 22 November 2021; Guyot interview by Sinsheimer, 36.

91. Asch and Musgrove, *Chocolate City*, 439–40; Hutto to Danielson, email, 26 November 2021; Alexander, "Provocative Figure," 3–5 (Guyot quotes); Laura Lang, Michael Schaffer, Elissa Silverman, and Erik Wemple, "Circling the Wagon," *Washington City Paper*, 6 February 1998, https://washingtoncitypaper.com/article/279407/circling-the-wagon/. Coumaris, a lawyer for the Internal Revenue Service, was himself convicted in 2002 for hiding a wanted bank robber (who was also his lover) from the police and helping him secure false identification. United States v. Coumaris, United States Court of Appeals, District of Columbia Circuit, No. 03-3024, 8 March 2005, https://caselaw.findlaw.com/us-dc-circuit/1222290.html.

92. Wemple, "Lawrence Guyot"; Alexander, "Provocative Figure"; Lauren Stephens, "Howard Student Elected ANC Commissioner," *Hilltop*, 19 November 2004, A1, A4.

93. Asch and Musgrove, *Chocolate City*, 442–46.

94. Asch and Musgrove, *Chocolate City*, 446–48 (quote on 447); Hutto to Danielson, email, 26 November 2021.

95. Asch and Musgrove, *Chocolate City*, 448, 452–57.

96. Mills, *This Little Light of Mine*, 374.

97. Funeral and Memorial Services Program for Fannie Lou Hamer, Ruleville, Mississippi, 20 March 1977, box 1, folder 1.1, Fannie Lou Hamer Collection; Payne, *I've Got the Light of Freedom*, 408.

98. Gail Hall and Carolyn McNair, "'Freedom Summer' of 1964 Revisited," *Jackson Advocate*, 8–14 November 1979, 1; Curriculum vitae of Clayborne Carson, Martin Luther King Jr. Research and Education Institute, https://kinginstitute.stanford.edu/institute/clayborne-carson/curriculum-vita/positions.

99. Transcript of AU 842, "Mississippi Freedom Summer Reviewed: Genesis of the Freedom Summer Project," 30 October 1979, 7–11, Tougaloo College, transcribed by John Jones, Mississippi Department of Archives and History, Jackson.

100. Transcript of AU 842, 19–20.

101. Transcript of AU 842, 42–43, 48. See chapter 5 for Guyot and Thelwell's collaboration in *Freedomways*.

102. Chafe, *Never Stop Running*, 100–102, 104–7; Paget, *Patriotic Betrayal*, 85–87, 306–7; Guyot interview by Sinsheimer, 35.

103. Transcript of AU 843, "Mississippi Freedom Summer Reviewed: Race Relations in Mississippi before 1964," 31 October 1979, Millsaps College, transcribed by John Jones, Mississippi Department of Archives and History, Jackson, 37–38. See also McMillen, *Citizens' Councils*.

104. Raines, *My Soul Is Rested*, 238–43, 286–90; Guyot interview by Ladner; Else, *True South*, 1–3, 66–69, 168–71; "Documentary Filmmaker Henry Hampton Dies," *Washington Post*, 24 November 1998, www.washingtonpost.com/archive

/local/1998/11/24/documentary-filmmaker-henry-hampton-dies/bc5ae34e-8555
-4b2d-b3d9-92f8721ae4f9/; *Eyes on the Prize: Mississippi*, season 1,
episode 5.

105. Guyot interview by Rachal; Program for "'We Shall Not Be Moved': The Life
and Times of the Student Non-violent Coordinating Committee," 1960–66, 14–16
April 1988, Trinity College, Hartford, CT; Linda Jones, "Professors Re-live Movement
through 'Legacy' Forum," *Hilltop*, 22 January 1993, A2; Lawrence Guyot, "A Veteran of
Mississippi's 'Freedom Summer' Remembers the Cause—and the Danger," *People*, September 18, 1989, 61–65.

106. Else, *True South*, 374–75.

107. Else, *True South*, 375–76.

108. Guyot interview by Nash and Taggart. For Evers, see Danielson, *After Freedom
Summer*, 54–65, 101–8.

109. Aprill O. Turner, "The Revolutionary," *Hilltop*, 20 November 1998, A1, A5;
Program for "A Celebration of the Life and Legacy of Victoria Jackson Gray Adams," 9
September 2006, box 9, folder 6, Virginia Gray Adams Papers.

110. Lawrence Thomas Guyot Jr. obituary, Lockett Williams Mortuary, www
.lockettwilliams.com/obituary/1863802; Hamil R. Harris and Matt Schudel, "Lawrence
Guyot, Civil Rights Leader and Community Activist, Dies at 73," *Washington Post*, 23
November 2012, www.washingtonpost.com/local/obituaries/lawrence-guyot-civil
-rights-leader-and-community-activist-dies-at-73/2012/11/23/93fc754a-35af
-11e2-bb9b-288a310849ee_story.html; "The IRS Investigates the NAACP," partial transcript of *The O'Reilly Factor*, Fox News, 29 October 2004, www.foxnews.com/story
/the-irs-investigates-the-naacp.

111. Segment summaries "Sizing Up New Orleans," "Col. Cowan's Rescue, Col.
Hunt's Assessment," and "Racial Tension from Katrina?," transcript of *The O'Reilly Factor*, 2 September 2005, www.billoreilly.com.

112. *Guyot's Newsletter*, December 2009 and January 2011, gift of Margaret Kibbee;
*Guyot's Newsletter*, April 2010, 2, box 14, folder 18, LG Papers; Lawrence Guyot to
Regina Knox Woods, 2 August 1996, box 16, folder 8, LG Papers; "The MFDP and the
Obama Campaign," box 18, folder 7, LG Papers; Guyot interview by Sinsheimer, 37.

113. *SNCC 50th Anniversary Conference*, vol. 10.

114. *SNCC 50th Anniversary Conference*, vol. 21; Citizens United v. Federal Election
Commission, 558 US 310 (2010).

115. Guyot interview by Moore and Dombrowski; Guyot interview by Bond; "Chaos
or Community."

116. Guyot interview by Bond, 43, 45.

117. "Robert 'Bob' Parris Moses (1935–2021)," www.crmvet.org/mem/mosesb.htm.

118. Payne, *I've Got the Light of Freedom*, 423–24; faculty bio for Nicolaus Mills, Sara
Lawrence College, www.sarahlawrence.edu/faculty/mills-nicolaus.html; John Dittmer,
review of *We Are Not Afraid: The Story of Goodman, Schwerner, and Chaney and the
Civil Rights Campaign for Mississippi*, by Seth Cagin and Philip Dray, *Journal of American History* 76, no. 2 (September 1989): 657.

119. Danielson, *Color of Politics*, 128–29. For Parker's voting rights consensus, see his *Black Votes Count*. For the legal case, see Northwest Austin Municipal Utility District No. 1 v. Holder, 557 US 193, 129 S.Ct. 2504 (2009).

120. Danielson, *Color of Politics*, 134–35. For Kousser's analysis, see his *Colorblind Injustice*. For the cases, see Shaw v. Reno, 509 US 630 (1993) and Bush v. Vera, 517 US 952 (1996).

121. Danielson, *Color of Politics*, 141–42. The case is Crawford v. Marion County Election Board, 553 US 181 (2008).

122. Guyot obituary; Guyot interview by Murray; Monica Land, "Memorials Planned for Civil Rights Activist Lawrence Guyot," *Mississippi Link*, 7 December 2012, www.themississippilink.com; Brentin Mock and Voting Rights Watch, "Voting Rights Icon Lawrence Guyot's Death Animates a Fight over the Future," *The Nation*, 6 December 2012.

123. Land, "Memorials Planned"; Hamil R. Harris, "Lawrence Guyot, Civil Rights Icon, Memorialized by Hundreds at D.C. Service," *Washington Post*, 15 December 2012.

124. Hunter Dawkins, "Pass Christian to Honor Civil Rights Leader Lawrence Guyot with Historical Marker," *Supertalk Mississippimedia*, 22 June 2023, www.supertalk.fm /pass-christian-to-honor-civil-rights-leader-lawrence-guyot-with-historical-marker /; Spencer Pullen, "Mississippi Freedom Marker Honors Lawrence Guyot in Hometown of Pass Christian," WXXV25, 10 July 2023, www.wxxv25.com /mississippi-freedom-marker-honors-lawrence-guyot-in-hometown-of-pass -christian.

## CONCLUSION

1. Shelby County v. Holder, 570 US 529 (2013); Mock and Voting Rights Watch, 6 December 2012; James Taranto, "Civil Rights Reactionaries: Nostalgia and the Voting Rights Act," *Wall Street Journal*, 29 November 2012.

2. Shelby County, 570 US 529; Vann R. Newkirk II, "How *Shelby County v. Holder* Broke America," *Atlantic*, 10 July 2018, www.theatlantic.com/politics/archive /2018/07/how-shelby-county-broke-america/564707/; Eric Bradner, "Discriminatory Voter Laws Have Surged in the Last 5 Years, Federal Commission Finds," CNN, 12 September 2018, https://edition.cnn.com/2018/09/12/politics/voting-rights -federal-commission-election/index.html; Brnovich v. Democratic National Committee, 594 US __ (2021).

3. Nicolas Reimann, "John Lewis Voting Rights Act Fails to Pass Senate," *Forbes*, 3 November 2021, www.forbes.com/sites/nicholasreimann/2021/11/03/john-lewis -voting-rights-act-fails-to-pass-senate/?sh=56e494fbb3d2; Horus Alas, "Report: Republican-Led State Legislatures Pass Dozens of Restrictive Voting Laws in 2021," *US News and World Report*, 2 July 2021, www.usnews.com/news/best-states/articles/2021 -07-02/17-states-have-passed-restrictive-voting-laws-this-year-report-says; Allen. Milligan, 599 US __ (2023); Sam Levine, "Alabama Discriminated against Black Voters, US

Supreme Court Rules," *Guardian*, 8 June 2023, www.theguardian.com/law/2023/jun/08/supreme-court-voting-rights-decision-allen-milligan.

4. Tonya Mosley and Allison Hagan, "How Black Grassroots Organizers in Georgia Changed Politics in a Longtime Republican Stronghold," WBUR, 6 January 2021, www.wbur.org/hereandnow/2021/01/06/grassroots-democrat-wins-georgia; www.onearizona.org.

5. Lawrence Thomas Guyot Jr. obituary, Lockett Williams Mortuary, www.lockettwilliams.com/obituary/1863802.

# BIBLIOGRAPHY

MANUSCRIPT COLLECTIONS

Victoria Gray Adams Papers. McCain Library & Archives, University of Southern Mississippi.

Billy Bourdin Historical Collections. Pass Christian Historical Society, Pass Christian, Mississippi.

Gloria Xifaras Clark Papers (MS 865). Special Collections and University Archives, University of Massachusetts Amherst Libraries. http://credo.library.umass.edu/view /full/mums865-b001-f002-i002.

Michael Davis Papers, 1965–1970. Box 1, folder 2. Wisconsin Historical Society, University of Wisconsin–Madison.

Delta Ministry Collection. Archives and Special Collections. Mitchell Memorial Library, Mississippi State University.

Lawrence Guyot Jr. Papers. Collection no. 130, DC Public Library.

Fannie Lou Hamer Collection. Department of Archives and Special Collections. J. D. Williams Library, University of Mississippi.

Fannie Lou Hamer Papers. Amistad Research Center, Tulane University.

Hancock County Historical Society, Bay St. Louis, Mississippi.

Charles Horowitz Collection. Mississippi Department of Archives and History, Jackson.

Mississippi State Sovereignty Commission Online, Mississippi Department of Archives and History.

R. Hunter Morey Papers. Wisconsin Historical Society, University of Wisconsin–Madison.

Segregation-Integration Miscellaneous Collection. Mitchell Memorial Library Archives and Special Collections, Mississippi State University.

Student Nonviolent Coordinating Committee Papers (microfilm).

## NEWSPAPERS AND PERIODICALS

*Atlantic*
*Benton County (MS) Freedom Train*
*Berkeley Barb* (University of California–Berkeley)
*Bolivar Commercial* (Cleveland, MS)
*Chicago Daily News*
*Common Denominator* (Washington, DC)
*Community News* (Howard University School of Communications, Washington, DC)
*Daily Californian* (University of California–Berkeley)
*Daily Egyptian* (Southern Illinois University, Carbondale, IL)
*Daily Princetonian* (Princeton University, Princeton, NJ)
*Daily Times Leader* (West Point, MS)
*Delta Democrat-Times* (Greenville, MS)
*Enterprise-Tocsin* (Indianola, MS)
*Forbes*
*Freedomways*
*Greenfield (MA) Recorder-Gazette*
*Greenwood (MS) Commonwealth*
*Guardian*
*Guyot's Newsletter* (Washington, DC)
*Hattiesburg (MS) American*
*Hilltop* (Howard University, Washington, DC)
*Hinds County FDP News*
*Jackson Advocate*
*Jackson Clarion-Ledger*
*Jackson Daily News*
*Liberation News Service* (Montague, MA)
*Liberty Bell* (Harrison County, MS)
*Massachusetts Collegian* (University of Massachusetts, Amherst, MA)
*Memphis Commercial Appeal*
*Mississippi Freedom Democratic Party Newsletter*
*Mississippi Link*
*Mississippi Newsletter*
*Movement* (SNCC of California)
*Nation*
*National Guardian*
*Neshoba Democrat* (Philadelphia, MS)
*New Left Notes* (Chicago, IL)
*New York Times*
*Oberlin Review* (Oberlin College, Oberlin, OH)
*Panolian* (Batesville, MS)
*Reporter*
*Sea Coast Echo* (Bay St. Louis, MS)
*Southern Courier* (Montgomery, AL)
*Southern Patriot*

*Student Voice*
*USA Today*
*US News and World Report*
*Voice of the Movement*
*Wall Street Journal*
*Washington Blade*
*Washington City Paper*
*Washington Post*
*Welfare Rights News* (Hinds County, MS)
*Winona (MS) Times*
*Wooster Voice* (Wooster College, Wooster, OH)
*The Worker* (New York City)


INTERVIEWS

Rueben V. Anderson. Interview by Jere Nash, 17 June 2004. Nash and Taggart Collection, Archives and Special Collections, University of Mississippi Libraries.

Unita Blackwell. Interview by Mike Garvey, 1977. Center for Oral History and Cultural Heritage, University of Southern Mississippi.

Luvaghn Brown. Interview by Paul T. Murray, 4 November 2022. Transcript in author's possession.

Peggy Connor. Interview by Jere Nash, 3 February 2005. Nash and Taggart Collection, Archives and Special Collections, University of Mississippi Libraries.

Danny Cupit. Interview by Jere Nash (part 1 of 2), 19 August 2004. Nash and Taggart Collection, Archives and Special Collections, University of Mississippi Libraries.

Felix Dunn. Interview by James Pat Smith, 25 October 2001. Mississippi Oral History Program, Center for Oral History and Cultural Heritage, University of Southern Mississippi.

Lawrence Guyot. Interview by Julian Bond, 30 December 2010. Civil Rights History Project, National Museum of African American History and Culture.

———. Interview by BB, n.d. Lawrence Guyot Jr. Papers, box 15, folder 9, DC Public Library, Special Collections Department, Collection no. 130.

———. Interview by Joyce Ladner, Joyce Ladner Collection, series 2, box 7, folder 39, Mississippi Department of Archives and History.

———. Interview by Joshua Moore and Diana Dombrowski, 23 September 2011. Samuel Proctor Oral History Program Collection. P. K. Yonge Library of Florida History, University of Florida.

———. Interview by Paul Murray, 25 July 2012. Washington, DC.

———. Interview by Jere Nash and Andy Taggart, 14 July 2004. Nash and Taggart Collection, Archives and Special Collections, University of Mississippi Libraries.

———. Interview by John Rachal, 1996. Mississippi Oral History Program, vol. 673, Center for Oral History and Cultural Heritage, University of Southern Mississippi.

———. Interview by Joe Sinsheimer, 4 February 1987. Washington, DC.

———. Unknown interviewer, 20 August 1986. Blackside Inc. Lawrence Guyot Jr. Papers, box 9, folder 23, DC Public Library, Special Collections Department, Collection no. 130.

———. Unknown interviewer, summer 1965. Mississippi Freedom Democratic Party Chapter 30. Stanford University Project, South Oral History no. 10, *New York Times* Oral History Program.

———. Unknown interviewer, 2 March 2006. Videotape, 53 minutes. Archives and Special Collections, L. Zenobia Coleman Library, Tougaloo College.

Jonathan Hutto. Interview by Chris Danielson, 16 June 2016, Washington, DC.

Staughton Lynd. Telephone interview by Chris Danielson, 13 March 2018.

Les McLemore. Interview by Jere Nash, 10 March 2004. Nash and Taggart Collection, Archives and Special Collections, University of Mississippi Libraries.

Robert Parris Moses. Interview by Anne Romaine, 1 April 1981. Mississippi Freedom Democratic Party, Mississippi Department of Archives and History, accession no. OH 81–08–11, Part 1.

Paul Ortiz. *"I Never Will Forget": Memories from Freedom Summer*. Samuel Proctor Oral History Program Collection. P. K. Yonge Library of Florida History, University of Florida.

Louis Joseph Piernas. Unknown interviewer, 1937 or 1938. Harrison County, Works Progress Administration Slave Narratives, MSGenWeb Library Slave Narrative Project. http://msgw.org/slaves/piernas-xslave.htm.

Claude Ramsey. Interview by Orley Caudill, 28 April 1981. Mississippi Oral History Program, University of Southern Mississippi.

Fannie Rushing and Peter Orris. Interview by Chris Danielson, 20 May 2015. Chicago, Illinois.

## VIDEORECORDINGS AND FILMS

"Chaos or Community: Where Do We Go from Here?" Third Annual Civil Rights History Panel. Delta State University, Cleveland, Mississippi, 20 June 2012. YouTube. https://www.youtube.com/watch?v=J2WnoEqzG1I.

Durrin, Ginny. *Promises to Keep*. Film. Washington, DC: Durrin Productions, 1988.

*Eyes on the Prize: America's Civil Rights Years*. Television documentary, PBS. Boston: Blackside, 1987.

Pincus, Edward, and David Neuman. *Black Natchez*. Videorecording, Amistad Research Center, 1967, Tulane University Digital Library.

*SNCC 50th Anniversary Conference*. Vol. 10, *Moving on Mississippi: "We Had to Be Strong."* Film. San Francisco: California Newsreel, 2011.

*SNCC 50th Anniversary Conference*. Vol. 21, *The Mississippi Freedom Democratic Party: "A Real Democratic Process."* Film. San Francisco: California Newsreel, 2011.

## GOVERNMENT PUBLICATION

US Senate. Committee to Investigate Senatorial Campaign Expenditures, 1946. *Testimony of Rev. George T. J. Strype, Pass Christian, Miss., Hearings before the Special Committee*. 79th Congress, 2nd Sess., 2–5 December 1946. Washington, DC: US Government Printing Office, 1947.

BOOKS

Allyn, David. *Make Love, Not War: The Sexual Revolution—An Unfettered History*. Boston: Little, Brown, 2000.

Andrews, Kenneth T. *Freedom Is a Constant Struggle: The Mississippi Civil Rights Movement and Its Legacy*. Chicago: University of Chicago Press, 2004.

Arsenault, Raymond. *Freedom Riders: 1961 and the Struggle for Racial Justice*. New York: Oxford University Press, 2006.

Asch, Chris Myers. *The Senator and the Sharecropper: The Freedom Struggles of James O. Eastland and Fannie Lou Hamer*. New York: New Press, 2008.

Asch, Chris Myers, and George Derek Musgrove. *Chocolate City: A History of Race and Democracy in the Nation's Capital*. Chapel Hill: University of North Carolina Press, 2017.

Barras, Jonetta Rose. *The Last of the Black Emperors: The Hollow Comeback of Marion Barry in the New Age of Black Leaders*. Baltimore: Bancroft, 1998.

Barry, Marion, and Omar Tyree. *Mayor for Life: The Incredible Story of Marion Barry, Jr.* New York: Strebor, 2014.

Beito, David T., and Linda Royster Beito. *Black Maverick: T. R. M. Howard's Fight for Civil Rights and Economic Power*. Urbana: University of Illinois Press, 2009.

Belfrage, Sally. *Freedom Summer*. Charlottesville: University Press of Virginia, 1965.

Blackwell, Unita, with JoAnne Pritchard Morris. *Barefootin': Life Lessons from the Road to Freedom*. New York: Crown, 2006.

Blain, Keisha N. *Until I Am Free: Fannie Lou Hamer's Enduring Message to America*. Boston: Beacon, 2021.

Blake, John. *Children of the Movement*. Chicago: Lawrence Hill, 2004.

Boyett, Patricia Michelle. *Right to Revolt: The Crusade for Racial Justice in Mississippi's Piney Woods*. Jackson: University Press of Mississippi, 2015.

Bracey, Earnest. *Fannie Lou Hamer: The Life of a Civil Rights Icon*. Jefferson, NC: McFarland, 2011.

Brady, John. *Bad Boy: The Life and Politics of Lee Atwater*. Boston: Da Capo, 1996.

Branch, Taylor. *Parting the Waters: America in the King Years, 1954–63*. New York: Simon & Schuster, 1988.

———. *Pillar of Fire: America in the King Years, 1963–65*. New York: Simon & Schuster, 1998.

Brodie, Fawn M. *Thomas Jefferson: An Intimate History*. New York: W. W. Norton, 2010.

Brooks, Maegan Parker. *A Voice That Could Stir an Army: Fannie Lou Hamer and the Rhetoric of the Black Freedom Movement*. Jackson: University Press of Mississippi, 2016.

———. *Fannie Lou Hamer: America's Freedom Fighting Woman*. Washington, DC: Rowman & Littlefield, 2020.

Brooks, Maegan Parker, and Davis Houck, eds. *The Speeches of Fannie Lou Hamer: To Tell It Like It Is*. Jackson: University Press of Mississippi, 2013.

Burner, Eric. *And Gently He Shall Lead Them: Robert Parris Moses and Civil Rights in Mississippi*. New York: NYU Press, 1994.

Caire, R. J., and Katy Caire. *History of Pass Christian*. Pass Christian, MS: Lafayette, 1976.

Califano, Joseph, Jr. *The Triumph and Tragedy of Lyndon Johnson: The White House Years*. New York: Simon & Schuster, 1991.

Campbell, Clarice T., and Oscar Allan Rogers Jr. *Mississippi: The View from Tougaloo*. Jackson: University Press of Mississippi, 1979.

Carmichael, Stokely, with Ekwueme Michael Thelwell. *Ready for Revolution: The Life and Struggles of Stokely Carmichael*. New York: Scribner, 2003.

Carson, Clayborne. *In Struggle: SNCC and the Black Awakening of the 1960s*. Cambridge, MA: Harvard University Press, 1981.

Chafe, William H. *Never Stop Running: Allard Lowenstein and the Struggle to Save American Liberalism*. New York: Basic Books, 1993.

Cobb, Charles E., Jr. *This Nonviolent Stuff'll Get You Killed: How Guns Made the Civil Rights Movement Possible*. New York: Basic Books, 2014.

Cobb, James C. *The Most Southern Place on Earth: The Mississippi Delta and the Roots of Regional Identity*. New York: Oxford University Press, 1992.

Cortner, Richard C. *The Apportionment Cases*. Knoxville: University of Tennessee Press, 1970.

Crosby, Emilye. *A Little Taste of Freedom: The Black Freedom Struggle in Claiborne County, Mississippi*. Chapel Hill: University of North Carolina Press, 2005.

Daniel, Pete. *Dispossession: Discrimination against African American Farmers in the Age of Civil Rights*. Chapel Hill: University of North Carolina Press, 2013.

Danielson, Chris. *After Freedom Summer: How Race Realigned Mississippi Politics, 1965–1986*. Gainesville: University Press of Florida, 2011.

———. *The Color of Politics: Racism in the American Political Arena Today*. Santa Barbara, CA: Praeger, 2013.

Davis, Cyprian. *The History of Black Catholics in the United States*. New York: Crossroad, 1990.

D'Emilio, John. *Lost Prophet: The Life and Times of Bayard Rustin*. Chicago: University of Chicago Press, 2003.

Dittmer, John. *The Good Doctors: The Medical Committee for Human Rights and the Struggle for Social Justice in Health Care*. New York: Bloomsbury, 2009.

———. *Local People: The Struggle for Civil Rights in Mississippi*. Urbana: University of Illinois Press, 1994.

Draper, Alan. *Conflicts of Interest: Organized Labor and the Civil Rights Movement in the South, 1954–1968*. Ithaca, NY: ILR, 1994.

DuPont, Carolyn, Renee. *Mississippi Praying: Southern White Evangelicals and the Civil Rights Movement, 1945–1975*. New York: New York University Press, 2013.

Else, Jon. *True South: Henry Hampton and "Eyes on the Prize," the Landmark Television Series That Reframed the Civil Rights Movement*. New York: Viking, 2017.

Estes, Steve. *I Am a Man! Race, Manhood, and the Civil Rights Movement*. Chapel Hill: University of North Carolina Press, 2005.

Evans, Sara. *Personal Politics: The Roots of Women's Liberation in the Civil Rights Movement and the New Left*. New York: Vintage, 1979.

Fage, J. D. *A History of Africa*. 3rd ed. New York: Routledge, 1995.

Findlay, James F., Jr. *Church People in the Struggle: The National Council of Churches and the Black Freedom Movement, 1950–1970*. New York: Oxford University Press, 1993.

Finnegan, Terence. *A Deed So Accursed: Lynching in Mississippi and South Carolina, 1881–1940*. Charlottesville: University of Virginia Press, 2013.

Fitzgerald, Michael W. *Urban Emancipation: Popular Politics in Reconstruction Mobile, 1860–1890*. Baton Rouge: Louisiana State University Press, 2002.

Foner, Eric. *Reconstruction: America's Unfinished Revolution, 1863–1877*. New York: Harper and Row, 1988.

Forman, James. *The Making of Black Revolutionaries*. Seattle: University of Washington Press, 1997.

Garrow, David J. *Bearing the Cross: Martin Luther King, Jr., and the Southern Christian Leadership Conference*. New York: Quill, 1989.

———. *Protest at Selma: Martin Luther King, Jr., and the Voting Rights Act of 1965*. New Haven, CT: Yale University Press, 1978.

Glatthaar, Joseph T. *Forged in Battle: The Civil War Alliance of Black Soldiers and White Officers*. New York: Free Press, 1990.

Goodwyn, Lawrence. *The Populist Moment: A Short History of the Agrarian Revolt in America*. New York: Oxford University Press, 1978.

Goudsouzian, Aram. *Down to the Crossroads: Civil Rights, Black Power, and the March against Fear*. New York: Farrar, Straus and Giroux, 2014.

Graham, Lawrence Otis. *Our Kind of People: Inside America's Black Upper Class*. New York: HarperCollins, 1999.

Halberstam, David. *The Children*. New York: Random House, 1998.

Hamlin, Françoise N. *Crossroads at Clarksdale: The Black Freedom Struggle in the Mississippi Delta after World War II*. Chapel Hill: University of North Carolina Press, 2012.

Henry, Aaron, with Constance Curry. *Aaron Henry: The Fire Ever Burning*. Jackson: University Press of Mississippi, 2000.

Herring, George C. *America's Longest War: The United States and Vietnam, 1950–1975*. 3rd ed. New York: McGraw-Hill, 1996.

Hill, Lance. *The Deacons for Defense: Armed Resistance and the Civil Rights Movement*. Chapel Hill: University of North Carolina Press, 2004.

Hirsch, Arnold R., and Joseph Logsdon, eds. *Creole New Orleans: Race and Americanization*. Baton Rouge: Louisiana State University Press, 1992.

Hogan, Wesley C. *Many Minds, One Heart: SNCC's Dream for a New America*. Chapel Hill: University of North Carolina Press, 2008.

Holt, Len. *The Summer That Didn't End: The Story of the Mississippi Civil Rights Project of 1964*. New York: Da Capo, 1992.

Howard, John. *Men Like That: A Southern Queer History*. Chicago: University of Chicago Press, 1999.

Human Rights Foundation and R. Hunter Morey. *Demystifying Homosexuality: A Teaching Guide about Lesbians and Gay Men*. New York: Irvington, 1984.

Hyra, Derek. *Race, Class, and Politics in the Cappuccino City*. Chicago: University of Chicago Press, 2017.

Jackson, Esther Cooper, ed. *Freedomways Reader*. Boulder, CO: Westview, 2000.

Jackson, Jessica Barbata. *Dixie's Italians: Sicilians, Race and Citizenship in the Jim Crow South*. Baton Rouge: Louisiana University Press, 2020.

Jaffe, Harry S., and Tom Sherwood. *Dream City: Race, Power, and the Decline of Washington, D.C.* New York: Argo Navis, 2014.

Jordan, Winthrop D. *White over Black: American Attitudes towards the Negro, 1550–1812*. Chapel Hill: University of North Carolina Press, 1968.

Joseph, Peniel E. *Stokely: A Life*. New York: Civitas, 2016.

———. *Waiting 'til the Midnight Hour: A Narrative History of Black Power in America*. New York: Henry Holt, 2006.

Kahrl, Andrew W. *This Land Was Ours: African American Beaches from Jim Crow to the Sunbelt South*. Cambridge, MA: Harvard University Press, 2012.

Katagiri, Yashurio. *The Mississippi State Sovereignty Commission: Civil Rights and States' Rights*. Jackson: University Press of Mississippi, 2001.

Kimbrough, Walter M. *Black Greek 101: The Culture, Customs, and Challenges of Black Fraternities and Sororities*. Danvers, MA: Rosemont, 2003.

Kimeldorf, Howard. *Reds or Rackets? The Making of Radical and Conservative Unions on the Waterfront*. Berkeley: University of California Press, 1988.

King, Martin Luther, Jr. *Stride toward Freedom*. New York: HarperCollins, 1987.

King, Mary E. *Freedom Song: A Personal Story of the 1960s Civil Rights Movement*. New York: William Morrow, 1987.

Kinoy, Arthur. *Rights on Trial: The Odyssey of a People's Lawyer*. Cambridge, MA: Harvard University Press, 1983.

Kirwan, Albert D. *Revolt of the Rednecks: Mississippi Politics, 1876–1925*. Lexington: University of Kentucky Press, 1964.

Kousser, J. Morgan. *Colorblind Injustice: Minority Voting Rights and the Undoing of the Second Reconstruction*. Chapel Hill: University of North Carolina Press, 1999.

Kunstler, William M., and Shelia Isenberg. *My Life as a Radical Lawyer*. New York: Birch Lane, 1994.

Lang, John H. *History of Harrison County, Mississippi*. Gulfport, MS: Dixie, 1936.

Langum, David. *William M. Kunstler: The Most Hated Lawyer in America*. New York: New York University Press, 1999.

Larson, Kate Clifford. *Walk with Me: A Biography of Fannie Lou Hamer*. New York: Oxford University Press, 2021.

Lawson, Steven F. *Black Ballots: Voting Rights in the South, 1944–1969*. Lanham, MD: Lexington, 1999.

Lawson, William H. *No Small Thing: The 1963 Mississippi Freedom Vote*. Jackson: University Press of Mississippi, 2018.

Lee, Chana Kai. *For Freedom's Sake: The Life of Fannie Lou Hamer*. Urbana: University of Illinois Press, 2000.

Lemann, Nicolas. *The Promised Land: The Great Black Migration and How It Changed America*. New York: Vintage, 1991.

Lester, Joan Steinau. *Fire in My Soul: The Life of Eleanor Holmes Norton*. New York: Atria, 2003.

Marsh, Charles. *God's Long Summer: Stories of Faith and Civil Rights*. Princeton, NJ: Princeton University Press, 1997.

Marshall, James P. *The Mississippi Civil Rights Movement and the Kennedy Administration, 1960–64: A History in Documents.* Baton Rouge: Louisiana State University Press, 2018.

———. *Student Activism and Civil Rights in Mississippi: Protest Politics and the Struggles for Racial Justice, 1960–1965.* Baton Rouge: Louisiana State University Press, 2013.

Mason, Gilbert R., and James Patterson Smith. *Beaches, Blood, and Ballots: A Black Doctor's Civil Rights Struggle.* Jackson: University Press of Mississippi, 2000.

Matusow, Allen J. *The Unraveling of America: A History of Liberalism in the 1960s.* New York: Harper & Row, 1984.

McAdam, Doug. *Freedom Summer.* New York: Oxford University Press, 1988.

McCord, William. *Mississippi: The Long, Hot Summer.* New York: W. W. Norton, 1965.

McGuire, Danielle L. *At the Dark End of the Street: Black Women, Rape, and Resistance—A New History of the Civil Rights Movement from Rosa Parks to the Rise of Black Power.* New York: Alfred A. Knopf, 2011.

McMillen, Neil R. *The Citizens' Councils: The Organized Resistance to the Second Reconstruction, 1954–64.* Urbana: University of Illinois Press, 1994.

———. *Dark Journey: Black Mississippians in the Age of Jim Crow.* Urbana: University of Illinois Press, 1989.

Michel, Gregg. *The Struggle for a Better South: The Southern Student Organizing Committee, 1964–1969.* New York: Palgrave McMillian, 2004.

Miller, Keith D. *Voice of Deliverance: The Language of Martin Luther King, Jr., and Its Sources.* Athens: University of Georgia Press, 1998.

Mills, Kay. *This Little Light of Mine: The Life of Fannie Lou Hamer.* Lexington: University Press of Kentucky, 2007.

Moody, Anne. *Coming of Age of Mississippi.* New York: Bantam Dell, 1968.

Moore, Leonard N. *The Defeat of Black Power: Civil Rights and the National Black Political Convention of 1972.* Baton Rouge: Louisiana State University Press, 2018.

Morrison, Minion K. C. *Aaron Henry of Mississippi: Inside Agitator.* Fayetteville: University of Arkansas Press, 2015.

Moye, J. Todd. *Let the People Decide: Black Freedom and White Resistance Movements in Sunflower County, Mississippi, 1945–1986.* Chapel Hill: University of North Carolina Press, 2004.

Musgrove, George Derek. *Rumor, Repression, and Racial Politics: How the Harassment of Black Elected Officials Shaped Post–Civil Rights America.* Athens: University of Georgia Press, 2012.

Nash, Jere, and Andy Taggart. *Mississippi Politics: The Struggle for Power, 1976–2006.* Jackson: University Press of Mississippi, 2006.

Newbeck, Phyl. *Virginia Hasn't Always Been for Lovers: Interracial Marriage Bans and the Case of Richard and Mildred Loving.* Carbondale: University of Southern Illinois Press, 2008.

Newman, Mark. *Desegregating Dixie: The Catholic Church in the South and Desegregation, 1945–1992.* Jackson: University of Mississippi Press, 2018.

Onaci, Edward. *Free the Land: The Republic of New Afrika and the Pursuit of a Black Nation-State.* Chapel Hill: University of North Carolina Press, 2020.

Oshinsky, David M. *"Worse than Slavery": Parchman Prison Farm and the Ordeal of Jim Crow Justice.* New York: Free Press, 1996.

Paget, Karen M. *Patriotic Betrayal: The Inside Story of the CIA's Secret Campaign to Enroll American Students in the Crusade against Communism.* New Haven, CT: Yale University Press, 2015.

Parker, Frank R. *Black Votes Count: Political Empowerment in Mississippi after 1965.* Chapel Hill: University of North Carolina Press, 1990.

Payne, Charles. *I've Got the Light of Freedom: The Organizing Tradition and the Mississippi Freedom Struggle.* Berkeley: University of California Press, 2007.

Pratt, Robert A. *Selma's Bloody Sunday: Protest, Voting Rights, and the Struggle for Racial Equality.* Baltimore: Johns Hopkins University Press, 2017.

Rader, Victoria. *Signal through the Flames: Mitch Snyder and America's Homeless.* Kansas City, MO: Sheed & Ward, 1986.

Raines, Howell. *My Soul Is Rested: Movement Days in the Deep South Remembered.* New York: Penguin, 1977.

Ransby, Barbara. *Ella Baker and the Black Freedom Movement: A Radical Democratic Vision.* Chapel Hill: University of North Carolina Press, 2003.

Reinhard, Rachel B. *The Politics of Change: The Mississippi Freedom Democratic Party—A Case Study of the Rise (and Fall) of Insurgency.* Edited by Mike Miller. Shorewood, WI: Euclid Avenue, 2020.

Robnett, Belinda. *How Long? How Long? African-American Women in the Struggle for Civil Rights.* New York: Oxford University Press, 1997.

Rosen, Ruth. *The World Split Open: How the Modern Women's Movement Changed America.* New York: Penguin, 2000.

Ross, Lawrence C., Jr. *The Divine Nine: The History of African American Fraternities and Sororities.* New York: Kensington, 2000.

Rothschild, Mary Aickin. *A Case of Black and White: Northern Volunteers and the Southern Freedom Summers, 1964–65.* Westport, CT: Greenwood, 1982.

Russell, Maud. *Men along the Shore.* New York: Brussel & Brussel, 1966.

Salter, John R., Jr. *Jackson, Mississippi: An American Chronicle of Struggle and Schism.* Hicksville, NY: Exposition, 1979.

Sanders, Crystal. *A Chance for Change: Head Start and Mississippi's Black Freedom Struggle.* Chapel Hill: University of North Carolina Press, 2016.

Sanford, M., and R. J. Caire. *The Past at the Pass.* Pass Christian, MS: Lafayette, 1980.

Sitkoff, Harvard. *A New Deal for Blacks: The Emergence of Civil Rights as a National Issue*, vol. 1. New York: Oxford University Press, 1978.

———. *The Struggle for Black Equality, 1954–1992.* Rev. ed. New York: Hill and Wang, 1993.

Smead, Howard. *Blood Justice: The Lynching of Mack Charles Parker.* New York: Oxford University Press, 1986.

Sojourner, Sue, with Cheryl Reitan. *Thunder of Freedom: Black Leadership and the Transformation of 1960s Mississippi.* Lexington: University Press of Kentucky, 2013.

Sokol, Jason. *There Goes My Everything: White Southerners in the Age of Civil Rights, 1945–1975.* New York: Vintage, 2007.

Street, Joe, and Henry Knight Lozano, eds. *The Shadow of Selma*. Gainesville: University Press of Florida, 2018.

Sutherland, Elizabeth, ed. *Letters from Mississippi*. New York: McGraw-Hill, 1965.

Todd, Lisa Anderson. *For a Voice and the Vote: My Journey with the Mississippi Freedom Democratic Party*. Lexington: University Press of Kentucky, 2014.

Umoja, Akinyele Omowales. *We Will Shoot Back: Armed Resistance in the Mississippi Freedom Movement*. New York: New York University Press, 2013.

Visser-Maessen, Laura. *Robert Parris Moses: A Life in Civil Rights and Leadership at the Grassroots*. Chapel Hill: University of North Carolina Press, 2016.

Waldschmidt-Nelson, Britta. *Dreams and Nightmares: Martin Luther King Jr., Malcolm X, and the Struggle for Black Equality in America*. Gainesville: University Press of Florida, 2012.

Walton, Hanes, Jr. *Black Political Parties: An Historical and Political Analysis*. New York: Free Press, 1972.

Watson, Bruce. *Freedom Summer: The Savage Season of 1964 That Made Mississippi Burn and Made America a Democracy*. New York: Penguin, 2010.

Watters, Pat, and Reese Cleghorn. *Climbing Jacob's Ladder: The Arrival of Negroes in Southern Politics*. New York: Harcourt, Brace & World, 1967.

Wendt, Simon. *The Spirit and the Shotgun: Armed Resistance and the Struggle for Civil Rights*. Gainesville: University Press of Florida, 2007.

White, Deborah Gray. *Ar'n't I a Woman? Female Slaves in the Plantation South*, rev. ed. New York: W. W. Norton, 1999.

Whitfield, Stephen J. *A Death in the Delta: The Story of Emmett Till*. Baltimore: Johns Hopkins University Press, 1988.

Williams, Michael Vinson. *Medgar Evers: Mississippi Martyr*. Fayetteville: University of Arkansas Press, 2011.

Williamson, Joy Ann. *Radicalizing the Ebony Tower: Black Colleges and the Black Freedom Struggle in Mississippi*. New York: Teachers College Press, 2008.

Wirt, Frederick M. *Politics of Southern Equality: Law and Social Change in a Mississippi County*. Chicago: Aldine, 1970.

Woodward, C. Vann. *The Strange Career of Jim Crow*. 1st ed. New York: Oxford University Press, 1955.

———. *Tom Watson: Agrarian Rebel*. New York: Oxford University Press, 1938.

Wright-Brown, Flonzie. *Looking Back to Move Ahead: An Experience of History and Hope*. Germantown, OH: FBW & Associates, 1994.

Young, Andrew. *An Easy Burden: The Civil Rights Movement and the Transformation of America*. 2nd ed. New York: HarperCollins, 2004.

Zinn, Howard. *SNCC: The New Abolitionists*. 2nd ed. Boston: Beacon, 1965.

Zwiers, Maarten. *Senator James Eastland: Mississippi's Jim Crow Democrat*. Baton Rouge: University of Louisiana Press, 2015.

## CHAPTERS IN EDITED COLLECTIONS

Branch, Carol D. "Variegated Roots: The Foundations of Stepping." In *African American Fraternities and Sororities: The Legacy and the Vision*, edited by Tamara L. Brown,

Gregory S. Parks, and Calrenda M. Phillips, 1–8. Lexington: University Press of Kentucky, 2005.

Cobb, James C. "World War II and the Mind of the Modern South." In *Remaking Dixie: The Impact of World War II on the American South*, edited by Neil McMillen, 3–20. Jackson: University of Mississippi Press, 1997.

Harris, Robert L., Jr. "Lobbying Congress for Civil Rights: The American Council on Human Rights, 1948–1963." In *African American Fraternities and Sororities: The Legacy and the Vision*, edited by Tamara L. Brown, Gregory S. Parks, and Calrenda M. Phillips, 211–29. Lexington: University Press of Kentucky, 2005.

Hirsch, Arnold R. "Simply a Matter of Black and White: The Transformation of Race and Politics in Twentieth-Century New Orleans." In *Creole New Orleans: Race and Americanization*, edited by Arnold R. Hirsch and Joseph Logsdon, 262–320. Baton Rouge: Louisiana State University Press, 1992.

McCoy, Marcella L. "Calls: An Inquiry into Their Origin, Meaning, and Function." In *African American Fraternities and Sororities: The Legacy and the Vision*, edited by Tamara L. Brown, Gregory S. Parks, and Calrenda M. Phillips, 331–50. Lexington: University Press of Kentucky, 2005.

McMillen, Neil. "Fighting for What We Didn't Have: How Mississippi's Black Veterans Remember World War II." In *Remaking Dixie: The Impact of World War II on the American South*, edited by Neil McMillen, 93–110. Jackson: University of Mississippi Press, 1997.

Mosley, Donald C. "The Labor Union Movement." In *A History of Mississippi*, vol. 2, edited by Richard Aubrey McLemore, 250–73. Jackson: University Press of Mississippi, 1973.

Parks, Gregory S., and Tamara L. Brown. "'In the Fell Clutch of Circumstance': Pledging and the Black Greek Experience." In *African American Fraternities and Sororities: The Legacy and the Vision*, edited by Tamara L. Brown, Gregory S. Parks, and Calrenda M. Phillips, 437–64. Lexington: University Press of Kentucky, 2005.

Pillar, James J. "Religious and Cultural Life, 1817–1860." In *A History of Mississippi*, vol. 1, edited by Richard Aubrey McLemore, 378–419. Jackson: University Press of Mississippi, 1973.

Rankin, David C. "The Politics of Caste: Free Colored Leadership in New Orleans during the Civil War." In *Louisiana's Black Heritage*, edited by Robert R. MacDonald, John R. Kemp, and Edward F. Haas, 107–46. New Orleans: Louisiana State Museum, 1979.

Smith, James Patterson. "Local Leadership, the Biloxi Beach Riot, and the Origins of the Civil Rights Movement on the Mississippi Gulf Coast, 1959–1964." In *Sunbelt Revolution: The Historical Progression of the Civil Rights Struggle in the Gulf South, 1866–2000*, edited by Samuel C. Hyde Jr., 210–33. Gainesville: University Press of Florida, 2003.

Strickland, Arvah E. "Remembering Hattiesburg: Growing Up Black in Wartime Mississippi." In *Remaking Dixie: The Impact of World War II on the American South*, edited by Neil McMillen, 146–58. Jackson: University of Mississippi Press, 1997.

Williamson, Joy Ann. "Black Colleges and Civil Rights Organizing and Mobilizing in Jackson, Mississippi." In *Higher Education and the Civil Rights Movement: White*

*Supremacy, Black Southerners, and College Campuses*, edited by Peter Wallenstein, 116–36. Gainesville: University Press of Florida, 2008.

JOURNAL ARTICLES

Bolton, Charles C. "Mississippi's School Equalization Program, 1945–1954: A Last Gasp to Try to Maintain a Segregated Educational System." *Journal of Southern History* 66, no. 4 (November 2000): 781–814.

Butler, Michael. "The Mississippi State Sovereignty Commission and Beach Integration, 1959–1963: A Cotton-Patch Gestapo?" *Journal of Southern History* 68, no. 1 (February 2002): 107–48.

Clune, Erin Elizabeth. "From Light Copper to the Blackest and Lowest Type: Daniel Thompkins and the Racial Order of the Global New South." *Journal of Southern History* 76, no. 2 (May 2010): 275–314.

Cobb, James C. "'Somebody Done Nailed Us on the Cross': Federal Farm and Welfare Policy and the Civil Rights Movement in the Mississippi Delta." *Journal of American History* 77, no. 3 (December 1990): 912–36.

Crouch, Robert F. "The Ingalls Story in Mississippi, 1938–1958." *Journal of Mississippi History* 26 (August 1964): 192–206.

Dailey, Jane. "Sex, Segregation, and the Sacred after *Brown*." *Journal of American History* 91, no. 1 (June 2004): 119–44.

Draper, Alan. "Class and Politics in the Mississippi Movement: An Analysis of the Mississippi Freedom Democratic Party Delegation," *Journal of Southern History* 82, no. 2 (May 2016): 269–304.

Elmore, Bartow J. "The American Beverage Industry and the Development of Curbside Recycling Programs, 1950–2000," *Business History Review* 86, no. 3 (Autumn 2012): 477–501.

Garrison, David F. "District of Columbia's Elected Advisory Neighborhood Commissions: An Unlikely Experiment in Governance at the Grassroots." *State & Local Government Review* 43, no. 2 (August 2011): 159–66.

Grim, Valerie. "Black Participation in the Farmers Home Administration and Agricultural Stabilization and Conservation Service, 1964–1990." *Agricultural History* 70, no. 2 (Spring 1996): 321–36.

Guyot, Lawrence, and Mike Thelwell. "The Politics of Necessity and Survival in Mississippi." *Freedomways* 6, no. 3 (1967): 120–32.

Hall, Jacquelyn Dowd. "The Long Civil Rights Movement and the Political Uses of the Past." *Journal of American History* 91, no. 4 (March 2005): 1233–263.

Hall, Simon. "'On the Tail of the Panther': Black Power and the 1967 Conference for New Politics." *Journal of American Studies* 37, no. 1 (2003): 59–78.

Hathorn, Billy Burton. "Challenging the Status Quo: Rubel Lex Phillips and the Mississippi Republican Party, 1963–1967." *Journal of Mississippi History* 47 (November 1985): 240–64.

Lowe, Maria. "'Sowing the Seeds of Discontent': Tougaloo College's Social Science Forums as a Prefigurative Movement Free Space, 1952–1964." *Journal of Black Studies* 39, no. 6 (July 2009): 865–87.

MacKenzie, Andre. "Community Service and Social Action: Using the Past to Guide the Future of Black Greek-Letter Fraternities." *NASPA Journal* 28, no. 1 (Fall 1990): 30–36.

Nelson, Bruce. "Organized Labor and the Struggle for Black Equality in Mobile during World War II." *Journal of American History* 80, no. 3 (December 1993): 952–88.

Rickford, Russell. "'We Can't Grow Food on All This Concrete': The Land Question, Agrarianism, and Black Nationalist Thought in the Late 1960s and 1970s." *Journal of American History* 103, no. 4 (2017): 956–80.

Saloman, Lester M. "The Time Dimension in Policy Evaluation: The Case of the New Deal Land-Reform Experiments." *Public Policy* 27, no. 2 (Spring 1979): 129–83.


THESES AND DISSERTATIONS

Buzard-Boyett, Patricia. "Race and Justice in Mississippi's Central Piney Woods, 1940–2010." PhD diss., University of Southern Mississippi, 2011.

Chesteen, Richard Dallas. "Change and Reaction in a Mississippi Delta Civil Community." PhD diss., University of Mississippi, 1975.

Davis, Vanessa Lynn. "'Sisters and Brothers All': The Mississippi Freedom Democratic Party and the Struggle for Political Equality." PhD diss., Vanderbilt University, 1996.

Gentine, Steven M. "The Mississippi Freedom Democratic Party's Congressional Challenge of 1964–65: A Case Study in Radical Persuasion." MS thesis, Florida State University, 2009.

McLemore, Leslie Burl. "The Mississippi Freedom Democratic Party: A Case Study of Grassroots Politics." PhD diss., University of Massachusetts, 1971.

Reinhard, Rachel B. "Politics of Change: The Mississippi Freedom Democratic Party and the Emergence of a Black Political Voice in Mississippi." PhD diss., University of California–Berkeley, 2005.

Sistrom, Michael Paul. "'Authors of the Liberation': The Mississippi Freedom Democrats and the Redefinition of Politics." PhD diss., University of North Carolina, 2002.

# INDEX

Abernathy, Ralph, 147

Abernethy, Thomas, 106, 109, 123

Adam, Bidwell, 28

Adams, Victoria Gray, 74, 83, 115, 120, 131; and Atlantic City, 89–90; and civil rights movement, 250, 251; and congressional campaigns, 82, 95, 106, 142; death of, 252; and other civil rights organizations, 182, 183; and relationship with Guyot, 147, 149

Adams Morgan (DC), 221

Advisory Neighborhood Commission (ANC), 1, 215, 228, 231–32

Afro-Academic Cultural, Technological, and Scientific Olympics, 213

Agriculture, Department of, 110, 144

Agricultural Stabilization and Conservation Service (ASCS), 144

Air Force Academy, 167

Alabama, 36, 59, 138, 145, 187, 253, 261, 262. See also Selma-to-Montgomery March

Albany Movement (GA), 136

Alcorn College, 41, 46, 191

Alexander, Yvette, 226

Allen, Anita Ford, 212

Allen, Elizabeth, 83

Allen, Louis, 83

Allen v. Milligan, 262

American Council on Human Rights, 33

American Federation of Labor–Congress of Industrial Organizations (AFL-CIO). See unions

American Legion, 123

American Missionary Association, 29

Americans for Democratic Action (ADA), 113

Ames, Adelbert, 9

Amherst College (MA), 110

Anacostia (DC), 215, 216, 218, 219

Anderson, Ruben, 25, 191

Aptheker, Herbert, 151

Arizona, 32, 262–63

armed self-defense, 161, 182–83, 184, 185, 188, 195; and Meredith March, 163–64; and Natchez movement, 133–34, 135–36, 137

Armstrong Tire and Rubber, 133

Arnold, Ed, 222

Asmard, Charles, 12

Asmard, Madelon, 12

Assembly of Unrepresented People, 121

Atlanta, 2, 41, 46, 86, 98, 125, 165, 189, 211, 217

Atlanta Project, 170

Atlanta separatists, 170, 207

Atlantic City, DNC convention in, 4, 90–92, 100, 109, 114, 145; background of MFDP delegates at, 104, 125–26, 147, 153–54, 192; and impact on and similarities to the congressional challenge, 106–7, 111, 113, 115, 124; and Guyot's views on convention compromise, 93–94; and MFDP fallout with white liberals and NAACP, 131–32, 161; and MFDP-SNCC split, 67, 92, 97, 103–5, 108, 254; preparations for, 84–85, 87, 89–90. See also Voting Rights Act of 1965

Atwater, Lee, 238–39
Auguste, Joseph, 14

Bailey, Howard Taft, 165
Bailey, John, 90
*Bailey v. Patterson*, 38
Baker, Ella, 73, 75, 240, 248; and founding of
SNCC, 36, 39; and MFDP, 89, 91, 116; and
sexism, 147, 171; and views on leadership,
40–41
Baker, James, 216
Baker, Robert, 125
Baker, Susan, 216
*Baker v. Carr*, 90, 145, 156, 166
Balance Agriculture with Industry, 17
Baldwin, James, 34
Banks, Fred, Jr., 25, 194
Barnes, Minnie, 154
Barnes, Thelma, 199
Barnett, Ross, 39, 51, 119, 225
Barry, Marion, 1, 3, 5, 209–11; and Guyot, 210,
212–13, 219–20, 224–25, 228–29, 231–32,
237, 259, 264; and LGBT rights, 226–27;
and political comeback, 231–32, 236–37;
and rise to power, 211–12; and SNCC, 40,
46, 54, 91, 104, 210–11, 212; and whites
in DC, 212. *See also* Donaldson, Ivanhoe;
Treadwell, Mary; Washington, DC
Basinger, John, 55, 72, 273n48
Batesville, MS, 118, 136, 154
Bay St. Louis, MS, 8, 10, 11, 16, 26
Beittel, Adam, 32, 34, 35, 53
Belafonte, Harry, 50
Bender, William Albert, 29
Bennett, Maybelle, 243, 246
Benton County, MS, 144
*Berkeley Barb* (newspaper), 154–55
Biami, Mary Evaline. *See* Guyot, Mary
Biden, Joseph, 262
Bilbo, Theodore, 26–27, 119
Biloxi, 12, 17, 18, 19–20, 31, 85, 142
Black and Tan Republicans, 19
Black Belt counties, 9, 137, 138
Black Belt Program, 98, 99, 100, 103, 109
Black History Month, 33, 252

*Black Natchez* (film), 135
Black Panther Party, 171, 192, 196, 208, 220
Black Power, 3, 5, 133, 162–63, 211, 252;
criticism of, 167, 175, 208; and damage
to MFDP, 175, 179, 187; and Guyot, 149,
163–64, 171–72, 191, 194, 196–97, 264; and
Loyalist Democrats, 204, 207–8; and New
Left, 183, 220–21; and relationship with
MFDP, 158, 164, 166, 170–71, 174, 182–84,
193, 223
Black Power conference (Newark),
182–83, 193
Blackwell, Unita, 3, 78, 93, 143, 147, 155, 250
Blanco, Kathleen, 253
Block, Sam, 42–43, 46, 50, 53, 81, 248
Bloody Sunday. *See* Selma-to-Montgomery
March
Board of Education (DC), 214–15, 230, 237
Bogalusa, LA, 134
Bolivar County, MS, 142, 154, 175
Bolton, MS, 181
Bond, Julian, 59, 173, 211, 227, 252–53,
255, 257
Borinski, Ernst, 29–30
bottle bill. *See* recycling, in Washington, DC
Bottle Initiative Committee (DC), 222
Borinski, Ernest, 29, 35–36
Bowers, Sam, 151
Branch, A. A., 34
Branch, Rose, 34
Branch, Taylor, 255
Brandon, Wiley, 52
Bright Star Baptist Church (Natchez),
135–36, 164
Brimmer, Andre, 233
Britt, May, 28
Britton, A. B., 159–60
Brookhaven, MS, 20, 131
Brooks, Lela, 174, 176
Brooks, Maegan Parker, 259
Brooks, Owen, 155, 171, 180, 181, 182, 189,
199, 206, 254
Brosse, Julia de La, 13
Brown, Ben, 179–80
Brown, H. Rap, 182, 184, 192–93, 194

Brown, John R., 120

Brown, Luvaghn, 3, 43, 44, 45, 54, 105, 109

Brown, Minniejean, 80

Brown, Otis, Jr., 173, 174, 176

Brown, Theresa, 215

*Brown v. Board of Education*, 19, 23, 24, 25, 27, 42, 133

Bruce, Walter, 117

Bryant, Carolyn, 23

Bryant, Roy, 23

Buffington, John, 201, 204

Bunche, Ralph, 34

Bush, George H. W., 5, 224, 227–28, 238–39

Bush, George W., 252–53, 258

*Bush v. Vera*, 258

Cagin, Seth, 257

Califano, Joseph, Jr., 139

California, 57, 91, 107, 128, 149, 154, 193

California Democratic Council, 80

Cameron, John, 82

Campbell, Cecil, 169

Camp Shelby, 18

Canton, 164, 170, 180, 192

*Capital City Magazine*, 218

Caribbean, 8, 239

Carmichael, Stokely, 2, 149, 173, 174; and Black Power, 133, 162, 167; and Black separatists, 170, 207; and celebrity status, 3, 162, 164–65; and Guyot, 65, 94–95, 154–55, 163, 180, 207; later life of, 247–48, 252; and Meredith March, 161–62, 163; and MFDP, 95, 137, 184; personality of, 86, 87; and Vietnam War, 123, 164

Carr, Oscar, Jr., 197, 203

Carroll County, MS, 57, 58, 125

Carrollton, 59

Carson, Clayborne, 248, 257

Carter, Hodding, III, 123, 126, 130, 197–98, 203, 204

Carter, Jimmy, 248

Carter, Tom, 152

Catholicism, 8, 213, 221, 259; and Gulf Coast, 12, 13; and influence on Guyot, 2, 16, 24,

27, 35–36, 76, 227, 263; and racism, 7, 8, 20, 24–27

Central Intelligence Agency (CIA), 191, 249

Chamber of Commerce, Biloxi, 20

Chaney, James, 87, 91, 199, 257

Charlot tract (Pass Christian), 13

Chavous, Kevin, 231, 235

Cheek, James, 238

Chicago, 20, 23, 42, 46, 51, 57, 183, 235. *See also* presidential election of 1968

*Chicago Daily News*, 62

*Chicago Defender*, 21

Child Development Group of Mississippi (CDGM), 151–52, 167, 168, 180, 192

Christian Life Commission, 25

Citizens Association of Georgetown, 223

Civil Rights Act of 1957, 158

Civil Rights Act of 1964, 136, 156, 195, 233

Civil Rights Commission, 65

civil rights conferences, 249–52, 254–55, 257

Civil Rights History Project, 227

Claiborne County, MS, 160, 167, 169

Clark, Ed, 195–96, 221

Clark, Jim, 115

Clark, Ramsey, 175

Clark, Robert, 187–90, 194, 199, 200, 201–2, 205

Clark, Septima, 73

Clarke, David, 234

Clarksdale, MS, 32, 197, 203

class, 5, 18–19, 74; and Black education, 13, 20, 187; and Guyot, 2, 7, 21, 30, 33, 41–42, 136, 147; and Howard University, 238, 243–44; and MFDP, 104, 126–27, 135, 146–47, 204; and SNCC, 71, 98; and Washington, DC, 213, 214, 222–23, 225, 232, 234; and white racism, 126, 132, 196, 221

Clay County, 201

Clayton, Claude, 72, 159

Clean Capital City Committee (CCCC), 222

Clergy against Initiative 28 (DC), 222

Cleveland, MS, 39, 41, 42, 43–44, 45, 116, 255

Cleveland, Grover, 10

Clifton Terrace Apartments, 213

Clinton, Bill, 233, 234, 235, 237

Coahoma County, MS, 32, 197

Coalition for the Homeless. *See* Washington, DC: and homelessness

Coates, TaNehisi, 243

Cobb, Charlie, 48, 71, 74, 83, 94

Coleman, J. P., 68, 119–20

Coles, Robert, 81

Collier, Clinton, 146, 155, 160, 161, 166

Colmer, William, 26–27, 82, 106, 146, 153, 155, 156, 160, 200

colorism, 8–9, 28, 30, 47–48, 238

Columbia Heights (DC), 213–14, 238, 244

*Commentary* (journal), 132

Commission on Latino Development, 230

communism. *See* Maoists; red-baiting

Communist Propaganda Control Law, 117

Community for Creative Nonviolence (CCNV), 213–17, 218–20

Compromise of 1877, 10

Confederate States of America, 8

congressional challenge, 2, 95, 97–98, 103, 146, 165, 210, 263; and antiwar movement, 121, 123; beginnings of, 106–7, 111; and Black Power, 158; and civil rights opposition to, 108–9, 111, 196; and Coleman nomination, 120; demonstrations supporting, 111–12, 118–19, 123–24; dismissal of, 124; and *Dombrowski*, 117, 119; and effects on funds and other projects, 110, 124–25, 130, 141, 154; and Freedom Vote, 99–100; Guyot's views on, 125–26, 192, 255; official opposition to, 113–14, 118, 123; and Selma, 115–16; support for, 121, 124, 130, 144; testimonies and preparation for, 109–10, 112–13, 115, 117–18; and Voting Rights Act, 124, 137–40

congressional elections, 1966. *See* Democratic primary (MS), 1966

Congress of Racial Equality (CORE), 48, 64, 100, 149, 184, 252; and relations with other civil rights groups, 39, 74, 107–8, 115, 134, 172–73, 193

Connor, Peggy, 91, 145, 149

*Connor v. Johnson*, 145

Constitutional Accountability Center, 261

Constitution of 1890, Mississippi, 9, 10, 19, 49, 149–50

Control Board (DC), 233–37

convention challenge. *See* Atlantic City

Conyers, John, 202

Cotton, MacArthur, 64–65

Coumaris, Tom, 245

Council of Federated Organizations (COFO), 44, 64, 90, 97, 99, 115, 122, 133, 136; and Agricultural Stabilization and Conservation Service, 144; and Atlantic City, 84–85, 97, 106; collapse of, 102, 113–14, 116, 119, 126, 129; and congressional challenge, 97, 106, 108, 113, 114–15, 116; formation of, 39; and Freedom Summer, 62, 67, 70–71, 80, 83–84, 87, 98; and Greenwood, 50, 52; and Gulf Coast, 85–86, 116; and Guyot, 39–40, 68, 69, 73, 82, 94, 130; and Hattiesburg, 74–78, 80; and homosexuality, 227; internal divisions in, 70–71, 74, 81–82, 97, 100, 107–8, 109, 110–11; legacy of, 155, 180–81, 248; and MFDP, 80–82, 108, 118; and voter registration, 39–40, 66, 67–68, 70, 184; and Young Democrats, 127–28

Courts, Gus, 20

Cox, Courtland, 97, 212

Cox, Harold, 82, 115

Cox, Minnie, 11

Crawford, H. R., 223, 229–30

*Crawford v. Marion County Election Board*, 258

Credentials Committee, 90, 91–92

Cropp, Linda, 246–47

Cupit, Danny, 200

Current, Gloster, 97–98, 99

Dahmer, Vernon, 73–74, 150–51

*Daily Californian*, 154

*Daily Times Leader* (West Point, MS), 154

Daley, Richard, 203

Darden, C. R., 32

Darrow, Clarence, 35

Davis, Charlene Drew, 246

Davis, Ossie, 110

Davis, Sammy, Jr., 28

*DCWatch* (magazine), 238

Deacons of Defense and Justice, 134, 137, 163–64, 185, 194

Dedeaux, Curtis, 19–20, 31–32

Defense Preparedness Subcommittee (US Senate), 127

Defner, Armand, 255

DeLay, Tom, 233

*Delta Democrat-Times*, 62, 123, 126, 167, 186

Delta Ministry, 134, 152, 176, 193; and Charles Evers, 172–73, 180; and Greenville sit-in, 152–53; and MFDP, 171, 181, 199, 200, 204, 206; and voter registration, 155, 162, 175, 197, 205

Delta State University, 255

Democratic National Committee, 131, 142

Democratic National Convention, 1964. *See* Atlantic City

Democratic National Convention, 1968. *See* presidential election of 1968

Democratic National Convention, 1996, 236

Democratic Party (MS). *See* Atlantic City; congressional challenge; Loyalist Democrats, Mississippi Freedom Democratic Party

Democratic Party (national), 196, 206–7, 263. *See also* Atlantic City; congressional challenge; Johnson, Lyndon Baines; Young Democratic Clubs of Mississippi (YDCM)

Democratic primary (MS), 1946, 21, 26–27, 29

Democratic primary (MS.), 1963, 68

Democratic primary (MS), 1964, 82–83

Democratic primary (MS), 1966, 142, 145–46, 154–56, 158–59, 160, 166, 167

Democratic primary (MS), 1967, 180–81

Democratic primary (MS), 1968, 199–200

Dennis, Dave, 39, 74, 100, 149, 252

Department of Human Services (DC), 216, 220

Derian, Patricia, 200

Detroit, 57, 149, 193, 194, 202

Detroit uprising, 184

Devine, Anne, 137, 143, 192, 206; and congressional challenge, 95–96, 106, 107, 112, 113, 115, 116, 123; health of, 250; and relationship with Guyot, 90

diGenova, Joseph, 218, 227

Diggs, Charles, 123, 212

Dilworth, Lee, 117

Dittmer, John, 255

Dixon, Sharon Pratt, 228, 229–30, 232

Doar, John, 52, 53, 59, 63, 72, 79–80, 82

Dole, Bob, 226

Dombrowski, Diana, 225

Dombrowski, James, 117

*Dombrowski v. Pfister*, 117, 119

Dominican Republic, 123, 128

Donaldson, Ivanhoe, 50, 71, 76, 212–13, 217, 218, 224, 237

Douglass, Jimmy Lee, 173

Downhill Battle, 251–52

Downtown Cluster of Congregations, 229

Dray, Phillip, 257

Drummond, Dock, 146, 166

Du Bois, W. E. B., 33

Dunn, Felix, 19

DuPont Circle (DC), 221

DuPont Circle Neighborhood Ecology Corporation (DC), 221, 222

Eames, Nik, 242–44

Eastland, James, 127, 131, 153, 173, 197, 198, 234; and congressional challenge, 123; and electoral campaigns, 140, 160, 166, 167, 169, 186; and federal registrars in Mississippi, 142, 175, 145; and judicial nominations, 115, 120, and red-baiting, 113–14, 151, 152

Edmonds, Stanley, 154

Edmund Pettus Bridge, 115, 250

educational levels, Black, 8, 16, 20, 24, 41, 173. *See also* Catholicism

Edwards, MS, 181

Eisenhower, Dwight, 72, 120

election of 1967 (MS), 172–73, 180–81, 185–90

election of 1971 (MS), 193–94, 206
Else, John, 70
Environmental Action Foundation, 222
Erwin, MS, 12
Euclid House, 213, 214
Evans, Rowland, 114, 128, 202
*Evening Exchange* (television show), 218
Evers, Charles, 76, 132, 150, 195, 211, 247–48;
    and cooperation with MFDP, 81, 118,
    119, 145, 151, 172–73; and Guyot, 161,
    165, 190–91, 207–8, 252; and hostility
    toward MFDP, 82, 123, 141, 161, 167–68,
    169, 177; and political organizing and
    patronage, 143, 155, 160, 167, 168, 169,
    181; and Republic of New Afrika, 193–94;
    and Third Congressional District election,
    190–92. *See also* election of 1967 (MS);
    Natchez; presidential election of 1968;
    Young Democratic Clubs of Mississippi
    (YDCM)
Evers, Medgar, 2, 27, 30, 31, 34, 77; and other
    civil rights activists, 37, 39; assassination
    of, 49, 59, 60, 67; and comparisons to
    Guyot, 41, 42
Ewing, Clay, 58
Ewing, F. C., 58
*Eyes on the Prize* (documentary), 251–52

Faircloth, Lauch, 236
Fairly, Kenneth, 204
Fanon, Franz, 183
Farmer, James, 64, 97, 111, 115, 116–17
Farm Security Administration, 146, 186
Fast for Freedom, 142
Fauntroy, Walter, 211, 217, 227, 228
Fayette, MS, 150, 191, 252
Federal Bureau of Investigation (FBI), 59, 83,
    89, 191, 199, 257; and Barry administra-
    tion, 216, 228, 238; and indifference to
    civil rights workers, 44, 83; and MFDP,
    91, 111; and murders of Black men, 31, 151;
    and white resistance, 46, 66; and Winona
    beatings, 57, 58, 59–60, 66
Fenty, Adrian, 246–47

Ferguson, Angella, 239
Fifth Circuit Court of Appeals, 73, 74, 82, 84,
    119–20, 169–70
Fifth Congressional District (MS), 73, 82, 85,
    106, 116, 146, 155, 156, 199, 200
Fifteenth Amendment, 111
Financial Responsibility and Management
    Assistance Authority. *See* Control Board
    (DC)
Finch, James, 78
First Amendment, 117
First Congressional District (MS), 106, 146,
    166, 199
First National Bank of Clarksdale, 203
Fitzgerald, Doll, 223
Fletcher, Arthur, 212
Ford Foundation, 252
Foreman, James, 52, 165, 252
Forrest County, MS,. *See* Hattiesburg
Forrest County Work Camp, 79
*Fortner v. Barnett*, 144–45
Fourteenth Amendment, 111, 117, 257
Fourth Congressional District (MS), 97, 106,
    146, 160, 161, 199, 200
Freedom Day, 74–76, 78, 79
"freedom high," 103, 105, 165, 245
Freedom Houses, 43, 74, 75, 77, 170
Freedom Information Service (FIS), 176–77,
    184
Freedom Rides, 36, 37, 38–39, 64
Freedom Schools, 72, 85, 87, 104, 108, 122,
    153, 171, 173
Freedom Summer, 107, 155, 171, 250, 257; an-
    niversaries of, 248–49, 251; and Atlantic
    City, 89, 91, 103; and COFO, 81–82, 84;
    and congressional challenge, 110; effects
    on participants in, 81, 105–6, 150; and
    Freedom Votes, 68, 69, 99–100; and
    Guyot, 82–83, 85, 86, 104–5, 136; and
    Martin Luther King Jr., 87, 89; and MFDP,
    66, 67, 80, 102; organizers of, 2, 69,
    97–98; and violence against participants,
    87; and Voting Rights Act, 137–38; and
    white volunteers, 70–72, 75–76, 110–11

Freedom Vote: (1963), 67, 68–71, 73, 75, 81–82, 158; (1964), 94, 95, 99–100, 104–5, 106, 107, 113
*Freedomways* (journal), 156, 163
free speech movement, 106
Fusco, Liz, 108
fusion (nineteenth century), 10
fusion (1968). *See* Loyalist Democrats

Gaither, Tom, 39
Galbraith, John Kenneth, 34, 173
Galler, Roberta, 57
Gamble, Larry, 125
GAP Community Child-Care Center, 230
Garriga, Lester, 26
Gary Convention (National Black Political Convention), 204
General Assembly (Howard University), 243
General Hospital (DC), 237
"genocide" bill. *See* sterilization
gentrification, 214–15, 239–40, 244
Georgetown (DC), 214–15, 218, 223
Georgetown Clergy Association, 214
Gerow, Richard, 24–25
gerrymandering, 258, 262
Giant Foods, 211
GI Bill of Rights, 41
Gingrich, Newt, 233, 234, 235, 236
Ginsburg, Ruth Bader, 262
Glover, Jesse James, 65
Glover, Thelma, 118
Goldwater, Barry, 94, 95
Goodloe, Flonzie, 192
Goodman, Andrew, 87, 89, 91, 199, 257
Goodman, Jan, 199, 202
Grant, Ulysses S., 9
Graves, Charlie, 154
Gray, Tony, 83
Gray, Victoria. *See* Adams, Victoria Gray
Gray, Vincent, 247, 259
Great Depression, 15–16, 22–23, 186
Great Society, 90, 120, 129, 156, 223
Greek fraternities, 32–33

Greene, George, 51, 133
Greene, Percy, 137
Greenville, MS, 62, 70, 72, 108, 128, 130, 199; sit-in, 152–53
Greenwood, MS, 26, 63, 68, 78, 81, 86; and civil rights reunions, 248; and comparisons to other Mississippi cities, 74; and Martin Luther King Jr., 87, 89; and Meredith March, 162; and MFDP, 142–43; and SNCC, 3, 38, 40, 42–45, 48–53, 62–63, 64–65, 94–95; and Winona beatings, 54, 55, 56, 57, 58, 59, 73
*Greenwood (MS) Commonwealth*, 45, 52, 155, 162
Gregory, Dick, 50, 51, 79, 173, 259
Grenada, MS, 162, 180
Griffin, Charles, 192
Guillot, August, 14
Guillot, Joseph, 14
Guinan, Ed, 213
Gulf Coast, MS, 1, 7, 38, 73, 103, 106, 126; and Black voting, 8–9, 14–15, 18–20; compared to rest of Mississippi, 2, 9–10, 11–12, 21, 27, 30–31, 41–42, 136, 263; economic and demographic changes in, 13, 16–18, 144–45; and French influence, 8–9, 12; and Guyot family, 14, 17–18, 29, 33–34, 41; and MFDP, 85–86, 155; and racial violence, 21–22, 31–32, 155
Gulfport, MS, 17, 18, 20, 23, 85, 155
Guyot, Albert (brother), 18
Guyot, Armand (great-uncle), 14
Guyot, Armand Arthur (great-grandfather), 11, 14–15
Guyot, Armantine (great-aunt), 14
Guyot, Arthur (great-great-uncle), 14
Guyot, Caesar (great-uncle), 14
Guyot, Edith (aunt), 15
Guyot, Elinore (grandmother), 15
Guyot, Elvina (great-aunt), 15
Guyot, Ernest (great-great-uncle), 14
Guyot, Jules (brother), 18, 172
Guyot, Julie (daughter), 210, 259, 260
Guyot, Lawrence, Sr. (father), 15, 16, 17

Guyot, Lawrence, Jr.: and absence from Atlantic City, 91, 92, 93; accomplishments of, 1–3, 206–8, 263–64; and Advisory Neighborhood Commission, 231–32, 239–40, 245–46; and armed self-defense, 135–36, 164, 185; and break with SNCC, 105, 165; and Catholicism, 24, 26, 221; childhood of, 17–18, 19–20, 21, 24, 26; children of, 210, 259; and civil rights movement, 247, 248–49, 249–52, 254–58; class biases of, 41–42; and colorism, 30, 47–48; and COFO, 39–40, 82, 108, 129, 130; commemoration of, 259–61; and Control Board, 233–34, 235–36; criticism of leadership style of, 116, 184–85, 195–96; death of, 259; and defeat in Natchez, 134–36; and disagreements with Bob Moses, 108–9, 254; and Sharon Pratt Dixon, 230, 232; and election bids, 146, 154–56, 160; and Charles Evers, 129, 143, 161, 180, 189–91; family of, 8–11, 14–16, 17–18, 21, 27–29, 172; and Adrian Fenty, 247; and James Foreman, 98–99, 103–4, 116–17; and Freedom Vote, 99–101; and gay rights, 226–27; health of, 79, 81, 205, 253–54; homeless advocacy of, 214–16; and Howard University, 239, 240–43, 244; and interracialism, 71, 170–71; and Johnson-Humphrey campaign, 93–95; and Monica Klein, 149, 154, 171, 227; and Latinos, 229–30; leadership style of, 122–23, 130, 143–44, 165–66, 187; and leaving the MFDP, 204–5; legacy of, 1, 264; and local DC politics, 225–26, 229, 230–31; and Martin Luther King Jr., 89, 134, 192; and Al Lowenstein, 71, 97, 248–49; and masculinity, 62–63, 171; and Glenn Melcher, 238, 245–46; and misidentification by Sovereignty Commission, 45–48; and Eleanor Holmes Norton, 58–59, 60, 236; and Barack Obama, 253–54, 259; oratory of, 75–76, 85–86; and Bill O'Reilly, 252–53; as overlooked as leader, 3–4, 250–52; and Parchman prison, 64–66; personality of, 48, 86–87, 94–95, 107–8, 176–77, 203, 244–45; pragmatism of, 184–85, 186, 197, 198–99; public testimony of, 83–84, 115; and Claude Ramsey, 126, 155, 189; and recycling, 222–24; and red-baiting of, 123, 151; and relocation to Newark, 205, 210; and relocation to Washington, DC, 212; as respectful of others in movement, 48; retirement of, 252; and SNCC work in Jackson, 38–39, 40; and Mitch Snyder, 218–20; and Vernell Tanner, 216, 217; and Tougaloo College, 29–31, 32–37, 53–54; and tours of US North and West, 80, 110, 141–42; as transformed by SNCC, 41–42, 106, 209; as transitional figure, 5, 209, 264; and Mary Treadwell, 238; and Jean Wheeler, 149; and white liberals, 131–32, 157, 203; and women, 147–48, 171–72. *See also* Barry, Marion; Black Power; congressional challenge; Freedom Summer; Greenwood, MS; Hattiesburg, MS; Mississippi Freedom Democratic Party (MFDP); Sunflower elections (1967); Winona, MS; Young Democratic Clubs of Mississippi (YDCM)

Guyot, Lawrence, III (son), 210
Guyot, Leonard (great-uncle), 14
Guyot, Mary (great-grandmother), 14, 15
Guyot, Monica (wife), 172, 240; children of, 210; and Guyot, 149, 154, 171, 227; and move to Newark, 205, 206, 210; and political races, 230–31
Guyot, Raymond (brother), 18
Guyot, Rosie (aunt), 15
Guyot, Thomas, Jr. (uncle), 15
Guyot, Thomas Eugene (grandfather), 15
*Guyot's Newsletter*, 253–54

Haddow, C. McClain, 219
Hall, Clarence, 100
Hamer, Fannie Lou, 82–83, 94, 168, 206; and comparisons to Guyot, 7, 263; and Guyot, 147, 171–72; and Hattiesburg, 74, 76; and Aaron Henry, 93; funeral of, 247–48; and indigenous leadership, 40; legacy of, 207, 247–48; and Loyalist Democrats, 198–99,

203, 204, 205; studies of, 2, 3–4, 247, 259; and Sunflower elections, 169–70, 174, 182; and voting, 41, 42, 161, 205, 265n1; on white participation in movement, 68, 71–72, 170. *See also* Atlantic City; congressional challenge; Democratic primary (MS), 1966; Winona, MS

*Hamer v. Campbell*, 169, 172

Hampton, Henry, 250, 251

Hancock, Milton, 55

Hancock County, MS, 9–10, 14, 21

Hancock County Republican Party, 11

Haralson, William, 78

Harlan, Stephen, 233

Harris, Joseph, 175, 181, 206, 182, 189, 204, 205

Harrison, Benjamin, 10, 11

Harrison County, MS, 23; and Black voting, 9–10, 19–20; early history of, 12; education in, 13, 21; and MFDP, 142; population of, 18; racial violence in, 22, 31–32

Harrison County Training School. *See* J. W. Randolph High School.

Harvey, Wilma, 230–31

Hatches, Henry, 183–82

Hattiesburg, MS, 68–69, 70, 83, 142, 199, 263; as compared to rest of Mississippi, 13, 18; Guyot's trial and imprisonment in, 77–79, 91; and SNCC operations in, 36, 40, 44, 67, 73–77, 79–80, 84; white violence in, 84, 155. *See also* Adams, Victoria Gray; Connor, Peggy Jean; Dahmer, Vernon

*Hattiesburg American*, 76, 77

Hawkins, Andrew, 143

Hawkins, J., 34–35

Hayden, Casey, 93, 105, 147, 171, 197

Hayden, Tom, 106

Hayes, Ralthus, 143, 146, 161, 165, 172, 186

Haynes, Curtis, 73–74

Head Start, 151–52, 192, 203

Health, Education, and Welfare (HEW), Department of, 110, 153

Health and Human Services, Department of, 215–16, 219, 220

Heath, B. F., 58

Heidelberg Hotel, 127, 129, 130

Henderson, Lenneal, 222

Henry, Aaron, 5, 36, 94, 120, 132, 182; and Atlantic City, 91–92; and COFO, 39, 114, 118; and congressional challenge, 95, 97–98, 106; and Freedom Vote, 68–69; and Guyot, 41, 126, 149, 202–3, 224; and Fannie Lou Hamer, 92, 93; and Hattiesburg, 73, 75, 77; and Hubert Humphrey, 197, 202–3; and life of, 31, 41, 227; and Loyalist Democrats, 126, 127, 180, 197–98, 199, 200, 202, 203, 205; and MFDP, 81, 89–90, 90–91, 109, 152, 155

Hernando, MS, 159

Herring, Hugh, 76

Hewes, Gaston, 28

Higgs, Bill, 110, 141–42, 227, 277n33

Highlander Center, 43, 70, 72

Highway 51 (MS), 159, 161, 162, 180

highway patrol (MS), 51, 54, 55, 72, 175

Hill, Al, 217

Hill, John, 233

Hillegas, Jan, 184–85, 195, 202, 206

Hinds County, MS, 177, 181, 183–84, 185, 186, 195

Hinds County Citizens' Action Committee, 180

Hinds County Democratic Convention, 85

*Hinds County FDP News*, 184

Hinds County Republican Party, 188

Hinds County Welfare Rights Movement, 182

historical memory. *See* civil rights conferences

HIV/AIDS, 223

Hogan, Wesley, 255, 257

Holbert, Annie, 22

Holbert, Luther, 22

Holly Springs, MS, 72, 146, 165

Holmes, Eleanor. *See* Norton, Eleanor Holmes

Holmes County, MS, 53, 143, 207, 225; and Black political candidates, 144, 160, 167, 169; and Robert Clark, 187–89; and county FDP, 161, 165–66, 170, 172, 186–87, 206

Holmes County Independent Campaign Committee, 188

Holt, Len, 80, 82

homelessness. *See* Washington, DC

Home Rule Act (DC), 212

homosexuality, 221, 223, 226–27, 229

Hoover, J. Edgar, 57, 59, 83, 89

Hopewell Baptist Church, 53, 64

Hopkins, A.L., 170

Hopson, Clint, 122–23

Houck, David, 259

House District Committee, 212

House Elections Subcommittee, 123–24

Houston, 17, 48

Houston, James Monroe, 82–83

Howard, H. L., 57

Howard, Perry, 19

Howard, T. R. M., 2, 41

Howardtown (DC), 239

Howard University, 30, 33, 48, 122, 149, 223, 233, 238–39, 240–44, 252

Howard University Community Association, 244, 246

Hughes, Langston, 33

Huguenin, Elizabeth, 216, 217

Human Services, DC Department of, 216, 220

Humphrey, Hubert, 114, 128, 132; and Atlantic City, 91–92; and MFDP support for in 1964, 93–95, 100, 103–4, 106, 108; and presidential election of 1968, 197, 199, 202–4

Hurricane Katrina, 253

Hutto, Jonathan, 240–44, 245, 247, 258

Imhoff, Gary, 238

Indiana, 258

Indianola, MS, 10, 19, 45, 296n75

Ingalls Shipbuilding Corporation, 16–17, 18, 29

Initiative 17 (DC), 214

Initiative 28 (DC), 222–23

International Longshoreman's Association (ILA), 17

International Woodworkers of America, 195

interracial marriage, 27, 149–50, 227

Iraq War, 252

Italians, 12

Itta Bena, MS, 46, 53, 64, 210

J. W. Randolph High School, 27

Jackson, MS, 25, 189–90; and Citizens' Councils, 19; and civil rights demonstrations, 32, 34, 37, 59, 60, 118–19, 180, 182; and COFO, 39, 44, 68, 70, 80, 85, 107–8, 114; and congressional challenge, 112–13, 115–16; and Freedom Riders, 36, 38, 60; and Guyot, 38, 40, 41, 43, 117, 150, 171, 172; and Jim Crow, 20, 30–31; and Martin Luther King Jr., 89; and Loyalist Democrats, 198, 200–202, 204, 205; and Meredith March, 159–60, 163, 164; and MFDP, 84, 89, 95, 134, 144, 146, 152, 155, 168; and reapportionment, 144–45, 166; and Republic of New Afrika, 223; and SNCC, 83; and Young Democrats, 127, 129, 130–31

Jackson, Jesse, 226, 231, 233

*Jackson Advocate*, 137, 175, 177

*Jackson Clarion-Ledger*, 112

Jackson County, MS, 13, 22, 155

Jackson Municipal Library, 32, 37

Jackson State College, 32, 37, 179–80, 186, 187

Jarvis, Charlene Drew, 228

Jefferson County, MS, 169, 208

Jenkins, Andrew, 225–26

Jenkins, Monroe, 150

John Lewis Voting Rights Advancement Act, 262

Johnson, June, 54, 57, 64

Johnson, Leroy, 115

Johnson, Lyndon Baines, 89, 120, 127, 138, 194; and James Coleman, 119–20; and congressional challenge, 111–12, 113; and Greenville sit-in, 152–53; and Meredith March, 159, 161, 162; and MFDP, 80, 90, 91–92, 93–95, 117–18, 142, 156, 223; and Vietnam War, 121, 123, 129; and Voting Rights Act, 124, 139–40; and Washington, DC, 211

Johnson, Paul, Jr., 68, 79, 95, 112, 118, 127, 133, 151

Johnston, Erle, Jr., 100–101, 112, 153, 190

Joint Un-American Activities Committee of the Louisiana Legislature, 117

Jones, Jim, 219

Jones, Print, 79

Justice, Department of, 51, 59, 76; and civil rights workers, 44, 52, 53, 55, 73, 79, 82, 84, 98; and Guyot, 94, 111; and harassment of Black elected officials, 217–18; and prosecutions of white supremacists, 63, 65, 66, 72, 151

Kant, Immanuel, 75, 76

Katzenbach, Nicolas, 142, 153

Keller, August, 10

Kelly, Sharon Pratt. *See* Dixon, Sharon Pratt

Kendall, Doug, 261

Kennard, Clyde, 64, 120

Kennedy, Anthony, 261–62

Kennedy, Edward, 203

Kennedy, John F., 39–40, 63, 68, 72, 90, 98, 136, 115, 120

Kennedy, Robert, 52, 59, 63, 66, 194, 197, 199, 202

Kenyatta, Jomo, 94, 279n67

Kerry, John, 253

Khayat, Edward, 155, 156, 160

Killingsworth, J. C., 199–200

Kimbrough, O. L., 51

*A Kind of Memo*, 147, 171

King, Clennon, 46, 119–20

King, Ed, 94, 119, 123, 138, 160, 247; and Atlantic City, 89, 90, 91–92; and electoral races, 68, 69, 146, 160, 166, 190; as MFDP officer, 89, 122–23, 126, 137; organizing of, 168, 182; and presidential election of 1968, 200, 204; and Young Democrats, 131

King, Martin Luther, Jr., 36, 72, 106, 115, 120, 123, 147, 227, 251; assassination of, 194, 199–200, 211; and Atlantic City, 91, 92; and Ella Baker, 36, 40; and comparisons to Guyot, 2, 7, 41, 76, 136, 263; and congressional challenge, 111, 118, 121, 138; and

Freedom Summer, 87, 89; and Greenville sit-in, 153; and Meredith March, 161–62, 163, 164; and Natchez campaign, 134; and Poor Peoples' Campaign, 192, 193; and Voting Rights Act, 139–40

King, Mary, 45, 69, 105, 138, 147, 171, 286n16

Kinoy, Arthur, 97, 106–24 passim, 210

Klein, Monica. *See* Guyot, Monica

Knoxville, 43, 164–65

Kousser, J. Morgan, 258

Kruse, Edwin, 129

Ku Klux Klan (KKK), 12, 33, 123; and violence against civil rights workers, 87, 89, 134, 151, 163; and white working class, 133, 195, 196

Kunstler, William, 97, 106, 109, 116, 117, 138, 142, 145

Labor, Department of, 211

Ladner, Dorie, 34, 37, 40, 60, 133, 134

Ladner, Heber, 99, 106

Ladner, Joyce, 34, 40, 93, 233, 234, 236, 250, 251, 259

Lafayette County, MS, 84

Lalande, Marie (Guyot's great-great-grandmother), 14

Lang, John, 12–13, 22

Lary, Curtis, 16

Latino Civil Rights Task Force (DC), 230

Latinos, 229–30, 239, 253

Lauderdale County Democratic Club, 129

Laurel, 22, 185, 195, 196

Lawrence, David, 142

Lawrence Guyot Way, 1

Lawyers Committee for Civil Rights under Law (LCCRUL), 190, 205, 210, 258

Lawyers' Constitutional Defense Committee (LCDC), 145, 205

Leadership Conference on Civil Rights (LCCR), 121, 124

LeDroit Park (DC), 1, 215, 228, 232, 239, 242–43, 246

LeDroit Park Civic Association (DC), 231, 240, 242

LeDroit Park Preservation Society (DC), 215, 240

LeDroit Park Initiative (DC), 242

Lee, Herbert, 36

Leflore County, MS, 42, 45, 49–50, 53, 64, 66, 69, 84, 161, 175. *See also* Greenwood

Lester, Julius, 171

Lewis, John, 68, 75, 92, 115, 117, 118

Lexington, MS, 53, 83–84, 186, 187, 205

LGBT rights. *See* homosexuality

Liddell, Colia, 32

Lightfoot, William, 225, 230

Lincoln, Abraham, 9, 112

Little Rock (1957 desegregation crisis), 30, 80

Long Beach, CA, 80

Long Branch, MS, 12

*Look* magazine, 23

Lorenzi, Henry, 165–66, 172

Lorenzi, Sue, 165–66, 172, 187

Lott, Hardy, 49

Louisiana, 7, 13, 14, 253; Black politics in, 8, 9; and Catholics, 25; and civil rights movement, 117, 134, 163; French influence in, 9, 14

Louisiana Subversive Activities and Communist Control Law, 117

Love, Edgar, 172

Love, J. P., 188, 189

Lowenstein, Al, 67–68, 69, 70–71, 97–98, 132, 248–49, 250

Lowndes County Freedom Organization, 187

Loyalist Democrats, 126, 180, 198–99, 200–204, 205, 207–8

Lynch, Terry, 229, 231

lynching, 21–23, 27, 31, 63, 250, 269n35

Lynd, Staughton, 93, 104

Lynd, Theron, 19, 73, 74–75, 76, 77, 79, 82, 118

Madison County, MS, 192

Magnolia Mutual Insurance Company, 41

Makin, Patricia, 215

Malcolm X, 110, 174, 251

Mangram, John, 30, 32, 34

Manna, Inc., 240

Maoists, 97, 114, 162, 195–96. *See also* red-baiting

March Against Fear. *See* Meredith March

March on Washington, 111–12, 132, 227

Marshall, Burke, 98

Marshall, Thurgood, 238

Marshall County, 144

Martin, Joe, 122

Mason, Gilbert, 20, 31, 198

Masonic Temple (Jackson), 80, 146, 180, 200

Masonite Corporation, 195–96

Matthews, Nate, 246

Mayor's Commission on the Homeless, 214

McCarthy, Eugene, 173, 194, 198, 199, 202–3

McComb, MS, 36, 40, 86, 106, 121–23, 128, 133, 136, 137, 184

McCormack, John, 113

McDew, Chuck, 134

McGee, Willie, 22

McGovern, George, 202

McKenzie, Floretta, 225

McKinley, William, 10–11

McLaurin, Charles, 176, 177, 181

McLaurin, Griffin, 188

McLemore, Les, 97, 107, 119; and Atlantic City, 89, 92–93; and Robert Clark, 187, 188, 189, 202; and congressional challenge, 121, 138–39; and congressional races, 156, 166; and Charles Evers, 81–82; and Loyalist Democrats, 185, 194, 198, 200, 201–2; and MFDP, 81, 84, 89, 122, 123, 149, 207; and Sunflower elections, 173, 174, 176, 189

McMillen, John, 212

McMillen, Neil, 249–50, 257

mechanization of agriculture, 130, 153, 156, 157, 167, 178, 206

Medicare, 90, 156, 235

Melcher, Glenn, 238, 245–46

Memphis, TN, 54, 59, 159, 160–61, 193, 194, 211

Meredith, James, 68, 72. *See also* Meredith March

Meredith March: in 1966, 133, 159–64, 166, 169, 185, 208; in 1967, 180

Metcalf, George, 133, 134

Methodist Council of Bishops, 25

*MFDP News*, 185

Migrant Farmer's Education Program, 187

Milam, J. W., 23

Miles, Robert, 136, 192

Mileston, 53, 99, 170, 189

Mills, Kay, 247

Mills, Nicolaus, 257

Millsaps College, 248, 249

Minnesota, 91

Mississippi Action for Progress (MAP), 152, 197, 200

Mississippi Baptist Convention, 25

*Mississippi Burning* (film), 257

Mississippi College, 192

Mississippi Democratic Conference (MDC), 126

Mississippi Freedom Democratic Party (MFDP), 1–4, 28, 66–67, 144, 153–54, 199–200; and armed self-defense, 135–36, 163–64; and break with SNCC, 102, 104–5; and criticism of Guyot, 165, 184–85, 195–96, 177; and election of 1966, 166; and end of, 204–6, 207; James Forman's criticism of, 103–4; founding of, 80–81; historical coverage of, 250–51, 254–55; independent strategies of, 142–43, 176–77, 180–81, 207; and Johnson-Humphrey campaign, 94–95, 97, 103–4, 108; and Meredith Marches, 159–60, 160–62, 180; and modern politics, 257, 262; out-of-state support for, 141–42, 154, 173; and reapportionment, 144–45, 166; and red-baiting, 151, 153; SNCC influence on, 104–5; SNCC support for, 99, 165; structure and ethos of, 103, 116, 136, 143, 156–58, 165, 208, 245; and support for impoverished people, 151–53; and Washington, DC, politics, 209, 211, 214, 218, 219, 224–25, 234, 242; and women, 146–47, 148, 171–72. *See also* Atlantic City; Black Power; congressional challenge; Council of Federated Organizations (COFO); Democratic primary (MS), 1966; election of 1967 (MS); Freedom Summer; Freedom Vote (1964); Loyalist Democrats; National Association for the Advancement of Colored People (NAACP); presidential election of 1968; Sunflower elections (1967); Vietnam War; Voting Rights Act of 1965; Young Democratic Clubs of Mississippi (YDCM)

Mississippi Freedom Labor Union (MFLU), 130, 144, 152–52

Mississippi Freedom Trail, 260

*Mississippi Newsletter*, 182, 184–85, 195, 197, 202

Mississippi Oral History Project, 251

Mississippi Progressive Voters League (MPVL), 18–19

Mississippi Southern College. *See* University of Southern Mississippi

Mississippi State Sovereignty Commission. *See* Sovereignty Commission

Mississippi Student Union, 127

Mississippi Teachers Association, 190, 198

Mississippi Voter Registration and Education League (MVREL), 155, 197–98

Mississippians United to Elect Negro Candidates, 181, 199, 205

Mitchell, Clarence, 142

Mobile, AL, 8, 9, 12, 24

Mondale, Walter, 91

Money, MS, 23

Montez, Antonio, 229

Montgomery, G. V. (Sonny), 160

Montgomery Bus Boycott, 30, 250

Moody, Anne, 23, 30, 36

Moore, Amzie, 39, 48, 76, 197, 263

Moore, Hazel Diana, 228

Moore, Jerry, 226

Moore, Joshua, 255

Moore (Hattiesburg fire captain), 68

Moorhead, MS, 168–69, 173, 174, 176, 178, 179

Morehouse College, 30

Morey, Hunter, 107–8, 128–29, 130, 131, 168, 227

Morgan, Romain, 10
Morris, Jesse, 107–8
Morsell, John, 97
Moss Point, 13, 85–86, 155
Mound Bayou, 20
Mount Beulah, 44, 152, 172, 192, 204
Mount Holyoke College, 110
Mount Pleasant, 221, 229–30, 239
multimember legislative districts, 145
municipal elections, 26, 117, 131, 169–70, 205.
    *See also* Sunflower elections (1967)
Murkowski, Lisa, 262
Murray, Paul, 3, 259

Natchez, MS, 12, 24; civil rights campaign in,
    102, 133–37, 143, 161, 164, 182, 185, 191,
    194
National Association for the Advancement of
    Colored People (NAACP), 20, 32, 38, 42,
    55, 77, 91, 138, 142; and Black Power, 163,
    167, 208; and COFO, 39, 81–82, 91, 114;
    and congressional challenge, 107, 109, 111,
    113, 114, 119, 121; and cooperation with
    MFDP, 155, 181, 182, 185, 188, 189–94, 195,
    264; election strategy of, 167–68, 169,
    172–73, 179, 180–81, 197, 205; and Medgar
    Evers, 2, 27, 42; and Hattiesburg, 74,
    150–51; and Loyalist Democrats, 198–201,
    204, 207; and Meredith March, 161,
    162; and Natchez, 133–35; and *O'Reilly
    Factor*, 252–53; and rivalry with MFDP,
    3, 97–98, 102, 109, 126–27, 141, 152, 159,
    160; and Tougaloo College, 30, 32; and
    Washington, DC, 213, 223; and Young
    Democrats Club of Mississippi (YDCM),
    130–31
National Black Government Convention, 193
National Black Political Convention (Gary
    Convention), 204
National Capital Revitalization Act of 1997,
    236
National Center for Neighborhood
    Enterprise, 253
National Committee for Free Elections in
    Sunflower, 173

National Conference for New Politics, 183,
    197, 220
National Council of Churches (NCC), 64, 67,
    75–76, 119
*National Guardian*, 176
National Lawyers Guild, 97, 98, 112, 114, 119
National Student Association, 249
National Youth Administration, 16
Nation of Islam, 212
Nazi Germany, 18, 35
Negro History Week, 33
Neshoba County, MS, 87, 89, 155
*Neshoba Democrat*, 162
*New America*, 177
Newark, NJ, 182, 184, 193, 205, 210
New Left, 3, 106, 154, 179, 183, 220–21
New Orleans, 2, 6, 12, 13, 17, 25, 41, 82; and
    Guyot family, 14–15; and Reconstruction,
    8–9
New Orleans Movement for a Democratic
    Society, 195
Newton, Huey, 193
New York City, 36, 86, 131, 173
*New York Times*, 26, 62, 111, 113, 125, 159
Nixon, Richard, 203–4, 212
Nnamdi, Kojo, 218
North Michigan Park Civic Association, 223
*Northwest Austin Municipal Utility District No.
    1 v. Holder*, 258
Norton, Eleanor Holmes, 173, 177, 228, 229,
    259; and DC Control Board, 234, 236, 237;
    and Winona, 58–59, 60
Nosser, John, 134
Novak, Robert, 114, 128, 202
Nystrom, Sandra, 173

Obadele, Imari, 194
Obama, Barack, 253–54, 259
Oberlin Action for Civil Rights, 142, 170
Oberlin College, 32, 142, 170
Ocean Springs, MS, 11, 126
Office of Economic Opportunity (OEO), 152,
    168
Office of Latino Affairs, 230
Office of Management and Budget, 237

Oliver, Spencer, 128–29, 130
Omega Psi Phi Fraternity, 33
Operation PUSH, 223
Operation Rolling Thunder, 121
O'Reilly, Bill, 252–53
Orris, Peter, 86–87
Oswald, Robert, 127, 129
Otero, Beatriz, 231
Our Lady of the Gulf Catholic Church, 8
Oxford, MS, 72, 106, 159, 169
Oxford, OH, 82

Page, Matthew, 198
Panola County, MS, 136, 153–54, 159, 192
Panola School District, North and South, 154
Parchman Farm prison, 28, 38, 57, 64–66,
    115, 263
Parker, Charles Mack, 31
Parker, Frank, 258, 262
Pascagoula, MS, 17, 18, 85
Pass Christian, MS, 2, 34; and Black voting,
    14–15, 19–20, 26–27, 266n7; Guyot child-
    hood in, 19, 20, 21, 24, 27–28, 65, 136;
    and Guyot commemoration, 259–60; and
    Guyot family, 10, 14–16, 18; history and
    development of, 8, 11–13, 18, 22
paternalism, 9, 10, 12, 22, 46–47,
    156–57, 249
Patridge, Earl, 55, 56, 57, 58, 66, 72
Patterson, Joe, 38, 90
Patterson, W. L., 175, 176
Payne, Charles, 255, 257
Peace and Freedom Party, 221
Peacock, Willie, 44, 45, 55, 56, 60, 71, 248
Pearl River, 31
Pearson, Drew, 113
Pearson-West, Kathryn, 223, 235
Peas, William, 12
*People* magazine, 251
Phelps, Emily, 261
Philadelphia, MS, 89, 146, 163, 199
Philadelphia, PA, 152
Phillips, Rubel, 68, 186, 188
Piernas, Henri, 19
Piernas, Julius "Jules," 16, 27, 194

Piernas, Louis, 8, 9–10, 16, 21
Piernas, Margaret, 10, 16, 17, 21, 27
Piernas, Mathilde, 16
Pleasantsville, NY, 162
*Plessy v. Ferguson*, 11
Plump, Robert, 76
Poe, Sole, 72
poll taxes, 20, 144, 146, 151, 169
Ponder, Annelle, 54–55, 57, 59, 72
Poor Peoples' Campaign, 192, 193
Poor Peoples' Conference, 152
Poplarville, MS, 31
Populist Party, 85
Porter, Tom, 245
Port Gibson boycott, 208
Posey, Buford, 199
Powell, Adam Clayton, 195
Pozzo, Theresa del, 108
Pratt, John (Jack), 73, 97
Presbyterian Church, 25, 75
presidential election of 1968, 91, 120, 131,
    197–99, 203–4; and divisions over can-
    didates, 199, 202–3; and MFDP-NAACP
    feud, 198–202; MFDP participation in,
    180, 185, 194, 196
Pride, Inc., 211, 212–23, 229, 250
Pride Economic Enterprises, 211
Prince George's County, MD, 232
Prince Hall Masons, 190, 198
Progressive Labor Party (PLP). *See* Maoists
Public Housing, Department of (DC), 236
Public Works, Department of, 222
Public Works Administration, 16

Quitman County, MS, 144

Raines, Howell, 250
Raleigh, NC, 36, 254
Ramsey, Claude, 131, 132, 190; and Holmes
    County, 188–89; and hostility toward
    MFDP, 123, 128, 129, 130, 155, 198–99, 204;
    and Mississippi Democratic Conference,
    126–27; and Young Democrats, 128–29,
    197–98
Randolph, J. W., 21

Rauh, Joseph, Jr., 89, 90, 91, 92, 97, 109, 114, 200
Ray, John, 232
Reagan, Ronald, 5, 213, 216, 217, 219, 224
reapportionment, 90, 144–45, 146, 156, 158. See also *Baker v. Carr*; *Reynolds v. Sims*
Reconstruction, 2, 7, 175, 258; and connections to civil rights organizing, 70, 89, 99, 101; and congressional challenge, 107, 111, 158; in Mississippi, 8–10, 12, 29, 188
Reconstruction Acts of 1867, 9
recycling: in Washington, DC, 221–24
red-baiting, 125, 137; and liberals, 97, 98, 114, 132, 249; and segregationists, 72, 113–14, 123, 151, 153, 177
Reed, Clarke, 167
Regional Council of Negro Leadership, 41
*Reporter* (magazine), 167
Republican Party, 94, 177; and Black and Tans, 19; and DC Control Board, 233–36; and early Black officeholding, 10–11, 37, 188; and MFDP, 113–14, 125, 167; Guyot's opposition to, 252–53, 254, 255, 257, 259; and Reconstruction, 9; and Mississippi elections in 1960s, 68, 155, 160, 167, 168, 181, 186; and presidential election of 1968, 203–4; and voter suppression, 258, 262; and DC municipal politics, 212, 219, 225, 226, 231, 232. *See also* Walker, Prentiss
Republic of New Afrika (RNA), 193, 196–97, 223
Reserve Officers Training Corps (ROTC), 33
Resnick, Joseph, 144
Revenue and Finance Committee (DC), 212
*Reynolds v. Sims*, 90, 145, 156, 166
Rhee, Michelle, 247
Rhodes, Alfred, 186, 190
Rivlin, Alice, 237
Robinson, Harry, 243
Robinson, Ruby Doris Smith, 128, 208
Roby, Harold, 106
Rodgers, Willie, 65
Roebuck, S. T., 100–101
Rolark, Wilhelmina, 231
Roosevelt, Franklin Delano, 16

Roosevelt, Theodore, 10–11
Ross, Holt, 17
Rottermann, John, 27
Ruffin, Susie, 185
Ruleville, MS, 41, 55, 93, 247–48
Rummel, Joseph Francis, 25
Rushing, Fannie, 42, 87, 106
Rust College, 146
Rustin, Bayard, 131–32, 200, 240
Rutgers University, 210
Ryals, W. C., 27
Ryan, William, 84

Saints Junior College, 187
Salter, Eldri, 32
Salter, John, Jr., 32, 36, 34–35, 50–51, 60
Sampson, Al, 134–35
Samstein, Mendy, 97, 98, 251
Sanders, Emma, 166
Saucier, Joseph, 10
Savio, Mario, 106
Scarbrough, Tom, 45–48, 50, 58, 64, 78
Schlesinger, Arthur, Jr., 98
school board races, 153–54, 167, 203–4, 206, 212, 224
School Governance Charter Amendment Act of 2000, 237
Schwartz, Carol, 232
Schwerner, Mickey, 76, 87, 89, 91, 199, 257
Schwerner, Rita, 76
*Sea Coast Echo* (Bay St. Louis, MS), 26
Seale, Bobby, 194
Second Congressional District (MS), 95, 106, 146, 200
Sellers, Cleveland, 161, 165, 207, 211
Selma-to-Montgomery March, 104, 115–16, 119, 138–39, 149, 153, 161, 250, 254
Senate Appropriations Committee, 152
Senate Internal Security Subcommittee, 197
Senate Judiciary Committee, 120, 127, 197
Senate race, 1978 (MS), 252
Sexton, John, 128
sexuality, 47, 62–63, 149. *See also* homosexuality
Simpson, Euvenester, 57–58

Sims, Charles, 134

Sistrom, Michael Paul, 255

sit-ins, 31–32, 60, 72, 153; and MFDP, 11, 138; and SNCC, 36, 39, 49; and Tougaloo College, 32, 33, 36, 37, 53–54

Shaw, John, 122

Shaw, Willie, 55

Shaw (DC neighborhood), 227

Shaw, MS, 130

Shaw University, 254

*Shaw v. Reno*, 258

Shelby, MS, 12

*Shelby County v. Holder*, 261–62

Sheridan-Kalorama (DC area), 239

Sherrod, Charles, 103

Sherzer, Bill, 170

Shields, Rudy, 137

Shirah, Sam, 85

Shriver, Sargent, 127

Shropshire, Claudia, 119

Shuttlesworth, Fred, 76, 194

Smith, Benjamin, 97, 106, 117

Smith, Doug, 116

Smith, Frank, 44, 98–99, 103, 182, 212, 224, 239, 242, 243

Smith, Lamar, 20

Smith, Mack, 129

Smith, R. L. T., 39, 94, 152, 161, 182, 197

Smith, Robert, 131

Smith, Steve, 203

Smith College, 110

Snyder, Mitch, 213–14, 215–17, 218–21, 264

Social Science Forum. *See* Borinksi, Ernst

Social Science Laboratory. *See* Borinksi, Ernst

Social Security, 44–45, 73, 255

Southern Christian Leadership Conference (SCLC), 36, 54, 60, 72, 136; and Black Power, 163; and congressional challenge, 118; conservatism of members of, 147, 224, 227; and other civil rights organizations, 104, 107, 134, 135, 168, 193; and Selma, 104, 115, 138, 139; top-down leadership structure of, 36, 40

Southern Conference Education Fund (SCEF), 117

Southern Illinois University, 80

Southern Student Organizing Committee (SSOC), 193

Sovereignty Commission, 20, 119; and James Eastland, 151, 152; and Greenwood, 50, 64; and Guyot, 45–46, 56, 58, 78, 100–101, 170, 182, 185; and Guyot relatives, 150, 171, 172; members of, 45, 78, 112, 137, 170, 177; and relations among civil rights groups, 129, 153, 190, 193, 199, 202–3, 208

Spann, John, 260

Spencer, Howard, 191

Spencer, Thomas, 19

Spock, Benjamin, 194

Stalin, Joseph, 162

Stallworth, Jessie Mae, 86

Stand Up for Democracy, 243

Stanford University, 69, 125, 142, 248

State Election Commission (MS), 166

Stavis, Morton, 174

St. Clare's Parish, 24

Steering Committee Against Repression (SCAR), 193

Stennis, John, 52, 82, 95, 106, 120, 123, 127, 152, 153

sterilization, 62, 115, 158

St. Joseph's Colored School, 24

St. Louis, 24

Stoner, Peter, 76, 79

St. Philomena's Catholic Church, 24, 26

Strype, George J., 26, 27

Students for a Democratic Society (SDS). *See* New Left

Student Nonviolent Coordinating Committee (SNCC), 4, 28–29, 47, 48, 132, 152, 173, 180; and armed self-defense, 133, 136; and Marion Barry, 40, 46, 54, 91, 104, 210–11, 212; and Black separatism, 170, 171, 172, 207; and H. Rap Brown, 182, 192–93; and COFO, 39, 126; and congressional challenge, 118, 119, 124; and Department of Justice, 44, 52, 65; founding of, 36, 39; Guyot as field secretary in, 1, 2, 40, 41–42, 53, 54, 263; and Howard University, 233, 240, 242, 244; and Indianola, 45–46; and

SNCC (*continued*)
    internal problems, 98–99, 100, 103–5; and
    Johnson-Humphrey campaign, 94–95,
    103–4, 108; leadership and decision-
    making styles in, 40–41, 71, 86–87, 104,
    116, 143, 165; and NAACP, 109, 113, 133, 135,
    172–73; and recruitment of Guyot, 37–38;
    reunions of veterans of, 248–49, 251,
    254–55, 257, 259; and sexism, 147, 171–72;
    transformative power of, 2, 3, 42, 105–6,
    209; and Vietnam War, 155, 164; and voter
    registration, 39–40, 48–49; white par-
    ticipation in, 70, 85, 93, 107–8, 128, 149,
    170; and Young Democrats, 127–28. *See
    also* Black Power, Council of Federated
    Organizations (COFO); Freedom Summer;
    Greenwood; Hattiesburg; Meredith March:
    in 1966; Mississippi Freedom Democratic
    Party (MFDP); Winona
Suarez, Matt, 108
summer project. *See* Freedom Summer; Black
    Belt Program
Sumrall, MS, 12
Sunflower County, MS, 45, 117, 184–85
Sunflower elections (1967), 124, 169–70,
    173–78, 182, 264; compared to Holmes
    County elections, 188, 189, 201–2; legacy
    of, 179, 181, 184, 195–96, 206, 207
Supreme Court, Mississippi, 25, 196
Supreme Court, US, 23, 117, 233; and interra-
    cial marriage, 28, 150; and reapportion-
    ment, 90, 145, 156, 166; and segregation
    rulings, 19, 25, 38; and voting rulings, 74,
    169–70, 258, 261–62
Surney, Lafayette, 76
Sutherland, Elizabeth, 85
Sutton, Percy, 174
Swygert, H. Patrick, 243

Taft, William Howard, 11
Talladega College, 32
Tanner, Vernell, 216, 217, 220
Taranto, James, 261, 262
Tate, Burrell, 187
Taylor, Ben, 50

Teamsters, 231
Tea Party, 254
Tennessee, 43, 72, 145, 217
term limits, 225
Thelwell, Mike, 107, 156–58, 163, 249, 254–55
Third Congressional District (MS), 146, 160,
    166, 190–92, 200
Thomas, Art, 152
Thomas, Barbara Ann, 77, 78
Thomas, Norman, 132
Thomas-Lester, Avis, 259
Till, Emmett, 23, 66, 149
Tillinghast, Muriel, 108
Todd, Lisa Anderson, 137–38, 139
Tougaloo College, 25, 50, 68, 76, 79, 128, 233;
    and civil rights, 29–30, 32, 34–36, 37,
    38, 60, 89; and Charles Evers, 191; and
    Freedom Summer panel, 248–49; and
    Guyot, 29–30, 32–36, 53–54, 76, 259, 262;
    and MFDP, 129, 143
Tougaloo Nine, 32, 37
Travis, Jimmy, 50, 51
Treadwell, Mary, 211, 213, 216, 217, 218, 238,
    245
Trinity College, 251
Trump, Donald, 255, 257, 262
Trumpauer, Joan, 37
Tucker, Stirling, 212
Ture, Kwame. *See* Carmichael, Stokely
Turnbow, Hartman, 53, 83–84, 93, 94, 186
Tuttle, Elbert, 120

understanding clause, 19, 20, 118
unions, 155, 160, 214, 231; and blue-Black
    coalition, 111, 130–31, 159, 188–89, 190,
    198; and Gulf Coast, 17, 29, 156; and oppo-
    sition to MFDP, 123, 126, 127–29, 132, 155;
    and white working-class racism, 127, 132,
    195–96. *See also* Ramsey, Claude
University of Alabama, 59
University of California, Berkeley, 106, 154
University of the District of Columbia, 235
University of Massachusetts, 110
University of Mississippi, 46, 68, 72, 119, 159,
    197, 200

University of Southern Mississippi, 64, 120, 249, 251

Urban League, 91, 161, 211

US Commission on Civil Rights, 112

*U.S. v. Patridge, Herrod, Surrell, Basinger and Perkins*, 72–73

Vardaman, James Kimble, 11, 47

Vicksburg, MS, 82, 89

Vietnam War, 127, 152, 156; and effects on the civil rights movement, 154–55, 164, 194; and Charles Evers, 191–92; Guyot's views on, 3, 121, 137; MFDP responses to, 121–23, 133, 156, 167, 183, 202, 203; and New Left, 154–55, 196, 220; and red-baiting of MFDP, 123, 151, 153; and Young Democrats, 128, 129

Voter Education Project (VEP), 40, 42, 52

voter ID laws, 255, 258, 262

voter registration, 20, 67, 115, 138, 175, 184, 249, 253; and Black Power, 162, 170–71; and Black vs. white registration numbers, 142, 153–54, 160, 174; and COFO, 66, 85, 87; and Greenwood, 42–43, 45, 49, 51, 53, 59, 63–64; and Gulf Coast, 14–15, 26–27; and Guyot's attitudes toward, 48–49, 129, 146; and Hattiesburg, 73–75, 77, 149, 151; and Holmes County, 53, 64–65, 187; and Jackson, 31, 129; and Meredith Marches, 161, 162, 180; and MFDP, 116–17, 118, 130, 142; and NAACP-labor alliance strategy, 127, 131, 155, 167, 172–73, 197–98; and Obama, 254; and SNCC, 36, 39–40, 86, 104; and Sunflower County, 174–75. *See also* Freedom Summer; Freedom Vote; Voting Rights Act of 1965

Voters League, 192

Voting Rights Act of 1965, 118, 124, 143, 159; and congressional challenge, 121, 123, 139; and effects on white Mississippians, 126, 151, 175, 181; and first Black candidates, 153–54; interpretations of passage of, 137–40, 254; and MFDP, 2, 101, 102, 124, 140, 141–42, 263; and reapportionment,

145; and renewals, 210, 213, 226, 258; roll-back of, 261–62

wade-ins, 31–32

Walker, Prentiss, 113, 123, 160, 167, 168, 169, 186

Wallace, George, 59, 203–4

*Wall Street Journal*, 177, 261

Waltzer, Bruce, 117

Ward 1 (DC), 222, 225, 230–31, 239–40, 245

Ward 1 Democrats, 224

Ware, Bill, 170, 207

War on Drugs, 227–28, 231

War on Poverty, 127, 153, 167

Washington, Booker T., 233

Washington, DC, 1, 24, 138, 264; antiwar protests in, 121, 123; and civil rights movement, 83, 98, 107, 110, 112, 114, 116, 124; and Control Board, 233–37; and corruption, 213, 217–18, 227–28, 237–38; and Sharon Pratt Dixon, 228–30, 232; and education, 225–26; and Adrian Fenty, 246–47; Guyot's move to and early life in, 3, 208, 209–10, 212; and Guyot's political career, 229, 244–46; homelessness in, 213–17, 218–21; and Howard University, 238–39, 240–44; and Latinos, 229–30, 239; LGBT community in, 226–27; and March on Washington, 111–12, 132; and Mississippi organizing, 4–5, 209, 210–11; and Poor Peoples' Campaign, 192; recycling in, 221–24

Washington, Walter, 211, 212, 214

*Washington City Paper*, 224, 245

*Washington Post*, 111, 125; on DC issues, 213, 215, 216, 217, 219, 223, 228, 230, 232

Watkins, Hollis, 34, 39, 40, 64–65, 71, 73–74, 181, 251, 252

Watts uprising, 133, 182

Waveland, MS, 24, 103, 104, 116, 147, 164

Weaver, Robert, 16, 167

Weber, Ed, 64

Weinberg, Arthur, 35

Wells, Will, 72–73

Welty, Eudora, 34

Wemple, Erik, 245
West, James, 55
West, Richard, 42
West Point, MS, 154
Wheeler, Jean, 149
Whirly Bird Café, 69
Whitaker, R. L., 167
White, Lee, 138
White Citizens' Councils, 19, 47, 56, 68, 126, 157, 173, 249–50
White Community (White Folks) Project, 85
White House Civil Rights Planning Conference, 143
Whitfield, Melvin, 127–28
Whitfield Hospital, 57, 119–20
Whitley, Clifton, 146, 160, 161, 166–67, 168, 169, 174, 200, 205
Whitman, J. J., 20
Whitten, Jamie, 82, 106
Wilkins, Roy, 114, 121, 133, 138, 161, 208
Wilkinson County, MS, 23, 167, 169
Williams, Anthony, 237, 246
Williams, Cleveland, 153–54
Williams, John Bell, 160, 166, 186, 188, 190, 192, 198, 200
Williams, Robert, 169
Williams, Robert W., 85
Willie Horton ad, 238–39
Wilson, T. B., 19
Wilson (unidentified woman), 152
Winona, MS, 2, 39, 64, 136, 172, 203, 228, 263; arrests and beatings in, 54–63; FBI investigation of, 65–66; Guyot's health problems from, 79, 81, 205, 206; and media coverage, 70; and post-trial legacy and testimony, 83, 115, 261; and trial of policemen, 72–73

*Winona (MS) Times*, 62, 63, 66
Winstead, Arthur, 106
Winter, Nadine, 215
Wisdom, John Minor, 120
women: activism of, in movement, 5, 84, 107, 147, 263; relationship of, with Guyot, 27, 89, 147–50, 171–72; and sexism in movement, 147, 171
Wood, Martha, 150
Woods, Mrs. L. E., 74
Woodson, Carter, 33
Woodson, Robert, 253
Works Progress Administration (WPA), 16
World War I, 15
World War II, 18, 20, 22–23, 28, 31, 32, 33, 41, 47, 153
Wright, Moses, 23
Wynn, Doug, 131

Xavier University, 41

Yale University, 58, 67, 69, 70, 97
Young, Andrew, 60, 86, 87, 110, 134, 224, 238, 248
Young, Charles, 141
Young Democratic Clubs of America (YDCA), 128–29, 131
Young Democratic Clubs of Mississippi (YDCM), 127–31
Young People's Socialist League, 132
Youth Services Administration (DC), 230

Zedong, Mao, 162
Zellner, Bob, 86, 257
Zinn, Howard, 37, 50, 54, 64, 70, 71, 75, 110